Patterns: Process and Change in Hum

MICHAEL CARR

Patterns

PROCESS AND CHANGE IN
HUMAN GEOGRAPHY

MACMILLAN

First published 1987
Reprinted 1988, 1989 (twice)

Published by
MACMILLAN EDUCATION LTD
Houndmills, Basingstoke, Hampshire RG21 2XS
and London
Companies and representatives
throughout the world

Designed by Roger Lightfoot
Cover design by Michael Russell
Design Associates

Printed in Hong Kong

British Library Cataloguing in Publication Data
Carr, Michael
Patterns: process and change in human geography.
1. Anthropo–geography
I. Title
304.2   GF41
ISBN 0–333–35013–8

Acknowledgements

The author and publishers wish to thank those publishers who have kindly given permission for their material to be used as a basis for the following illustrations: Fig. 1.6 Existing Water/Sanitation Services, WHO; Fig. 1.7 What is Primary Health Care? From Situation of Children in the Developing World 1979: UNICEF. The State of World Population 1980 UNFPA; Figs. 7.4, 7.5 from *The Study of Urban Geography*, H. Carter, Edward Arnold, 1972; Fig. 8.3 a model of Latin American City Structure, Griffin and Ford, *Geographical Review*, 1980; Fig. 10.1 from *A Geography of Economic Behaviour*, M. E. Hurst, Duxbury Press, Mass., 1972; Fig. 12.3b from *South American Development — A Geographical Introduction*, Bromley, CUP, 1982; Fig. 15.4 from *Land and Water Resources of West Africa*, Hocking and Thomson, Murray House College of Education, 1979; Fig. 19.4 Commission of Energy and the Environment 1981; Fig. 19.18 British Wind Energy Association; Fig. 20.1 from *The Marine Environment*, Levihan and Fletcher, Blackie, 1977; Case Study 8.1 from *An Emerging World City*, Masser, Town and Country Planning; Case Study 20.1 from *Forestry, Fishing, Mining and Power*, G. Dinkele, Harrap Reform Geography series, Nelson; Case Study 21.1 from *Transport Geography*, White and Senior, Longman, after Hilling 135 in Hoyle and Hilling 1970, and after Bird 1963.

The author and publishers wish to thank South American Pictures for the photographs shown on page 74.

Illustrations by Taurus Graphics.

The publishers have made every effort to trace the copyright holders, but where they have failed to do so they will be pleased to make the necessary arrangements at the first opportunity.

Personal Acknowledgements

I am very conscious of and grateful for all the help and support I have been given in the course of completing this text. My thanks go especially to the following – Gus Caesar and Emrys Jones for the grounding in geography I was privileged to receive from them, to colleagues and students at Homerton especially Mike Younger who advised on some of the sections, to Elaine Butt for numerous draft diagrams, to Mary Coburn who kindly typed some of the draft, to Penny Farrant, Lindsey Charles and Susie Williams for their editorial advice and good humoured patience with my idiosyncracies. Above all I should like to acknowledge the help, encouragement and support of my wife Zena to whom with love, together with the four girls in our lives — Jayne, Elizabeth, Joanne and Sally, I dedicate this text.

Michael Carr
Cambridge 1987

Contents

SECTION 3   MANUFACTURING AND INDUSTRIAL LOCATION

SECTION 4   AGRICULTURE

SECTION 5   MANAGEMENT AND DEVELOPMENT OF RESOURCES

SECTION 6   TRANSPORT AND COMMUNICATION NETWORKS

SECTION 7   INTERNATIONAL TRADE

List of Illustrations

To the Reader

Though this text has been written especially for advanced level study in geography, it is suitable for others seriously concerned with the contribution the subject can make to an understanding of many of the issues and problems facing the world and its peoples at this present time.

A systematic approach is taken, beginning with population since people lie at the heart of all human geography. Here as elsewhere in the text the interactions between people and the environment are explored with a view to bringing out locational aspects and the resultant distribution patterns and spatial relationships which occur.

In this approach the text remains true to human geography tradition. But also fundamental to it is an awareness of the rapid changes which are going on in the world today and out of which emerge important issues and problems for which the geographer, along with those from other disciplines, must have concern. Hence emphasis throughout the text is placed on change and the processes underlying it which alter the spatial relationships lying at the core of geography.

Case Studies are introduced throughout the book, since we must ultimately go beyond generalities to the implications they have for particular people and places. Exercises devised around tables and diagrams are suggested either for the reader individually or as part of a group to stimulate closer study of the relevance and importance of the figures or material provided to points being made in the text. It is thereby hoped the reader will be saved from the temptation to 'skim' over tables, diagrams and Case Studies assuming them simply to be supplementary material. They are an important and integral part of the book deserving of as close a study as the general text. Use of the Contents and the Index will also be of help in finding material when exploring a particular theme or concept.

Given the size of the task undertaken and the limited space available in the book, only the basic points can be explored and exemplified. It must be left to the reader to explore them more fully, not only in the available texts, but also in the more accessible journals and news publications which provide the most update information and observations on the themes in the book. A general guide to further reading is therefore given at the back of the book.

It is assumed that the reader in any event will have to hand an atlas, without which it is difficult to appreciate sufficiently the locational and spatial aspects raised in many of the discussions. Access to an atlas is also useful in placing many of the map diagrams for specific areas into their wider world context.

Michael Carr
1987

1   People and World Health

POPULATION GEOGRAPHY

'Numbers, densities and qualities of the population provide the essential background for all geography. Population is the point of reference from which all other elements are observed and from which they all singly and collectively derive significance and meaning.' (Wrigley)

People are the starting point for geography and much of the data used in population geography comes from demographers — specialists in population studies. But whereas demographers are essentially concerned with the enumeration of populations and changes in the population structure, geographers are mainly interested in population density distributions and aspects of these, including changes in them over time. They are also concerned to explain them. Hence the geographer is involved not only in the ways in which population densities are related to the environment and its resources from one region to another, but also with the whole process of development whereby people endeavour to increase those resources and thereby living standards.

It is thus useful at the beginning of this first section to summarise these concerns before we go on to look at them in more detail (Figs. 1.1, 1.2).

Where the resource base for a country's population is inadequate, this is most directly reflected in poor health standards and low levels of welfare provision as has been illustrated from the television coverage of the famine in Ethiopia and Sudan. In turn poor health and welfare provision directly influence vital population rates such as the number of deaths, including incidences of infant mortality, life expectancy and much less obviously birth and fertility rates. Health standards thus provide an important indication of the relation between population and resource levels.

Location, Distribution and Characteristics of Population e.g. nutrition and health levels, sex, age, ethnic composition, natural increase rates.

Changes in Distribution over Time resulting from regional differences in rates of natural increase and net migration rates.

The Relationship of Population to the Environment and its resources from which people gain a living.

Population Migration and Urbanisation as processes related to the comparative development of countries and their societies.

N.B.   Information about the population of a country is gained largely from taking a periodic census. But the amount and kinds of information obtained varies from one country to another as does its reliability.

Fig. 1.1   Components of population geography

Malnutrition and world food supplies

Malnutrition

Human beings need not only proteins and energy foods, but also certain vitamins and minerals. Whilst proteins are vital for body building, the most critical element in any diet is the energy giving carbohydrates, because if this falls below minimum needs the body functions will divert some of the protein intake in an effort to make up this deficiency. If protein and carbohydrates are adequate, minimum vitamin and mineral needs will also be met from the food consumed.

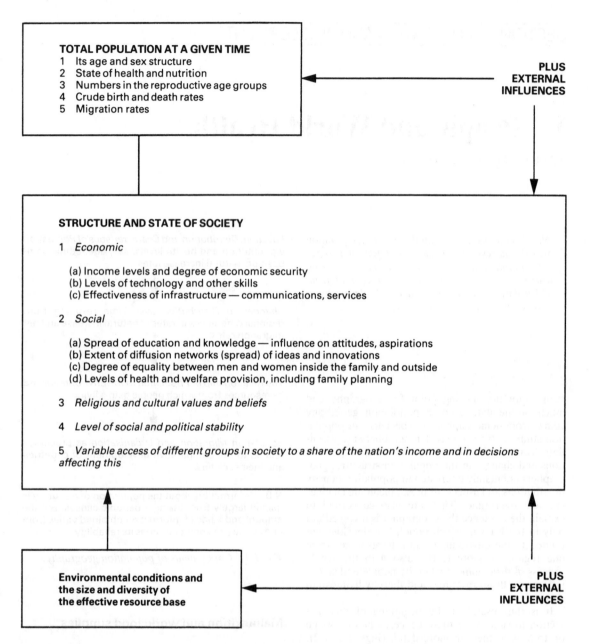

TOTAL POPULATION AT A GIVEN TIME
1 Its age and sex structure
2 State of health and nutrition
3 Numbers in the reproductive age groups
4 Crude birth and death rates
5 Migration rates

PLUS
EXTERNAL
INFLUENCES

STRUCTURE AND STATE OF SOCIETY

1 *Economic*

(a) Income levels and degree of economic security
(b) Levels of technology and other skills
(c) Effectiveness of infrastructure — communications, services

2 *Social*

(a) Spread of education and knowledge — influence on attitudes, aspirations
(b) Extent of diffusion networks (spread) of ideas and innovations
(c) Degree of equality between men and women inside the family and outside
(d) Levels of health and welfare provision, including family planning

3 *Religious and cultural values and beliefs*

4 *Level of social and political stability*

5 *Variable access of different groups in society to a share of the nation's income and in decisions affecting this*

**Environmental conditions and
the size and diversity of
the effective resource base**

PLUS
EXTERNAL
INFLUENCES

Fig. 1.2 Factors affecting density, distributions and changes

Since carbohydrate intake is so critical, this is generally the nutrition measure used to show differences in diet and food intake levels from one part of the world to another. It is given in calories, a common energy measure.

Fig. 1.3 shows how this varies from country to country and particularly highlights those populations where malnutrition is a problem. People in the more advanced countries have more than their fair share of the world's food; indeed, it is overeating which causes more health problems than malnutrition.

The link between food level intakes on the one hand and vital population rates as indicated by mortality rates and life expectancy on the other is indicated in Fig. 1.4. Within any country there are

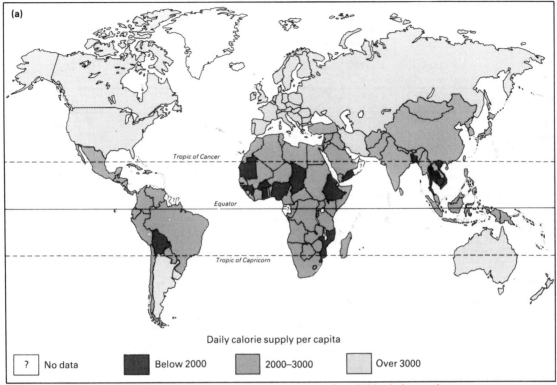

Daily calorie supply per capita

? No data   Below 2000   2000–3000   Over 3000

N.B. The daily intake of calories necessary to sustain a person averages about 2200 calories per day

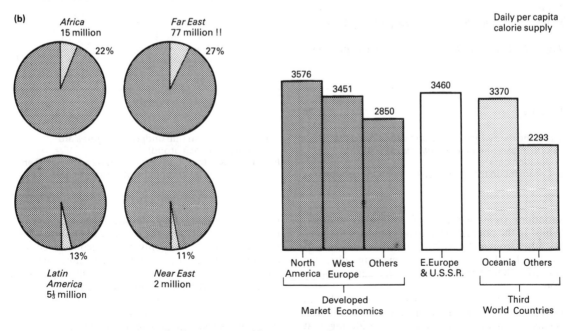

Fig. 1.3   Food consumption levels as measured by energy intake
(a) Daily calorie supply per capita of the population, 1977
(b) People with energy intake below critical min. limit

	Daily calorie supply as % of requirements (1981)	Infant mortality rate (aged under 1) per 1000 of live births (1982)	Life expectancy at birth (1982)
Low Income Countries	91	114	51
Ethiopia	76	122	47
India	86	94	54
Bangladesh	84	133	49
Kenya	88	77	57
Vietnam	90	53	64
Middle Income Countries	111	76	59
Egypt	116	104	57
Bolivia	91	126	51
Malaysia	121	29	67
Mexico	121	53	66
Portugal	110	26	70
Industrialised Countries	132	10	74
Italy	150	14	74
United Kingdom	132	11	74
Japan	117	7	76
United States	138	11	75
Denmark	133	8	75

Source: World Development Report (O.U.P.) 1984

Fig. 1.4   Infant mortality and life expectancy rates relative to calorie intake

Exercise

Using the data which shows on the one hand the calorie intake, and on the other two sets of vital population data —
a Comment on the difference between the groups of countries shown (the underlined figures are averages for each group).
b Indicate whether there appears to be a link between calorie intake levels and the other sets of data.

variations from one part of society to another. Whilst in the poorest developing countries the masses suffer from malnutrition, a small wealthy minority live lavishly — conversely even in advanced countries there are cases of poverty and malnutrition.

The main source of carbohydrates is cereals and thus the levels of world production and distribution, relative to demand are critical. Considering that 40% of the world's population suffers from malnutrition, it is surprising to find the World Action for Development Group making the point that throughout this century, despite huge increases in the world's population, the capacity to produce food has kept ahead. Not only have record levels of production in rice, wheat and coarse grains, such as barley, consistently been reached, but large cutbacks in planting have been made amongst some major producers for fear of an over-supply occurring. In the light of these facts the stark conclusion is that there is a serious problem of maldistribution of cereal foods relative to the distribution of needs. The problem could possibly be solved in a number of ways.

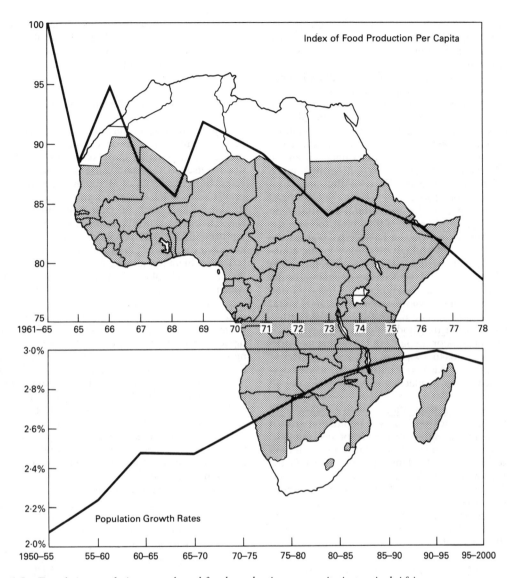

Index of Food Production Per Capita

100
95
90
85
80
75

1961–65 65 66 67 68 69 70 71 72 73 74 75 76 77 78

3·0%
2·8%
2·6%
2·4%
2·2%

Population Growth Rates

2·0%
1950–55 55–60 60–65 65–70 70–75 75–80 80–85 85–90 90–95 95–2000

Fig. 1.5 Trends in population growth and food production per capita in tropical Africa

1 <u>Direct transfer of surplus food from one part of the world to another</u>. But this is not feasible for a number of reasons — the chief being the enormous cost of transferring the estimated 120 million tonnes needed by the poorest countries. Another is the difficulty of persuading traditional eaters of one type of grain, e.g. rice, to eat another, e.g. wheat, of which there are the largest surpluses. Only in emergency disaster cases affecting a limited part of the world is direct transfer of food a feasible solution e.g. Ethiopian famine.
2 <u>Increasing food production in countries where</u> <u>shortages occur</u>. It is generally accepted that developing countries do have the physical potential to produce enough food for their populations. Technological advances are enabling higher yields to be obtained from existing land as well as more land to be brought under cultivation. Yet the gap between food supplies and population need has not been closed, indeed in some African countries it is widening (refer to Fig. 1.5). Some of the reasons for this are as follows:
a) Too little investment has gone into expanding agricultural production. Until recently, with one or

5

two exceptions such as Tanzania and China, developing countries have concentrated on industrialisation and prestige projects in their search for economic growth.

b) Too much of the land under cultivation is given over to export crops in response to the demand from advanced countries for certain tropical products. Despite independence overseas multinational companies still control a significant part of agricultural production in some developing countries. Even where this is not the case governments look to agricultural exports as a way of earning much needed foreign currency. There is thus the paradoxical situation of some countries in the Caribbean and Africa being major agricultural exporters and yet having to import some of their basic food needs.

c) Advanced countries on balance have given the wrong kind of aid and advice to developing countries — including shipments of food rather than agricultural tools, and finance investment in prestige projects and advice benefiting only those of the farming community who have the skills and capital to benefit from it. The poorest have gained little.

3 Better use of the food which is produced. It is estimated that poor methods of harvesting and storage of food leads to a waste of well over a quarter of the food grown. Also poor nutritional practices destroy much of the goodness and nutritional value in the food eaten.

4 Slowing down population growth to allow food production to catch up. Rates of population growth are beginning to slow down but not fast enough. Poverty hinders the spread of education and fetters the desire for smaller families — a crucial factor towards lowering birth rates. Higher income would bring about social development including more rights for women — giving them a greater say in how many children they will bear. However, as Tarrant indicates, population control takes time to work itself through and therefore is only of importance in the long term:

'The number of people on the earth at present plus the slow rate of change in the factors controlling population growth means that significant changes in rates of growth will be unlikely over the next thirty to forty years. The population to be fed from the earth's food supply will more than double regardless of the success or failure of any present efforts to control population growth. The importance of these programmes will not be felt until well into the next century. The population structure of the developing world is dominated by children.'
(Tarrant, J. Food Policies, p. 181, John Wiley, 1983)

In summary, closing the gap between population numbers and food supplies and also improving the health of the mass of the population in the least developed countries depends crucially on raising the incomes of the poor to allow them to produce and buy enough food for themselves. The achievement of this is inextricably linked with the whole development process in a country and includes not only economic but also political and social change.

Disease from water supplies and sanitation

Though malnutrition directly contributes to the higher death rates in developing countries and makes the population more susceptible to disease, disease itself is the main cause of higher mortality rates. Moreover 80% of all disease occurrences are preventable being directly attributable to impure drinking water, lack of sanitation and to disease carrying insects which breed in contaminated water. An estimated 25 000 people die every day through not having access to pure drinking water. (Fig. 1.6)

The problem is not only one of providing the large financial, technological and managerial outlays which are needed to provide a pure water supply and safe sanitation but also of changing people's personal habits. It has been observed in Bangladesh for example that villagers may shun a perfectly good piped water supply, preferring to walk a mile or more to a polluted well simply because traditionally it is not only a source of water but also of gossip. 'Drinking water is one thing: the meaning of drinking water is another.' Besides diseases associated with malnutrition, water and sanitation, there are a variety of others with the same debilitating effects, including a drastic lowering of the physical and mental energy needed for work. In South East Asia for example 45% of all the people are infected by soil transmitted worms — a fact very rarely commented on by health authorities.

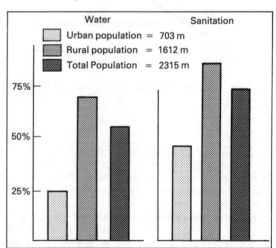

Fig. 1.6 *Population of developing countries (excluding China) lacking access to community water supply and sanitation services, 1980*

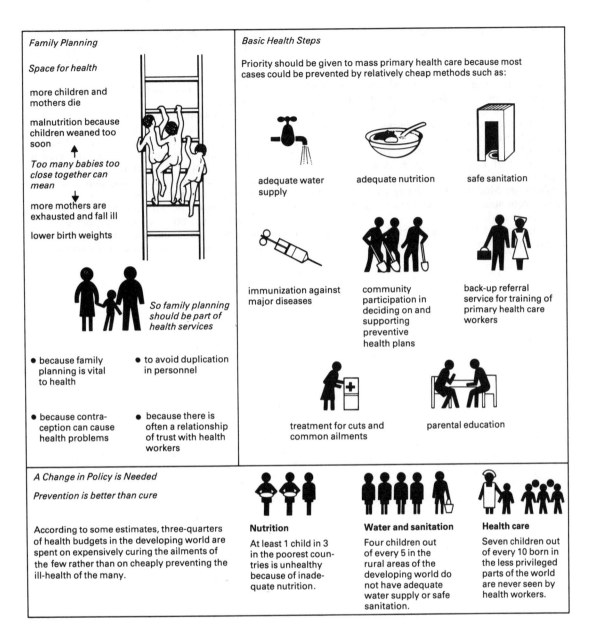

Family Planning

Space for health

more children and mothers die

malnutrition because children weaned too soon

↑

Too many babies too close together can mean

↓

more mothers are exhausted and fall ill

lower birth weights

So family planning should be part of health services

- because family planning is vital to health
- to avoid duplication in personnel

- because contraception can cause health problems
- because there is often a relationship of trust with health workers

Basic Health Steps

Priority should be given to mass primary health care because most cases could be prevented by relatively cheap methods such as:

adequate water supply

adequate nutrition

safe sanitation

immunization against major diseases

community participation in deciding on and supporting preventive health plans

back-up referral service for training of primary health care workers

treatment for cuts and common ailments

parental education

A Change in Policy is Needed

Prevention is better than cure

According to some estimates, three-quarters of health budgets in the developing world are spent on expensively curing the ailments of the few rather than on cheaply preventing the ill-health of the many.

Nutrition

At least 1 child in 3 in the poorest countries is unhealthy because of inadequate nutrition.

Water and sanitation

Four children out of every 5 in the rural areas of the developing world do not have adequate water supply or safe sanitation.

Health care

Seven children out of every 10 born in the less privileged parts of the world are never seen by health workers.

Fig. 1.7   Primary health care concerns

Primary health care in developing countries

Very real progress is being made in solving some of these problems. International institutions as well as national governments are backing the development and extension of primary health care which is well summarised by a centre-page spread in Unicef News Issue 108, 1981/3. (Fig. 1.7) The most encouraging feature is the direct participation of organisations set up by the people themselves on a local level. The 'grass roots' are making their needs known, successfully exercising pressure on governments and others holding power in society, as well as taking inexpensive steps in the local community.

A number of developing countries are following programmes on the Chinese model. (However it must be noted that health improvement in China only came as a result of a strategy for total development.)

The Chinese Health Care Model

In the pre-1949 period China's mortality and poor health figures attested to the wide occurrence of poverty and suffering. But by 1956 under a communist regime China had virtually eradicated the most prevalent communicable diseases and built up a strong preventive network in both urban and rural areas across the whole country. The success was based on four health care principles which have become internationally known as the Chinese Health Care Model and are being studied with regard to community health schemes being developed in other countries.

1　Same type of health care for all.
2　Prevention was to receive priority.
3　Uniting of Western and traditional Chinese medicine — there were 500 000 existing medical practitioners compared to 20 000 western trained doctors.
4　Community participation in health care including:—
(a)　Mass campaigns in which all the people became production units participating in ridding the country of disease carriers such as rats, flies, bedbugs and in sweeping streets and cleaning them of rubbish. The campaigns also became vehicles for mass health education and experience in eradicating diseases.
(b)　'Barefoot doctor' policy — a part-time health worker chosen by and responsible to the community who could undertake general health care and had the confidence of the community.

2 Population Change and the Demographic Transition

Introduction

Demographers have recognised a general pattern in the way crude birth and death rates per thousand of the population, and therefore natural rates of increase, have changed over time as countries have undergone development. Though essentially based on the experience of industrialised societies, it has until recently, been seen as a transition pattern, applicable to countries in general including those in the developing world. The demographic transition model Fig. 2.1 is used not only for describing and predicting population change, but also as a kind of explanatory framework for it.

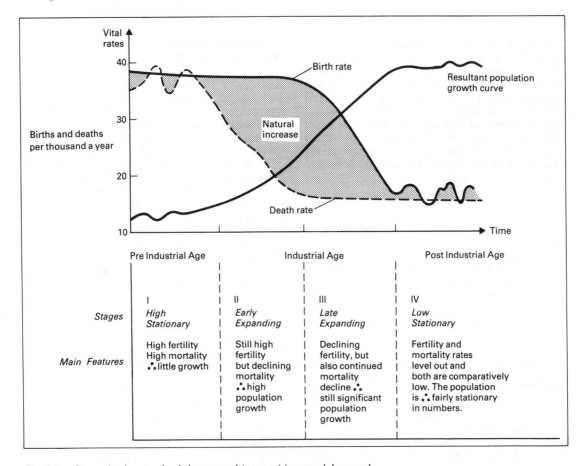

Fig. 2.1   Stages in the standard demographic transition model or cycle

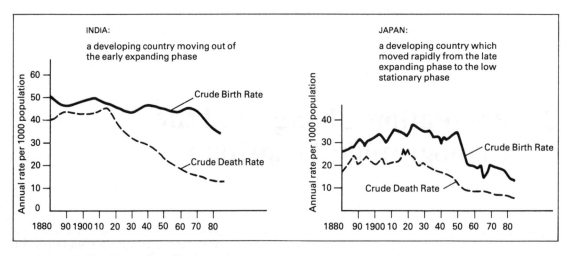

Fig. 2.2   Demographic transition for India and Japan, 1880–1980

But there are however, significant differences particularly between the change as seen in older nations which are now towards the end of demographic transition and the trends for newer nations still in the midst of it. In general for the older advanced nations the transition was slower than the present pace of change for developing nations. This is not surprising in view of the fact that these nations are able to learn from the earlier experiences of the older developed countries and have the benefit of modern skills and technology.

Exercise

Look at Fig. 2.2 and try to explain why by 1978 the two countries were at different stages of their demographic transition. Comment on any differences you are able to note between the shapes of the graphs.

Variations in the pace and shape of change in the demographic transition cycle are linked to the rates and kinds of social and economic development. In particular there are variations between developing nations and advanced countries.

The graphs shown in Fig. 2.2 indicate change in crude birth and death rates, the difference between them giving the amount of natural increase at any one stage in the cycle.

Population change and development in the developing world

There are a number of reasons why birth rates are high amongst traditional societies in the developing world. There is a general desire for a large family, the need for labour to work in the fields and in local small-scale industry and also the need for enough children to survive into adult life to support parents in their old age. Until colonial times death rates were also high due to limited food supplies and an even higher incidence of disease than now.

But the introduction of better health measures from the developed world during this century has brought some decline in the death rate. However, until recently birth rates have shown little signs of decline, since many people remained dependent on a subsistence type of economy and retained their traditional view of the family. Now, except in parts of Africa, birth rates are beginning to fall. There are signs that the demographic cycle can be accelerated to bring population to within manageable numbers and release enough resources to allow for a rise in the standard of living of the mass of the population.

To ensure this happens, planners and others concerned with population have increasingly realised the need to do more than try and implement family planning campaigns as they have done in the past. There is now a better understanding of the complex interrelationship of factors which affect birth and fertility rates (i.e. the number of children born relative to the number of women of child bearing age (15–44 years) in the population). The most

10

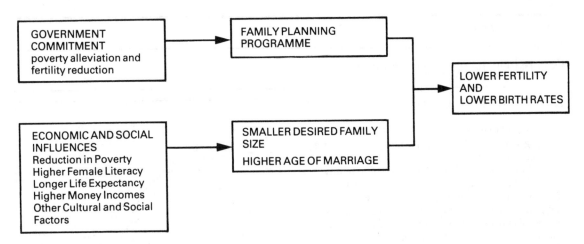

```
┌─────────────────────┐          ┌─────────────────────┐
│ GOVERNMENT          │          │ FAMILY PLANNING     │
│ COMMITMENT          │ ────────►│ PROGRAMME           │
│ poverty alleviation and│       └─────────────────────┘
│ fertility reduction │                                      ┌─────────────────────┐
└─────────────────────┘                                      │ LOWER FERTILITY     │
                                                             │ AND                 │
                                                   ────────► │ LOWER BIRTH RATES   │
┌─────────────────────┐          ┌─────────────────────┐     └─────────────────────┘
│ ECONOMIC AND SOCIAL │          │ SMALLER DESIRED FAMILY│
│ INFLUENCES          │ ────────►│ SIZE                │
│ Reduction in Poverty│          │ HIGHER AGE OF MARRIAGE│
│ Higher Female Literacy│        └─────────────────────┘
│ Longer Life Expectancy│
│ Higher Money Incomes│
│ Other Cultural and Social│
│ Factors             │
└─────────────────────┘
```

Fig. 2.3   Factors lowering fertility and birth rates

important features of this interrelationship are shown in Fig. 2.3.

Efforts are also now being directed towards raising standards of living including levels of literacy and improving the position of women in society. It has been pointed out that women are the forgotten half. 'Centuries of cultural conditioning have relegated women to the roles of child bearing and servant to their husband. It is imperative to give them more rights and an equal say in family matters if the aim of smaller families is to be met.'

Progress towards more comprehensive planning and the effect of wider social and economic influences on birth rates can be summarised for Sri Lanka, where over the last decade there has been a marked fall in the birth rates. (Case Study 2.1)

Population change in the developed world — the case of West Germany

Whilst most developing countries are trying to control population growth, there is concern in the developed world about the levelling out of growth and even a decline in population numbers. The circumstances under which this has occurred are broadly similar for Western European countries, though as we shall see in the case of West Germany there are also factors particular to one country. Whilst economic change is an important factor, it is bound up with disruptions caused by the two World Wars and changes in the views and attitudes of society.

Germany's population growth rate began to slow down after the First World War. This was partly due to so many young men being killed which reduced male numbers in the reproductive sector of the population. The war was followed by the uncertain-

ties of the economic depression of the 1920s and 1930s. These made couples anxious about the number of children they could support and encouraged many young adults to emigrate overseas namely to U.S.A. and Latin American countries. Thus birth rates fell in the inter-war period despite some limited recovery towards the end of the 1930s. At that time the Nazi Government, as part of its expansionist policies, was actively encouraging couples to have more children.

Then came the Second World War when Germany lost nearly 3 million people, most of them from the reproductive sector of the population. For a time this was compensated for by the temporary rise in birth rates which usually follows the return of men home from the armed forces and by a major influx of refugees, including those from East Germany and other Eastern bloc countries which came under communist regimes. The population rose in this period of 1945–1960 from 42 million to 55 million.

During the postwar economic boom, labour shortages persuaded the German government to take in a sizeable immigration of guest workers from a number of other West European and Mediterranean countries including Turkey. But these were regarded as a temporary addition to the population and added little growth to the birth rate.

Indeed beneath this upsurge in total numbers, the 1960s witnessed a sharp fall in the birth rate from 18/000 to 14/000 and by 1980 it had fallen further to 10/000, insufficient to replace losses due to a death rate staying at around 11/000–12/000. (Fig. 2.4)

Such a decline is too great for it to be wholly explained by the fewer women coming into the reproductive age group as a result of the earlier falls in the birth rate.

11

2:1 SRI LANKA

Factors influencing family planning

A GOVERNMENT COMMITMENT

1 Fear of overpopulation (15 million) in an agriculturally based economy with increasing need of food imports.
2 Well established health network and family planning campaign even if of limited success.

But Government failed to give recent Preethi campaign full backing due to Buddhist opposition (immoral and against will of deity) and fear from Sinhalese minority that if it does not continue to increase, Tamil majority in population will gain power.

B FAMILY PLANNING

1 Despite clinic network, in 1970 only ⅓ of couples used a family planning method which required a visit to clinic or doctor.
2 Government media campaign
3 Preethi (Happiness) campaign launched to mass advertise, visit and sell male contraceptives through ordinary shop outlets cheaply (subsidised) — supported by IPPF (International Planned Parenthood Federation) and marketed by British Firm Reckitt and Colman. Highly successful. Mithuri (Friend) — pill campaign now launched.

C POVERTY REDUCTION

1 Malnutrition and disease reduced *but* incomes still low $230 per capita. Severe inflation and rising unemployment.
2 High literacy and awareness — 78% adult literacy.
3 Expanding education — 86% primary education rate.
4 Knowledge of family planning — high percentage 86%.
5 No absolute social barriers — but fear effect on male virility.

D SMALLER DESIRED FAMILY

1 Awareness high (86%) and desire high (63% of couples) 1971.
2 Further prompted by rising food costs and unemployment — fear cannot support a large family.

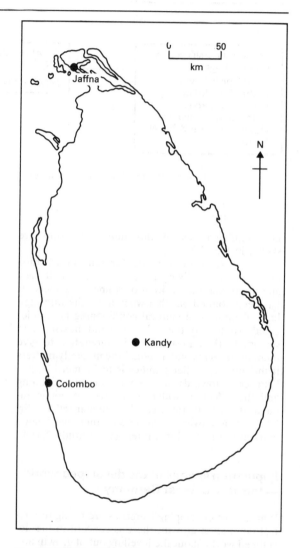

E HIGHER AGE OF MARRIAGE

1 Age rising — in 1977 average age of women 25 years.

F LOWER FERTILITY

(birth rates)
1960 = 36/000
1983 = 28/000

(a)	Year	Population ('000s)	Birth rate (per 1000)	Death rate (per 1000)	Nat. increase/decrease (per 1000)
	1946	46 190	16.1	13.0	3.1
	1950	50 173	16.2	10.5	5.7
	1955	52 383	15.7	11.1	4.6
	1960	55 433	17.4	11.6	5.8
	1965	58 619	17.7	11.5	6.2
	1970	60 651	13.4	12.1	1.3
	1975	61 829	9.7	12.1	−2.4
	1980	61 300	10.0	12.0	−2.0

Source: Statistisches Jahrbuch: Bevölkerungsbewegung

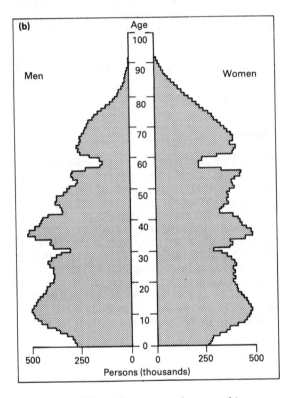

Fig. 2.4 (a) West Germany — demographic statistics, 1946–80
(b) West Germany's age structure, 1975

The main cause, as elsewhere in the developed world, is said to be the marked rise in affluence amongst the population during the postwar years. This has increased the desire for the good life in terms of consumer goods and material comforts. In turn this has led couples to postpone having children until later in marriage and to a desire for a small family. Good job opportunities for women, many of whom now look to continuing a career after marriage, has also been a significant factor.

There are other factors, including the uncertain political future of a divided Germany, which is located in an exposed position between the NATO forces of the West and the Communist bloc in the East.

Now, Germany has an ageing and a slowly declining population with little chance of this trend reversing, either by net-migration or by an up turn in the birth rate. This has important social and economic implications. With the growth in technology labour shortages are not likely to be too serious a problem except in lower paid service occupations. However, as more people enter the older age bracket beyond retirement and life expectancy continues to increase with better health care and welfare support, so a greater burden will fall on those same services requiring the switching of resources. Other implications are a changing pattern of consumer spending and housing needs, as well as some political anxiety over a decrease in population.

Exercises

1 Graph the post 1945 birth and death rate figures given above and discuss some of the possible reasons for the changes shown.
2 Try to indicate how fluctuations in the rate of population growth and the shape of the age sex pyramid for the West German population in 1975 are related.

The demographic transition model — limitations and usefulness

Limitations

Accepting that the population change for a country tends to follow the pattern depicted in the standard demographic transition model, there are bound to be variations in the rate and pace of change from one part of the world to another, even amongst

Natural increase rate (%)		Population (estimate 1981)	Annual addition
Group 1			
Egypt	3.0	43 500 000	1 305 000
Uganda	3.0	14 100 000	423 000
Venezuela	3.0	15 500 000	465 000
Group 2			
Mauritius	2.0	1 000 000	20 000
Indonesia	2.0	148 800 000	2 976 000
Thailand	2.0	48 600 000	972 000
Group 3			
Uruguay	1.0	2 900 000	29 000
Poland	1.0	36 000 000	360 000
Ireland	1.0	3 400 000	34 000

Fig. 2.5

advanced countries. For example Japan by conscious government planning, and effort from its peoples, using a variety of easily available birth control methods, went through the later expanding phase of its population much more rapidly than the earlier industrialised nations. Again, in the developing world not only are social and economic conditions different from the developed world, but countries are being assisted by international aid and finance to bring their populations under control. Thus those same industrial nations which in colonial days 'catapulted' territories into the rapidly expanding phase now contribute to slowing down that population growth.

In using the transition model as a framework for studying and comparing population changes from one country to another we should therefore be aware of these variations, as well as other limitations due to errors of exclusion. For example, absolute growth in population is not simply a matter of the rate of natural increase, i.e. differences in birth and death rates, but is also related to the size of the base population to which this relates as shown in Fig. 2.5. In each group the rate of natural increase is the same but because of different base populations, the annual addition to this varies considerably.

The transition model too includes no reference to the effects of migration in and out of a country. Yet for countries in the New World during the 19th and early 20th centuries this was the major cause of population growth as more recently it was for Israel, with its influx of Jews after the Second World War. Conversely it was a contributory factor to falling population rates in countries supplying these migrants. Further, since migrant populations are predominantly made up of young adults and young families, migration trends also have an important effect on natural rates of increase which form the basis of the transition model.

Usefulness

Provided it is used with caution, the transition model can provide a useful comparative framework within which to study some aspects of the population geography of countries, e.g. for relating population change to social and economic change.

Commonly the comparisons made have been between countries at varying stages in their development. But particularly for developing countries where there are marked regional variations in the rate of development, the demographic transition model can be used to highlight these as well as some of the wider dimensions of population change. This is illustrated in the following case study on Brazil.

2:2 BRAZIL

Regional aspects of demography

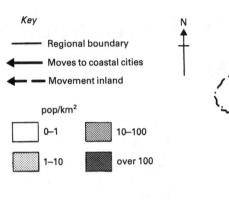

DENSITY DISTRIBUTION
main migration flows

THE INTERIOR — NORTH/CENTRE WEST

Least developed — sparse population, most at subsistence level.

Birth and death rates remain high ∴ limited natural increase. But since 1960s efforts to develop interior including new capital Brasilia, led to in migration and ∴ population increase. Emerging centres contrast with rest of interior.

NORTH EAST

Apart from the coastal region much of the population lives at subsistence level.

Whilst birth and death rates remain high inland, on the more developed coast death rates have fallen due to better medical facilities and higher incomes and there is ∴ a marked natural increase overall.

SOUTH EAST

The most industrialised region.

Marked contrast demographically between richer well educated minority and impoverished masses.

But generally birth and death rates are lower than in the North East and Interior and there is still a significant natural increase.

SOUTH

Many Western European settlers e.g. Dutch, German. Highly commercialised mixed economy — agriculture and industry.

Demographic structure is akin to developed countries but less so in the coffee lands bordering the South East.

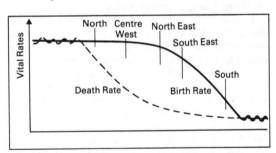

Suggested position of each region along the
Demographic Transition Cycle

N.B. Regional contrasts in economic development and opportunities have led to strong migration flows to the more industrialised South East and other coastal regions. This is only partly compensated for by a counter settler flow to the interior. Thus migration also affects the population structure of different regions.

Exercise

● On the basis of the information given identify the salient features in Brazil's population geography and try to account for them.

3 Population Density, Distribution and Carrying Capacity

Population and resources

'The clock is ticking,
Every day there are 200 000 more births,
Six million more every month!!'

Malthus and the fear of overpopulation

Whilst half the world is virtually uninhabited, the principal concern is that there are too many people for the world to support. Overpopulation, over-crowding and resultant poverty are said to be at the root of many of the major social and economic problems facing countries today.

This fear of overpopulation is not new. As long ago as 1798 Malthus caused a furore with his *Essay on the Principles of Population*. In it he stated quite simply that the growth in numbers will always keep a population's mass living standards at subsistence level, because whilst the 'passions between the sexes' would remain constant leading to population increasing in a geometric ratio (i.e. 1, 2, 4, 8, 16 etc.), the limit to increasing food supplies for them would be set by the limited amount of new land available for cultivation, so that food supply would increase only in an arithmetic ratio (i.e. 1, 2, 3, 4, 5 etc.). Population would so press on resources that the natural and positive checks famine, pestilence, war and higher mortality amongst the weak and diseased would operate, supported only to a small extent by a conscious reduction in early marriages amongst the more educated in society and voluntary restraint from intercourse.

In the developing world there is evidence of Malthusian checks operating especially in some of the drought ridden areas of Africa like the Sahel bordering the Sahara and stretching through to Sudan and Ethiopia. But much of the world, because of technological and social progress as well as new discoveries, has been able to escape the misery Malthus foretold. Population growth has long been under control in the developed world and there are signs of this happening elsewhere in the world, most notably in China and India, the world's most popu-lated countries. Food production has risen and new resources are constantly being added to the world's disposable wealth. The misery and hunger seen in the world today is not so much due to insufficient resources but to its unequal distribution amongst peoples both within and between countries.

Population — technology, resource, relationships

However, Malthus did highlight the close rela-tionship which exists between population numbers and the resources available to support those num-bers. To this simple relationship can be added a third element — namely advances in technology. These include not only new techniques aiding eco-nomic growth but also others such as new birth control methods and health measures like the use of D.D.T. to eradicate malaria. These directly affect the population element in the relationship.

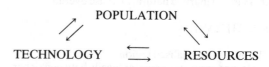

Whilst it is important to appreciate these basic relationships, it soon becomes apparent in any effort to explore these in real world situations, that a simple population-resource — technology frame-work is inadequate. Its dimensions need more detailed specification. Also some references are needed to show how interactions are modified from one situation to another by cultural differences be-tween societies and by external factors. Hence an elaboration of the basic framework just given is shown in Fig. 3.1, together with a schematic applica-tion of it — the United Kingdom (Fig. 3.2) exem-plifying an industrial nation and India (Fig. 3.3) exemplifying a country in the developing world.

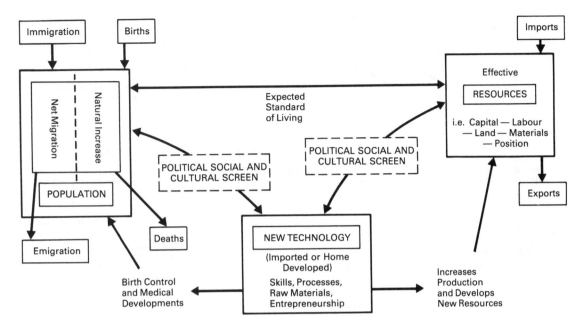

Fig. 3.1   Population, resource, technology relationships

Exercise

Study Figs. 3.2 and 3.3. Briefly highlight the significance of the relationships shown for each country and compare and contrast India and the United Kingdom in the light of the information given.

Rate of increase % per annum	Number of years to double population
2	35
3	23
4	18

Density and the concept of carrying capacity

The most elementary index of population distribution is that of crude density, i.e. the number of persons per unit area, usually expressed per km² (Fig. 3.4). But as it simply relates people to an area of land, taking no account of the capacity of that land to support the population or the standard of living at which the population expects to be supported, the crude density index is of very limited value. We must therefore consider density in terms of the carrying capacity of the land.

Carrying capacity is an ecological concept. It is used for example to identify the number of livestock which an area of grazing land can support, but it has proved useful too in the study of human populations.

Biologically a population can in theory expand indefinitely at an exponential rate soon doubling itself as the following example shows:

In reality, however, as environmental limits take effect the exponential curve for any living species will level off. But the point at which this occurs will vary from one type of species to another and from one kind of habitat to another. It will depend on the food requirements of a species on the one hand and environmental conditions on the other. These will include not only the amount and dependability of the food supply in any habitat, but also such things as climatic conditions, the threat of predators and competition from other species for the same food supply.

Once the population has reached the ceiling limit for a particular habitat, growth will level off and the population stabilise. Any temporary increase in population due to unusually favourable conditions, such as a good growing season for vegetation and wildlife, will ultimately be wiped out through natural checks and outmigration when conditions return to normal. Conversely any temporary deterioration in conditions, for instance a prolonged drought, will also bring about the operation of natural checks and outmigration as seen in the case of livestock and human populations occupying marginal land.

Where such natural checks and outmigration are in evidence over a period of time, whether of wild-

17

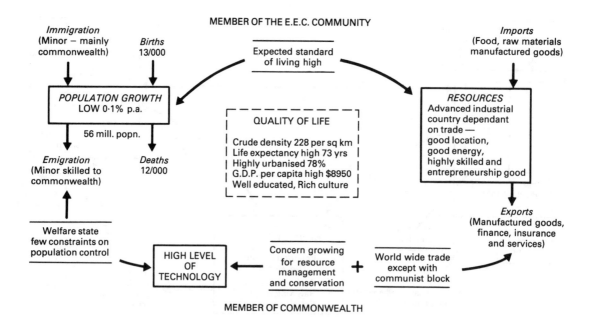

Fig. 3.2   The United Kingdom — population, resource, technology relationships

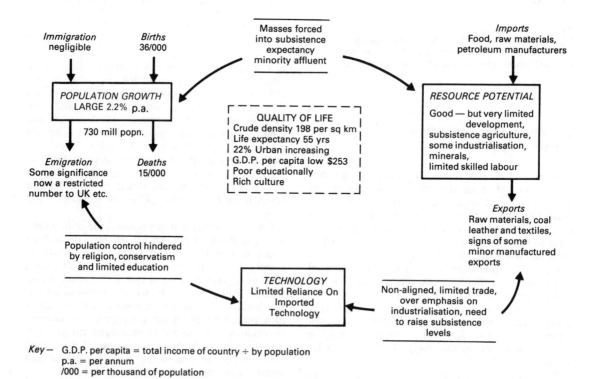

Fig. 3.3   India — population, resource, technology relationships

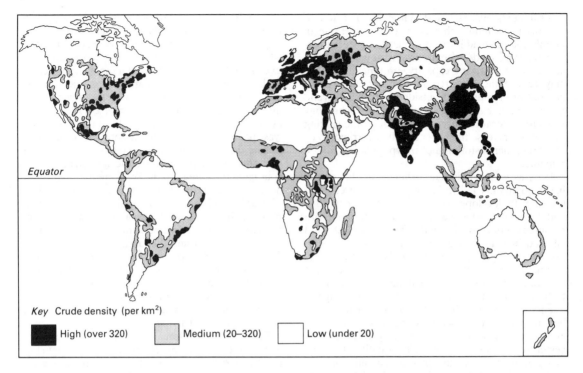

Key Crude density (per km²)

■ High (over 320)   ▨ Medium (20–320)   ☐ Low (under 20)

Fig. 3.4   Population density distribution

life or human populations, this is a sure sign that the carrying capacity of that particular environment has been reached. For human populations this means that there is enough food for survival but not for vigour or optimum growth and any slight unfavourable change in environmental conditions could be disastrous. Today there are undoubtedly populations in this situation, notably in the drier lands of Africa. Clearly this concept of survival carrying capacity is a useful one and it is worth mentioning here two associated concepts, optimum carrying capacity and tolerance capacity.

Optimum carrying capacity occurs when numbers are below the survival carrying capacity, allowing for adequate nutrition and individual growth. In effect for human populations, it is a situation allowing for a rise in the standard of living and so is akin to the concept of optimum population used by demographers.

However amongst any population, quality of living is not simply a matter of material well-being but also of feelings — of psychological well-being. This applies as much to animals as to human beings and for this, the term tolerance capacity is used. Stresses and strains of high density living for instance, may lead to feelings of dissatisfaction and depression prompting migration to areas with more tolerable conditions. Thus tolerance capacity is a useful and appropriate concept in relation to the urban overcrowding of populations.

Related concepts of optimum, over- and underpopulation

Having discussed the useful link between population and the capacity of the environment to carry that population, we may briefly consider the density terms exclusively used for human populations but closely allied to the concept of carrying capacity already outlined.

Whilst optimum population is synonymous as a term with optimum carrying capacity, under- and overpopulation refer not simply to carrying capacity but also to the standard of living at which the population can be supported. Thus overpopulation occurs where a reduction in numbers would lead to a rise in the standard of living for the remaining population by releasing some resources for investment in further development. Underpopulation occurs where an increase in numbers would enable more utilisation of resources again leading to a rise in the standard of living.

Overpopulation

It is easy to appreciate that high densities of population may lead to situations of overpopulation, but not so easy to appreciate that it may also occur where densities are low. For example in harsh

19

environments such as desert margins basic resource support is so limited that even a small increase in population can lead to overpopulation. Alternatively in the same kinds of environment, as we have seen in relation to carrying capacity, prolonged drought may reduce the resource support for an existing population. However, if outside agencies intervene by bringing in basic food supplies or the technology to increase local resources e.g. through the sinking of wells to increase the water supply for irrigation or livestock, then a situation of overpopulation can be remedied.

It is, as we have stated earlier, a matter of the basic population — technology — resource relationship. In developed countries capital, technology and knowledge have enabled the utilisation of more resources both locally and from overseas and allowed increasing population densities to be supported at improving living standards. Yet overpopulation may still occur in the sense that whilst material standards may be maintained, overconcentration causes other stresses and strains lowering the quality of life. The level of population has gone beyond tolerance capacity. A check on population growth or active decentralisation away from congested regions would improve the quality of living.

Different situations in which overpopulation currently occurs are illustrated in Fig. 3.5. These cases however also indicate that situations are never static and therefore overpopulation itself is a relative term not only in the locational sense but also within the dimension of time.

Overpopulation creates the most problems and therefore receives most attention. But there are regions where underpopulation occurs, requiring governments to instigate policies designed to increase populations.

Underpopulation

Underpopulation usually occurs where despite the resource potential to support a higher density, a region is unattractive when compared with more settled areas. It may be the area is a frontier region awaiting development or a longer settled area which has lost population to more attractive areas.

Frontier regions

The remoter areas of Australia and Siberia have rich mineral and other resources awaiting development, but one of the problems is attracting enough labour. People are reluctant to move from the more favourable urbanised areas into these harsh environments. By improving communications, including light passenger planes, and by offering very high wages, some labour is attracted but it is usually only temporary. Population numbers remain low.

A similar problem has been recognised in Brazil, where an extreme population imbalance exists between the heavily settled coastal regions, particularly the south east and the sparsely populated interior including Amazonia. In an effort to attract people into the interior, the new capital of Brasilia was established in the 1960s 960 km from the coast and it was made a focal point for a network of highways linking the interior and coastal regions. It was hoped that this would provide a basic infrastructure encouraging the spread of the settlement and development to areas around Brasilia and further afield.

Brasilia itself now has a population of around 1.3 million. But it is only the area immediately around the city that has attracted some further settlement and development and this partly in response to the expanding market offered by the capital for foodstuffs and other produce. Indeed Brasilia has to some extent produced a counter effect on further areas, encouraging rural depopulation this time to the new capital in the hopes of employment and a better standard of living.

Brazil has therefore more recently adopted a wider and more comprehensive regional development programme for the interior involving Amazonia as well as the plateau interior. In addition to extending the major highway network, further secondary growth points promoting rural development will be set up. But so far these efforts have met with only limited success.

Underpopulation brought about by depopulation

Underpopulation is not a feature of frontier areas only, it also exists in long settled regions as depopulated rural peripheries in the advanced countries of Western Europe show. In the United Kingdom, for example, wages are on an average lower and unemployment higher in the peripheral south west, rural Wales and the Highlands of Scotland than for the rest of the country, excepting older declining industrial areas.

Resultant outward migration becomes self perpetuating unless something is done to stem the flow — fewer people mean a decreasing demand for services — the lower level of services reduces the viability of the community encouraging further outmigration.

Factors influencing population density

We may usefully close this section on population density by summarising the environmental and human factors influencing the population density which can be supported in contrasting situations (Figs. 3.6, 3.7).

Indicators	Chad	Bangladesh	Hong Kong	Netherlands
Population 000	4647	92 619	5233	15 020
Birth rate	44	47	17	13
Death rate	24	18	5	8
Natural increase % per annum	2.0	3.1	2.7	0.7
Crude density per sq. km	3.5	623	4900	349
Income				
Gross national product per capita in dollars	172	121	3809	10 624
Growth rate of economy % per annum	3.3	6.2	9.2	3.1
Food				
Calorie intake per capita as % of minimum requirements	75	84	100+	129
Employment %				
Primary	41	53	1	4
Manufacturing	13	7	27	29
Services	46	40	72	67

Sources for 1983

CHAD
Low density and low standard of living

Harsh desert margin environment — pastoralism — cultivation in watered areas

Drought disasters leads to forced outmigration

Emergency food relief — longer term improvement through secure water supply and better agriculture

BANGLADESH
High density — low standard — crowded population onto alluvial lowlands — mass depend on subsistence rice farming

Flood/typhoon hazards

Relief and rise in living standard sought through Green Revolution and birth control

NETHERLANDS
High density at a high standard of living

Ranstaadt example of overcrowded urban living — social-psychological pressures and inner city problems — long distance commuting

Solution sought through decentralisation — green belt and other planning controls

HONG KONG
High density — rising incomes but extreme overcrowding on limited site — urban high-rise blocks

Island site spreading to mainland — dependent on industry and trade — rising prosperity

Overcrowding exacerbated by refugee influx from China and Vietnam

Relief sought through control on immigration — planned new towns and tunnel linkage on New Territory mainland

Exercise

What are the criteria on which an area may be classed as overpopulated? Discuss the ways in which over-population may be solved. (Refer to Fig. 3.5.)

Fig. 3.5 *Different situations of overpopulation*

Physical Factors		Human Factors	
Negative Influences	*Positive Influences*	*Negative Influences*	*Positive Influences*
Steep mountainous terrain	Lowland — undulating terrain	Too many people giving little surplus of production	Numbers sufficiently below survival capacity to allow for a surplus to sell, giving finance for further development
Severe climatic conditions — severe cold and aridity	Absence of temperature extremes, sufficient precipitation and high enough temperatures to encourage plant growth throughout the year (plus irrigation facilities where a dry season occurs)	Ageing labour force subject to disease and apathy	Healthy young labour force
		Low levels of literacy and education making use of more advanced techniques difficult	Adaptable educated workforce
Dense forest vegetation which combined with a constantly high humidity is detrimental to health	Easily cleared vegetation such as savanna		
Infertile soils	Easily worked fertile soils such as alluvium and loams	Poverty, therefore limited purchasing power and limited finance for investments and improvements	Rising income levels and access to investment funds
Poor drainage — swamp and marsh	Well drained soils but sufficiently retentive of moisture for crop growth	Poor entrepreneurship (management skills etc.)	Improving entrepreneur skills and good advisory services
Absence of complementary fishing resource	Presence of fishing opportunities, lake, river or sea access	Poor infrastructure including communications	Good basic infrastructure
Absence of mineral or energy deposits	Presence of mineral or energy deposits	Absence of export markets	Expanding home and export markets
		Overdominance of multi-national companies 'creaming' off profits	Equitable share of invest-ment and control of country's assets
		Political instability	Political stability

Location and Accessibility Factors

Negative Influences	*Positive Influences*
Isolated from outside influences	Open to outside influences including perhaps a history of colonisation

Fig. 3.6   *Developing regions largely dependent on primary activities*

Human Factors

Negative Influences	Positive Influences
Poverty and low purchasing power	Affluence and high purchasing power
Low levels of education and a high illiteracy rate	Good level of general education, together with higher and technical education and research facilities
Poor communication network and overall infrastructure (i.e. services etc.)	Well integrated communication network and a good integrated and flexible infrastructure
Limited entrepreneurship (i.e. business, sales and innovative skills)	High level of entrepreneurship together with international linkages via multinational corporations etc.
Newly independent politically or with a history of political dependency. (There may be social and political instability)	Mature politically and socially with stability
Poor level of international trade with emphasis on primary exports and import of technology, manufactured goods and aid/investment	Specialisation and a strong reliance on international trade and exchange. Export emphasis on skills manufactured goods, technology, services and overseas investment

Physical Factors

These were of importance but outside of rural regions are now secondary to accessibility and human influences

For rural activities they are similar to those for developing regions (opposite)

But as a basis for manufacturing they include the presence or absence of such things as mineral and power resources, an adequate water supply, extent of available level and accessible sites, difficulty or otherwise of terrain for constructing a communication network

Location and Accessibility Factors

Negative Influences	Positive Influences
Inaccessible and far inland	Accessible, coastal estuary locations

Fig. 3.7   *Developed countries largely dependent on manufacturing and services (and newly industrialised countries)*

Exercise

On the basis of material given in the text and Figs. 3.6 and 3.7, compare and explain the population density distribution for two countries, one from the developing world and the other from the developed world.

4 Migration and Urbanisation

'*Human beings have always been migrants...Indeed, one of the oldest of human rights is mobility — the right to move.*'
(Palmer, M. — *The Guardian*, 28.8.79)

What is migration?

The term is frequently used to cover any kind of movement by people, but most writers concerned with population study agree that its use should be restricted to moves involving a permanent change of residence. (The United Nations constitution defines 'permanent' as a change of residence lasting more than a year.) It does not then cover temporary movements. Thus such things as pastoral nomadism, seasonal movement of labour, commuting to work and tourism do not strictly come under the heading of migration, since they are of a short term and temporary nature and involve a return to a previous location. These are better termed circulatory movements and are dealt with elsewhere.

Permanent migrations can be basically classified on three counts:

1 Cause of the move, i.e. whether voluntary from choice or involuntary as a result of being forced out of an area.

2 The distance over which the migration occurs — the main differentiation being between international migrations where national frontiers are crossed and those internal to a country. This internal kind of move is further divided between localised and longer inter-regional migration.

3 By the type of area from and to which the migration occurs

On the basis of these criteria an overall classification of the different kinds of migration can be made.

A BASIC CLASSIFICATION OF MIGRATION

Cause		Distance	
		Internal to a country	
		Regional	*Local*
VOLUNTARY	*International* (across national frontiers)	rural—rural	rural—rural
		rural—urban	rural—urban
	Overseas — Continental	urban—rural	urban—rural
		urban—urban	intra-urban
		frontierwards	(i.e. within an urban area)
INVOLUNTARY	*International*	*Regional*	*Local*
	Overseas — Continental		

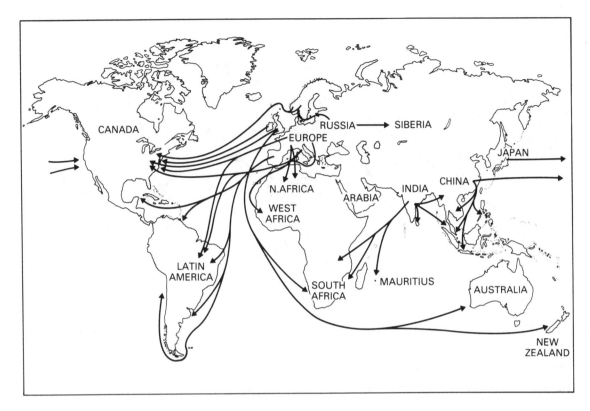

Fig. 4.1   Main world migrations

Patterns of migration

As we have already begun to see, patterns of migration are complex, even bewilderingly so if we remember that such movements have gone on throughout history involving peoples of varying nationality, race and colour and affecting every inhabited corner of the globe. The main directions of international migrations for recent times are shown in Fig. 4.1.

Within any country the various kinds of migration flows seem to be related on the one hand to major growth centres, in particular large metropolitan core regions, and on the other to peripheral-frontier regions. Most migration is associated with growth centres and its various kinds are shown in Fig. 4.2. In the case of developing countries inmigration flows dominate for large urban centres but for the older advanced countries outmigration is overtaking inmigration.

The kinds of patterns shown could in modified form also be used for other types of core growth regions such as a mining centre or a newly industrialised area.

As we saw earlier, frontier or peripheral regions may also be affected by in- and outmigration. Whilst these may be related to what is happening in growth centres, frontier or peripheral migration patterns are of secondary importance.

Towards an explanation of migration

Given the complex pattern of migration and the variety of influences at work, it is not surprising that it has proved difficult to provide a generally satisfactory framework or model within which to explain these various kinds of migration.

One of the most basic attempts has been to see migration as a response to a simple push-pull mechanism. Negative factors in the losing area are seen as forcing or encouraging people to move in response to the pull of better opportunities, whether real or perceived in the receiving area. Whilst useful as a starting point it is too deterministic an explanation giving little attention to the process by which individuals or groups weigh up the situation and then decide whether to move or not. Lee in his theory of migration on the other hand, focusses attention on the decision taking process with the individual, family or group weighing up the pros and cons of moving in the light of a whole range of

25

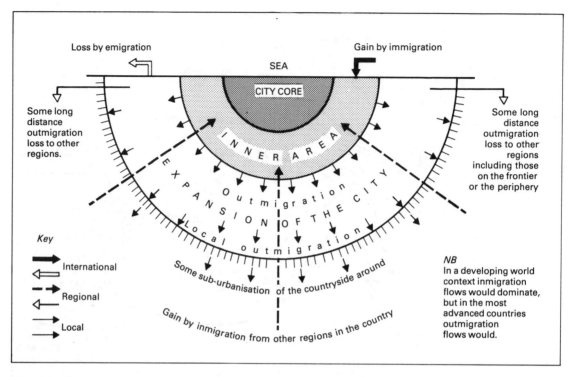

Fig. 4.2   Broad patterns of migration for a large coastal metropolitan centre

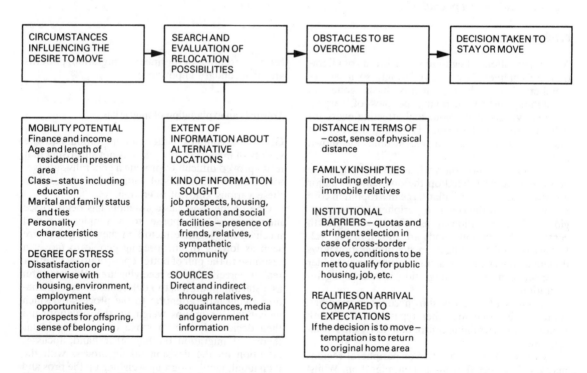

Fig. 4.3   Factors affecting the decision whether to migrate or not

factors, one set in the home area at one end and the other in the contemplated prospective receiving area(s). He then also introduces the idea of there being a number of personal and environmental obstacles both real and perceived which have to be overcome before migration takes place. The longer the distance of the contemplated move the greater are the real and perceived obstacles which need to be overcome. So much so that initial moves tend to be over a limited distance.

Faced with making the kinds of decisions which are outlined in Lee's theory some families and individuals will be in a better position than others to move. These are the ones whose circumstances make them highly mobile. In contrast there are others whose circumstances make it unlikely they will move — these are the immobile — the stayers.

The reasons for staying or leaving are summarised in Fig. 4.3. Given this more detailed kind of framework we can now consider the migrations which have and are helping to shape the population geography of different countries — taking firstly the case of developed countries and secondly that of developing countries.

Mobility and migration in developed countries

Historically the main streams of migration concerning the countries of Western Europe and North America have been those associated with the period of the Industrial Revolution and the emergence of Nation States in Central Europe during the 19th century. Economic and political circumstances, together with the pressure of growing population numbers led to mass migration overseas from Europe to the New World, following in the wake of the earlier colonists including those such as the Pilgrim Fathers seeking freedom from religious persecution. But at the same time as these overseas migrations, an equally massive but internal migration was taking place from the countryside into the cities. The growth of industries provided expanding employment opportunities to those pushed off the land because of the enclosures and mechanisation associated with the agricultural revolution.

Whilst well into the 20th century overseas migration and urbanisation remained the dominant kinds of migration associated with advanced countries, in the aftermath of the Second World War these gave way to other lesser but still important movements in the immediate postwar years and the 1960s. These included movement and resettlement of refugees, labour migrations of foreign workers into countries with labour shortages such as Germany and France, some of whom settled permanently. Perhaps most significantly for the United Kingdom there was the influx of many coloured migrants from Commonwealth countries such as India, Pakistan, and the Caribbean.

But both in the New World and Europe these have largely come to an end, with even some return migration of refugees and longer term migrants to their countries of origin. Today most attention in developed countries seems to be centred on problems of rural depopulation from peripheral regions and the decentralisation or counter urbanisation flows from the congested and decaying inner areas of the largest cities to the outer suburbs and nearby rural areas. Whilst much of this is spontaneous, some of it is planned decentralisation associated with the establishment of new towns and expansion of smaller towns in the more accessible areas.

The most interesting case in these respects, because of its history, size and diversity of population, is the United States.

The case of the United States

No other country perhaps better demonstrates not only the whole variety of migration indicated in our initial classification, but also the depth of human searching and the will to survive encompassed in the kinds of decision taking processes people go through about whether to migrate or not.

The United States (of which the Red Indians, the indigenous inhabitants, are now but a small underprivileged ethnic minority) is frequently held up as a nation and society founded on human rights — including that of freedom of movement. However, many of the migrations which went towards the building of this nation were not voluntary, but forced migrations. The most notable of these was the negro slave trade which provided the labour for the cotton and sugar plantations in the south. But from the middle of the last century there have also been waves of refugees from Europe fleeing from war, and religious and political persecution. There were also those forced to migrate to avoid the starvation and hardship engendered among the masses by social and economic systems emerging out of the industrial and agricultural revolutions occurring amongst the new nation states of Europe — first in the West and then in Eastern and Central Europe.

So forced as well as voluntary migrations contributed to the melting pot, out of which the American nation was made. Today the main streams of international migration have dwindled, but internally the melting pot process goes on. All but the lowest paid and underprivileged have increasing potential and opportunity for movement and many are seeking new growth areas and a more amenable environment. So the westward movement to occupy new lands during the 19th century and the first half of the 20th century and the build up of industrial cities in the north east, has now given way to a shift of population to the sunnier climates and new growth areas on the Gulf Coast and in the west. These migrations increasingly include people moving on

27

retirement. The second change in migration has been the dispersion of people away from the large cities to more rural suburbs and smaller towns around the main centres.

These changes summarised in Case Study 4.1 (p. 32, 33) partly reflect not only spatial shifts in the economy, with older areas relatively declining and others emerging elsewhere based on new technology, but also reflect changes of aspirations amongst the population. Unfortunately the poorer classes in American society, such as the negroes in the ghettos of Detroit and other large cities, the recently arrived ethnic minorities such as the Puerto Ricans, and the poor whites of Appalachia and the south, have no way of realising their aspirations. They therefore represent the 'stayers' amongst the population.

Migration, mobility and urbanisation in developing countries

Kinds of migration past and present

Apart from circulatory movements associated with seasonal changes in agriculture or land exhaustion, and forced migrations associated with inter-tribal wars and the slave trade, most of the major migration flows in the developing world date from European intervention and colonisation. Whilst much of the attention today is focussed on the process of urbanisation now well advanced in Latin America and parts of Asia but still gathering momentum in Africa, there have been and are other important migration flows. These are illustrated in Case Study 4.2 (p. 34, 35), together with some of the basic causes and consequences.

Urbanisation

Broadening the concept

In its simplest form urbanisation is the process of population concentration into cities and the sprawl of urban land uses into the countryside. But increasingly urbanisation is also being seen as a dynamic force in society whereby values and behaviour patterns recognised as 'urban' are propagated and cultural changes take place. The urban environment involves not only a change of life style for the newcomers but also the stresses and strains adjustment to city life brings. This has frequently implied the break up of the extended family and of the communal group which underpinned the old rural life the migrant left. But ties do remain. Many immigrants coming to the city initially seek security with relations and other people from their own home area, who have already settled in the city.

Furthermore contact with the home area is maintained — money is sent back and many hope some day to return with their fortunes made to buy land and end their days peacefully amongst their own folk and surroundings.

The pace of urbanisation

From 1850–1900 world population increased by about 37% but the number of people living in cities increased by over 200%. From 1900–1950 it escalated further to 250% for urban centres in comparison to a 50% growth in world population as a whole. Whilst the trend towards large cities in most developed countries is now being reversed, in developing countries it is still gathering momentum (see Fig. 4.4).

Concern at the rate of urbanisation

In the move from a basically subsistence and self-sufficient economy to one based on specialisation of activities and exchange, the concentration of people in particular localities is inevitable. Industry and commerce on any large scale can only take place where there is the opportunity for contacts and linkages of a varied and complex kind. As developing countries progress along the path of modernisation, urbanisation will gather momentum until its peak is reached.

At present the inability of cities in the developing world to absorb the influx of people has created many problems associated primarily with unemployment and overcrowding. So much so that government policies are directed towards finding ways of stemming rural urban migration altogether rather than focussing on the central issues of how to accommodate those who have already arrived.

Whilst most of those experienced in attempts to cope with this rapid influx, recognise the need to control the pace of urbanisation, they also see some continued urbanisation not only as inevitable but even desirable. They claim that even with all the problems, the lot of the migrant is on the whole better than it would be back in the rural area. Further by relieving pressure on these areas it allows for some improvement in conditions for those left.

This more positive view of urbanisation is well summarised by Souza, one of the developing world's most experienced city planners and a former Managing Director of the 'New Bombay' built to relieve some of the problems of the overcrowded old city.

'Properly we ought to lament the influx only if migrants to cities consequently live more wretched lives than they would if they stayed at home in the villages. Clearly they do not, because they would in that case go back, and we could suspend our lament. So that even after allowing for all the miseries they suffer, you must conclude that they

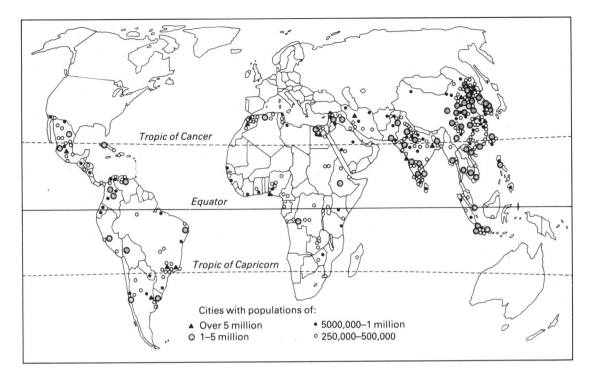

Fig. 4.4   Developing world cities

are better off than they were in the villages. Their employment opportunities have increased immensely, and so have their access to drinking water, to health services, to schools and to entertainment. The new options, the vistas of opportunities that the cities offer them, are a welcome escape from the irrational conventions and social taboos that rural society often imposes on poor people.

The rural influx then is not the continuing disaster we are told it is. It is the natural search for equilibrium in an unequal situation. Yet there is cause for concern.'

(From D'Souza, J.B., 'Half the World in Cities' *New Internationalist*, No. 88 June 1980)

Urbanisation in Africa

Growth rate

Whilst only about 20% of Africa's population lives in urban environments compared with, for example, 64% in Latin America, the current rate of urbanisation is high — around 6% annually taking all sizes of urban areas, and 8.5% for the major cities. If this pace continues the urban population of Africa will have doubled in a decade and will be greater still for West Africa where much of the urban growth is taking place (see Fig. 4.5).

Direction and character

Most movement is to the largest cities, but it is not a simple movement from the rural areas. Udo indicates that migrants come from both rural areas and the smaller urban centres where opportunities are limited. Frequently the migration may be in stages with a first move being to the nearest large town and from there as hopes of employment are dashed to the largest centres. In Africa (unlike parts of Latin America) the overseas migration component is not important. Of the African migrants themselves most come from the young sector in the population, aged 15–35. There tends to be a predominance of males, partly because wives and children are left behind until the husband is permanently settled, but also because free movement of single women is frowned on in parts of Africa, particularly in Muslim areas of West Africa.

On arriving in the city the tendency is not to settle initially in one of the peripheral shanty town areas that characterise every large city in a developing country, but to join relatives or friends usually already living in the main inner areas. Kinship and tribal links remain important, for many migrants need support until they have found a job or become accustomed to city life. It is generally only after they have been in a city for a time that migrants leave friends or relatives and try to find somewhere to live

	Estimated population in thousands			
	1950	1960	1970	1980
Ibadan	430	550	750	1100
Addis Ababa	350	500	850	1300
Lagos	250	600	1600	3000
Kinshasa	220	500	1400	2700
Khartoum	210	380	650	1100
Dakar	180	380	600	950
Accra	160	390	740	1100
Luanda	150	250	470	750
Harare	140	280	400	800
Nairobi	130	270	510	900
Abidjan	80	220	600	1200
Dar es Salaam	80	170	380	800

Note: Figures are for the whole urban agglomeration.

Fig. 4.5   Population growth in tropical African cities, 1950–80

themselves. It is then that they may become squatters with their families in some shanty area, building their own makeshift home.

Consequences of urbanisation

Demographic

Unlike some areas such as Sao Paulo and Rio de Janeiro in Brazil or Bombay in India where natural increase is now the dominant factor, migration remains the essential cause of the urban population explosion in Africa. The natural rate of increase of the population already settled in the city is a secondary though significant influence. Fertility rates are generally lower than in rural areas but because of better health facilities mortality rates are also lower.

In the long run urbanisation is likely to lead to a slowing down of population growth in Africa just as it has and is doing elsewhere. But at the present time the continued influx of young migrants offsets lower mortality and fertility rates so that the major cities in general have a similar age population structure to the national average.

Positive social and economic effects

It has already been noted that urbanisation has advantages. It hastens the modernisation process for the country as a whole, brings people into contact with more job opportunities as well as better health, education and other welfare services.

Urbanisation is also not quite the disruptive influence on family and tribal life that it appears to be in some of the literature. Whilst important changes inevitably take place there is a transition phase where links with family, the tribe and the home are maintained by many. The family is an active agent in the process of urbanisation. Able members are sponsored to migrate in search of urban employment and members in need are supported by the kin network. Migrants remain dependent on the goodwill of those at home.

Whilst unemployment is high, there is much informal employment which helps to sustain at a basic subsistence level all but the most disadvantaged migrant groups. Many seek casual employment often below the minimum legal wage. Others engage in petty self employment such as newspaper selling and portering. The range of opportunities available outside the organised labour market is so wide that few of the 'unemployed' are totally without some form of income. Overall there is sufficient cash surplus to sustain the wide practice of sending money back home to families and dependent relatives in rural areas, thus bringing some benefit to rural areas.

Detrimental effects

Too rapid urbanisation is the crucial problem. Job opportunity cannot be expanded fast enough to keep pace with it and though housing and other service facilities are increasing these are not sufficient either. Also the actual planning and administrative framework within which authorities try to grapple with over rapid urbanisation are quite unsuitable for the size of the organisational and financial problems this has brought.

There is therefore mounting unemployment, as well as pollution and other health hazards from casual efforts to set up a variety of small scale businesses. The waste from these is either tipped into cesspits or runs down the alleyways in the poorer inner quarters or in the shanty towns on the periphery.

There is a serious shortage of housing. Few dwellings have an interior water supply and many no access to a running water supply at all. In Freetown 95% of the inhabitants in 1970 shared latrines and in Abidjan 65% of the sewerage ended up in unlined pits and water courses.

The sheer growth of large urban centres also creates overall infrastructure problems well illustrated in Lagos. The journey to work is a nightmare for many poorly paid workers living in shanties at a distance from industry and employment in the city centre. Bus services are infrequent and too expensive. Highways become clogged with traffic increasing social and economic costs to workers and businesses.

Towards a solution

A recent World Bank Report looking at the problems of tropical Africa suggests the following points as part of an urban strategy which would help to bring the problems under control.

An overhaul of administrative and planning structures

Many are legacies from an earlier colonial period and cover an inadequate area, urbanisation having overflowed into the surrounding areas. Further, various departments compete against each other or are unaware of what is happening so that comprehensive planning becomes exceedingly difficult. Alongside this there is the need for a reform in rating and taxation laws to bring in more finance.

Realistic servicing

There are two sides to this. On the one hand at present many of the migrants coming in are highly motivated and have high expectations, therefore they expect a higher level of services than it is realistic to expect. On the other hand many authorities have concentrated on the wrong type of servicing and housing. For example, during the period before independence, the Colonial Development Corporation financed national housing corporations and building societies which constructed housing of a standard and price which only the better off could afford. Also until recently the answer to shanty town growth has been the bulldozer and expensive comprehensive redevelopment on the site or, as in Bombay, the building of a new town nearby.

Recently a more realistic sites and service approach has been advocated, whereby the local authority or the government supply the site foundations and services but the people themselves do the building on a self-help basis. In this way costs are kept down, building is more rapid, the people are directly involved and are more likely to be able to afford housing. Areas can later be up-graded to receive other services — schools, shopping centres and clinics etc. A crucial need is for people to have a secure tenure of the land on which their homes are built.

Employment

Whilst efforts should be made to expand employment in established sectors developing countries should encourage the informal sectors too, because activities in this sector are labour intensive and the cost of job creation is low. Examples include small businesses, the construction industries involved with low cost housing, and small scale cottage industry. These activities largely arise from the entrepreneurship of individuals, many of them one time migrants now settled in the city. Entrepreneurs until now have been discouraged by unnecessary regulations. Credit needs to be given and low cost loans under a 'cost-recovery scheme'.

Slowing down the rate of urbanisation

Slowing down rural – urban migration will also help to keep existing urban problems nearer more manageable levels. This inevitably involves authorities giving more attention and finance to improving conditions in rural areas. Some cash flow already takes place back to the countryside from relatives settled in the cities and the growth in urban populations is providing a market for cash crops in rural areas nearest to the cities. But these are not enough to persuade people that rural areas hold a better future for them than the cities. Recently there have been encouraging signs that national development planning is being reorientated to take more account of rural needs (see Section 4). More capital is being invested in agricultural improvement schemes and in local market towns to encourage small scale industry and commerce.

But political and financial power still effectively resides in the hands of a few who mainly live in the large urban centres and are swayed by the voice of business interests and the more educated and wealthy minority. Thus resources are still disproportionately allocated to the urban sector, mainly the large capital cities. Thus any major change must involve a shift in the balance of power. This happened in Nigeria in 1983 where a military coup overthrew the established corrupt government. One of the specific objectives of the new regime was the redistribution of wealth away from the privileged few, towards the mass of the people, including those in rural areas. So far huge external debt commitments and the need for austerity measures to combat inflation and other internal problems have limited progress in this direction. However increasing support for the agricultural sector is bringing some benefits to rural areas.

4:1 THE UNITED STATES

Migration

WHITE MIGRATION

1 1800-1910 (40 million from Europe), to 1890 mainly from West Europe: some forced by disasters (Irish potato famine 1840) and wars. But most seeking new opportunities.

2 Settled initially in North East Sea Board to work in industry and on the land. But as the West was opened up and population increased by births and immigration move Westward to Mid-West and onward to California, aided by railways at close of 19th C.

BLACK MIGRATION

1 1750-1850 15 million slaves from West Africa mainly to the South plantations.

2 After the Civil War (1865) and abolition of slavery, many moved to industrial cities in North — peak reached 1910 — settled in inner cities — black ghettos.

3 Since 1945 move West to large metropolitan centres of California eg. San Francisco.

4 Recent counter migration back to South attracted by oil and technology boom on the Gulf coast and psychological pull of the South.

3 Later immigration from Europe more selective, some refugees but flow restricted by quota and slowing down of population growth in Europe. After 1945 — 9 million came.

4 Recent internal migration to sunbelt of West and South — for retirement and to new industrial growth and desire to move out of large cities.

CONSEQUENCES

1 Brought capital, expertise and manpower to open up continent.

2 Money resources and products shipped back to Europe helped further growth of the country.

3 Rich culture/political mix.

4 Rising living standards except for poor whites in rural backwaters of the South Appalachia and the inner cities.

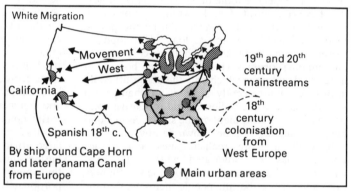

White Migration

Movement West

California

Spanish 18th c.

By ship round Cape Horn and later Panama Canal from Europe

19th and 20th century mainstreams

18th century colonisation from West Europe

Main urban areas

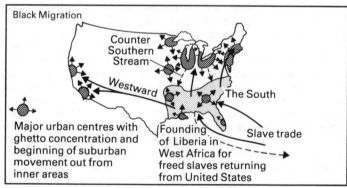

Black Migration

Counter Southern Stream

Westward

The South

Slave trade

Major urban centres with ghetto concentration and beginning of suburban movement out from inner areas

Founding of Liberia in West Africa for freed slaves returning from United States

CONSEQUENCES

1 23 million (10% of total population) increasing as higher fertility rate than whites.

2 Rich labour resource for the South and industrial cities.

3 Rich contribution to United States culture.

4 Offset by racial tension, discrimination, plight of black inner city ghettos.

Recent migration trends

1. To California and the Gulf
2. Decentralisation from the large cities
3. Recent immigration of Mexicans, Puerto Ricans etc. seeking work — Mexicans in agriculture of South West — others in the cities.

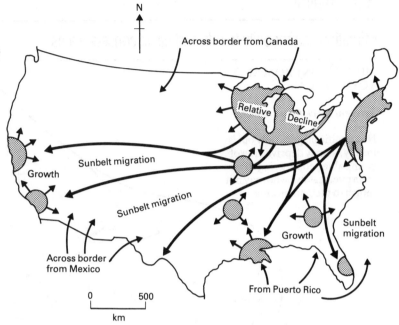

DECENTRALISATION FROM AND WITHIN THE LARGE CITIES 1970-80

Change 1970-80 (per cent)

Region	Total urban areas	Central city	suburbs
N East	−4.9	−12.3	+1.0
N Central	+0.3	−14.1	+10.5
South	+19.8	+2.4	+35.3
West	+17.7	+8.1	+24.3
U.S.A. Total	−6.9	−4.9	+10.0

	1970 Population (millions)	1980 Population (millions)	Change 1970/80 per cent	Per cent of U.S. Total 1980
Main met. areas	153.7	169.4	10.2	74.8
Other areas	49.6	57.1	15.1	25.2
U.S.A.	203.3	226.5	11.4	100.0

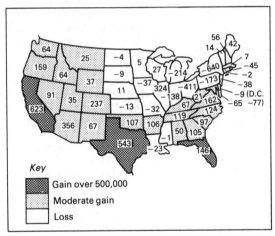

Regional net gains and losses by migration 1970–1976 by 000's

Exercise

● Analyse and try to account for the main trends in migration.
● To what extent does the history of migration to and within the United States support the classification and explanatory models of migration outlined earlier?

4:2 AFRICA

Migration and mobility trends and basic consequences

MIGRATION FROM AND TO OVERSEAS

3 Recent Black Migration Out

Not significant generally but is locally, as may deprive area of young able people going to train overseas but who may not return to their home area.

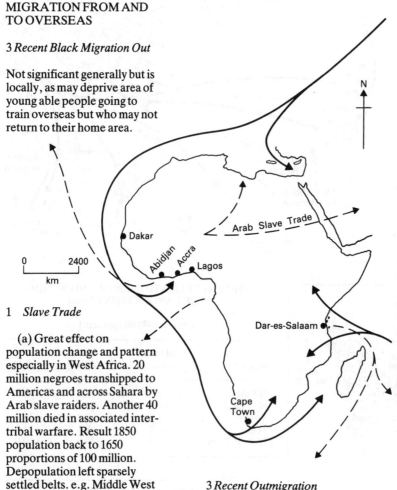

1 Slave Trade

(a) Great effect on population change and pattern especially in West Africa. 20 million negroes transhipped to Americas and across Sahara by Arab slave raiders. Another 40 million died in associated inter-tribal warfare. Result 1850 population back to 1650 proportions of 100 million. Depopulation left sparsely settled belts. e.g. Middle West Africa.

(b) Disrupted development in Africa. In 16th Century Africa had as progressive an economy and culture as rich as that in Europe and the Mediterranean. Slave trade caused loss of labour and abandonment of agricultural land. Barter trade by Liverpool ships etc. engaged in trade brought in cheap goods which adversely affected home craft industries e.g. textile and metal working.

3 Recent Outmigration

of Asians and Whites mainly to UK and Australia.

Key

1 To mid 19ᵗʰ century
2 Late 19ᵗʰ century to 1950
3 Post 1950

←– – Emigration

←— Immigration

2 European Penetration

(a) Settlement only in climatically favourable highlands of East Africa and South Africa.

(b) Brought some benefits opening up areas — some education and health measures but on balance African geographers Udo and Mabogunge claimed detrimental, disrupting economic and social development and making Africa subservient to European modernisation to provide minerals and agricultural products in exchange for manufactures which undermined Africa's traditional home industries.

(c) Communication network developed not to serve Africa but European needs — geared to coastal outlets.

(d) Some of the best land taken over for plantations and in East and South Africa by White settlers.

(e) Racial discrimination

(i) Against indigenous black population

(ii) After Independence reverse discrimination against Asians and whites leading to counter migration flow 1960s onwards from East Africa.

(iii) Apartheid in white dominated South Africa — greatest economic progress occurred here using mineral and other resources to build up a modern economy which black population only just beginning to share.

REGIONAL MIGRATION AND URBANISATION

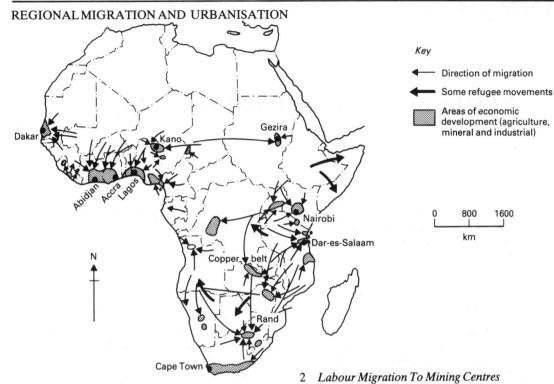

Key

← Direction of migration

◄ Some refugee movements

▨ Areas of economic development (agriculture, mineral and industrial)

0   800   1600
km

1 Rural to Urban Migration

Not as urbanised as other continents but the pace is quickening mainly due to pressure of population on rural areas with insufficient land to go round and hopes of employment and further advancement in towns.

Some Basic Causes

(a) Pressures occur on good subsistence farmland e.g. Kikuyu areas in Kenya highlands (density 300 per sq km) — fragmentation of holdings, soil impoverishment, declining crop yields fuelled by high birth rates in rural areas and backward farming methods.

(b) Pressures in marginal areas heightened by harsh environmental conditions including periodic drought e.g. Okore highlands Uganda and Mali in West Africa.

(c) Some of the best land is under commercial farming increasing land shortages among peasants.

Some Consequences

Relieves pressure on rural areas and some cash sent home to pay taxes, for education etc. but may create problems in towns e.g. Lagos due to insufficient jobs, housing and services for numbers coming.

2 Labour Migration To Mining Centres

Causes similar to that for general urban. Migration to mining areas Copper belt, the Rand and West Africa — male dominated. Provides valuable source of labour in mining areas but disrupts tribal and family life in losing areas.

3 Rural To Rural Migrations

From subsistence areas which are overpopulated to plantation, timber, road construction schemes. Some seasonal, but much long term e.g. 70% of Ivory Coast coffee and cocoa plantation workers were from poor neighbouring countries — Mali, Burkina Faso and Guinea. Relieves population pressure on losing area and some cash flow back. Provides labour in rural economy of receiving area but any political instability may lead to ethnic/tribal clashes.

4 Refugee Movements

Civil wars have brought variety of refugee movements —
Angola to Zaire
Ruanda to Uganda
Zimbabwe to Botswana
Little benefit but grave disadvantages — disruption to home and tribal life, burden of refugee camps, hunger and disease — latest in Ethiopia and Somalia.

5   Settlement Patterns and Change

For some purposes it is useful to distinguish between urban and rural settlements. But because in any area there are close links between settlements, it is important also to see the settlement pattern as a whole. This is done here in two ways: firstly, by considering the sorts of settlement patterns which may develop and secondly, through use of the central place concept, the relationship which links settlements into a functioning system.

Rural settlement is then briefly dealt with, but the rest of the section is devoted to various facets of urban areas which today increasingly dominate both the overall form of settlement patterns and also the structure of society.

Factors influencing settlement patterns

Any pattern reflects not only current influences but also past influences and the physical constraints which operated as the settlement pattern developed. The formative influences are summarised in Fig. 5.1 – noting that though the nature of these may vary they still continue to influence the way the pattern is changing today. They have affected the initial siting of settlements, their situation relative to other settlements, the way they have developed and the transport network linking them.

In remote areas of difficult terrain and with harsh climatic conditions settlement patterns are thin.

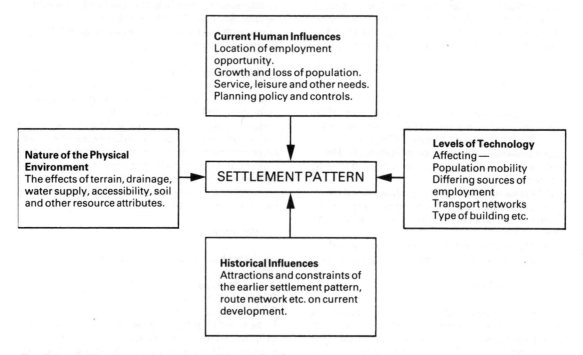

Fig. 5.1   *Factors affecting the shape and form of settlement patterns*

What settlements there are are closely related to the few locations which are accessible and offer more favourable physical conditions than surrounding areas. A well structured and closely linked settlement pattern is unable to develop. Indeed over time population may be lost to areas of greater opportunity so that some of the smallest settlements, individual homesteads and small hamlets may disappear altogether. This may be illustrated from Case Study 5.1 of the Scottish Highlands, but is a common feature of all peripheral highland regions. Even where there is some impetus for growth such as the development of a mineral resource it tends only to affect one or two settlements and not the settlement pattern as a whole. For example, in the Australian Outback — Alice Springs has recently expanded because of a growth in tourism but it has had little effect on the isolated settlements around.

Where physical conditions are favourable to settlement a more structured and fuller settlement pattern can develop over time. It is possible to recognise a hierarchical arrangement within the settlement pattern beginning with the towns which act as regional centres, passing down through villages, then to hamlets and finally to farms and other individual dwellings. If the area is uniformly favourable it may also be possible to recognise order too in the spatial arrangement of settlements, though local variations and physical conditions may produce some modifications. This type of pattern is typical for agricultural areas such as East Anglia.

Where the economy of a region is dominantly urban based the settlement pattern as a whole is strongly permeated by urban influences with town suburbs increasingly taking over the rural fringe and dormitory settlement the nearby villages. The main features in the settlement pattern are that of decreasing intensity with distance from the major urban centre and disruption of the hierarchy with the urban population component swamping the lower order of rural settlements. Because of the fear of too much urban sprawl the settlement pattern is also increasingly controlled by planning policy decisions. These are concerned with such things as maintaining a Green Belt to separate the town from the countryside and designating those villages where some dormitory growth may be allowed, as opposed to those protected from further expansion by conservation orders.

Physical conditions and past historical influences in the case of urban dominated patterns tend to be overshadowed by current influences. Though differentiated by scale, areas dominated by the largest conurbations do exhibit many of the features of areas centred around smaller but still dynamic urban centres, such as Cambridge, which illustrates this type of settlement pattern. (Case Study 5.2 p. 42)

Central Place theory and the pattern of settlement

The size order, spatial distribution and interrelatedness of settlements within an area or region are the key issues at the heart of much of the theory about settlement patterns, most notably the Central Place theory expounded by Christaller and others.

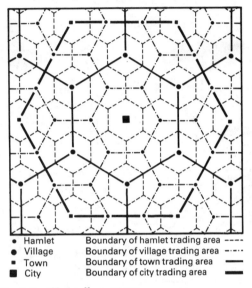

• Hamlet	Boundary of hamlet trading area ----
● Village	Boundary of village trading area -·-··
▪ Town	Boundary of town trading area ——
■ City	Boundary of city trading area ▬▬

Fig. 5.2 Christaller pattern

Because the Central Place theory still exercises an important influence on thinking about settlements, it is worth exploring it in more detail.

Fig. 5.3 illustrates a simple functional interdependence of settlements within a hierarchy. The farms

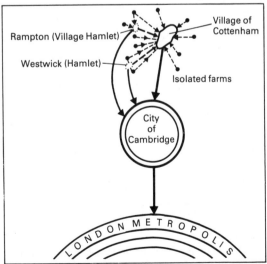

Fig. 5.3 A simple functional interdependence of settlements

5:1 GLEN LYON, PERTHSHIRE, SCOTLAND

Highland settlement

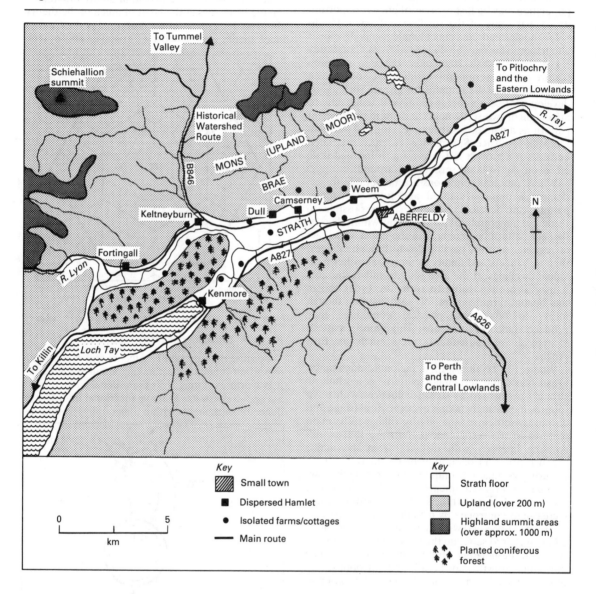

Key
- ▨ Small town
- ■ Dispersed Hamlet
- ● Isolated farms/cottages
- — Main route

Key
- ▢ Strath floor
- ▨ Upland (over 200 m)
- ▨ Highland summit areas (over approx. 1000 m)
- ♠♠ Planted coniferous forest

0 — 5 km

A SPARSE SETTLEMENT PATTERN — CHARACTERISTICS

Linear along the lower valley edge apart from the small market centre of Aberfeldy at a route node and bridging point.

Settlement units are of marginal viability, based on primary occupations — agriculture and forestry. But now heavily reliant on external support socially and economically through subsidies, grants and tourism Population temporarily swollen in the summer, including second home occupancies.

FACTORS AFFECTING THE SETTLEMENT PATTERN

The Physical Environment

Harsh dissected highland above the valley areas repels settlement — infertile, poorly drained, much of it with difficult access. Uncertain climatic conditions — wet with over 1270mm precipitation, hard winters and frequent storms. Terrain — acidic, rough and poorly drained.

Settlement concentrates on the accessible valley edge with its more fertile soils and milder climate — most is on the sunny south-facing side. Avoidance of the valley floor due to liability of flooding. Settlement decreases westward into the highland proper.

Aberfeldy's location favoured by a bridging point and focal position, a dry terraced site and a sheltered aspect.

Human And Historical Influences

Apart from emergence of Aberfeldy (18th Century) and some depopulation especially from higher marginal settlements, pattern has little altered from the 15th Century.

Phase 1   Celtic settlement from the West with some later Nordic infusion from the East — a self sufficient agriculturally based economy with Weem of ecclesiastical and military prominence.

Phase 2   A clan feudal system to the mid 18th Century — summer grazing on upper slopes and peat for fuel, mixed farming on lower slopes, water mills for local craft work. Drove road links to outside world.

Phase 3   Depopulation following Jacobite rebellion causing the break up of clans — conversion of upland to sheep runs and grouse moors.

Phase 4   20th Century rise of Aberfeldy following railway link of 1856 — marginal hillfarming, forestry, hydro-electric schemes and tourism supports sparse settlement.

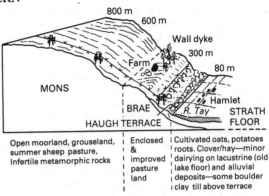

| Open moorland, grouseland, summer sheep pasture, Infertile metamorphic rocks | Enclosed & improved pasture land | Cultivated oats, potatoes roots. Clover/hay—minor dairying on lacustrine (old lake floor) and alluvial deposits—some boulder clay till above terrace |

AN INTERRUPTED AND TRUNCATED SETTLEMENT HIERARCHY

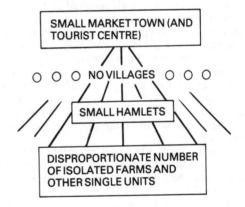

and smaller settlements depend on nearby Cottenham and Cambridge itself for such things as weekly shopping and secondary education. Cottenham like other villages and the smaller settlements depends on Cambridge for more specialist services such as hospital treatment and entertainment. However, the whole Cambridge region looks beyond to London, a still higher order centre, for certain very special services such as opera and first division football, entertainment and very special shopping such as at Selfridges and Harrods Department Stores. Here the choice and quality of goods and services on offer are much greater than in Cambridge.

This dependency relationship exists because of the inability of smaller settlements further down the hierarchy to provide some of the more specialist services required by their populations. This is simply because it would not be viable for anyone to set up specialist services in a small settlement centre — not enough people would use this service to make it a worthwhile profitable venture. Hence the more expensive and less frequently required goods and services are made available at large centres where the resident population provide a market demand which is further reinforced by people coming in from the smaller settlements. When concerned with places as service centres the term 'central place' is used. Hence central place theory is concerned with settlements as service centres — places where goods and services are offered and bought, either by the public coming to the centre or the supplier going to the consumer.

For urban centres the most important part of the catchment area is the population of the centre itself as a Lincolnshire shopping survey illustrates below.

Also within any one town, in addition to the main centre – the Central Business District — there is also a hierarchy of sub-centres for the provision of lower order goods and services for the people living within reach of them. These are part of the total pattern of service centres completed by other sub-centres within the region around the central city which is at the head of the service centre hierarchy.

Principle ideas associated with Central Place theory

The centrality of a place refers to its functional importance and this clearly depends on the number and variety of goods and services it provides for the people resident there, and the area around.

Threshold population is the minimum number of people needed to support any good or service outlet established at a central place. The frequency with which a good or service is required and its cost determines the size of the threshold needed to support one outlet. For example, if a good is bought at any one time by only a few people out of all the potential buyers in an area, then the threshold population will need to be large to ensure that there are sufficient customers.

The minimum range of a good or service is defined by the distance of the boundary needed to enclose the threshold population for the outlet providing it. The maximum range of a good or service is the furthest distance measured in time and cost over which either a customer would be prepared to travel to obtain it or a supplier travel to provide it.

The concept of range or sphere of influence is closely related to the cost of a good or service. It is only common sense that for something cheap and frequently needed such as a daily newspaper, people will not expend much time or money travelling to obtain it. The range, therefore, of a lower order good like this one is small. Also because of this and the fact that most people in an area will buy that good nearly all central places including even villages will have shops and outlets selling low order goods such as newspapers, sweets, cigarettes and everyday groceries. In contrast, high order goods of a larger range are those which cost more and which are not required very frequently, hence people will be prepared to travel a longer distance for them. The catchment area or hinterland for such a good or service must be sufficiently large for this type of outlet. Thus whilst every central place will have lower order outlets only the larger central places will have the higher order ones.

Lincolnshire Shopping Survey — Place of Residence

	Distance from town centre				
	Lincoln	Up to 8 km	8–16 km	Over 16 km	Total
Number of shoppers	284	63	38	15	400
Expressed as a percentage	71.0	15.8	9.5	3.8	100

Source: Dalton, R. et al, *Sampling Techniques in Geography,* Philip, 1975

Settlement form	Distance apart (km)	Population	Tributary area size (km^2)	Population
Market hamlet (Markort)	7	800	45	2 700
Township centre (Amtsort)	12	1 500	135	8 100
County seat (Kreistadt)	21	3 500	400	24 000
District city (Bezirksstadt)	36	9 000	1 200	75 000
Small state capital (Gaustadt)	62	27 000	3 600	225 000
Provincial head capital (Provinzhaupstadt)	108	90 000	10 800	675 000
Regional capital city (Landeshaupstadt)	186	300 000	32 400	2 025 000

Source: E. L. Ullman, *Amer. Jour. Sociology* 46 (1941), 857.

Fig. 5.4   The urban hierarchy in SW Germany (after Christaller)

The Central Place hierarchy

Within any region the hierarchy of central places can be established by classifying each central place according to the highest order good or service it supplies. At the apex of the hierarchy there will be the largest central place in a region, with a catchment area not only large enough to support more than one outlet for all the orders of goods and services present in a centre smaller than it, but also at least one outlet for each of the higher order goods and services not present in these smaller centres. Below this leading central place the hierarchy progressively descends to the lowest order (see Fig. 5.4).

It follows that at each level in the hierarchy a central place will support not only an order of outlet not present in central places of lower levels, but also all the types of outlets evident in these smaller central places.

From his studies in South Germany, Christaller was able to show that within a central place hierarchy there was not only regularity in the size order of places and the number of places found at each level of the hierarchy, but also regularity of the spatial distribution of central places for any one level and between different orders of central places.

When attributing to places only a service site function Christaller termed the resultant theoretical hierarchy and spatial order pattern as a K3 system. This was because any central place at one order level required within its catchment area three times the population of a central place of the next lower order. Christaller envisaged a hierarchy of central places such that a number of them rose in a geometric progression from the highest to the lowest order. The geometric progression for a K3 system would involve the following sequence: 1, 2, 6, 18, 54, 162 etc. He also put forward the K4 system based on the transportation function the centre might provide and a K7 one based on its administrative function.

In respect of the spatial network formed by a hierarchy he envisaged this as a hexagonal pattern with every place at one hierarchical level being equidistant from the others at that level. To minimise the number of central places so that they were equidistant from one another required them to be at the corner of equilateral triangles which together formed the hexagons. Such an arrangement meant there would be no over-lapping of trade areas and the smaller hexagons would pack or nest within the larger hexagonal areas in a way conforming with the K3 principle where service functions were concerned. (Refer back to Fig. 5.2.)

It was left to Lösch to attempt to incorporate the K4 and K7 networks with the K3 one into a total settlement system. Clearly a network which incorporated the marketing, administrative and transport functions was closer to reality than any single type of network proposed by Christaller. To achieve the composite network, Lösch rotated superimposed K3, K4 and K6 networks to allow for what he called 'city rich' and 'city poor' areas within the system since he felt this was closer to the distribution pattern in real situations.

Some basic underlying assumptions

Just as for the purposes of identifying certain principles of his theory Christaller tried to disentangle one important function from the rest, he also made other assumptions about an area. These included regarding the area upon which a central place pattern developed as a homogeneous plain (an isotropic surface), with equal ease of travel in any direction away from the centre. He also assumed free market competition in that both supplier and customer would make decisions entirely on economic grounds.

5:2 CAMBRIDGE AREA

A dynamic settlement pattern

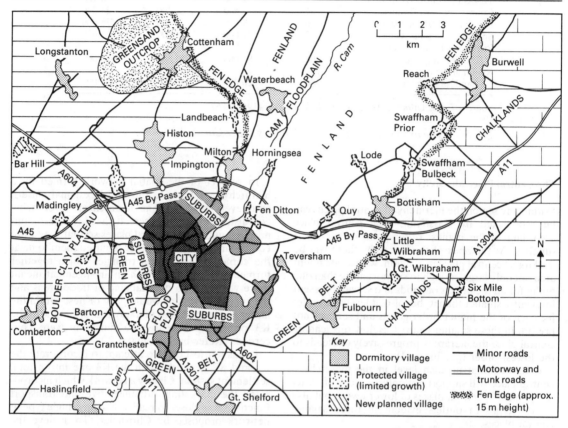

Key

	Dormitory village		Minor roads
	Protected village (limited growth)		Motorway and trunk roads
	New planned village		Fen Edge (approx. 15 m height)

CHARACTERISTICS

A well settled and well defined pattern influenced by terrain and drainage, increasingly submerged beneath the invasion of urban dormitory influences.

Strong viable community structures — fenland still primarily agricultural, but others under urbanisation pressures having a dual community structure, even in 'limited villages' protected by planning.

Cambridge — controlled size at 110 000, overspill to dormitory villages of 1000-2000, controlled villages at approximately 200-600.

INCOMING MIGRATION DOMINANT
but including a retirement element ∴ balanced communities generally

---

A WELL DEFINED AND ORDERED SETTLEMENT HIERARCHY (MODIFIED BY PLANNING INTERVENTION)

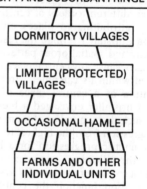

CITY AND SUBURBAN FRINGE

DORMITORY VILLAGES

LIMITED (PROTECTED) VILLAGES

OCCASIONAL HAMLET

FARMS AND OTHER INDIVIDUAL UNITS

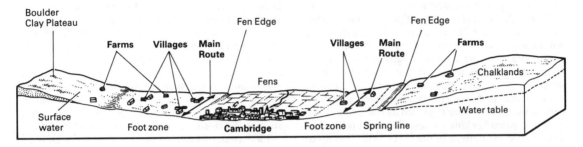

Cross-section showing broad relation of settlement to physical features in the landscape

Key

Village = Human elements in the landscape

Foot zone = Physical features

FACTORS AFFECTING THE SETTLEMENT PATTERN

INFLUENCE OF PHYSICAL ENVIRONMENT

Still apparent in pattern of settlement location but increasingly overshadowed by human influences, especially with suburban and dormitory spread from Cambridge.

Physically favourable areas are chalk — fen edge for eastern settlement and boulder clay plateau plus greensand outcrops to West — firm dry, well drained, water supply (spring line and well) — on line of access.

Negative areas are lowlying fenland and Cam flood plain — liable to flooding.

Nodal growth of Cambridge on terraces and chalk spur either side of bridging point.

HISTORICAL AND HUMAN INFLUENCES

Phase 1 to mid 19th Century   Settlement had its economic base in agriculture — fertile fen edge soils and rich fenlands once drained — chalkland and plateau mixed farming — Cambridge had dual function of long established market town and ecclesiastical/university centre.

Phase 2 1875-1945   Surburban growth of Cambridge takes in near villages e.g. Cherry Hinton, through ribbon development. Some town industry but still strong agricultural base.

Phase 3 1945-present   Continued suburban pressure controlled by planners — greenbelt and limited villages — dormitory and light industrial growth in others. London commuter influence to South.

The limitations and use of Central Place theory

To avoid any unwarranted and superficial criticism of Christaller's work it is worthwhile emphasising that, as with other theories, Central Place theory is not meant to have universal validity. Nor can it be regarded as offering a total explanation of a settlement pattern in any region. Its purpose is to identify some of the salient elements in certain types of patterns and some of the factors which might lie behind them. It is to be regarded as one of the tools available when seeking to describe and understand some particular pattern in the real world. It is up to the potential user to decide whether the theory would be of use in any particular situation or not. Whilst, for example, the Central Place theory would be a useful analytical tool in the study of a region where the marketing function is important in the economic basis of settlements, it clearly would be of very limited value if a settlement pattern were say dominated by industry. For example, Dickinson working at the same time as Christaller in the 1930s did identify a Central Place type of pattern in the agricultural region of East Anglia where towns were important market centres. But in an industrial region such as the North East of England the market function was submerged beneath manufacturing influences and therefore Central Place theory would be of very limited use.

Further, even when a potential user has identified the region as being amenable to a Central Place type of analysis, it is important that as study and analysis proceeds, some of the underlying assumptions made by Christaller should be relaxed to allow the modifying effects of reality to come into play. For example, starting from the assumption of an isotropic plain may lead to some identification of a regular hierarchical network, but recognition of irregularities in the terrain of the area is needed to help understand why distortions from the theoretical hexagonal pattern occur. It would also be necessary to recognise that distortions will occur because total free competition does not exist and people are motivated by social and attitude influences as well as economic considerations.

However, even given user awareness, there are today progressively fewer situations in which Central Place theory can offer a useful framework. Times have changed since Christaller formulated his theory in the 1930s and therefore the underlying circumstances affecting settlement patterns are different.

Demand patterns for services and goods have altered because of affluence, changes in taste and preferences and greater mobility enabling people to travel further to do their shopping and obtain other services. Technological progress has also brought changes in the ways provision of goods and services are organised and located. For instance to obtain benefits of economies of scale, provision of services is centralised into fewer and larger units of which the hypermarket and supermarket now located away from town centres are good examples.

Because larger centres are now more accessible and offer a greater variety of choice of goods and services these are increasingly attracting customers away from smaller centres. Even for lower order goods and services such as weekly shopping, smaller towns are losing some of their functions to larger towns. At village level other losses are occurring such as the closing of primary schools, pubs, shops.

Increased government intervention through planning measures and other legislation has also interfered in the operation of the market forces which help to shape the Central Place system. Witness, for example, the effect of locating a planned town of the size of Milton Keynes with a quarter of a million people within the East Midlands settlement pattern. Other planning decisions affect such things as out of town shopping centres and the future growth of various settlements around the town.

However despite these recent changes, Central Place theory does have some value as an analytical tool. It can still help identify more clearly the role of settlements as places of trade and exchange and the extent to which this has influenced the nature of the settlement pattern developing in a region. It also helps us to identify some of the important principles or concepts inherent in settlements functioning as Central Places — such concepts as threshold population, range of a good and frequency of demand are useful in their own right apart from any Central Place theory. It also encourages us to think of individual settlements in their wider context and to seek above all some order in the spacing and interrelatedness of settlements.

Rural settlement and change

Under the pressures of modern day living, with its advances in technology including the spread and speeding up of communications and the increasing erosion of the countryside by urban influences, the character of rural settlements is changing. Nevertheless it is possible to recognise certain fundamental features both in the pattern of settlements and structure of communities which have persisted over a long period. These are most apparent in areas furthest away from our large cities but also remain as significant features even in areas where settlements are rapidly being transformed into dormitories for the masses commuting back into the city for work.

Nucleation and dispersion

In seeking to clarify rural settlement patterns geographers have traditionally distinguished between nucleated and dispersed settlements. The highland in the west of Britain for example is generally characterised by a dispersed settlement pattern and the Eastern scarplands and lowlands as a nucleated one, whilst other areas such as the Midlands are a mixture of the two (see Fig. 5.5). Examples of dispersed and nucleated patterns are given in the following Case Studies together with brief summaries of formative forces. But in both cases as elsewhere the pattern has become increasingly modified by external influences. In the Teify valley for example there has been abandonment of uneconomic and socially remote upland marginal settlements and the intrusion of second home buyers and tourist services into others lower down. In lowland areas like County Durham the spread of cities into the countryside exercises an all-pervasive influence which goes beyond the extension of the built up area and dormitory extension to villages. It has had deep effects on the character of communities and the structure of society in hitherto rural settings.

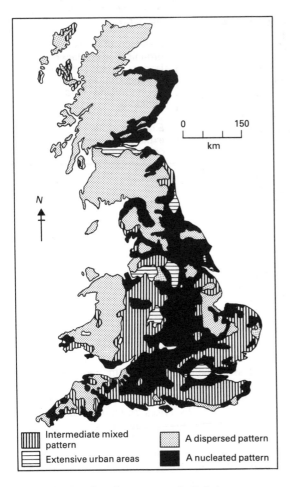

Intermediate mixed pattern

Extensive urban areas

A dispersed pattern

A nucleated pattern

Fig. 5.5   Rural settlement types in Britain

The changing social geography of rural areas

Life in a rural community is frequently contrasted with city living. Within sociological studies the idea of a rural community based on everyday neighbourly contact and an accepted order of society, is set against the more impersonalised urban living where status depends upon achievement rather than inheritance. Tonnies' characterisations of the ideal rural community (Gemeinschaft) and of urban living (Gesellschaft) are perhaps the most well known.

But a simple classification of this kind tends to hide the variety and complexity so evident today in all but the remotest communities. Mass media, better means of transport and greater mobility have taken urban aspects of living into the countryside.

Many people work in the town and live in the countryside and many town dwellers have retired there. Thus many rural communities contain a mixture of newcomers and old established families still with some links to the land. Social institutions have as a consequence become more varied in the more accessible rural communities, in particular dormitory villages close to larger cities.

Something of Tonnies' 'Gemeinschaft' however remains in the more isolated rural areas regardless of where in the world. It is that of kinship. Rees, commenting on the reasons for stability and immobility amongst Welsh upland communities makes the point rather well.

'The solidarity of the family, the bonds of kinship and the individual status among his neighbours — all ties him to his locality and makes life incomplete elsewhere.'

In contrast in areas within reach of cities a dual social structure frequently develops with middle and working class groups having their own separate social organisations. This division seems to be becoming more significant than the hitherto recognised division of newcomers and established villagers. However both characteristics may be present making a social and spatial mix of the community even more complex.

Given this complexity and the variety of rural communities it is quite evident that Tonnies' simple description of the ideal rural community i.e. Gemeinschaft is quite inadequate. Mitchell has recently suggested a fourfold classification of rural communities based on first the extent to which rural communities may be receptive to outside influences and secondly upon the extent to which there is evidence of an integrated community feeling. Whilst the four typologies may be somewhat different in the situation of the developing world, the two criteria of degree of openness to outside influences and extent of community feeling may well also provide a basis here for classifying rural communities (see Fig. 5.6).

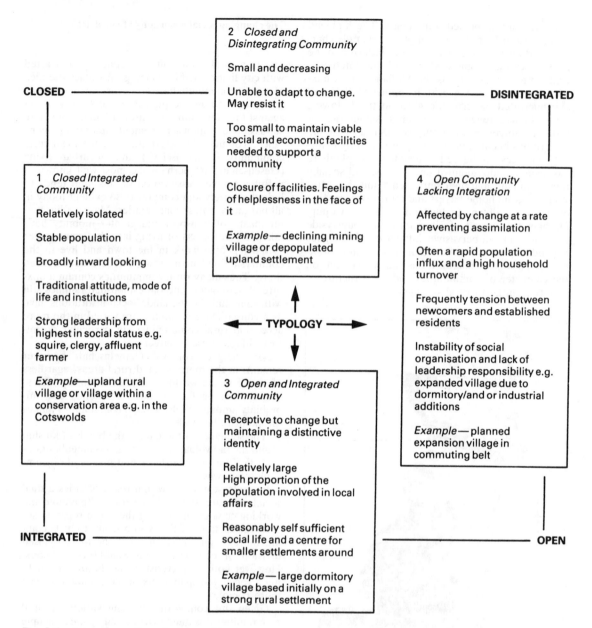

Fig. 5.6 *A typology of rural communities*

However, there is one set of external influences over which rural communities have only limited control and which are increasingly affecting the structure of the community. These are the actions and policies of the various central and local government institutions. For example, to prevent rural areas near towns being swamped by dormitory spread there is planning legislation under which some rural settlements are protected from any dormitory development whilst others may be designated as suitable for it. Also in the more remote rural areas strenuous efforts have been made through various measures such as subsidising agriculture and social services, to maintain the viability of rural life and small communities.

Thus over time not only do rural settlement patterns tend to become more complex, but so does the social geography of the communities living in the settlements.

5:3 THE MIDDLE TEIFY VALLEY, WALES

Dispersed settlement

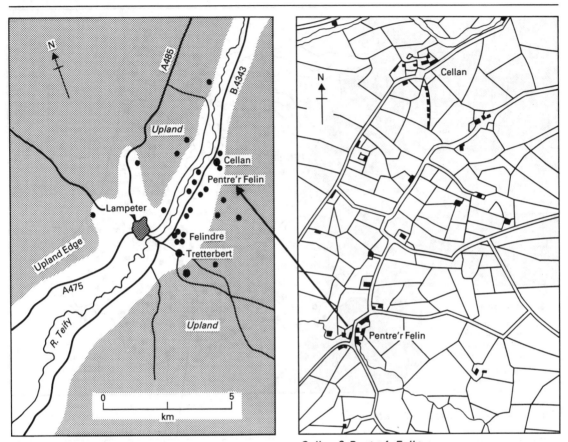

Part of the dispersed settlement

*Cellan & Pentre'r Felin
Hamlets in more detail*

SOME FACTORS LEADING TO A DISPERSED PATTERN DEVELOPING

Historical and cultural influences
Celtic land tenure system meant each male on marriage could claim a homestead site (tyddyn). On the death of the head of the family the territory would be further divided encouraging more settlement dispersion.

Hamlets frequently marked the site of a holy place (later replaced by a church or chapel) or the site of a tribal group pre-dating Celtic colonisation.

The lower valley as part of a main route into Wales was subject to later external influences e.g. cathedral town of Lampeter was established in Norman times and market towns such as Tregaron as part of the cattle trade to the fattening areas of the English lowland.

Physical influences
Poor inhospitable upland terrain with harsh and wet climatic conditions supported only a sparse population, which was dispersed so that each family could obtain enough land for subsistence, based on rearing of livestock and the cultivation of a patch near the homestead.

The lower valley being sheltered, more fertile and accessible attracted most settlement. These lay above the areas of the valley floor liable to flooding.

Where tributary valley routes met the main valley route as at Lampeter, a town might develop.

5:4 COUNTY DURHAM

Nucleated settlement

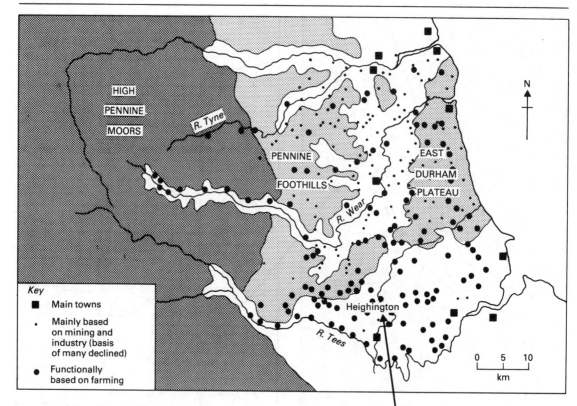

Key

■ Main towns

· Mainly based on mining and industry (basis of many declined)

● Functionally based on farming

County Durham — Nucleated settlement

SOME FACTORS LEADING TO A NUCLEATED PATTERN

Nucleated rural settlements are characteristic of the Southern part of the county, especially in the middle and lower Tees valley — the deep glacial drift soils provided good mixed farmland encouraging settlement of a nucleated kind.

Characteristic form of settlement is the green village with homesteads clustered round a grassy open space. Probably dates from the Anglian conquest — the settlement clustered partly for defence against cross-border raiders, with the 'village green' a sheltered night compound for the cattle.

Rural settlement in the centre and North of the County overshadowed by mining villages and industrial settlement based on the exposed coalfield in the centre and concealed part further East.

The upland Pennine moorlands in the West have settlement only in sheltered valleys.

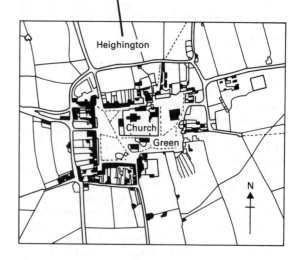

A nucleated village developed round a broad green

6   Urban Places — People in the City

'Each urban place is a very dense concentration of
people and homes, plus their attendant work-
places, centres of trade, entertainment and recreation and the many facilities and utilities needed to
service all these.'
Spatial Structures, Johnston, R.J. p. 56
(Methuen), 1973

Spatial inequalities

Without people and their needs there would be no
urban places, and the structure and functions of any
town or city have developed over time in response to
these needs. Thus it is people who form the starting
point for urban studies and in looking at the social
geography of the city, in particular housing patterns,
many geographers have been concerned with the
fact that the needs of certain groups or classes are
much better served than those of others. The rich
and comfortably off not only have access to the most
favoured housing areas, but have much better service provision than the poor, be they shanty dwellers
in some developing world city like Calcutta, or slum
dwellers in an inner city slum or ghetto of a city such
as New York. Social inequalities are mirrored in
unequal access to space and desirable locations, so
that spatial and social inequality go together.

As a result a number of geographers have adopted
a more radical approach in urban geography and a
concern for welfare geography. Bunge was so struck
by the inequalities emerging from his study of Detroit that he adopted rather emotive terms for his
division of the city and emphasised the ways in
which the poorer income groups and ethnic minorities of the city were being 'exploited' by the rest of
the city, particularly by the elite business, entrepreneurial and professional classes occupying his 'city
of superfluity' — pleasant suburbs and rural dormitory areas. (Fig. 6.1)

This concern for social inequalities and for what
Harvey calls 'social justice in the city' is not new.
Indeed it lies at the core of urban structure models

which figure so prominently in urban geography and
which have their beginnings in the work of Burgess
and Park, two eminent sociologists studying the
social problems of Chicago during the 1920s. It is to
their work we now turn because they identified some
of the important processes which still help us to
understand the way in which cities are residentially
zoned and why inner city areas are characterised by
special types of social problems such as poor housing, racial tension, and social deprivation by way of
insufficient medical and other welfare facilities.

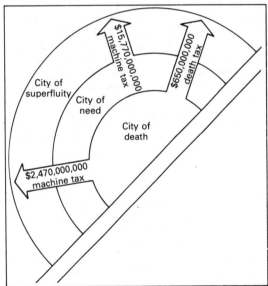

Fig. 6.1   Bunge's view of exploitation and
inequality in the city
(His 'machine tax' represents the profits
made from exploiting the labour of poorer
groups living and working in the inner
areas of the 'city of death', whilst his
'death tax' indicates the rate and other
taxes imposed on inner areas without an
equivalent recompense in adequate health,
education and other welfare services.)

49

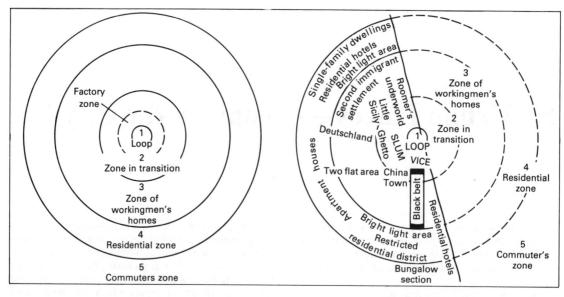

Fig. 6.2   Burgess' model of the city

The concentric ring model — Burgess and Park

In the process of collecting data about social conditions in Chicago during the 1920s Burgess and Park were able to identify something of the structure of the city. At the time the city was experiencing mushroom growth due to the influx of migrants flocking in, attracted by booming industries and job opportunities.

They were also able to recognise some of the processes underlying the ways in which the population was being spatially sorted out into different housing zones. The terms used by Burgess for the zones he identified not only indicate the unequal struggle between different groups for housing space, but also the desire of most groups to escape from the worst areas near the centre of the city.

The following is the city's residential structure as seen by Burgess and Park (refer to Fig. 6.2):
1. 'Within, the central business district (the loop) is the "main stem" of "hobohemia" the teeming Rialto of the homeless migratory man of the Middle West'.
2   In the zone of deterioration including the central business district are always to be found the so-called 'slums' and 'bad lands'.
3   A third area is inhabited by the workers in industry who have escaped the area of deterioration.
4   Beyond this zone is the 'residential area' of high class apartment buildings of exclusive 'restricted' districts of single family dwellings.
5   Still farther out beyond the city limits is the commuters' zone — suburban areas or satellite cities — within thirty to sixty minute ride of the C.B.D.

This movement to the periphery has been sought by people from all walks of life. Beginning with the most well-off, suburbanisation has moved progressively over time down the social scale as real incomes have risen and better transportation has increased mobility, allowing home and workplace to be at some distance from one another. But there remain disadvantaged groups trapped by circumstance in decaying inner city areas both in the old and the new world. They are unable to move either because they cannot afford it or because they are being discriminated against in the housing market.

Burgess was centrally concerned with the influx of people into the city including black people and other minorities and the problems associated with the dynamic growth of the city which ensued from this continued influx. From his studies he emphasised the still important processes of invasion and succession, concentration and deconcentration which occurred as incoming migrants sought to live close to the city centre — the economic, social and political heart of the community. In the face of continued invasion, frequently by poorer coloured and other ethnic minorities, established residents who could afford to moved out into the suburbs and nearby countryside, commuting from there daily to work in the city. Using Burgess' own words written in the mid 1920s the newcomers went into 'the areas of deterioration which were not many years ago the zone inhabited by independent wage earners and within the memories of thousands of Chicagoans, contained the residence of the best families.'

We thus see a historical process going on, with the city growing outward by a process of accretion as particular groups or classes sought to segregate themselves from other groups whose life style was very different and considered inferior. Incoming families sought security and identification with their own kind in inner areas but were also relegated to these locations because they could not afford to live in better housing areas further out, nor afford the cost of travelling into inner areas and the centre of the city where most of the job opportunities were. Ultimately as they established themselves in the city Burgess saw many families like those before them moving out. However certain groups were forced to stay in inner areas which not only over time physically deteriorated but were 'invaded' by commercial usages overflowing from the bulging Central Business District or downtown area. Ghettos developed where a particular ethnic minority such as the negroes or Puerto Ricans concentrated. Other disadvantaged groups found in the zone of deterioration were the aged and unemployable as well as transients occupying lodging houses and apartments. In this twilight or transition zone vice, violence and disease flourished in the 1920s.

Similar problem areas can be found today in the world's larger cities but they are not confined to inner areas. They are now found on the periphery. In the developing countries these include shanty areas sited on marginal land normally unsuitable for building, such as the steep slope behind Rio de Janeiro in Brazil or lowlying areas liable to flooding. In advanced countries they take the form of large low cost housing estates frequently including high rise blocks and built hurriedly on the edge of cities to meet housing shortages in the 1950s and 60s. Much of it, such as that at Speke, outside of Liverpool, was built by Local Authorities to house the homeless, including those from inner slum clearance areas. Unfortunately the sheer size of estates, the psychological pressures of high-rise living, faulty building, isolation from familiar surroundings and too few social amenities have resulted in many of these becoming serious problem areas. More recently here and on the continent, rising unemployment has aggravated the problem.

Alternative models

Others since Burgess and Park's pioneering work of the 1920s, have produced alternative models of city structure. Like the concentric ring model they are viewed as ecological models in that they incorporate the same ecological processes of establishment round a core, together with accretion, invasion, succession and deconcentration, as well as the adaptation by new groups, of the existing areas they have occupied.

Whilst differing in form from the concentric ring model, other ecological models are variations upon

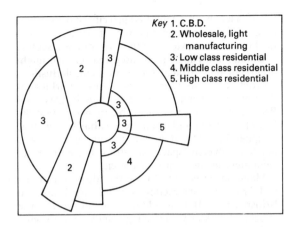

Fig. 6.3   Hoyt's sector model of urban structure

it rather than new structures. All incorporate the idea of different classes of residential areas based upon inequalities of opportunity and access between one group or class and another. Moreover as we have seen, the same broad processes are recognised as shaping the form of the city.

Hoyt introduced the idea of sectors as well as Burgess' concentric rings, in the zonation of urban places. This was in part based on the idea of unequal access to the city, with main routes favoured thus attracting wholesale and manufacturing activity along them with the low class housing for the workers next to the zone. But it was also in part based on the recognition that once a certain class of residen-

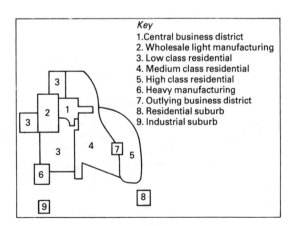

Fig. 6.4   Harris and Ullman's multiple nuclei model

51

tial area had been established in a city, it would over time attract accretionary growth of similar residential housing thus extending the zone out as a sector.

Ullman and Harris recognised that growth might occur not only around the main Central Business District, but also round sub-centres. Working as they were at a much later date than Burgess and Park or Hoyt, they were also able to incorporate the fact of industrial and commercial suburbs as well as peripheral residential growth, as some usages could not find sufficient space nor afford the cost of development at the centre of the city.

Mann has attempted to use the ideas of Burgess and Hoyt in constructing a model applicable to British cities. But in addition he allows for the effects of westerly prevailing winds, encouraging higher income groups to live upwind of the smoke and grime from industry near the centre. He also allows for the rather different housing sectors present in British towns compared with their American counterparts.

However times and circumstances change so that it is only to be expected that models need updating if they are to serve any useful purpose. Fig. 6.6 is a

suggested structure model to reflect in a general way the present structure and residential pattern in developed cities.

There have also been efforts to generalise about developing world cities where social and cultural forces are more prominent than in developed cities. (Refer to Fig. 8.3 p. 72.)

An alternative approach — social area analysis

Over recent years there has been increasing concern about the inadequacies of these older classical models of city structure in relation to the variety of urban patterns evident today. Attempts have been made to superimpose such models on cities which because of their smaller size or recent origin do not respond to processes in the same way as did the large cities developing from the turn of the century in America, where most of the earlier studies took place.

Thus social area analysis has increasingly been seen as an alternative and more flexible way of

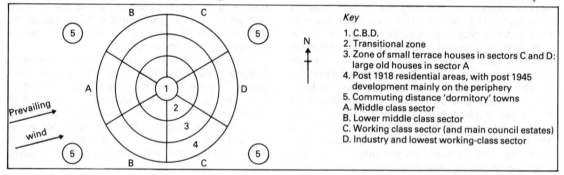

Key

1. C.B.D.
2. Transitional zone
3. Zone of small terrace houses in sectors C and D: large old houses in sector A
4. Post 1918 residential areas, with post 1945 development mainly on the periphery
5. Commuting distance 'dormitory' towns
A. Middle class sector
B. Lower middle class sector
C. Working class sector (and main council estates)
D. Industry and lowest working-class sector

Fig. 6.5   Model of a British city (based on Hoyt and Burgess)

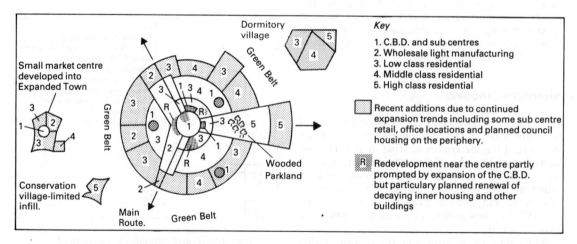

Key

1. C.B.D. and sub centres
2. Wholesale light manufacturing
3. Low class residential
4. Middle class residential
5. High class residential

Recent additions due to continued expansion trends including some sub centre retail, office locations and planned council housing on the periphery.

Redevelopment near the centre partly prompted by expansion of the C.B.D. but particularly planned renewal of decaying inner housing and other buildings

Fig. 6.6   Urban structure — modifications based on Hoyt's sector model

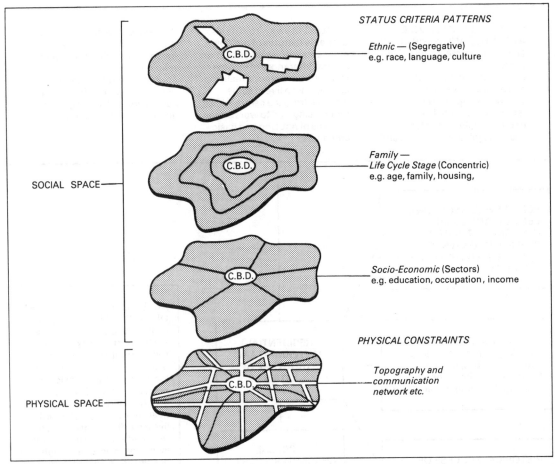

STATUS CRITERIA PATTERNS

Ethnic — (Segregative)
e.g. race, language, culture

Family —
Life Cycle Stage (Concentric)
e.g. age, family, housing,

Socio-Economic (Sectors)
e.g. education, occupation, income

PHYSICAL CONSTRAINTS

Topography and
communication
network etc.

SOCIAL SPACE

PHYSICAL SPACE

Fig. 6.7   Social area analysis model showing the 3 social·space components and the physical space map onto
which they can be superimposed

studying residential patterns, in cities. In this approach the factors (variables) influencing a family or household's residential location have been grouped as three contributory components, each of which when mapped produces a regular spatial pattern (Fig. 6.7). Firstly the socio-economic status component, including occupation of the head of household, when mapped tends to result in a sector pattern. Secondly the effect of the stage reached in the life-cycle component produces a ring pattern. The third ethnic or segregation component exhibits a nucleated pattern with alike households wanting to locate in the same area. These sector, ring and nucleation components, when superimposed onto a map of the physical characteristics of the city including terrain variants and its established layout (including its transport network), result in a generalised urban structure for the city.

The social area analysis approach has yielded useful generalisations in a variety of situations over the world, including those of different cultures. When applied it reflects more thoroughly the local conditions present for a particular town or city than can any of the older classical models. This is because it is based on data about the actual urban structure being studied and not some earlier study of a North American city.

An open factors approach

In some cases a more basic approach to the residential patterning and structure of cities might be appropriate. In this case some of the underlying processes already identified both within the ecological models framework and social area analysis might be combined with the constraints exercised by the physical environment on patterns of growth and modification to provide the kind of framework indicated in Fig. 6.8.

53

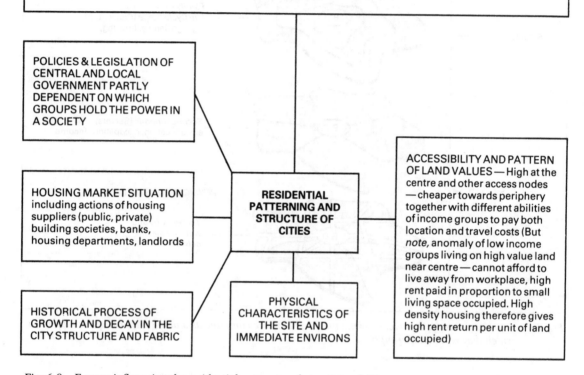

HUMAN CIRCUMSTANCE, ATTITUDES AND ASPIRATIONS
Levels of income, stage in life, life style
Degree of mobility, attitudes and aspirations lead to —
1   Competing desires of different groups to live near enough to city core to have access to job opportunities and services but away from its less desirable features of run down inner areas, noise and pollution
2   But differences of income result in some groups realising aspirations to live at some distance from the centre whilst others relegated to worst areas in terms of housing and basic amenities
3   Segregation tendencies of groups distinguished by income, life style, ethnic origin, religion etc
4   Processes of concentration decentralisation — invasion and succession of one group over another in a part of the city

POLICIES & LEGISLATION OF CENTRAL AND LOCAL GOVERNMENT PARTLY DEPENDENT ON WHICH GROUPS HOLD THE POWER IN A SOCIETY

HOUSING MARKET SITUATION including actions of housing suppliers (public, private) building societies, banks, housing departments, landlords

RESIDENTIAL PATTERNING AND STRUCTURE OF CITIES

ACCESSIBILITY AND PATTERN OF LAND VALUES — High at the centre and other access nodes — cheaper towards periphery together with different abilities of income groups to pay both location and travel costs (But *note,* anomaly of low income groups living on high value land near centre — cannot afford to live away from workplace, high rent paid in proportion to small living space occupied. High density housing therefore gives high rent return per unit of land occupied)

HISTORICAL PROCESS OF GROWTH AND DECAY IN THE CITY STRUCTURE AND FABRIC

PHYSICAL CHARACTERISTICS OF THE SITE AND IMMEDIATE ENVIRONS

Fig. 6.8   Factors influencing the residential patterns and structure of cities

7   The Economic Basis of Cities

The concentration of economic activities in cities

The more developed a country the more its economic activity is located in and around urban centres. This is because for a variety of reasons the tertiary (service) and manufacturing activities which increasingly dominate the economy require an urban location. For one thing most of the market demand for goods and services is increasingly located in urban areas. Also as nodal or route centres, towns provide much of the infrastructure required by manufacturing and services, including an adequate transport network.

Another reason is that the linkages which are needed between a variety of activities, draw them to a common urban location. This encourages further expansion making the city an even more attractive location. A process of cumulative causation may thus be set in motion, diversifying and strengthening the economic base. Even where a city is noted for one particular activity such as motor manufacturing or as a resort, it is still surprising what a range of other activities are also present.

Location of economic activity in the city

Given the functional diversity of most cities it is not surprising to find the locational pattern of economic activity is quite complex. But it is possible to identify certain favoured locations:
1   In and around the Central Business District.
2   Along main routes leading out from the centre.
3   At route nodes on the periphery particularly where ring roads round the city intersect with routes leading out from the centre.
4   Sub-centres of shopping and service provision in certain residential areas to serve local needs.

These can be schematically represented as shown in Fig. 7.1.

However, the functional pattern for any particular city will vary from this according to local circumstances. It may particularly deviate where a town or city is dominated by some specialist function.

Location of tertiary (service) activities

Accessibility is the key to the location of retail, office and other service activities. They must be located where they can best serve the needs of the population dependent on them, and where the work

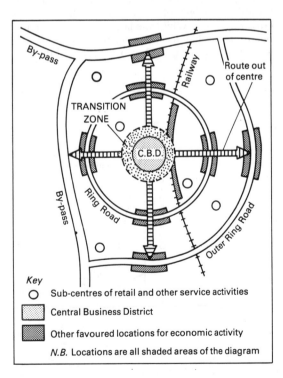

Fig. 7.1   A model of the location of economic activity in a typical town or city

55

force can easily commute from the residential areas around.

In the classical models of city structure, the Central Business District (C.B.D.) and the transitional area around it are identified as the most accessible locations in the city. These are the most sought after locations, with different usages competing with one another for sites. Within this competitive situation the usages most likely to occupy a central location will be those which can most profit from it, since these will be able to outbid other usages relegating them to a position progressively further out from the city centre.

Commercial activities like high order retailing, banks, other financial institutions and certain office activities are held to profit most from a central location. These therefore dominate the core or centre of large cities, with lesser order usages and those requiring large site areas being pushed out to other locations. Residential usage is the least profitable one and therefore in city structure models residential zoning makes up the outer rings or sectors of land used.

This process of land use sorting with service activities dominating the C.B.D. is demonstrated in the bid rent curve diagram in Fig. 7.2.

But today the core is not the only or even the most accessible location. Others occur along access routes into the centre and increasingly at nodal points out towards the edges of the city where these routes cross ring roads. Whilst the latter increase the number of accessible locations on the periphery, the accessibility of the C.B.D. is being reduced through increasing traffic congestion and its attraction as a potential site through soaring rents and rates.

Paradoxically more widespread car ownership, whilst contributing to city centre congestion, has increased customer mobility and favoured out of town shopping and service expansion. The increasing dispersion of population away from older inner residential areas towards the suburbs and dormitory settlements in the countryside beyond the city has also favoured peripheral locations.

Of the activities now looking towards a peripheral rather than city centre location, those requiring comparatively large site areas are most attracted, since land is cheaper and more plentiful on the fringe of the city. These include super and hyper-markets, warehouses and certain kinds of light industry such as furniture assembly. City centre locations are therefore being increasingly left to those specialised activities with high turnover and profit margins, which require only a limited amount of space and which need to maintain linkages with similar activities. This is particularly well illustrated by financial institutions.

The concentric arrangement therefore suggested by the simple bid-rent curve needs to be modified as indicated to reflect current location patterns for tertiary activities (Fig. 7.3).

The Central Business District

The Central Business District has usually developed around the historical core of the town. The location of this has itself been influenced by physical circumstances such as a dry site overlooking the bridging point across a river. As the town grows the C.B.D. expands around this core, frequently extending out for a way along the main access routes into the centre. However, with modern day pressures and changes in methods of retailing and servicing, part of the old C.B.D. or part of the transitional zone nearby may be re-developed to produce a second and new planned core. Some cities, therefore, have two centres of contrasting appearance, in effect a dual C.B.D.

Whether a simply structured C.B.D. or a more complex one, it will be dominated by commercial activities. But it may include certain non-commercial activities which for historical or other reasons can continue to occupy land of high value which in a free market situation would be given over to commercial activities. For instance churches and municipal parks or gardens may still be found in the city centre, since they are now protected by conservation legislation. There may also be public administration offices to which people need easy access. Whilst these do not earn a large profit in a commercial sense, the high cost of the site is paid out of rates and other public funds.

Fig. 7.2 Bid rent graph and resultant ring zoning

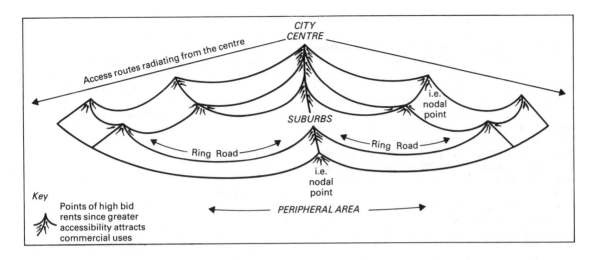

Fig. 7.3   Bid rent curves for a city based on varied accessibility

Functional concentrations within the C.B.D.

In larger cities where the demand for central area functions is high, it is possible to identify two ways in which some spatial sorting out can occur. Firstly specialist retailing activities need to attract custom off the street and thus generally occupy the ground floor of buildings fronting on to the main thoroughfare. The upper floors are usually occupied by offices which, whilst needing a central location, do not require constant contact with the general public. Away from the centre where rents are not so high office as well as retail activities may occupy the ground floor of buildings.

Secondly clustering of the same functional activity or of linked activities may occur as is shown for Cardiff in Fig. 7.4. For instance civic administration may have become clustered around an historical site such as a castle or market place and the financial quarter in an old merchanting area. Once established, the reputation of an area for a particular activity tends to attract more of the same and ensure its continued importance. However other clustering is of linked activities which need quick personal contact and which may be visited by the same clientele. One of the best examples of such clustering is that of solicitors, estate agents and insurance offices which may be concerned with a common business such as a house sale. In Sheffield for example solicitors and some estate agents have taken over the Georgian houses in Paradise Square behind the Cathedral but still close to the city centre.

Other clustering occurs because an activity benefits from the large flow of customers drawn to the area. Despite competition between retail outlets located together in the area, each attracts sufficient trade from the large number of potential customers

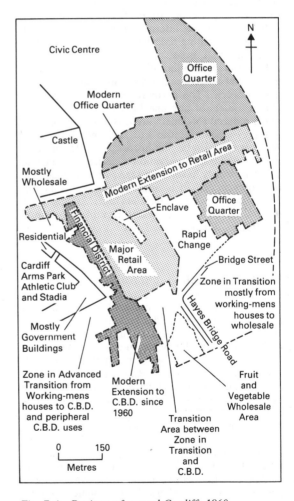

Fig. 7.4   Regions of central Cardiff, 1960

and makes a greater profit than it would be likely to do if sited on its own.

In the streets leading off the major thoroughfares rents and rates are lower than on the main frontages. These side streets therefore attract highly specialised shops, such as antiques or rare books serving a restricted clientele rather than depending on passing custom. Some low order retail services such as sweet shops and small cafes may also be found off the main street, simply because their turnover is insufficient to pay the higher rents on a main street location. They must rely on sufficient customers turning down the street from the main pedestrian thoroughfares.

Service and light industry activities with lower profit margins per unit area occupied, and in need of comparatively large areas tend to be pushed to the margins of the C.B.D. and into the transition zone. A number of such activities can be identified — grocery supermarkets, discount stores, betting shops, second-hand goods shops, spare part sales, small warehouses and printing firms, bingo halls etc. Here they may be intermixed with older housing areas some awaiting redevelopment, others adapted for commercial usage.

However in smaller cities particularly historical market towns such spatial concentration and sorting may not occur. This partly reflects the smaller number of outlets of any one kind needed to serve a much reduced catchment area. But it also indicates less pressure for central sites and therefore lower rents. It may also be that historical constraints such as old buildings, conservation measures and ancient street networks have encouraged only a piecemeal development of C.B.D. functions in a central core. These smaller central business districts are more difficult to define and less susceptible to general description. Each tends to have a character of its own.

The changing C.B.D.

Because of the increasing cost and shortage of land in the centre of cities, older buildings of one or two storeys have increasingly been replaced by new multi-storey developments including skyscraper blocks in some of the largest cities such as New York and Tokyo. Hence the C.B.D. can now be identified as much by the distinctive height of its skyline as by the concentration of commercial activity within it.

But with continued expansion of cities and economies, such has been the pressure on C.B.D.s that more comprehensive redevelopment has frequently taken place. This is because there is a limit to the modification that can be made to an existing town plan and existing buildings. Redevelopment has included not only the building of large under-cover

shopping precincts, but also a redesigning of the street layout to segregate pedestrian and vehicle flows.

In addition a number of usages commonly found in the C.B.D. have found it more convenient and as profitable to locate outside the C.B.D., leaving it for the highest profit making concerns such as banks and other financial institutions and large department stores.

The transitional zone

In earlier times as Burgess' city structure model shows, much of the transitional zone was occupied by housing and industry. Working class neighbourhoods grew up next to the factories. But today transitional zones tend to be more diversified. They now also include commercial activities which have overflowed from the C.B.D., as well as some vacant lots and derelict sites awaiting redevelopment. More recent additions have been multi-storey car parks and temporary car parking on vacant ground to serve the needs of workers, shoppers and others using the nearby C.B.D.

The transitional zone may vary from one part to another depending on whether expansion pressures on the C.B.D. are occurring or not. Evidence from studies of American cities indicates that pressures are greatest on those parts of the transitional zone adjacent to higher status areas, since this attracts offices, new hotels and speciality shops seeking this more favourable environment. In contrast, in lower status areas of the transitional zone delapidated housing may be intermixed with incoming usages such as bars, bingo halls and discount stores. Elsewhere in the more static parts of the transitional zone small scale industry may still persist.

However, many of the older small scale works and warehouse premises are characterised by frequent change of use as some small businesses go bankrupt and other new enterprises take over. These are frequently seed-bed industries i.e. new businesses being set up in some expanding sector of the economy such as electronics, and computing. This is because the cheaper rents and smaller premises found in the transitional zone attract new firms which if succeeding may then move out to larger premises on the edge of the city. This type of change is particularly noticeable in the inner transitional zone of old industrial cities such as Birmingham and Manchester in the United Kingdom and Boston in the United States.

The varied rate of change and usage from one part of the transitional zone to another has been summarised in the generalised pattern of land use shown in Fig. 7.5.

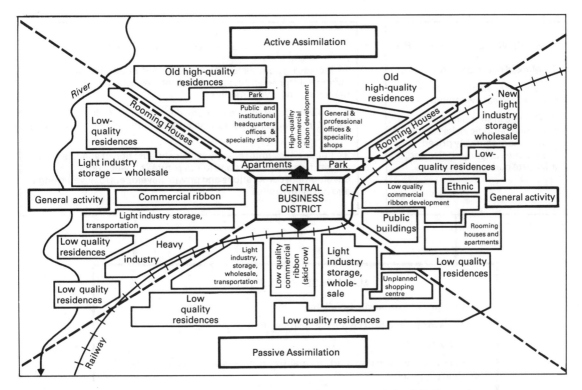

Fig. 7.5   Generalised pattern of land uses in the transitional zone around the C.B.D.

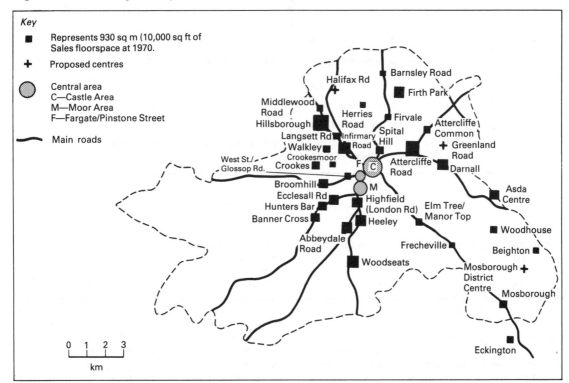

Fig. 7.6   The large sub-centres of retail activity for Sheffield

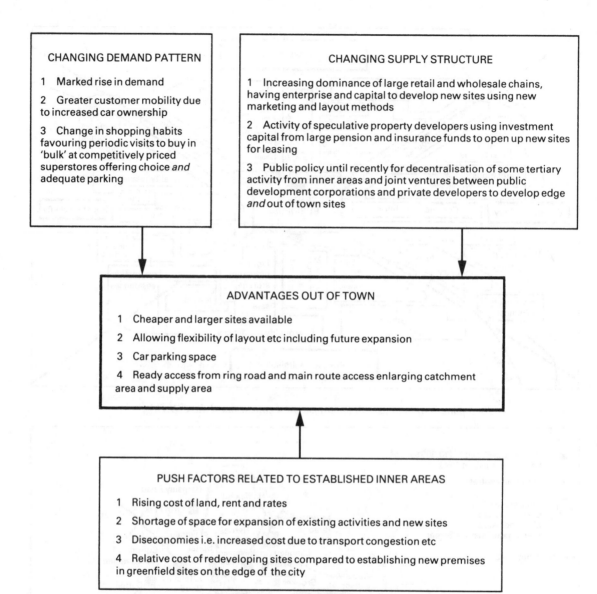

Fig. 7.7   Factors influencing the growth of peripheral and out-of-town centres

Commercial activity in the suburbs and on the edge of the city

Sub-centres occur outside the C.B.D. to serve local catchment areas. They vary in size but it is possible to recognise some hierarchical order along central place lines, beginning with the lowly corner shop providing everyday needs such as newspapers and groceries for the immediate neighbourhood; through to small shopping parades with a wider catchment area and right up to sub-centres equivalent in size to the C.B.D. of a small town. Such centres include not only the usual convenience shops but also local branches of banks, estate agents and insurance offices, as well as more specialist shops.

Some of the more important sub-centres for Sheffield are shown in Fig. 7.6. The details of floor space given can provide some indication of the relative importance of each centre. As the diagram shows points of good accessibility are favoured locations. Some centres such as Mossborough have been planned to serve new housing areas but most sub-centres have grown along with the expansion of the city itself. Centres such as Woodhouse and Hillsborough may have begun as shopping centres for independent settlements in the areas around Sheffield and then along with the settlement itself been incorporated into the city as it later expanded.

Out-of-town shopping centres and offices

The increasing location of certain tertiary activities on the margins of cities or in the nearby countryside has been one of the outstanding features of recent urban development. This includes not only shopping complexes centred on a supermarket or hypermarket but also wholesale services and offices.

This out-of-town development is basically due to the rapid advancement of tertiary activities relative to manufacturing in the growth of the economy. As people have become more affluent a greater propor-

tion of their income is spent on retail goods and services; consequently there has been a marked rise in demand for premises which could not be fully met in central areas where space is both limited and costly. Consequently other locations have been sought, most notably on the margins of cities where reasonably priced land is available and where new ring-roads and other improvements in transport have made such sites increasingly accessible. These and other factors summarised in Fig. 7.7 help to explain such growth.

As regards retailing, a distinction should be made between supermarkets, hypermarkets and regional shopping centres, whether associated with central area redevelopment schemes or out-of-town locations. Difference of size basically distinguishes supermarkets and hypermarkets. Hypermarkets have a minimum area of 2500 square metres, at least 15 check-out points and while specialising in food may offer a variety of other goods and services. The parking area is at least three times the size of the retail selling area and may include a petrol station and kiosk. The whole complex is usually located on a good access route 3 to 6 km from the town centre, for example Chandler's Ford in South Hampshire.

Regional shopping centres like the Parly Deux near Versailles in France are located outside established urban areas and are defined as a shopping complex. Again good accessibility is essential. Brent Cross, though not strictly outside London, is classed as a regional shopping centre because of the number of retail outlets it contains. It is near the junction of the M1 motorway and the North Circular Road in north west London.

Examples of wholesale and warehouse developments outside of urban centres includes the relocation of the London Covent Garden Vegetable Market at High Elms and its Paris equivalent at Rungis close to Orly Airport and on a main autoroute from Paris.

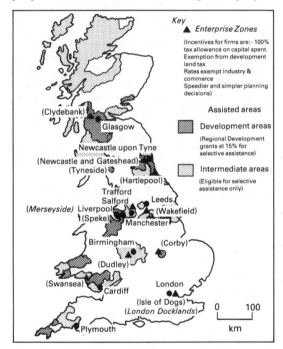

Fig. 7.8   Enterprise Zones in relation to Assisted Areas
(Enterprise Zones are part of a wider Urban Programme under which additional Urban Grant Aids can be made especially for regeneration of inner urban areas. Merseyside and the London Docklands now have their own Development Corporations. In turn aid for urban areas can be set within the broader Regional Industrial Policy measures under which two tiers of Assisted Areas were identified towards the end of 1984.)

Over dispersion

Inner city areas including some parts of established C.B.D.s have recently declined so much in importance that there are fears about over dispersion of tertiary activities. It is not simply a matter of vacant lots and physical deterioration, particularly of inner transitional zones, but also the loss of employment opportunity and rate revenue with which to maintain the necessary services such as roads and lighting. Many people among the poorest groups have no choice but to live in poor housing near the centre of cities and now face also declining job prospects with removal of too many job opportunities to the outer suburbs. The situation is further compounded by the economic recession which has especially hit some older sources of employment in inner areas.

61

Such have been the concerns that there is now some reversal of decentralisation policies. Inner areas are being revitalised. Some are now classed as special enterprise zones allowing subsidies and other inducements to be offered to attract employment back into the centre and other inner areas of older cities (Fig. 7.8). Two examples in this country are the London Dockland Scheme and the Tyneside Enterprise Zone. Similar policies are also now being followed in other EEC countries as well as in America.

Within such schemes there has been a return to intermixing of new housing with business premises, offering therefore employment opportunity in the same area. As at Hillfields close to the centre of Coventry re-development frequently includes setting up small industrial units as well as service activities alongside small scale housing schemes. In this way it is hoped the close community sense engendered in the earlier neighbourhood of 19th century terrace housing and workshops may be recaptured giving cohesion and purpose to the developed area.

Manufacturing and its location within the city

As city size increases so does the variety of its manufacturing and its occurrence in several distinct locations. Most explanations centre round some

form of cumulative causation whereby once industry is established and the city prospers, more activity is attracted to it until a stage is reached when, to an important extent, growth is self sustaining (Fig. 7.9). It is a basic fact that though small cities may decline through failure of some specialist industry such as heavy metals or chemicals, large cities never do. They may go through periods of difficulty and re-organisation of their economic base as is the present case with large conurbations such as Tyneside and Merseyside, but they continue to grow or at least to survive.

As cities have grown, the locational pattern of industry like that of service activities has become more complex. In the beginning industry would be concentrated round the initial core of the city and nearby along a waterway, rail line or some other land route which provided the cheapest transport for the raw materials needed and the finished product. But over time shortage of land, congestion and other problems associated with older industrial areas, together with the development of rapid road transport and technological changes have led to the decentralisation of industry. Established industries have moved out and together with new industries occupied more peripheral locations. Though there has been some recovery and return of small industry to the inner areas of cities, the overall trend has remained one of decentralisation.

Despite the greater complexity of intra-urban patterns of industry it is still possible to identify some of

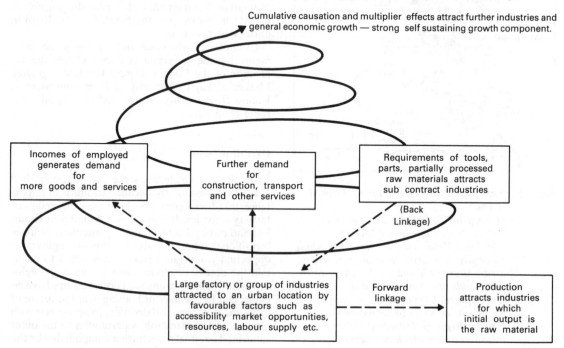

Cumulative causation and multiplier effects attract further industries and general economic growth — strong self sustaining growth component.

Incomes of employed generates demand for more goods and services

Further demand for construction, transport and other services

Requirements of tools, parts, partially processed raw materials attracts sub contract industries

(Back Linkage)

Large factory or group of industries attracted to an urban location by favourable factors such as accessibility market opportunities, resources, labour supply etc.

Forward linkage

Production attracts industries for which initial output is the raw material

Fig. 7.9 Cumulative to self-sustained growth

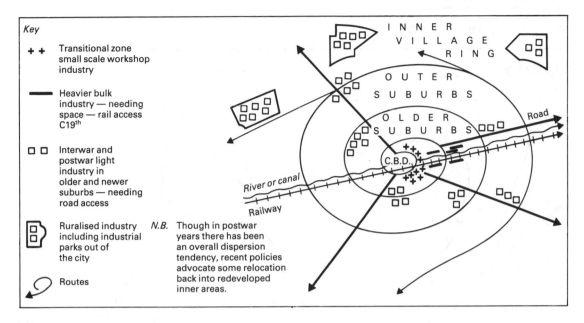

Fig. 7.10   A model of industry in the intra-urban setting

its salient features. These are diagrammatically summarised in Fig. 7.10 and illustrated in the Case Study of Sao Paulo (p. 64), one of the major industrial cities in Latin America. It indicates that many of the processes which have influenced urban industrial location in developed countries over a much longer period of time are also evident in the developing world.

Central locations for industry

The oldest industrial zone is usually situated around the C.B.D. of the city. It may include a mixture of small and large firms, many in old and dilapidated buildings, some close to the railway termini and canal basins which used to serve them. But there may also be a considerable number of small new industries set up in converted housing or in factories of the former older industries. There is frequently quite a high turnover amongst small businesses as some fail while others expand and require larger premises. The older inner area is therefore one where new industry may be spawned as well as the scene of the former industry on which the city initially depended.

The reasons for the original location of this older industry near the centre are various. Initially the zone around the C.B.D. would be the fringe zone around the then small city giving good locational access, cheap sites for development and a ready labour supply. Until the end of the 19th century there was no compelling reason for industry to move out. Today some industry, especially small scale industry remains, particularly where close links are

needed with activities located in the C.B.D. area and with other workshops in the production process. This is the case for example with bespoke tailoring, printing and craft manufacturing such as jewellery or small precision tools.

In the transition zone too, small rented accommodation is available close to the city centre and nearby warehouses, reducing the need for a canteen for workers, parking and storage space — all factors important to businesses with little capital. Such premises are attractive to 'seed bed' industries i.e. small industries arising from new technologies and using an adaptable labour force available at central locations. Seed bed industries include electronics, scientific instruments and pattern making as for example in Little Sheffield on the western margin of Sheffield's C.B.D. and initially the location of the early cutlery and small metals industry.

In respect of heavy industry such as heavy metals like iron and steel or timber works established near rail sidings and canal docks, the zone frequently extends radially out from the inner site alongside the railway and canal. Industry was attracted here not only because of access to raw material supplies and markets but also by vacant and cheaper level land along the valley next to the railway or canal access. This can be seen along the Don Valley below the centre of Sheffield and along the canals near the centres of Birmingham and Tyneside.

Such a pattern was typical in North America and Europe and is today also seen in developing countries where urbanisation and industrialisation have occurred this century as for instance in the case of Sao Paulo in Brazil. In respect of heavy industry,

7:1 SAO PAULO, BRAZIL

Distribution of industry

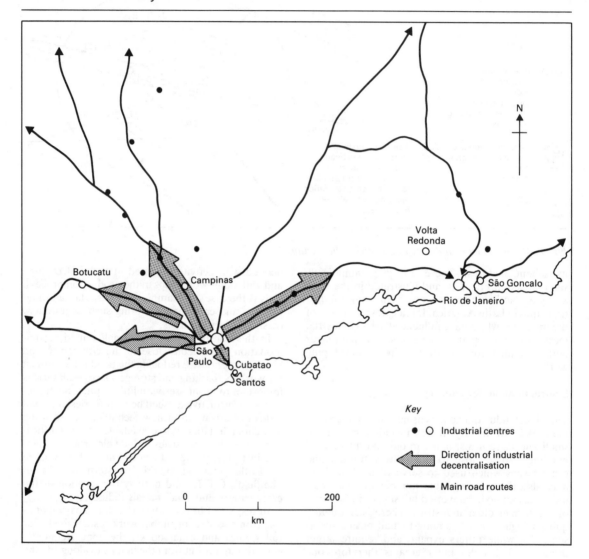

Key

● ○ Industrial centres

⬅ Direction of industrial decentralisation

─── Main road routes

0 ─── 200
km

LOCATION CONTEXT

INITIAL AND CUMULATIVE ADVANTAGES

Initial — situated in the favoured South East region — growth and wealth arising from the coffee industry — export corridor via its port of Santos — capital available for industrial development.

Cumulative — attractive to investors — with an established and growing market for varied industries expanding labour pool, good infrastructure — government support and financial backing for further development.

DYNAMIC GROWTH CENTRE — 40% of Brazil's industrial output with much foreign investment in branch plants etc. — good capacity for self sustained growth. Population 10.5 million current increase 500 000 annually.

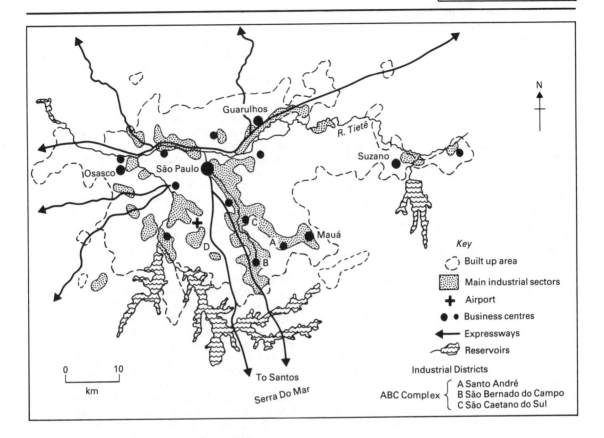

Key

◌ Built up area

▦ Main industrial sectors

✚ Airport

● ● Business centres

◀— Expressways

🌫 Reservoirs

Industrial Districts

ABC Complex {
A Santo André
B São Bernado do Campo
C São Caetano do Sul
}

CHANGING PATTERN OF INDUSTRIAL DEVELOPMENT

Stage 1 — Central development

Locations on terrace site south bank of the R.Tiete — diversified range of industries — engineering, textiles, consumer goods etc.

Stage 2 — Suburban spread

By 1930s satellite centres to the South East — metal works, chemicals, engineering etc. — some area specialisation.

1950s — further development here plus on access routes to the East and West of the Triangulo Central Area — further diversification under government stimulus e.g. motor vehicles, electrical goods.

Stage 3 — Comprehensive planning

Pressures and diseconomies led to the 1963 Plan for multi-centred growth (polynuclear) — especially

centres to the South, along arterial road and central redevelopment.

Stage 4 — Decentralisation

Further decentralisation beyond Sao Paulo e.g. towards Santos etc. — further diversification e.g. high technology — national market now served.

Stage 5 — National planning

of counter growth poles to reduce pressures.

Exercise

● Assess the relative importance of factors influencing the growth and location of manufacturing in the Sao Paulo region.

capital investment in buildings, equipment and other factors may maintain the location there despite the growing disadvantages associated with an ageing site and a change in transport methods. Hence industrial inertia may be an influential factor in the present siting of old heavy industry towards the inner area and centre of cities.

Suburbanisation of industry

In general there has been a marked suburbanisation or decentralisation of industry. This has gathered momentum and is now affecting large cities all over the world. Some of this change is due to the relocation of industry moving from inner sites, some of it branch factory establishments by national and multinational companies and the rest new industry to meet changing tastes and a growing demand. Keeble, in his study of the north west London suburbs, found for example that whereas in 1914 there were only a handful of firms, by 1960 there were many employing nearly a quarter of a million people altogether.

Most industry in the suburbs is of a lighter kind, located on purpose built industrial or trading estates segregated from other land usages though often close to residential and retail areas. Buildings are single storey incorporating office space planned with car parking provision and services laid on. They can be found in the older inter-war suburbs as well as in newer ones and more recently on the rural fringe surrounded by green fields or located on the edge of a village.

The deliberate decentralisation of industry into new towns and expanded towns at some distance from a main conurbation can be viewed as a logical extension of this radial outward movement of industry which has been going on from the end of the First World War. Much of it concerns newer consumer industries such as cosmetics, electrical assembly, light engineering and food products.

There are a number of reasons for the suburbanisation of industry and these can be summarised under pull and push factors. Pred emphasised changes in transport as one of the pull factors. Provision of bus and rail services increasingly enable the workforce to live in the suburbs and travel into the work. Now industry has followed the workforce out to the suburbs. The development of lorry transportation also freed industry from traditional sites close to water and rail, giving greater flexibility in both siting and access to raw materials and markets.

Land is also cheaper in suburban locations and more plentiful compared to the inner city areas, allowing therefore for the one storey and continuous assembly processes modern industry frequently requires as well as space for further expansion. Transport access has been further increased by the development of ring-roads, motorways, as well as by-passes linking into a national motorway network widening markets.

Push factors from the inner area have been increasing land shortages, the difficulties of adapting or expanding old buildings, increasing traffic congestion and urban renewal programmes. Many small factories are forced to close while redevelopment took place and then found that on new sites in redeveloped areas rents had so increased that they could no longer afford to go back to an inner location. For example, Edge, investigating the location of industry in Birmingham indicated that in the St. Paul's and Newtown area, old single workshop sites which before development cost £500 or so per annum were replaced by modern flatted built factories with rents at £3000 per annum. Interestingly most firms which have moved out from the centre have tended to move to sites further out on the same side of the city in order to tap the established labour force, especially where it was highly skilled and therefore difficult to replace.

Increasing concern however, has been expressed about the loss of industry, like other employment facilities, from inner areas. There is now a campaign in most advanced countries to attract industry back into the city and to redevelop sites such as closed railway stations and sidings, or slum clearance areas. Local authorities frequently work in conjunction with property developers on comprehensive schemes in which small units are being offered to small businesses on very advantageous terms. Thus though the overall trend has been towards dispersion of industry there is, as we have already seen in respect of tertiary activities, some revival of the initial and older inner areas which were discussed at the beginning of this section. This is to be seen for example in the redevelopment plans for the old inner areas of Coventry such as Hillfields.

Transport networks and movement

In discussing the economic basis of cities particular emphasis has been placed on accessibility and the effect of developments in transport on the pattern of economic activity.

Their influence on residential patterns has been equally significant, allowing for example the increasing separation of residence and workplace and with it suburbanisation and dormitory growth. But whilst communications have a direct influence on location, communication networks warrant attention, as the pattern of traffic flowing along them between different parts of the city helps to show how it functions. For example, commuter flows indicate the link between residence and workplace and shopping trips and service centres, including the C.B.D. Thus through a study of the transport network we see the city as a functioning system, its different parts not only interrelated but also interdependent. Any urban transport network has to be capable of catering for a variety of traffic, each competing with the other for travel space. Also it has to cater for many different patterns of journey. It is commonly assumed that the most used routes are those to and from the city centre, but surveys show that cross traffic in larger cities is even greater. There is also 'all through' traffic flow as well as that along link roads.

Given all this volume of traffic and the complexity of journey patterns a very flexible mode of transport is required. Hence the increasing emphasis on roads and motor vehicles while other types of transport though secondary are still of significant importance to this. For example suburban underground and rail facilities in large cities such as London and Tokyo are vital in helping carry commuters to and from work.

So rapid has been the growth in the volume of traffic, that much of the planning since the war has been concerned with solving the problem of too much traffic in our cities. This has also been associated with safeguarding the rights of pedestrians and cyclists who make up the bulk of movements over short distances in a city. For example, a quarter of the journeys of under 1.5 km in the City of London are by foot.

Improvements to city transport systems

Accommodation of motor vehicle traffic

This has involved complete systems of ringways and by-passes to divert through traffic away from the city centre, and facilitate cross-city traffic movement (Fig. 7.11). There is usually an inner ring-road for local traffic and an outer ring-road also serving local traffic but particularly to allow through traffic to bypass the most built up areas of the city. There may also be freeways of dual carriageway proportions into the heart of the city, traffic gaining easy access by clover-leaf type junctions where the freeway intersects ring-roads (Fig. 7.12).

These kinds of improvement may bring benefits but they are costly not only in economic terms but also socially. Valuable urban land has been used up, housing cleared to make way for motorways and communities divided by new routes crossing through the middle of some residential areas. There is also the problem of increased noise and high levels of pollution from exhaust fumes. Frequently it is the poorer housing areas which are most seriously affected whilst it is businesses and the more affluent car owning sectors of society who benefit most. For example London's Westway — a six lane elevated dual carriageway has been carved right through

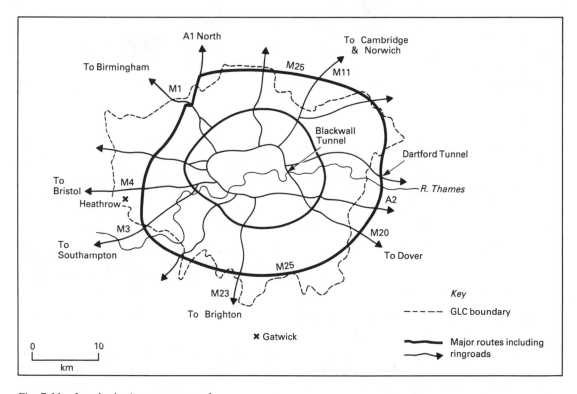

Fig. 7.11   London's ringway proposals

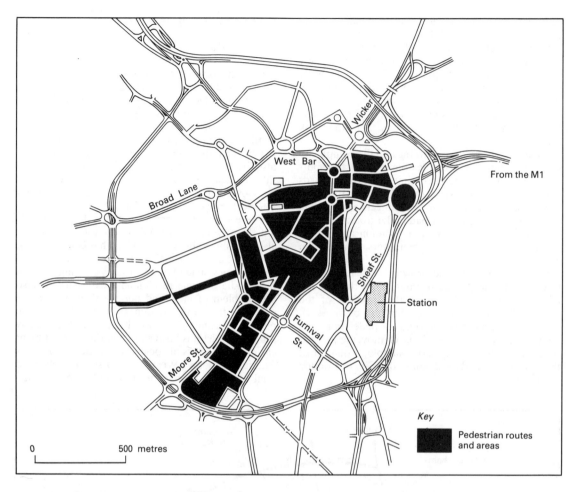

Fig. 7.12   Sheffield's new central traffic system and pedestrian area

North Kensington and Paddington's poorer housing areas and prompted the following observations:

'The construction of a new motorway is a type of modern parable using public funds to make life easier for the rich and harder for the poor'.

Increased parking space is also needed in the city. Frequently this is in the transitional zone next to the C.B.D. using up land which may be needed to provide more housing for lower income groups.

Alternative transport provision

Until recently the needs of those walking or cycling in the city have been given comparatively little attention, but further measures have followed on from the idea of helping those on foot by providing some pedestrian precincts and subways under busy roads. Now a number of pedestrian ways are being weatherproofed, as well as some being built above

ground level. In highly congested areas like The Bank in London, conveyor belts are also being installed over short distances.

Whilst the Netherlands has long had its cycle ways, these are another recent innovation in most European cities. The new town of Milton Keynes has an extensive network of cycle ways. But so far only a few of the older towns are attempting to provide them to segregate the cyclist from vehicle traffic. In Cambridge, however, a cycle way network is well advanced hastened by the abnormal number of cyclists because it is a University town — one fifth of all journeys are by cycle.

For longer journeys the main alternative provision to private cars has been the extension of the suburban and underground rail networks. In Hong Kong for example a complete new system has been installed (Fig. 7.13). In London the network has been improved by the new Victoria and Heathrow Airport lines. Elsewhere in England the most no-

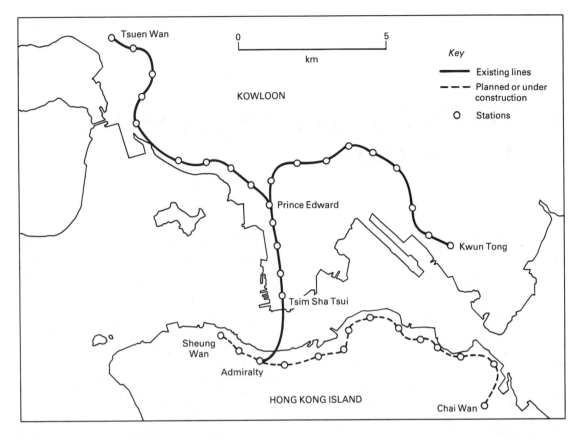

Fig. 7.13 Hong Kong's mass transit railway system

ticeable scheme has been that for Tyneside to which bus-feeder routes have been added.

In conclusion it can be seen that strenuous efforts are being made to cope with increased town traffic, but perhaps the biggest contribution to a long term solution will be a further decentralisation of employ- ment and service facilities bringing them into closer proximity to residential areas. This will then perhaps not only reduce some of the need for people to travel by car into the more congested central areas, but also reduce the amount of freight which must be transported across the city.

8 The Form and Future Shape of the Modern City

Past constraints

During the 20th century the pace of modernisation has so quickened that simple accretionary growth and adaptation of existing buildings in towns are no longer sufficient to meet the changing needs of society. Consequently we are seeing not only wholesale redevelopment of older and even comparatively recent city areas, but also the development of new kinds of cities. To some extent these are based on the Garden City movement which had its beginning in the 1930s with the work of Ebenezer Howard and other pioneers.

However, change still has to take place within the constraints left by the past. The existing built form of a city, including the street plan and general layout which make up the morphology or physical structure of a city, cannot simply be swept away. Apart from groups pressing for conservation of what is considered best of the past, the existing built form represents a massive financial investment some of which must continue to be used where possible. Thus to understand the nature of present change we do need to have some regard for the past.

The past and urban structures

The form of any urban place depends, to some extent, on how old it is. The older the city, the greater the number of morphological (historical) periods which have contributed to its makeup. New towns such as Milton Keynes in the U.K. and Brasilia, the new interior capital of Brazil, are a product of the present but older cities like London or Rio de Janeiro are products of a number of morphological periods. In inner areas the street plan and some buildings even pre-date those main phases of the 19th century — inter-war and post 1945 — which have made the greatest contribution to the shape of cities in the developed world.

When looking at cities it is possible from the shape and style of buildings as well as the nature of the street plan to recognise which historical phase contributed most to the character of a city. But it is difficult to pick out phases of growth clearly, partly because succeeding development not only adds further accretionary growth onto the fringes of a city but may also bring some redevelopment and adaptation in existing areas. Furthermore every period of growth tends to throw out certain usages to the fringe, e.g. obnoxious sewer and gas works, mental hospitals, allotments and playing fields. Thus each morphological period tends to have its fringe belt which during the following phases of expansion gets filled in with new development and encapsulated into the city. Thus besides the usual zonation of cities it is possible to recognise old fringe belts of mixed use, which mark the outer limits of a city or town at different phases in its development.

Forms in the developing world

Phases of growth and fringe development may also be seen in cities of the developing world but here the morphological form of cities is frequently complicated by colonial and post colonial influences which have introduced elements of a 'Western' cultural form to many cities. Sometimes indigenous and external influences may be spatially separated giving a distinctive dual structure to the city, as in the case of Bombay in India and Kano in Nigeria (Fig. 8.2). But more usually influences are mixed, though there may be distinct native and European quarters.

Most recently continued pressures have brought redevelopment in the centre and the spread of suburbs. Thus many of the larger cities in a developing world such as Rio de Janeiro and Mexico City have newer areas, including high rise development, which make them very reminiscent of modern cities in the developed world. Unlike the latter there has been the additional development of shanty areas both on the edge and further in where difficult terrain hitherto deterred building.

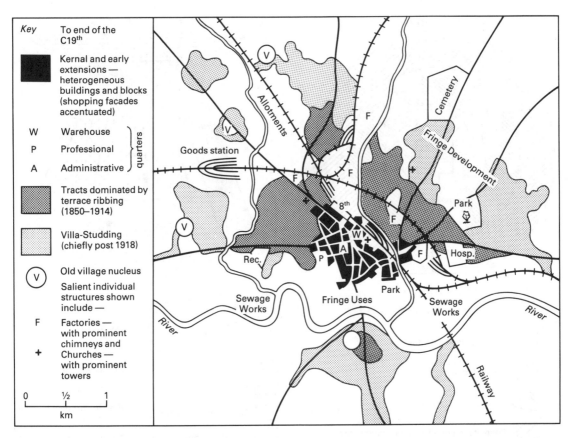

Fig. 8.1   The morphology of a typical county town including fringe belt development (after Smailes)

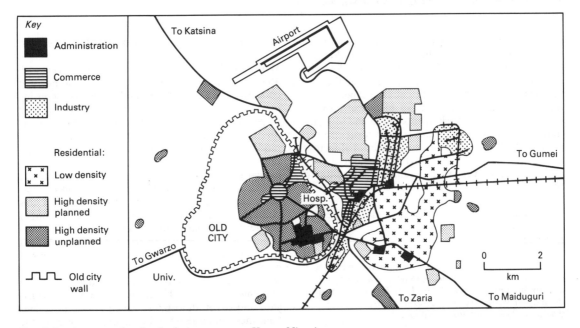

Fig. 8.2   An example of a dual city structure, Kano, Nigeria

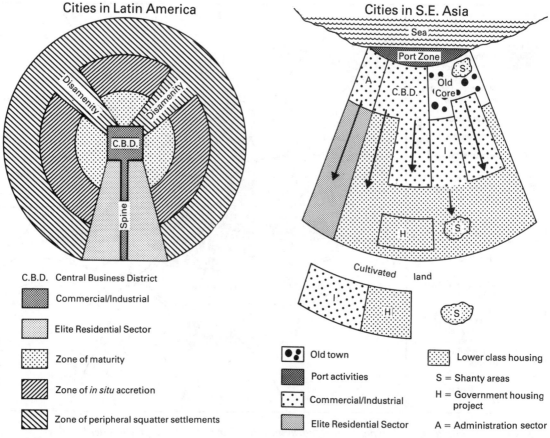

Cities in Latin America

Disamenity

Disamenity

C.B.D.

Spine

C.B.D. Central Business District

Commercial/Industrial

Elite Residential Sector

Zone of maturity

Zone of *in situ* accretion

Zone of peripheral squatter settlements

Cities in S.E. Asia

Sea

Port Zone

A

C.B.D.

Old Core

S

H

S

Cultivated land

I

H

S

Old town

Port activities

Commercial/Industrial

Elite Residential Sector

Lower class housing

S = Shanty areas

H = Government housing project

A = Administration sector

Fig. 8.3   City structure models for the developing world

Attempts have been made to produce generalisations of city structures for the developing world (Fig. 8.3). Though these contain ring and sector elements similar to those city structure models in the developed world and to some extent are shaped by the same processes such as rates of historical growth, social processes of invasion, succession and segregation as well as economic forces, city form is more varied. This is due to some of the additional factors already noted, such as dual indigenous and outside influences and over-rapid urbanisation leading to shanty growth.

Exercise

Comment on the form of the city suggested in the models in Fig. 8.3 and indicate in what ways they are similar and dissimilar from those for cities in the developed world. Try and account for any dissimilarities which you identify.

City redevelopment in the developed world

Whilst much of the present redevelopment is associated with run down areas of the city, some of it concerns areas of high rise and other mass housing put up within the last twenty-five years. In the rush to provide housing (after the Second World War) for the many homeless and those in unfit accommodation, many defects occurred — faulty building, over-large estates, as well as the social and psychological problems associated with living in high rise blocks and on impersonal large estates. Consequently some wholesale clearance of the worst of this building is now occurring in certain of the larger Western European cities such as Liverpool and Hamburg. In the new development there has been a reversion to the construction of smaller scale units of more traditional design in response to pressure from ordinary families and other concerned groups. Such building gives some chance of recreating the courtyard and street atmosphere which led to the neighbourliness and a sense of belonging so valued in the past.

IS THE FUTURE OF OUR HOMES SECURE?

Your Residents' Association Committee feel there may be some doubt in the Council's mind. It is nearly two years (January 27th, 1971) since Councillors and officials promised that our area would be improved.

Nothing has been heard since. How long do we have to wait?

Our homes are not getting any younger. New houses at the end of the street and factories each side of us. Are the Council hoping now to run the area down for redevelopment?

WHAT CAN WE DO?

After taking advice your committee have found out that our Residents' Association with professional voluntary help can legally submit a report to the Council asking for the declaration of these streets as a General Improvement Area. (G.I.A.)

HOW WOULD THIS HELP?

* It would mean a secure future for our homes for 30 years at least.

* The area would be given a facelift because £28,000 would be made available to be spent on cleaning up derelict sites and streets, new fences and back jetties.

* We would have a say in what other things ought to be done and how this money is spent.

THE DRAWBACKS?

- rents and rates may go up if your landlord improves the house.

- some residents may not want the mess or bother of improving the area or their home.

- it may encourage new families into the area and landlords to sell.

THE NEXT STEP _ _ _ _ _ _ _ _ CUT HERE _ _

The Committee need to know the following: (please tick boxes)

(1) DO YOU WISH TO STAY IN THE AREA?   YES [ ]   NO [ ]

(2) WOULD YOU LIKE TO SEE THE AREA IMPROVED?   YES [ ]   NO [ ]

(3) IF THE COUNCIL IMPROVED THE AREA WOULD IT ENCOURAGE YOU TO MODERNISE YOUR HOUSE OR ASK YOUR LANDLORD OR AGENT TO DO SO? (FOR THOSE WHO HAVE NOT ALREADY HAD COUNCIL GRANTS FOR IMPROVEMENTS).   YES [ ]   NO [ ]

If people wish to stay and improve the area then your Committee will call a public meeting to talk about the next step.

A MEMBER OF THE RESIDENTS COMMITTEE WILL BE CALLING ON YOU IN THE NEXT FEW DAYS TO GET YOUR ANSWERS.

This is not a Council leaflet – issued by the Hartlepool Road Redcar Road, Stockton Road Residents' Association Committee.

NAME ....
ADDRESS ....

Fig. 8.4 *Community participation and inner city renewal (issued by Hartlepool and Stockton Residents Association, Coventry)*

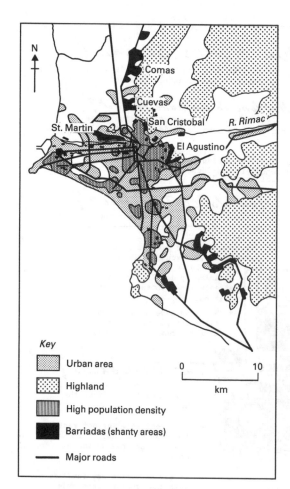

Key

- :::: Urban area
- ⋰ Highland
- ‖‖ High population density
- ■ Barriadas (shanty areas)
- ── Major roads

0 ──── 10

km

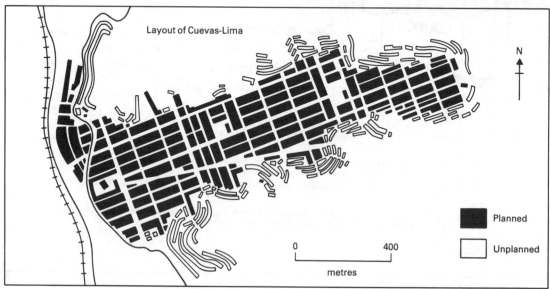

Layout of Cuevas-Lima

■ Planned

□ Unplanned

0 ──── 400

metres

Fig. 8.5 Shanty and self-help housing in Lima, Peru

There have also been efforts to stop wholesale clearance of older housing which, though short in certain basic amenities such as an interior toilet and bathroom, was still structurally sound. In the United Kingdom some older inner areas have been classed as Community Improvement Areas and Housing Action Areas where grants and subsidies can be made to allow housing to be improved up to present day standards. Also street improvement schemes have been undertaken to provide a better environment including safe playing areas for children.

Thus some areas are now mixed reflecting a successive change of policy from one postwar government to another in response to increasingly informed public opinion, effective pressure groups and the need for planning authorities now to consult the public through structure plans (Fig. 8.4).

Spontaneous and self-help housing in the developing world

Shanty areas perhaps pose the most serious problem to the local and metropolitan authorities of developing world cities. Until recently policies have been rather negative. Attempts have been made to prevent more people coming in and established shanty areas have either been bulldozed down or ignored. In the face of the continued influx of people into the cities and growing health and other problems in shanty areas, more constructive policies are being adopted. However, there are insufficient funds to allow enough local authority housing projects of the kind undertaken in the developed world. So the main impetus has increasingly been towards self-help schemes (see Fig. 8.5).

The authorities provide basic services such as sanitation and a water supply whilst the shanty dwellers improve existing make-shift dwellings or build new ones on plots to which they are given some security of tenure. Credit loans are provided for materials and advisory as well as other support services given such, as community health and education. In Calcutta and Madras 'Bustee' improvement schemes have also included workshops to provide some kind of employment. So far, however, only modest progress has been made.

In Peru where shanty developments not only grew up haphazardly but also as a result of a planned invasion and squatting on vacant lots by whole communities as at Villa El Salvador which now houses 200 000 people 32 km from Lima, co-operatives have been formed by groups of families. These co-operatives with some credit provided by a National Housing Bank acquire land, submit plans to the local authority and allocate plots to individual families. The families can then construct basic housing to suit their present needs and have enough space on the plot to allow for later additions to it. The problem is that many of the 30% of Lima's households who live in the shanty areas (Barriadas or Pueblos Jovenes) have no cash of their own which makes it difficult to qualify for a government credit grant. Thus the needs of the most under-privileged sector of the population are still not being met.

New and expanded towns in developed countries

As we have seen, where urbanisation has passed its peak there is a natural movement of people away from overcrowded cities into the countryside. It had already begun in Western Europe at the turn of the century and gathered momentum in the inter-war years, when improvements in road transport and rising affluence among ordinary people led to the rapid spread of suburbs around major cities. This has continued into the postwar years. It is not only evident in the sprawl of outer suburbs but also in the dormitory growth of villages in the nearby countryside. Greenbelt restrictions imposed on the further growth of built up areas and the Town and Country

Fig. 8.6 New towns in the United Kingdom

75

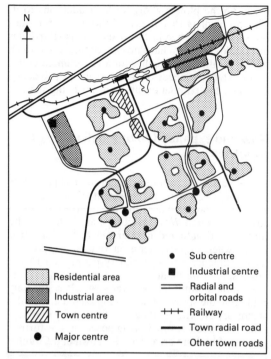

Key:
- Residential area
- Industrial area
- Town centre
- Major centre
- Sub centre
- Industrial centre
- Radial and orbital roads
- Railway
- Town radial road
- Other town roads

Fig. 8.7   The earlier pattern for Harlow new town (based on Gibberd's Plan, 1947)

Planning legislation begun in the late 19th century but implemented in a more determined fashion after the Second World War, served only to put pressure on the villages and nearby small towns immediately beyond the greenbelt.

This pressure, combined with that on the older areas in cities, forced governments to adopt a more positive approach which would actively encourage decentralisation away from major cities. It needed to be planned towards locations which could readily absorb and benefit from such growth. New towns were developed on virgin green-field sites in the country or adjacent to small settlements as in the case of Harlow and Stevenage which were built to accommodate some of London's over-spill. These towns (see Fig. 8.6) were laid out along lines pioneered by Ebenezer Howard and others of the Garden City movement begun in the inter-war years, and which itself was responsible for the Garden City of Letchworth.

In addition a number of small market towns in need of further growth and better economic prospects were earmarked to receive over-spill from London and other large cities under the Expanded Towns Act of 1953. For example some of the older market towns of East Anglia such as St. Neots, Haverhill and Huntingdon have been expanded to take in over-spill population from greater London together with some businesses.

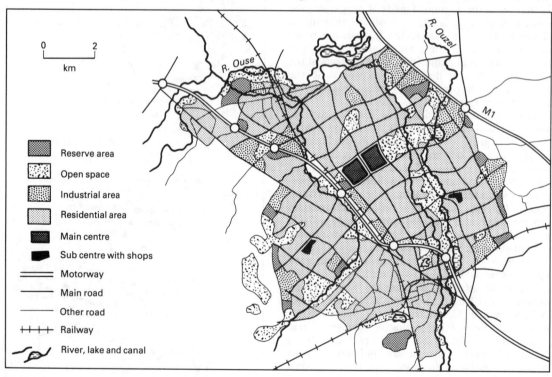

Key:
- Reserve area
- Open space
- Industrial area
- Residential area
- Main centre
- Sub centre with shops
- Motorway
- Main road
- Other road
- Railway
- River, lake and canal

Fig. 8.8   The later pattern for Milton Keynes

Despite the individual success enjoyed by certain new and expanded towns, overall the policy has only been partially successful in relieving pressure on the largest conurbations. For one thing insufficient employment opportunities were available and also some of the new towns were too close to a main conurbation. Many who lived in new and expanded towns continued to commute back to work in the large cities and this has placed a severe strain on the transport network. It has also encouraged the continued setting up of offices and expansion of factories in the conurbations despite the planning restrictions against them.

As a consequence in Britain and on the continent a second generation of new towns were planned, this time sufficiently far from established conurbations to be independent of them and large enough to truly act as counter-magnets to them. So much so that they would eventually generate further growth without government support and financial aid. The best known of these second generation new towns in this country is Milton Keynes in Buckinghamshire which was designated in 1967 (Fig. 8.8). It is planned to house a quarter of a million people. Despite the economic recession and a downward turn in the country's population growth this, the last of Britain's new towns, already has a population of 100 000. It is continuing to grow at the rate of 7000 a year. Milton Keynes has an imaginative layout and a diverse range of housing. The old idea of large neighbourhood shopping precincts incorporated into the planning of the early new towns has been abandoned in favour of central shopping backed by a fast public transport network from residential areas to it.

Though Milton Keynes was started as a result of state intervention and planning, private investment has been attracted on a large scale since the late 1970s, indicating the capacity for self-sustaining growth. In the early 1980s private investment was running at £80 000 000 a year and all current housing development is being undertaken by private enterprise. Furthermore Milton Keynes is rapidly becoming a regional shopping centre and has attracted a range of firms and offices including some growth industry of Information Technology.

Its success is partly due to its central position in the Midlands and a fast and efficient road and rail service to different parts of the country, in particular London. It is also due to the vigour and initiative shown by the first chairman of the Development Corporation, Lord Campbell, and his team who have adopted an aggressive growth and advertising policy. Furthermore they have encouraged the use of modern technology both domestically and in the servicing in the new town as a whole. For example, it was the first city centre to have solar heating built into some of the housing developments, the first city to have cable television on any scale and

a network of television communication for business purposes.

In a number of ways, therefore, Milton Keynes marked the transition phase towards the city of the future which may take a widely dispersed form, housing and business areas being separated by green leisure zones and open spaces. The future may see dispersed cities which will be interlinked by a modern communication network along which not only goods and people may flow, but also masses of information. Indeed it is envisaged that an increasing number of businessmen and executives may live and work at home communicating and exchanging information with office headquarters by telex lines and computer linkages.

Dispersion and new towns in the developing world

Though for some time decentralisation policies have been adopted in the Western world, reinforcing the spontaneous de-urbanisation which has also occurred, it is only really since the 1970s that such policies have been widely adopted in the developing world. Today planned suburban dispersion, dormitory growth and new towns are characteristic of most developing countries. This may be illustrated from the case of South Korea where planned dispersion of further growth from Seoul, the capital, is being undertaken. (Case Study 8.1)

South Korea like other developing countries such as Brazil and India is adopting decentralisation policies similar to those in developed countries. But developing countries may well run into the same problems with continued growth of the primate city due to self-sustained growth through natural increase amongst the population already resident. There is also the likely problem of siting future growth too close to the capital as was the case with the first new towns built around London. Thus urban sprawl could continue. Indeed there is evidence in the developing countries that greenbelt restrictions placed on large cities to prevent further development have been overtaken by events with the city continuing to sprawl and take up much of the greenbelt areas.

Exercise

In what ways do new towns differ from older established cities. What are the problems which may be associated with them?

8:1 SEOUL, SOUTH KOREA

Dispersion from a capital city

A *The Growth of Seoul Relative to Total Population*

	Growth in South Korea (pop in 000s)					
	1952	1960	1965	1970	1975	1980
Seoul City	1575	2445	3470	5433	6879	8367
South Korea	21502	24954	28327	31435	34681	38723
% of national population living in Seoul	7.3	9.8	12.2	17.2	19.8	21.6

B *The need for planned dispersion*

Seoul, South Korea's capital with a metropolitan population of over 11 000 000, nearly one fifth of the country's population, now ranks as one of the largest urban concentrations in the world. Yet twenty years earlier it had only 1.5 million people.

Growth on this scale has brought enormous problems compounded by the restriction of rocky hill ranges on all sides, canalising building along the floors of valley corridors and splitting up the urban fabric of the city. There is chronic traffic congestion, overcrowding and pressure on public utilities.

C *Government policies for dispersion*

1 Aims to place much of the future growth of the city to the south bank of the River Han and away from the North which as the historic core has experienced most growth.
2 In addition by 1986 it is expected to have diverted an additional 4.3 million people to other centres in the total metropolitan region. These centres are also seen as future economic growth areas for industry etc.
3 A new administrative capital is to be built on a site beyond Seoul.

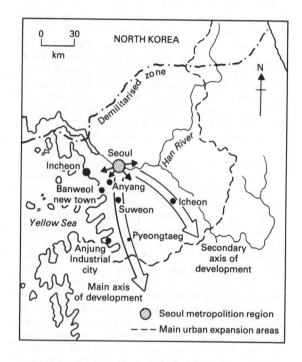

Exercise

● Suggest reasons why Seoul has experienced such rapid growth and consider whether the government policies outlined are likely to provide a successful solution to the problems this rapid growth has brought.

9   Manufacturing and Industry

THE PROCESS OF CHANGE AND LOCATIONAL INFLUENCES

The manufacturing process: industrialisation

Industry as a term, besides referring to manufacturing can also be used to refer to other economic activities such as mining, construction and public utilities including gas and electricity supplies. In this section however we are concerned only with manufacturing industry, that is the making of a product under factory conditions. Various inputs (factors of production) such as raw materials, power, labour and capital are brought together in the production process from which there emerges an output — the product. (Refer to Fig. 9.1.)

Frequently the output of one manufacturing industry becomes one of the raw materials of another. Steel for example is used to make car bodies and is therefore one of the inputs needed by the automobile industry. The market for many industries is another industry and only certain manufacturing firms such as those concerned with food processing and furniture making sell directly to the public. Such industries are referred to as consumer industries.

It is usual to divide manufacturing into heavy and light industry, consumer manufacturing being part of the latter. This simple division is to some extent based on the weight of inputs and output but also involves the notion of heavy industry as the basic

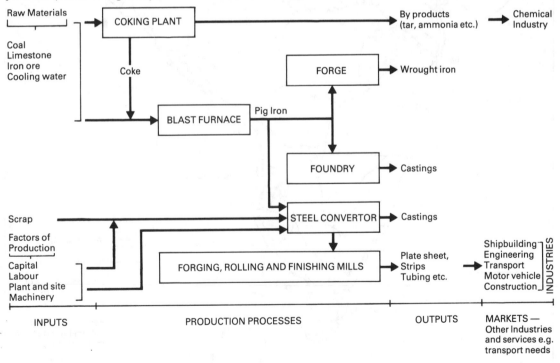

Fig. 9.1   Simplified production flow for iron and steel

9:1 INDIA

Major industrial regions

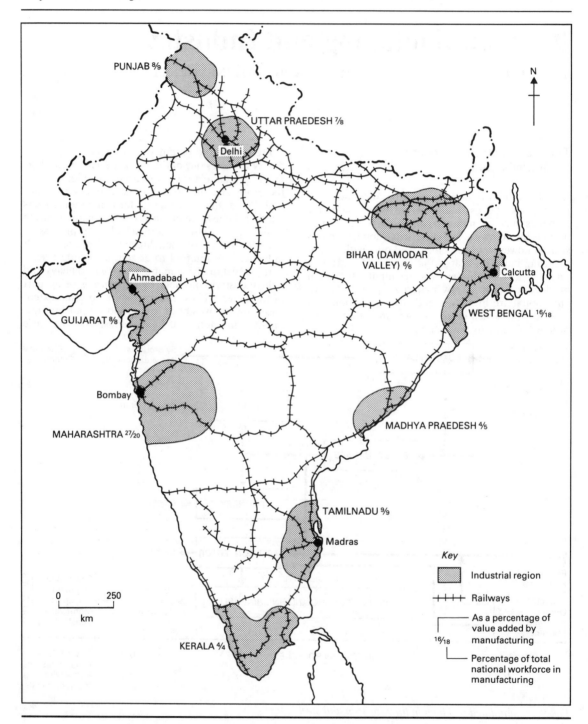

PUNJAB 8/9

UTTAR PRAEDESH 7/8

Delhi

BIHAR (DAMODAR VALLEY) 9/6

Ahmadabad

Calcutta

GUIJARAT 8/8

WEST BENGAL 16/18

Bombay

MADHYA PRAEDESH 4/5

MAHARASHTRA 27/20

TAMILNADU 9/9

Madras

KERALA 4/4

0   250

km

Key

Industrial region

+++++ Railways

16/18

As a percentage of value added by manufacturing

Percentage of total national workforce in manufacturing

STRUCTURAL ORGANISATION OF INDIA'S INDUSTRIAL ECONOMY THREE LEVELS IDENTIFIED

Lowest — village and household — based mostly on hand labour with little capital and a localised market e.g. textiles and metal working.

Middle — small scale with limited technology — located in urban areas — government aid via 'Small Industries Development Organisation' — light industrial estate units to let. Employs 30% of manufacturing labour. Very varied products — serving local market but increased sub-contracting to large industry. Also serves agriculture e.g. hand tools.

Large — scale industry
Found only in big cities — taking advantage of scale economies. Increasingly concentrated on new sites specifically for industry.
(a) Private enterprise e.g. Tata — dominant in electrical, vehicle and machine tools.
(b) Government/public ownership — iron and steel, non-ferrous metals, heavy engineering.
(c) Mixed ownership — aluminium, chemicals, road and sea transport.

Increasing cooperation with and investment from multinational companies — U.S.A., UK, Germany, Japan plus cooperation with USSR.

CHARACTER AND LOCATIONAL INFLUENCES FOR MAJOR REGIONS

Maharashtra (Bombay and Pune)

Textiles were dominant now diversified — electrical, mechanicial engineering, vehicles, durable consumers e.g. pharmaceuticals.
Aided by good port access, proximity to cotton areas etc. — cumulative advantages include growing domestic market, labour pool, infrastructure including electrified rail, power — oil, nuclear and H.E.P.

West Bengal (Calcutta, Hooghlyside)

Very diversified including textiles, synthetic fibres, engineering machinery, typewriters, oil refinery — petro-chemicals and consumer goods.
Historically favoured as port and commercial centre, access to jute area, cumultive effects include large market, scale economies, outport of Haldia — diseconomies now due to overconcentration.

Bihar (Damodar)

Initially heavy industry based on local coal, iron-ore, H.E.P. and access to Calcutta market. More industry added on this base — heavy engineering, chemicals, bricks, locomotives, toolmaking, radio, etc.

Other regions (including Delhi, Madras, Ahmadabad)

Favoured by government emphasis on more decentralisation, but with a range of industries also based on accessibility, power, raw materials etc. — capacity for further growth.

Exercise

● On the basis of the information given and access to relevant atlas maps, identify the salient features in the distribution of manufacturing in India and try to account for them.

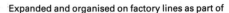

Expanded and organised on factory lines as part of

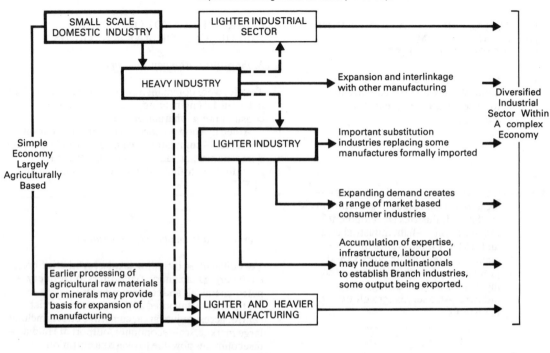

Fig. 9.2   Industrialisation in a developing country

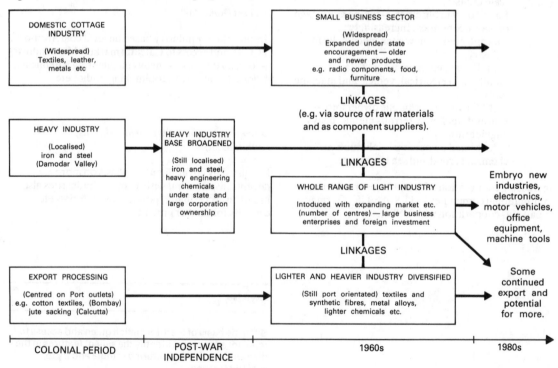

Fig. 9.3   Industrialisation process in India

manufacturing sector upon which many lighter industries depend. Consequently countries seeking to industrialise have given special attention to the development of a heavy industrial sector, even when few natural advantages by way of raw materials and power resources were available and the capital investment needed was in short supply. Once underway further industrialisation led to development of a variety of lighter industries in response to both the needs of already established industries and the demand for goods by an increasingly affluent population. Other factors too played their part such as the acquiring of entrepreneurial skill and investment capital together with an improvement in infrastructure facilities.

The main general features associated with this industrialisation process are shown in Fig. 9.2. We may now move on to consider the locational pattern arising from it, the principal feature being the concentration of most of the manufacturing into a few locations as for example in the case of India which has undergone rapid industrialisation since the 1950s. (Refer to Fig. 9.3.)

Locational influences

Much of the literature on industrial location focuses on the individual firm or industry. These aspects are dealt with in the next two chapters. Here we are concerned with the general pattern of industry and this requires a more comprehensive approach than is possible by either a systematic treatment of factors or the use of classical industrial location theory commonly used for an individual industry or firm.

We need firstly to see any general pattern as the cumulative result of a wide range of forces operating in an inter-related way over a substantial period of time. Secondly, we need to be able to home in on its salient features which as the Case Study of India shows is the marked concentration of industry into a few locations and a more recent tendency to some dispersion. A reasonably comprehensive framework is suggested in Fig. 9.4 and each of its salient features are explained later.

It centres on forces associated with the process of cumulative causation together with some subsequent dispersion due to the associated diseconomies arising from over-concentration. But it also includes a whole range of wider forces operating both at international and national levels and which lie behind any cumulative causation process. Whilst there is not the space to deal in any detail with these wider influences, their effects can be traced through the decisions of multinational corporations which today control much of the world's major industries and the actions of governments which have the power directly and indirectly to affect the location of manufacturing.

The cumulative causation process and its associated features

In the search for an explanation as to why manufacturing is mainly concentrated into a few growth centres a number of writers, including Myrdal, an economist, have identified a set of inter-relating factors operating in a kind of cumulative process. They see three stages in this process of cumulative growth. Firstly there is one of early growth based on the initial advantages one region has over others. Then there is a middle one of rapid growth, when derived advantages flowing out of this earlier concentration of activity reinforces the initial advantages and leads to a multiplier effect being set in motion. Then there is a final one in which so much concentration has occurred that problems arise leading to some dispersion of manufacturing to the periphery of the region and further afield.

Initial advantages include both natural and man-made ones. In the case of the Bombay region of India, for example, its natural advantages included a harbour inlet and a west coast position facing the main trading routes to Europe, together with proximity to the rich cotton growing areas inland from it. Man-made initial advantages were added when Britain as the colonial power, made Bombay one of the main export points for India as well as an important commercial and administrative centre. This led to the setting up of a strong infrastructure including a good transport network focusing on the port of Bombay. As a consequence textile and other manufacturing developed from the turn of the century leading to a rapid rise in the population and an expansion of a labour pool. To these derived advantages were added the entrepreneurship and capital of influential families such as the Tata family concerned with textile manufacturing in Bombay. As a result further expansion of industry and power resources occurred. Today Bombay has a wide range of industries in addition to the textile industry which lay at the core of the port's initial industrialisation. But there are already many signs of over-concentration leading to the dispersion of some industry, including that to the new town lying outside Bombay.

Some of the mechanisms associated with cumulative causation

Derived advantages result from external economies of scale outside the firm. These enable a firm to produce each unit of its output at a lower cost than might otherwise be the case. (There may also be internal economies of scale but these result from enlarging and reorganisation of the production process within the firm and will be dealt with later.)

External economies of scale include such things as

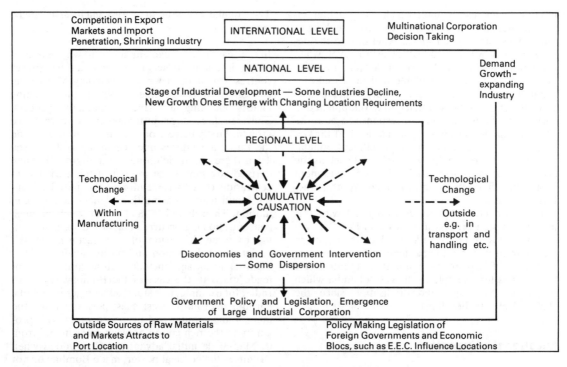

Fig. 9.4   (a) Factors at different levels affecting manufacturing and its location

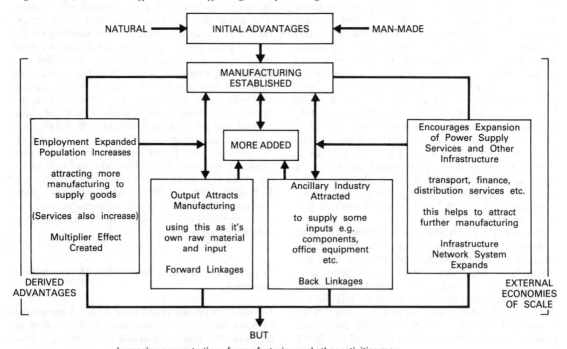

Fig. 9.4   (b) Factors influencing the concentration of manufacturing

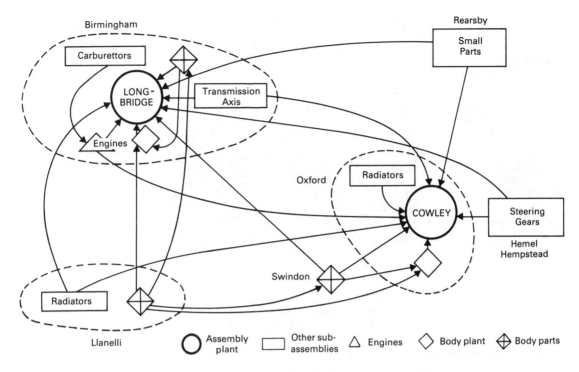

Fig. 9.5   Linkages between component suppliers and British Leyland car assembly plants

the existence of a good transport network and handling facilities which saves a firm having to install its own system. Other less obvious economies arise from making use of such things as the research, insurance and credit facilities already present in the region.

External economies of scale are also to do with the linkages enjoyed by a firm in the manufacturing region. In addition to marketing, financial and other commercial linkages there are also those directly concerned with the production process. These include vertical linkages whereby a series of processes are linked together contributing to the gradual transformation of the raw material inputs into the finished product, as for example in the iron and steel industry. Lateral or horizontal linkages involve industries producing parts or accessories feeding into different aspects of the assembly process, as in the motor vehicle industry (see Fig. 9.5). There are also diagonal linkages in which specialist trades or services such as repair firms do the same job for a number of different industries.

Over-concentration of manufacturing

Whilst we have so far concentrated on the agglomerative advantages resulting in a piling up of manufacturing and other economic activity in a location,

if growth continues over-concentration can occur leading to what are called diseconomies. These not only raise the cost of manufacturing and therefore must be increasingly set off against the savings firms have hitherto enjoyed as a result of the agglomerative influences, but they also involve a social cost to the community which may require considerable public expenditure if the situation is to be ameliorated.

All large concentrations of manufacturing experience diseconomies. But the point at which this leads to some dispersion of industry depends on the extent to which economies of scale savings are being eroded away. There must come a point where an alternative site is looked for, but there are cases of firms remaining in a location for some length of time after this point has been reached. This is the result of an inertia factor at work — plant owners do not want to write off the capital they have invested in building plant and machinery on the old site, nor may they wish to leave the pool of skilled labour that has been acquired over a long period of time.

Much of the dispersal of industry which has occurred has been over a short distance so that firms have been able to shed the effects of diseconomies and yet retain some of the benefits of close proximity to the established growth centre. However, the actions of multinational corporations which control much of industry today and those of government have led to dispersion of operations further afield.

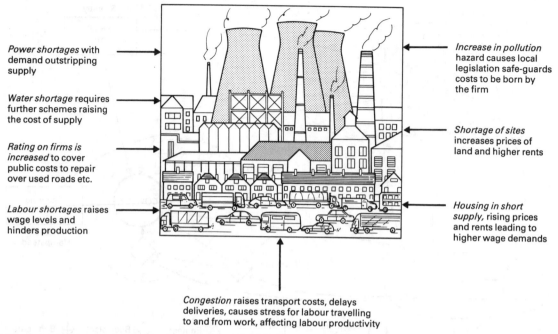

Power shortages with demand outstripping supply

Water shortage requires further schemes raising the cost of supply

Rating on firms is increased to cover public costs to repair over used roads etc.

Labour shortages raises wage levels and hinders production

Increase in pollution hazard causes local legislation safe-guards costs to be born by the firm

Shortage of sites increases prices of land and higher rents

Housing in short supply, rising prices and rents leading to higher wage demands

Congestion raises transport costs, delays deliveries, causes stress for labour travelling to and from work, affecting labour productivity

Fig. 9.6   Overconcentration leads to diseconomies of scale and increasing costs

The role of multinational corporations

Changes have been taking place within the organisation of manufacturing which greatly affect its distribution pattern. Despite the continued existence of many small scale industries, most of the manufacturing of today, whether expressed by value or volume of output, is under the control of large corporations many of which are multinational. Such corporations control a range of manufacturing and have branch plants not only in the parent country but abroad. For example 43% of Canada's manufacturing employment in the mid 1970s was in foreign owned plants, particularly those owned by large corporations with headquarters in the United States. In India much of the investment expansion of industry comes from foreign investment including link-ups with domestic firms and a setting up of branch plants by multinational corporations. It is illustrated by Japanese link-ups to expand the motor cycle and motor vehicle industry (Fig. 9.7) Another way of expressing the worldwide spread of multinational corporations is to indicate the location of patterns for one. The Japanese Matsushita Electrical Industrial Company Ltd., trading under the brand names of National Panasonic, Technics and Quasar, produce a wide range of products within consumer electronics, industrial equipment, business machines, home appliances, lighting equipment, systems products, electrical components, motors and batteries. It has branches all over the world. In all there

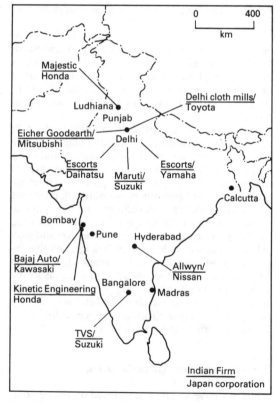

Fig. 9.7   Japanese links with the Indian vehicle industry

are 110 manufacturing departments in different parts of Japan employing 107 000 and 39 manufacturing companies overseas employing another 33 000 with sales in 1980 valued at $US13.9 billion. This gives some idea of the scale of operations of a multinational corporation.

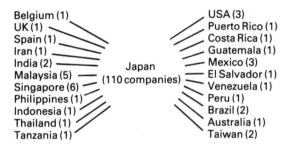

Belgium (1)
UK (1)
Spain (1)
Iran (1)
India (2)
Malaysia (5)
Singapore (6)
Philippines (1)
Indonesia (1)
Thailand (1)
Tanzania (1)

Japan
(110 companies)

USA (3)
Puerto Rico (1)
Costa Rica (1)
Guatemala (1)
Mexico (3)
El Salvador (1)
Venezuela (1)
Peru (1)
Brazil (2)
Australia (1)
Taiwan (2)

Fig. 9.8   Branches of the Matsushita electronic corporation

This organisation of manufacturing on a large scale, under corporate ownership can be regarded as a further development of a process which has been going on ever since the Industrial Revolution. With the advances in technology that have continually occurred, much larger capital investment in specialised machinery and plant have been required together with highly organised research, sales and administrative back-up forces, catering for world as well as home markets. Also only large companies and corporations have the capital and expertise to make many of the types of products on the scale present market demands require.

By operating on such a large scale these corporations can achieve important internal economies of scale leading to a decrease in the average cost per unit of output as the quantity of output or volume increases. Average costs tend to decrease with an increase in the scale of operations. The general reasons why this occurs are related to four important cost components — specialisation, discount on bulk purchase of raw materials, vertical integration linking all processes together on a production line and the possibility of standardisation. For example, in a small firm one person may have to do several jobs, but in a large firm one can specialise in a job and thereby be that much more efficient and produce more output per man hour than the non specialist who has to spend time moving from one job to another.

The decisions of large corporations involved with locating branch plants will be different from those of an individual small firm. For one thing larger factories mean larger sites, access to more raw materials and more infrastructure. Whilst large corporations may have the capital to develop industry in new locations it is usually more economic to locate

within or near the established large centre which can provide the necessary infrastructure linkages, size of labour and other requirements. There have been instances, however, where a corporation has set up a new growth centre particularly when tapping a mineral source or locating on a new deep water coastal site, as in the case of multinational oil corporations. Whether at an established or new centre, the location of branch plants by multinational corporations will attract further growth contributing to the cumulative causation process. For example the growth of Aberdeen as a result of North Sea oil operations has brought with it further expansion from support companies being set up, service back-up and other infrastructure developments.

The scale of operations undertaken by multinational corporations also has other implications for the location of industry. Whereas the board of a single firm can consider a location solely on the needs of the one plant, the board of a multinational corporation when setting up a branch plant or contemplating closing one must consider it in the context of the corporation's whole operations. Thus it is quite common for them to shut down a plant in an established area even though it is making a profit and open up a branch plant elsewhere where better proximity to the market and lower labour costs ensure greater profits. Examples are plentiful and they include the Ford Motor Corporation reducing its capacity in the United States and the United Kingdom and opening up new factories in the cheaper production areas of Spain and Brazil.

The influence of governments and supranational public bodies

During the postwar years governments have been preoccupied with two major concerns in relation to manufacturing. One was to do with the problems arising from over-expansion and concentration in new industrial areas and the decline of older ones. The other was to ensure the build up of certain basic and strategic industries such as iron and steel.

In the United Kingdom the first comprehensive attempt to tackle the problem of over-expanding and declining regions stemmed from the Royal Commission into the Distribution of Industrial Population and the associated Barlow Report in 1940. The report linked the loss of jobs between the wars in old industrial areas such as the North East and South Wales to the over-concentration of job opportunities in the South East and Midlands, both of which had attracted the new market orientated growth industries in the economy such as the motor vehicle industry and electrical engineering. Under the Distribution of Industry Act of 1945 which followed the Barlow Report, older depressed industrial areas which had already been granted special area

9:2 MARSEILLE AREA

Development as a manufacturing region

Post 1945 Fos Port and industrial complex — iron and steel, other metallurgy, heavy engineering, petro-chemicals, chemicals (plant branches of multinational firms and large corporations).

1930s and post 1945 L'Etang de Berre — oil refining petro-chemicals. (Mainly branch plants of large corporations).

Decentralisation — postwar industrial estates (mixture of branch plants and individual enterprises).

Long established major port — processing industries (vegetable oils, flour milling, sugar refining) marine engineering, ship repairs (individual enterprises).

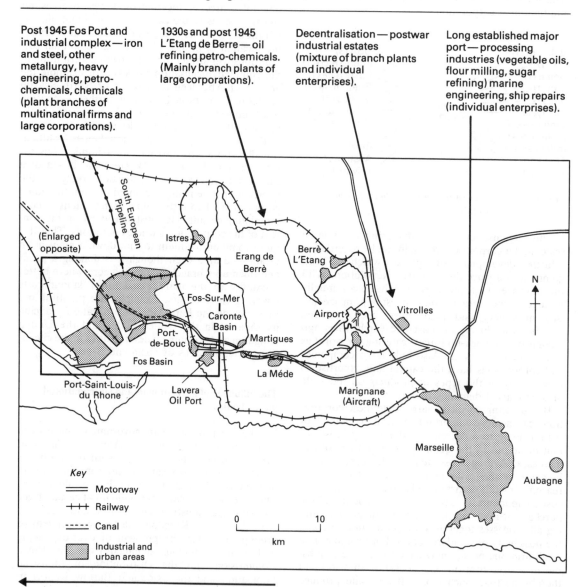

Key

═══ Motorway

+++ Railway

----- Canal

▨ Industrial and urban areas

0   10

km

Over time a westward shift in industrial development has occurred due to port diseconomies at Marseille and insufficient deepwater access — heavier newer and specialised industries at Etang de Berre and Fos Port and industrial complex.

Until recently this newest heavy industrial complex enjoyed high growth attracting capital intensive industries using modern technology.

Exercise

● Explain why the Marseille region has developed into an important industrial region.
● Why has this development not led to significant spread effects to the surrounding areas? What types of investments and schemes might benefit these surrounding areas?

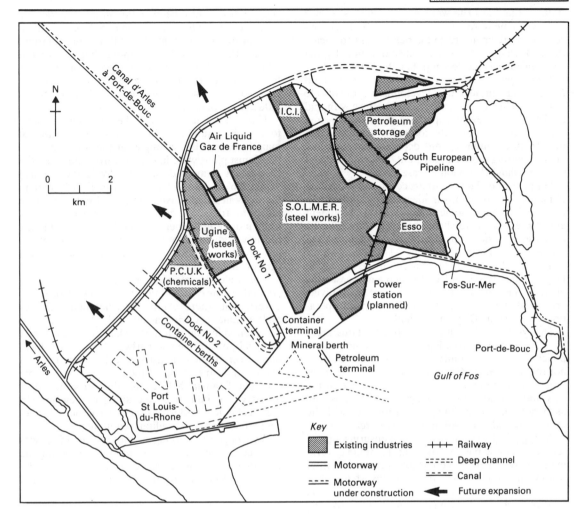

The map labels include:

- Canal d'Arles à Port-de-Bouc
- N
- 0   2 km
- I.C.I.
- Air Liquid Gaz de France
- Petroleum storage
- South European Pipeline
- S.O.L.M.E.R. (steel works)
- Esso
- Ugine (steel works)
- P.C.U.K. (chemicals)
- Dock No 1
- Dock No 2
- Container berths
- Power station (planned)
- Fos-Sur-Mer
- Container terminal
- Mineral berth
- Petroleum terminal
- Port-de-Bouc
- Arles
- Port St Louis-du-Rhone
- Gulf of Fos

Key
- ▨ Existing industries
- ═ Motorway
- ═ ═ Motorway under construction
- +++ Railway
- ===== Deep channel
- ─── Canal
- ◀ Future expansion

The Fos-Sur-Mer Port industrial complex

Factors influencing the cumulative growth of the Marseille region and the westward shift of industrial development.

1. Initial advantages of Marseille's location and growth as a port and industrial centre serving France's home and overseas markets.
2. As market opportunities expanded the Port Authority of Marseille developed sites on the Etang de Berre and then looked to the Gulf of Fos for further development as it offered large areas of level, ample water and deepwater access for imports and exports.
3. Multinational corporations involved in steel, petroleum and petro-chemicals based largely on imported raw materials, valued these attributes for scale of operations planned.
4. Government viewing such growth as vital to the Marseille region and areas around had already enhanced its attraction by funding etc. of Rhône-Durance as inland water route. Then proceeded to plan and finance the Fos-Sur-Mer complex. Attracted multinationals and set up its own S.O.L.M.E.R. integrated steelworks there.
5. Cumulative growth as advantages of an established region attracted more growth to existing centres. But region as a whole has gained limited benefits as new industries are not labour intensive and serve markets beyond and not essentially within the region.

status during the 1930s were given further assistance as Development Areas. Loans, grants and tax concessions were made to industries willing to locate there. Perhaps the most significant action by the government was the decision that all planned industrial development in excess of 5000 square feet would require an Industrial Development Certificate (I.D.C.). The government could therefore withhold an I.D.C. to prevent expansion in a growth area where there was already too much industry and thereby direct industry into depressed or marginal areas requiring more employment opportunities and a more balanced economic base.

In practice the large business corporations such as ICI and Fords frequently made a compromise agreement and accepted some direction to development areas in exchange for being allowed some modest expansion in the more prosperous regions of the South East and the Midlands. The Ford Motor Company, for example, based in England at Dagenham in Essex, agreed to open a new assembly plant in the North West at Ellesmere near Liverpool, and in return was allowed to expand operations at its main Dagenham plant.

Though the delimitations of special status areas have since changed (see Fig. 7.8), the same general policy of government intervention remains. But it is not the only policy. Government intervention takes other forms too as we have seen in the case of the new and expanded towns policy (p. 75 ff.), as well as a whole range of planning legislation to do with the location of industry within an urban area.

As regards the second concern of ensuring a more secure economic base for the country, some governments have taken certain staple industries either wholly into public ownership or invested public funds in them to obtain some measure of direct control. In the United Kingdom most of the iron and steel industry has been nationalised and despite recent Conservative government policies of privatisation the government also still has an important share in the motor vehicle, ship-building and aircraft industries. Other Western European countries have to a varying extent adopted a similar policy whilst in Communist countries, of course, public control of industry is complete.

Through public ownership the government is able to exercise another influence on the location of manufacturing. For example, at the time when expansionist plans were in hand for iron and steel, the British government decided to divide the planned expansion in coastal sites between Port Talbot in South Wales and Ravenscraig on Clydeside in an effort to trigger a multiplier effect which would bring more employment into both areas. During the recent worldwide depression, closure of some plants has set the multiplier effect into reverse bringing further unemployment.

The scale of intervention has now further increased because in addition to the action of single governments there is now the combined action of multinational agencies including the EEC and similar economic communities. Their legislative and financial policies have a marked effect on the location of certain new industry and the rationalisation of older industry. Recently the EEC has for example extended financial help to the ailing iron and steel industry and influenced the siting of new growth high technology industries such as computing, telecommunications and military equipment.

We can see something of these wider influences and that of cumulative causation by considering the growth of one industrial complex — that of the Marseilles-Etang de Berre – Fos area in the South of France.

10 Industrial Location Theory — a Critical Review

Until recently explanation of the location of an individual firm or industry was sought mainly through classical location theory. Whilst many of the widespread forces for change identified in the previous chapter may have increasingly limited the value of such theory, some discussion of it is warranted — partly because it still holds a place in the literature, but more importantly because there have been attempts to update it, thus bringing theory closer to reality.

Weber's Least Cost Theory

Basic principles

Classical location theory is rooted in economics and owes much to the work around the turn of the century of a German economist, Alfred Weber. In the search for the best location for a firm, Weber focused on a least cost approach, seeing the most favourable location as the one where costs could be minimised. To him the most important costs were transport costs, but he also took into account the supporting or offsetting effects of the cost of labour together with what he termed agglomerative (concentrating) and deglomerative (dispersion) costs.

To focus attention on these central influences, Weber neutralised or held constant the effects of secondary influences, by making certain assumptions along lines similar to other classical location theorists. These included free competition, all decision-taking to be based solely on economic reasoning and the existence of an isotropic (uniform) plain. As analysis proceeded, these assumptions could be relaxed to allow for the effects of secondary influences.

Weber saw the identification of a least cost location as a resolving of competing location pulls — on the one hand that of raw material sources and on the other the pull of a market location. These he saw as occurring at fixed points rather than spread over an area, except for certain raw materials which were to be found everywhere such as air and water — these he termed ubiquitous and therefore of no consequence in deciding a firm's location.

In order to resolve the problem of opposing locational pulls, Weber developed as the central feature of his least cost theory a material index. Taking the transport cost of raw materials and the finished product as a function of weight per unit and distance over which it had to be transported, the material index for a firm could be obtained by dividing the weight of localised raw materials needed for one unit of output by the weight of that unit of output. Clearly where the answer exceeded one, the weight of raw materials is greatest and the firm concerned is dealing with a weight losing product as is the case with iron and steel for example. In this case the industry would be drawn towards a raw material rather than a market location. Conversely if the material index is less than one the product is a weight gaining one as for example in the case of brewing where water is added during processing and the product has to be bottled for shipment. In this case the pull would be towards the markets. The higher the material index the greater the pull towards a raw material location whilst once the index drops below one the more potent the location to market pull. However, as indicated earlier labour cost considerations and/or agglomerative and deglomerative influences could modify the result. If suffficiently important and operating in a counter manner to the material index, these other cost factors could in fact result in an opposing location to that decided on the material index alone. Examples of different situations and locations for a firm are indicated in Fig. 10.1.

In order to identify points of least cost for a manufacturing firm Weber devised a useful technique involving isotim lines and isodopanes (see Fig. 10.2). Each isotim line connects points of equal transport costs. Isotim lines can be drawn to show how transport assembly costs change with distance from raw material sources on the one hand and on

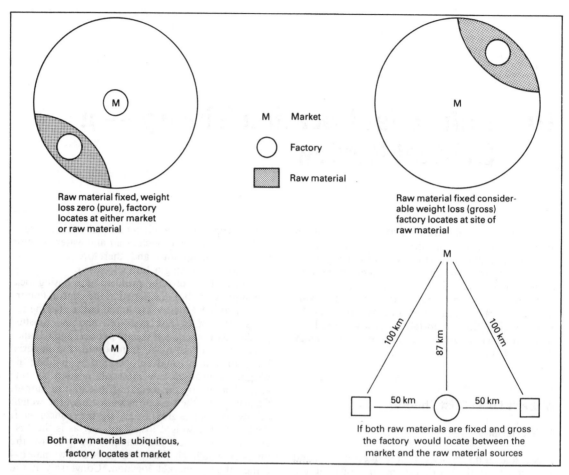

Fig. 10.1   Factory locations as determined by raw material and market pulls

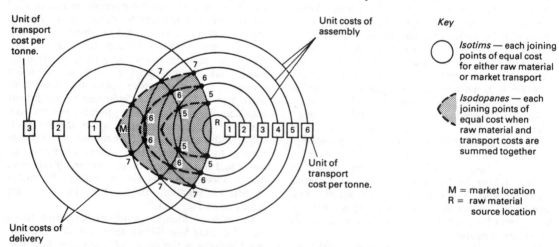

Fig. 10.2   Assembly and delivery costs related to a market and a raw material source
(In the example given, the isodopanes (equal combined transport cost lines) progressively decrease
in the direction of the raw material source indicating the cheapest location for a factory i.e. towards
this source and enclosed by the '5' value isodopane line.)

the other how delivery charges change with distance from market. In the simplest case in which a firm deals with only one source of raw material and one market there would thus be two sets of isotim lines. On the basis of where these intersect, it is possible to construct the isodopane lines, each joining points of equal transport cost over all. From these isodopane lines the least cost location can be found.

However, in reality there may not only be a number of raw material sources and markets but also cost lines for access to a labour pool as well. Thus reaching any diagrammatic solution using isotim and isodopane lines can be a complex process. Add to this the influence of agglomeration which firms might enjoy through locating close together rather than each in its own location and the complexity increases. Weber himself recognised no less than fourteen different locational types resulting from the influence of different combinations of transportation costs, labour costs and agglomeration economies.

Use and limitations

Whilst Weber's is a useful approach in that it identifies certain basic influences, its value is now limited — partly because of certain inherent weaknesses in the theory but also because circumstances have changed since the turn of the century when Weber published it.

Weber's material index was too crude a measure — transportation costs are not directly proportional to distance and not equal for given weights of materials. More important still, transport costs are rarely a basic criteria for the location of a firm today. Though varying from one kind of firm to another it is estimated that on average, transport costs make up only 5% to 12% of a firm's budget. It is not only that technological improvements have relatively reduced transport costs, but it is also because of changes in other things making up total costs, particularly those to do with the actual manufacturing process, the internal organisation and external links of the firm.

Also by concentrating too much on minimising costs, Weber's theory fails to identify the revenue aspects of a firm's operation which also directly affects the profitability of a firm. The theory, therefore, gives an unbalanced approach to the question of location.

The agglomerative and deglomerative influences already identified in our early discussions on cumulative causation now occupy a far more central position in location decisions than allowed for by Weber. Furthermore, some of the secondary influences suppressed in the assumptions Weber made, also have an important effect. Political, social and other human considerations including imperfect knowledge of situations, are all recognised today as significant in deciding the location of a firm or a branch plant.

Consequently efforts have been made to modify and update Weber's work. As a result other models of industrial locations have emerged bringing the theoretical approach increasingly closer to the real situations of today.

Lösch's Market Area or Profit Maximisation Approach

Having felt that Weber had overemphasised the cost factor, and unrealistically seen a market as a point rather than a demand spread over an area, Lösch sought to draw attention to the marketing factor and the idea of maximum profits related to sales revenue. Thus he held production costs constant in his initial analysis and indicated the optimum location for a firm as being where the largest possible market area could be monopolised or controlled. However, it should be noted that revenue would fall off with distance from the point at which the firm chose to locate in the market area, because of the cost of transporting the product to the consumer. One could thus initially envisage a simple revenue cone covering the market area, as shown in Fig. 10.3.

The market demand factor would encourage firms in any one industry to disperse across a region so that each could have control of its own market area. But Lösch saw that firms from different industries by congregating together at the same location in any one market area, could also benefit from agglomerative economies.

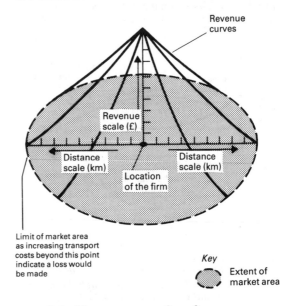

Fig. 10.3 The revenue cone for a firm

Whilst Lösch emphasised a different approach to that of Weber some of Lösch's simplifying assumptions were similar, such as perfect competition and rational economic man, and thus the theory suffers similar defects. Moreover Lösch's calculation of market demand was too crude and ignored many of the difficulties an entrepreneur would encounter in trying to estimate demand as a basis for his locational decision. Consequently later workers like Isard and Greenhut modified Lösch's theory in an attempt to make it more realistic, but with limited success. However the market orientated approach does have some validity for consumer industries such as brewing, furniture assembly and baking and in this sense complements Weber's Least Cost Theory which is more suited to heavier industry.

The Spatial Limits Model

By now the reader will be aware that a better model could result if the best of Weber's Least Cost Model could be combined with the best of Lösch's Profit Maximisation Model. Later alternative approaches such as that by D.M. Smith do attempt this. But additionally it is accepted that an entrepreneur is unlikely to have full knowledge of the facts needed for a firm to be located at its optimum point.

Once we have accepted that firms may be located in other than the optimum location, not one but a range of possible locations are evident. This can be illustrated from Smith's simple model of industrial location which introduces the idea of spatial margins, locations outside of which would result in the firm making a loss, but inside which the extent of profit making based on the difference between costs and revenue would vary according to the location chosen (see Fig. 10.4).

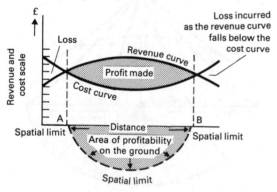

Fig. 10.4 Revenue/cost curve for a firm indicating spatial limits to a profitable location (A firm could locate anywhere within A–B and still make a profit though the amount would vary according to the location chosen.)

It is accepted then that entrepreneurs may choose locations which will satisfy them because reasonable profits can be made though they may not be the 'optimum' profit maximisation locations. Once this is recognised we have entrepreneurs as 'satisfiers' instead of 'economic optimisers', which lies at the basis of earlier location theory. It is but a short step then to also seeing entrepreneurs as consciously allowing other factors than economic ones to influence their decision taking. Then it is not only limited perception of a situation which results in a less than optimum location being chosen, but also to some extent a conscious decision to attempt this if other non-economic benefits can be gained, such as a pleasant location in a socially desirable area.

We can see that these spatial margins models by allowing for a range of possible sub-optimum locations and the influence of non-economic factors in the decision taking process, are more realistic than the earlier classical location models out of which they grew. But they still have the weakness of concentrating on the location of a single firm and the actions of individual entrepreneurs. Yet as we have seen in an earlier section, much of industry is under the control of large organisations, including in some countries varying degrees of state ownership. Thus it is to be anticipated that the most recent work attempting to produce a meaningful theoretical framework within which industrial location can be studied, should include extensive reference to the organisation of industry within large corporations including the multinationals. Despite this, links remain with earlier theories in that the behavioural approach already evident in spatial margins theory, dealt with above, is developed further.

The behavioural approach — locational decision making

This approach places emphasis on the way an individual or groups of individuals reach decisions. It takes into account the perception they have of situations and such things as the way their attitudes and values affect decision taking. Whilst earlier behavioural work was concerned with the individual entrepreneur and the single firm, more recently much has been about the corporate decision taking process in the large scale multi-plant, multi-functional and multinational organisations which control much of industry.

In pursuit of the specific goals sought for the corporation as a whole, the decision about the location of one branch plant (the equivalent of the single firm), is but a small part of the decision taking process as a whole. Indeed it is but one of the decisions which need to be made about setting up a particular branch plant. Others would include the nature of the product to be manufactured, the way

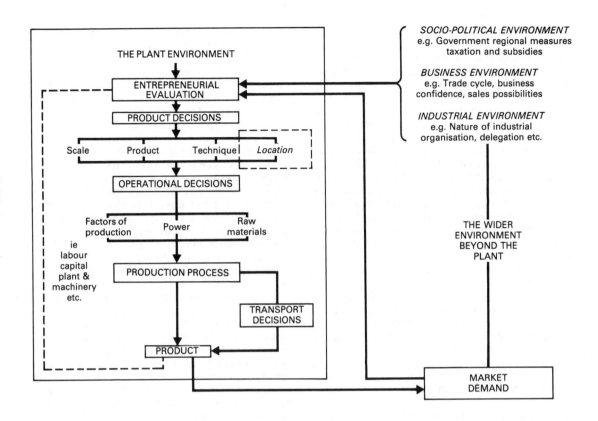

Fig. 10.5   Location decisions as part of the total investment process (based on Gold)

production should be organised and the scale or size of the plant. Such considerations as well as the overall goals of the organisation must have a bearing on the question of location. Thus to understand why one location is ultimately chosen in preference to another we need to be aware of the whole decision taking process. (Refer to Fig. 10.5.).

Moreover whilst a large industrial organisation is essentially motivated by a search for profits its goals cannot be wholly divorced from political and social considerations. This is clearly indicated in Gold's diagram in which decisions about location are seen as part of the overall investment process and but one of the four product decisions which have to be made about any contemplated new branch plant and industrial output overall. It will be noted that many of the wider influences discussed in the previous section are now given a place in a general framework. But also the character of the people involved and the kinds of decision taking procedures pursued have an important bearing on the ultimate choice of locations for branch plants.

The plastics industry has been one of the growth industries of the postwar years, and North in a United Kingdom study indicates the procedure and

Exercise

Using the framework in Fig. 10.5 as a guide consider the circumstances leading to the establishment of a branch plant or small industrial firm of which you have same personal knowledge.

influences at work for locational decision taking in this industry. He thus provides a useful framework within which to study the location of branch firms and, if modified, also one suitable for the location of an independent firm.

Other important results of North's work were to show that even within large corporations, with all their expertise and communication technology, the search began with the local and familiar, and that decisions were taken within the limited context of a highly parochial and partial schema. Further, quick and satisfactory solutions rather than optimum solutions were sought. Personal preference also played an important part in the decision taking.

Other studies including one within the Unilever

Corporation have supported North's findings; the Unilever study for example found that senior and middle management personnel were opposed to a move to northern England, largely on the grounds that the social environment would not be stimulating nor did they think schools for their children of as good a quality as in the south.

It would thus appear from recent studies that the kind of wider behavioural approach outlined by Gold and others, is more likely to provide a fuller and more realistic context for the study of industrial location than the more narrowly based and theoretical models developed earlier by Weber, Lösch and others. But it must be remembered that it was criticism of these which paved the way for the more realistic behavioural approach. Thus earlier work retains its usefulness as a starting point for further research and the continued search for a more updated and comprehensive body of industrial location theory.

The search will go on. Already the behavioural approach is under heavy criticism for centring attention only on the decisions of entrepreneurs and management having little regard to the role of labour and the needs of society.

Towards a more radical view

Reisser and others concerned with the welfare and prosperity of society as a whole deplore any approach which centres on business and its goal of maximum profits. Reisser points out, for example, that the massive monopolies which increasingly control much of economic activity not only continue to search for profit maximisation (though ultimately accepting less than this), but do so by increasingly manipulating consumer demand through such mechanisms as media advertising. Thus for many industrialists it is not so much now a matter of responding to a market demand but of creating that market demand. The reader may no doubt be able to identify a number of recent growth industries for which this appears to be the case.

Not only this but the 'risk taking' which in the ideology of capitalism justifies the owner and shareholders receiving a much greater share of the revenue from the sale of goods than the workers whose labours have helped to produce those goods, is stated by critics of the capitalist approach as now very much reduced. State support for industry by way of subsidies and grants; price support systems and the like have seen to this. Thus workers are entitled to a greater share of business income as well as a share in decision taking.

Whether one goes all the way with such criticism or not, it has to be accepted that the needs of interests of workers as well as of society in general, should have a place in the study of economic activity. Indeed trade union activity as representative of labour and intervention by the state in the location and organisation of economic activity in the interests of society as a whole mean that these other voices have already an important place (whether directly or indirectly) in decision taking procedures. Hence any change in the way geographers approach the question of location must recognise the central parts government and trade unions play. Some of these additional influences will be seen in the study of selected industries which follows.

11   The Changing Pattern of Selected Industries

A study of a few different industries will help to show how the relative importance of locational factors differs from one industry to another and also how changes over time occur bringing shifts in the distribution of an industry. It can also further emphasise why earlier location theory, though still of some value, is being replaced by a more dynamic and comprehensive approach.

Changes in the United Kingdom iron and steel industry

The iron and steel industry perhaps more than any other, has been used to illustrate the validity of Weber's Least Cost Theory. Being a weight losing industry, its material index is greater than one resulting generally in a location pull towards raw materials. This was initially towards fuel sources of charcoal and later coal. Then as technological developments reduced fuel requirements the shift has been towards iron ore sources, partly to the Jurassic ore fields of the East Midlands but also increasingly to coastal locations where imported ores could be brought in. But other influences were significant and in particular instances resulted in some small works remaining on coalfield sites or being orientated towards markets.

The structure and distribution pattern of the industry has undergone further significant changes since the 1950s. Whilst access to raw materials remains important, the changes that have taken place have had more to do with market competition and the policy decisions of the large corporations which together with governments now control much of the world's iron and steel making. This is particularly well illustrated from the United Kingdom iron and steel industry. Fig. 11.1 summarises the way in which the structure and pattern of the industry has changed over the postwar period, as well as indicating the principal factors underlying these changes. The way these came about is discussed more fully below.

Changes 1950–1973

In the 1950s, though some steel was being made in electric arc furnaces which used scrap, most was produced in oxygen steel furnaces using pig iron coming from iron smelting works. In iron smelting approximately three and three quarter tonnes of raw material were needed to produce one tonne of pig iron and since iron ore was the largest single item this was the strongest single influence on the location of industry. Hence the two major types of location on the low grade jurassic ore fields and near to or on tidewater locations, where high grade ore could be imported and which required less fuel in smelting than home ores. (A few iron smelting works such as those at Consett, Chesterfield, Stoke on Trent, remained on the coalfields, kept there by forces of inertia including invested capital and availability of a trained labour force but originally located because of coal as a power source and associated Coal Measure black band iron ore.)

In 1967 the bulk of the iron and steel industry was nationalised and placed under the control of the British Steel Corporation (B.S.C.). So in future, government policies and investment plans would play an important role in the structuring and distribution of the industry. Whilst the B.S.C. in its Ten Year Development Strategy Paper (1973) saw the medium term outlook for world steel as promising, in its efforts to maintain a hold on home markets and secure a share of world markets, it faced severe competition from cheaper overseas producers. The major one was Japan, where the steel industry was being rapidly expanded and which was capturing more of world markets, but also certain developing countries such as Brazil, India and South Korea were emerging as significant steel producers. These had the advantage of invested foreign capital and skill being combined with rich domestic ore resources and cheaper labour costs.

In order to be competitive the B.S.C. saw it as essential to follow the same kind of development strategy already proving successful in Japan —

A. LOCATION

Progressive shift to a few coastal sites with only small specialised works remaining inland

1. Forces for a dominant coastal pull and large integrated works
   a) A Coast site — imported ores and coke, cooling water, large areas of level land, agglomerative effects of technological changes.
   b) Increasing overseas markets
   c) Competition from overseas producers
   d) Government policy and investment

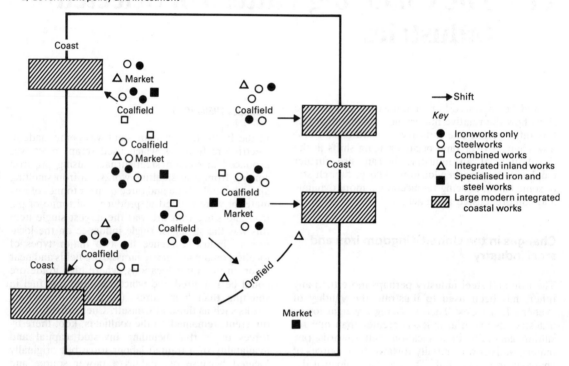

2. Forces for some specialised inland works remaining
   a) A particular market
   b) Scrap available
   c) Skilled labour
   d) Inertia and social factors
   e) Private and public investment

B. RATIONALISATION INTO FEWER WORKS

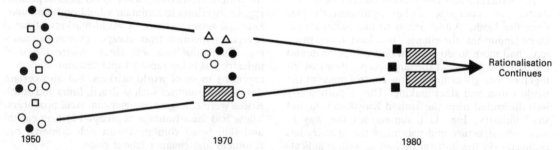

Note Until 1980 the British Steel Corporation was organised on a regional basis, but alongside site rationalisation, the management of B.S.C. was re-organised on a vertical basis according to product made i.e. Strips Product Division, General Steels, Tubes Division, B.S.C. Holding (specialised steel). Each division is responsible for its own profitability.

Fig. 11.1   Changes in the structure and location of the British iron and steel industry

(a) *Layout of the Plant and Production Flow*

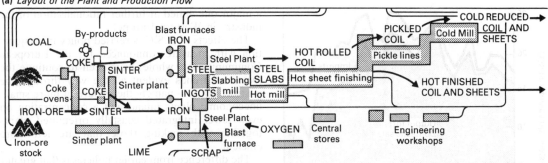

(b) *Factors Influencing Location and Production*

1. Availability of a large coastal site 5·5 km × 1·2 km.

2. Pool of experienced labour and B.S.C. management.

3. Government financial investment.

4. Raw material inputs-
   a) Coal from South Wales average journey 60 km.
   b) Iron-ore imported from Labrador, Venezuela, Peru, W. Africa, Australia, U.S.S.R. discharged at Port Talbot and transferred 80 km by rail to the works.
   c) Limestone available locally.

5. Abundant cooling water.

6. Power-thermal from oil, and local coal.

7. Markets for steel coil and sheets-
   South Wales, Midlands & South East via efficient motorway and rail freight networks.

Fig. 11.2   *A modern integrated steelworks, Llanwern, S Wales: (a) Layout of the plant and production flow; (b) Factors influencing location and production*

namely to take advantage of recent technology developments and concentrate production on a few larger integrated works in coastal districts though not necessarily on tidewater sites. During the 1970s therefore the B.S.C. concentrated its bulk steel making production on five main integrated coastal district sites giving increased economies of scale which would help reduce costs per unit output and make the industry more competitive. Costs were further reduced by using mainly fuel saving rich foreign ores imported to deep water sites on bulk carriers, together with an increasing import of coke for the smelting of that iron ore, but only two of the five integrated works were actually on tidewater locations i.e. Port Talbot and Lackenby – Redcar. Of the others, Llanwern (Fig. 11.2) relied on iron ore brought 80 km from Port Talbot whilst the two more inland sites at Ravenscraig and Scunthorpe were dependent on ore brought from specially constructed ore terminals at Hunterston and Immingham. As a result of this reorganisation of the industry it was hoped to expand steel production from 28 million ingot tonnes in 1973 to 36 million tonnes by 1988–91. But the other side of this rationalisation programme involved contraction and in a number of cases the closure of older and smaller inland iron and steel works such as Ebbw Vale, Shotton and Consett. Even though some as individual works might still be operated at a profit, in the total plan of the corporation most were seen as uneconomic. It

was cheaper where needed to transport semi-finished steel from the new large integrated works to the inland rolling and forging mills to be converted into finished specialised steel, rather than maintain steel furnaces at these inland sites. Thus the corporation closed 23 inland works between 1973 and 1980 which together with a modernisation programme of the works that were left resulted in a reduction of the workforce of 336 000 to 162 000 in 1980. Since then a further 100 000 jobs have been lost in the steel industry bringing severe problems to towns which had been particularly dependent on the steel works, for example Corby.

Whilst a substantial number of finishing mills were retained inland, only small specialised steel works using scrap and electric furnaces were left open. These like some in the private sector such as Hatfields at Sheffield, had a capacity of a few hundred thousand tonnes a year and were competitive for a limited range of specialised products such as alloy steels. The electric arc method was a rapid, flexible and cost effective process, scrap was within easy reach and locations also had a pool of highly skilled labour.

1973–today — further rationalisation

During the 1970s world steel markets did not develop as expected. Instead, at a time when steel

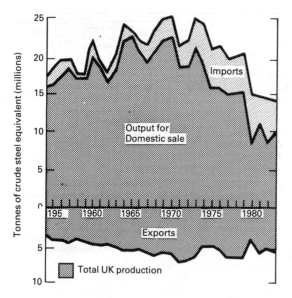

Fig. 11.3 Steel production, imports and exports for the United Kingdom, 1954–83

production capacity was being rapidly expanded home demand dropped dramatically due to the economic recession and the United Kingdom's share of overseas markets also declined. Steel consumption at home peaked in 1973 and then fell back to its level of 1950 (Fig. 11.3). For example, the motor vehicle industry which took 1.6 million tonnes of steel in 1967, in 1980 had reduced its demand to 0.62 million tonnes. Also increasing amounts of cheaper foreign steel were coming in and imports trebled during the 1970s.

Despite some recovery in the world economy during the 1980s the basic problem of over capacity remains. The world steel industry in 1982, excluding the Communist bloc, had the capacity to produce 650 million tonnes but world consumption was only 400 million tonnes. Furthermore, production continues to expand amongst new lower cost producers in the developing world where contrary to general trends demand has risen over the 1970s by 50%. Given the security of an expanding home market certain of the new developing world producers are in a good position to penetrate other world markets. For example the Pohang Steel Corporation of South Korea now exports steel plate and strip to Japan, the leading steel producer among the developed countries.

In the face of these problems of excess capacity and increasing overseas competition, the B.S.C. has had to drastically revise its plans for the industry. But since Britain is part of the EEC, the future of the country's steel industry is also bound up with the future of the European Community's steel industry as a whole. It is, therefore, subject to the EEC agreements, of which the Davignon Plan of 1977 was

a major one aimed at further rationalisation of the industry in Western Europe.

The effects of B.S.C.'s revised policy in conjunction with measures announced for the European Community as a whole, have been to continue the locational trends evident all the way through the postwar years — namely the closure of more small, uneconomic plants inland and a concentration on even fewer integrated coastally orientated plants together with making those that are left more efficient.

The difference from earlier policies is that greater efficiency means not only further modernisation and re-organisation of the management structure of the industry but also reducing the capacity of the remaining coastally orientated plants. Work forces have been further reduced raising productivity per man from 14 man hours per tonne of steel in 1980 to 4 man hours in 1984. New fuel saving and other techniques have also been adopted and more money has gone into research backup and marketing.

But whilst the Llanwern and Lackenby–Redcar plants have been particularly successful in raising productivity the smaller Ravenscraig plant has continued to lose money (£40 000 000 in 1983/84). This is partly because of its poorer location inland and loss of nearby markets with the slump in the motor vehicle and engineering industries in Scotland. Ravenscraig has been kept open so far to avoid further unemployment in the region. But on all economic grounds it should have closed and is likely to do so in the near future.

The other additional feature of the industry has been financial assistance to cushion the effects of these revised policies. The steel industry has been subsidised to slow down closures and it enjoys some protection from overseas competition. For example, a reduction in the amount of American steel allowed into the EEC. Also both the British government and the European Community have put a great deal of effort into financing the attraction of new industry into declining steel areas. This has met with variable success, one of the more successful locations being Corby.

Future trends

Whilst there is an economic future for a much reduced iron and steel industry, it is clear world market demand will be increasingly met from the newer industries in developing countries. The most important ones are likely to be Brazil, India, China, the Philippines and South Korea. It is generally accepted amongst developed countries that it may be more economic in the future to allow import penetration of these cheaper steels from overseas. Developed countries cannot compete on price with foreign imports. The cheaper imported steel could be used to manufacture high technology goods and other export products for which there is an expanding overseas market and thereby bring in overseas earning. In addition, as is already happening, more overseas earnings could also be obtained by the advanced countries exporting their technical know-how, capital equipment and investment finance to these new steel producers.

The structure and distribution of the industry in these newer producing developing countries is emerging as similar to that in the developed countries. A dual structure exists with large integrated plants such as that of China Steel in Taiwan (3.3 million tonnes capacity) generally orientated to coastal areas or on inland sites with waterway access and a few mini steel plants market orientated to meet specialised requirements.

The motor vehicle industry — a barometer for change

The motor vehicle industry is essentially made up of three sections – parts making, body making and motor vehicle assembly. Whilst the latter is dominated by a few large companies, eight of which control 70% of the world's output, they are dependent on a vast number of parts makers with whom they must maintain close links. Thus we must see the motor vehicle industry as having a dual structure in which a few large companies are supported by a large range of small firms. It is estimated that worldwide 3.5 million people are employed in the assembly industry and another 7 million in the supporting industries.

The motor vehicle industry is the most important single consumer industry in developed countries and has been seen until recently as the main driving force in the manufacturing economy. Basic industries like steel and petroleum refining are dependent on it as a market whilst any significant decline in motor vehicle assembly has serious effects in supporting ancillary industries — the more so because of the marked concentration of the industry into a few regions.

Trends in distribution

Perhaps better than any other industry it illustrates some of the processes which are generally affecting industry and its locational pattern. Whilst the industry remains to an important extent market orientated and located where agglomerative benefits can be obtained along lines indicated in the Least Cost Theory, the actions of multinational corporations and governments have brought a trend towards establishing branch plants in countries such as Spain and Brazil, hitherto of little importance as motor vehicle producers.

Motor vehicle production is now controlled by a few large multinational corporations with branch plants and link-ups in a number of countries. Thus any decision taking in relation to one factory must be seen as part of wider policy making, as for example in the case of the American based General Motors siting of a new large plant near Saragossa in Spain (Fig. 11.4), to supply the European market, and its link up with the giant Japanese company Toyota, which in turn is setting up a plant in the United States to tap this market. This organisation into large corporations and what has been described as a spider's web of collaborative agreements between producers are not simply to do with the economies of scale which large scale mass production can bring. It is also to do with the heavy capital investment and technological know-how needed, if a corporation is to remain competitive in a rapidly changing industry.

The motor vehicle industry illustrates how important direct and indirect government action is in influencing not only the size of the industry itself in any country but also the success or otherwise with which foreign competition can penetrate markets. British Leyland the only big United Kingdom producer is still largely government owned, as is Renault, France's largest producer. Others like the German Volkswagen-Audi corporation are part government owned, whilst without government financial backing the large American Chrysler Corporation would no longer exist.

Clearly with such direct intervention governments have an important influence on locational as well as other decisions. Also with the motor vehicle industry being such an important part of the economy and so much employment dependent on it, public intervention is also exercised in many other ways; via such things as taxation, legislation, import and export regulations.

As world demand continues to rise the locus of production is changing. The United States and Western European producers, original founders of the motor vehicle industry, are now being overtaken by Japan (Fig. 11.5). Until the 1950s Japan's motor vehicle industry was a minor one, but from then on it has rapidly expanded with production doubling in the 1970s, mostly at the expense of American manufacture. Production reached 8 million vehicles in 1978 and rose to 11 million in 1981. Japan now accounts for approximately 30% of world production, with much of it from its two largest corporations Nissan (Datsun) and Toyota.

Another change is also evident again mirroring a general trend. Whilst demand will continue to rise, albeit slowly in the developed countries, there is evidence that the largest potential market expansion will occur in the developing countries (Fig. 11.6). Some of the more rapidly developing of these countries are likely to be affected by the kind of consum-

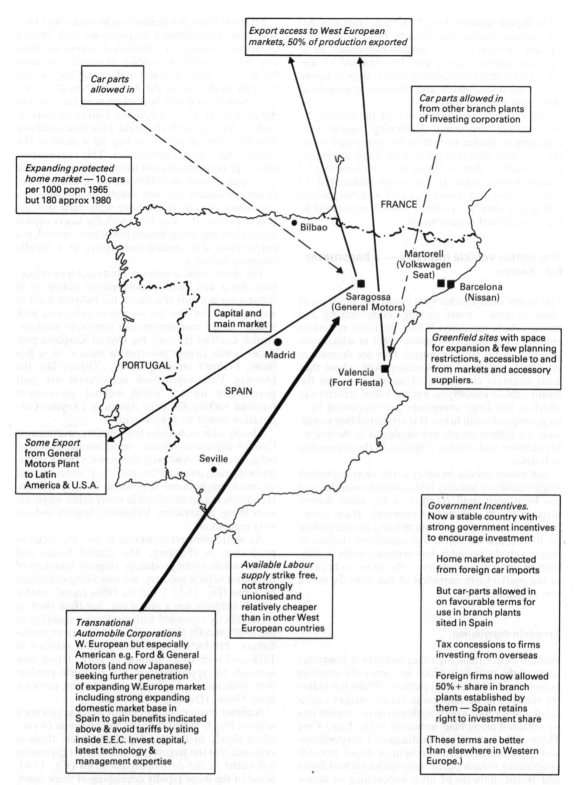

Export access to West European
markets, 50% of production exported

Car parts
allowed in

Car parts allowed in
from other branch plants
of investing corporation

Expanding protected
home market — 10 cars
per 1000 popn 1965
but 180 approx 1980

FRANCE

Martorell
(Volkswagen
Seat)

Barcelona
(Nissan)

Bilbao

Saragossa
(General Motors)

Capital and
main market

Greenfield sites with space
for expansion & few planning
restrictions, accessible to and
from markets and accessory
suppliers.

Madrid

PORTUGAL

Valencia
(Ford Fiesta)

SPAIN

Some Export
from General
Motors Plant
to Latin
America & U.S.A.

Seville

Government Incentives.
Now a stable country with
strong government incentives
to encourage investment

Home market protected
from foreign car imports

But car-parts allowed in
on favourable terms for
use in branch plants
sited in Spain

Available Labour
supply strike free,
not strongly
unionised and
relatively cheaper
than in other West
European countries

Tax concessions to firms
investing from overseas

Foreign firms now allowed
50%+ share in branch
plants established by
them — Spain retains
right to investment share

Transnational
Automobile Corporations
W. European but especially
American e.g. Ford & General
Motors (and now Japanese)
seeking further penetration
of expanding W.Europe market
including strong expanding
domestic market base in
Spain to gain benefits indicated
above & avoid tariffs by siting
inside E.E.C. Invest capital,
latest technology &
management expertise

(These terms are better
than elsewhere in Western
Europe.)

Fig. 11.4   Location factors of General Motors and Ford (U.S.A.) in Spain

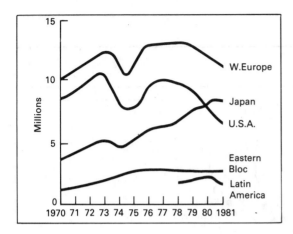

*Fig. 11.5   World motor vehicle production,
1970–81*

er boom in demand that occurred in the developed countries during the 1950s and 1960s. Consequently the large corporations are busily establishing branch plants in such areas — Brazil, Mexico and India being but three examples where recent expansion has occurred. But the practice of branch plant establishment overseas is not restricted to developing countries. Where labour costs and other savings are to be had plants are being established not so much to supply a domestic market but for export markets in European areas also. Spain, where labour costs are cheaper than elsewhere in Western Europe, has recently emerged as a major car producer and is now ahead of the United Kingdom in output. In Brazil it is estimated that labour costs are one sixth of those in Western Europe and one eighth of those in the United States, hence to some extent the reason why Sao Paulo has become one of the leading world centres for motor vehicle production with a range of foreign corporations investing these — Volkswagen,

Fords, General Motors and Fiat. Brazil has also its own motor vehicle manufacturers in the firms of Gurgel and Puma which are state supported.

Regional location factors

The motor vehicle industry is essentially an assembly industry and it is thus cheaper to locate near a large market where parts can be most easily assembled. But also since the motor vehicle industry is dependent on generally labour intensive firms providing many of the parts needed and which historically are located in the large urban regions this was a further incentive to a market orientation. In the mid 1970s parts supplies made up over half the production cost.

Assembly labour costs have significance despite the move to computer control some machinery and the introduction of robots in some factories. Again this favours large urban regions where a pool of labour is likely to be available.

These combined influences are thus important in explaining the concentration of motor vehicle manufacturers into a few centres, but as we shall see from the Japanese Case Study, historical and entrepreneurial influences have also been very significant.

Exercise

From Fig. 11.6 identify the estimated changes in the share of production for different regions up to the end of the century. On what factors do you think the estimates are based?

OECD PROJECTIONS OF WORLD AUTOMOBILE DEMAND, 1979 TO 2000
A = million units % = per cent of total

	1979		1985		1990		2000	
	A	%	A	%	A	%	A	%
North America	11.6	38	12.4	35	12.5	33	13.4	29
Latin America	1.8	6	2.5	7	3.3	9	5.4	12
Western Europe	10.3	34	11.2	32	11.8	31	13.6	29
Asia	4.4	14	6.2	18	7.0	18	8.7	19
Africa	0.5	2	0.8	2	1.0	3	1.4	3
Eastern Europe	2.0	7	2.1	6	2.6	7	3.9	8
TOTAL	**30.5**	**100**	**35.2**	**100**	**38.1**	**100**	**46.6**	**100**

Note: Figures may not add due to rounding.

Fig. 11.6   Current and future demand trends

11:1   JAPAN

Car industry

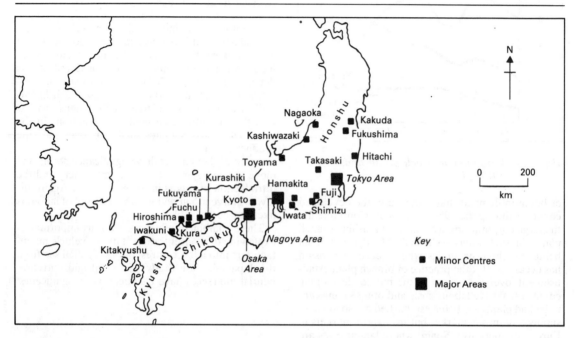

Location of the Japanese Car Industry

**MAIN PRODUCERS—
%age SHARE**
of the home market (1982)

Toyota	40.7
Nissan	29.9
Mitsubishi	7.2
Toyo Kogyo (Mazda)	8.2
Honda	6.9
Isuzu	2.4
Daihatsu	1.8
Fuji (heavy industry	1.6

IMPORTANCE AND GENERAL LOCATING FACTORS

1   One of Japan's leading industries employing a workforce of 650 000.
2   Concentrated in the Nagoya and Tokyo regions close to much of the home market and major export outlets.
3   Initially developed in the Tokyo region with the Nagoya region developing later—
  (a)   based on existing skills and business interests in cycle and small engineering workshops, the presence of an adaptable labour force and an expanding home market;
  (b)   cumulative and agglomerative advantages for these regions followed — e.g. linkages to component suppliers, access to research institutes and government agencies.
4   Modern line assembly methods requiring more space led to dispersion of assembly plants to the periphery of the producing regions but still within easy reach of component suppliers and markets. (Most minor producing regions are also well linked by rail and road to the major home markets.)

**EXPORTS BY %age
DISTRIBUTION**
1980

North America (U.S.A. 34)	37
Europe	19
S E Asia	
Africa	44*
Oceania	
Latin America	

*20% in knockdown form

N.B. Exports equal just over half total production

FORCES FOR REGIONAL LOCALISATION ILLUSTRATED FROM THE TOYOTA CITY REGION

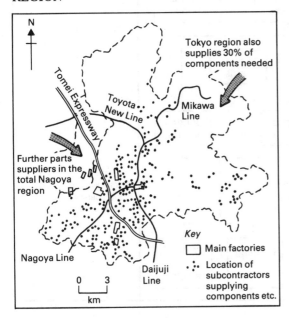

Tokyo region also supplies 30% of components needed

Tomei Expressway

Toyota New Line

Mikawa Line

Further parts suppliers in the total Nagoya region

Nagoya Line

Daijuji Line

Key

☐ Main factories

∴ Location of subcontractors supplying components etc.

0   3
km

Historical 'reservoir' of entrepreneurship

The Toyota motor company grew out of the Toyada weaving and corn industries which included many small craft and engineering firms in the 1930s. The family based concern then moved into steel and aircraft manufacture. By 1950s had the basis for expansion into a large corporation.

Policy of high investment to maintain technological advance — had the backing of 50 Japanese banks.

Organised as one 'mammoth production system' centred on one head office — good labour relations. Management and labour united on goals.

Given government financial backing etc. and protected by restriction on foreign imports.

Links overseas with General Motors etc. — design research etc.

Toyota City is the sixth largest industrial city in Japan and lies approx. 250 km south of Tokyo. 90% of its workforce is connected with the motor industry with production of 3 million vehicles a year it is the country's largest producer and now has overseas branches in Costa Rica, Brazil, Peru, Australia and Thailand.

Labour force available — previously an agricultural region with a large adaptable workforce — reliable and hardworking.
Company provides security of employment, housing, some shopping facilities, health and recreation provision.

Expanding home demand with the increasing affluence of post war years and Toyota City commands a central position in the Pacific Industrial Belt where most of the demand is.

Close communication and information links with the Tokyo region — research, secretariat and sales force in Tokyo itself.

Excellent communication network and infrastructure including export points.

Space and facilities for mass production — initally centred on small town of Koromo, its local authority was influential in attracting Toyota Motors to the site in the 1950s.
Plenty of land was available cheaply, dam built to supply adequate water, parking and other facilities, new highway built and a rail line extension encouraged.

Local labour organisation helpful — Association of Wage Earners active in promoting industry and encouraging amalgamation of neighbouring districts to form 'one enclosed life support system'.

Exercise

- Account for the continued rise of Japanese automobile production into the 1980s whilst production in other developed countries has fallen.

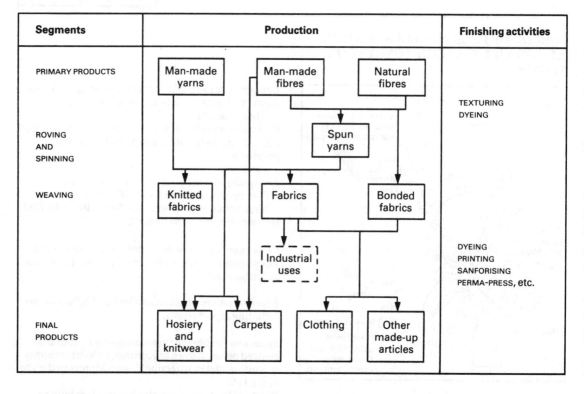

Segments	Production			Finishing activities
PRIMARY PRODUCTS	Man-made yarns	Man-made fibres	Natural fibres	TEXTURING DYEING
ROVING AND SPINNING		Spun yarns		
WEAVING	Knitted fabrics	Fabrics	Bonded fabrics	
		Industrial uses		DYEING PRINTING SANFORISING PERMA-PRESS, etc.
FINAL PRODUCTS	Hosiery and knitwear	Carpets	Clothing	Other made-up articles

Fig. 11.7   *The manufacturing process of textile products*

The textile industry

Its importance in the industrialisation process

The textile industry is usually defined as a processing industry concerned with the production of textile fabrics, but it is difficult to divorce discussion of this from the side of the industry which makes up the fabric into the final products, such as household goods like carpets, and industrial ones such as car seating (see Fig. 11.7). This is because changes in the demand for these products and the introduction of new products made from non-woven fabrics such as Typan sheeting to strengthen foundations in airport runways and roads, have a basic effect on the structure and pattern of the industry as a whole.

The textile industry is considered one of the staple industries in an expanding and industrialising economy. This is partly because of the widespread general demand for textile products as population increases and a cash economy develops. It is also because in the past, textile industries could be established with limited investment and were labour intensive providing alternative employment to agriculture and other traditional occupations. Thus the growth of the textile industry has been an important part of the industrialisation process for countries.

This was so in Western Europe in the late 18th and 19th centuries, also later in the industrial development of Japan and since the Second World War in the further industrialisation of Southern and Eastern European countries such as Italy and Poland as well as developing world producers like South Korea, Taiwan and Hong Kong.

These newer emergent producers now have lower cost advantages in textile production, combining cheaper labour costs with the benefit of up-to-date techniques transferred from older producers. But as we shall see the fall in the latter's share of world textile markets and the changes that have taken place in an attempt to maintain a viable textile industry in the United Kingdom cannot simply be explained in terms of cheaper competition from overseas. It is only one of a number of factors (see Fig. 11.9).

The textile industry — forces leading to change

Changing market demand

It is commonly assumed that the recent problems of the textile industry in developed countries are pri-

	Textile industry		Clothing industry	
	1963	1980	1963	1980
Developed market economies[b] of which:	57.5	48.2	70.2	52.3
OECD Europe of which:	27.9	20.5	24.7	17.9
(EEC)	(23.4)	(15.7)	(22.1)	(14.4)
North America	21.7	20.2	42.6	31.8
Japan	6.4	6.7	2.1	2.6
Centrally planned economies[c]	28.6	37.5	24.7	41.0
Developing countries of which:	13.9	14.3	5.1	6.7
Asia	5.4	5.4	2.1	2.8

Production: value added in constant prices.
a) Excluding China and other centrally planned economies in Asia.
b) OECD countries plus South Africa and Israel.
c) Soviet Union and 6 European members of CMEA.

Source: United Nations: Yearbook of Industrial Statistics.

Fig. 11.8 Textile and clothing industries (% share in world[a] production)

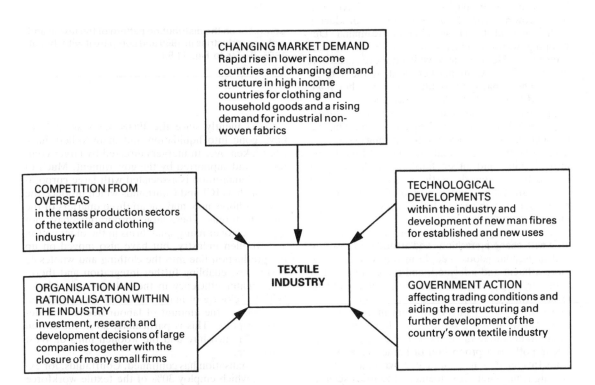

Fig. 11.9 Factors affecting the structure and location of the textile industry

marily due to successful competition from expansion of textile production among developing countries. In fact a more central cause has been a relative decrease in home demand compared to other parts of the world. This is a result of a combination of factors including slower population and income growth, and a change in the pattern of consumer expenditure in developed countries, more being spent on consumer durables like cars, electrical appliances and services. In contrast, as incomes rose amongst less well-off peoples in Eastern and Southern Europe and certain areas of the developing world particularly in South East Asia, domestic demand has risen considerably providing the basis for expansion and development of a modern textile industry in these countries.

Given a rising and secure home demand combined with modern mass production methods, foreign investment by large corporations and cheaper labour costs than in developed countries, these newer producers have been able to penetrate export markets. Thus foreign competition is a significant secondary factor following on from changing domestic demand patterns. In EEC markets competition has largely come from Southern European producers, in particular Spain and Italy. Italy is now the world's leading exporter of textiles and clothing. These are part of the EEC and therefore not subject to rigorous tariff and quota restrictions. Under bilateral and other agreements, exports have also been growing from Eastern European producers such as Poland, Czechoslovakia and Rumania. Developing world producers such as South Korea, Taiwan and Hong Kong have been more successful in South East Asian markets and in the United States where, partly for political reasons, they have received favourable trading conditions.

The export earnings of these newer producers have been further increased by them extending the production process beyond the primary stage of making fabric to the actual making up of the fabric into clothing and other finished products again helped by a strong domestic demand. Thus fabric exports are falling and export of finished articles rising especially in casual clothes as fashions change in western and other markets.

A further important market factor is also associated with changing fashions and attitudes to clothing and household goods. People in the west are now more affluent and informed, and therefore demand a bigger range of choice and respond rapidly to fashion changes. Hence retail outlets stock a wide range of choice by buying in from more suppliers thus making it more difficult for home manufacturers to dominate the market. For example, in the UK imports as a proportion of home demand rose from 16% in 1968 to 35% in 1980 with most of this coming from other EEC member countries such as Italy, Belgium and France.

The influence of large corporations and governments

In the face of declining home demand and overseas competition, private companies and governments are being faced with the need to restructure the industry in older areas in an effort to make it more efficient. This was also needed to take advantage of technological developments in the industry and the new kinds of market demand already indicated.

Until the 1950s the industry in the UK, as in other Western European countries such as Belgium, was characterised by small to medium sized businesses each specialising in one part of the production process. Though regionally concentrated — cotton in South Lancashire, woollens in West Yorkshire, and hosiery and knitwear in the East Midlands and Central Scotland — the industry was thus fragmented into small but closely linked divisions in which capital investment was small relative to the large amount of labour employed, much of it female. The scale of efficiency was low compared to manufacturing generally, labour inputs being too high, much of the machinery outdated and the size of processing units too small to provide much in the way of economies of scale.

Exercise

Comment on the distribution pattern of the textile and clothing industries in 1980 and compare it with that of 1963. (Refer to Fig. 11.8.)

Consequently since the 1960s many small firms have gone into liquidation and many others have been taken over in mergers directed by larger companies and supported by the government. Much of this rationalisation is associated with large corporations such as ICI and Courtaulds which produce the artificial fibres now making up three quarters of the fabric materials. These large corporations have not only taken over many small firms in the older cotton and woollen industry, but have also moved on up the production line into the clothing and wholesale businesses, enabling further integration and therefore greater efficiency in the industry as a whole. With the closure of many works and modernisation of processes the amount of labour needed has declined rapidly. This is particularly so in the cotton areas of Lancashire and the woollen mills of West Yorkshire.

Rationalisation has continued. Courtaulds, for example, which employ 30% of the textile workforce have closed over a quarter of their plants since 1970.

But along with other large concerns Courtaulds has also sought to expand the market through new uses of non-woven materials such as glass and carbon fibres in industry, services and in the home.

Though much of the textile industry is being concentrated into large modern units, there does however remain one sector of the industry in which the smaller firms can succeed. This is the one of smaller volume higher price quality fabrics and clothing. Here design flair, flexibility for responding to new fashion fabrics and close liaison with retailing outlets are important. These are attributes in which small firms with longstanding experience and good entrepreneurship usually have the advantage over larger ones and foreign competitors. Moreover the range of quality goods is widening, varying now from new casual wear in denims and corduroys for example, to household textiles, jersey fabrics, knitting and hosiery, and knitwear.

Government action to help the industry has usually been of three kinds — protective measures, aid for restructuring it and help to cushion the effects of job losses.

We have already noted some of the tariff and quota agreements taken to protect the industry from foreign imports, but too much protection means higher prices to the consumer and therefore affects demand. Over-protection also shields inefficient producers, therefore slowing down the restructuring the government is seeking.

Regional development funding has helped to attract new plants and other industry through capital grants, depreciation grants and rates concessions. Subsidies have also been paid to employers to slow down rates of redundancy and encourage other employers to take on unemployed textile workers. A variety of retraining grants are also available including those from the European Social Fund.

Whilst to some extent cushioning the worst effects of a rundown in this industry, on the whole the government's efforts to restructure it have been successful. As we have already seen the industry has been rationalised into larger units using modern methods and its overall character has changed.

There has also been an end to the well defined regional concentrations which had continued over more than two centuries and which were still visible in 1970. Decline of textiles and the introduction of a variety of other industries in the old cotton areas of South Lancashire and the woollen districts of West Yorkshire mean that these have ceased to be leading textile regions. The East Midlands now has the largest proportion of workers in textiles. This is partly due to the decline of Lancashire and Yorkshire, but also because places such as Nottingham and Derby in the East Midlands have been more successful in retaining their share of knitwear and hosiery as well as obtaining a significant proportion of non-woven materials based on artificial fibres.

A summary of changes

In the foregoing discussions we have been concerned with a range of factors which have led to the decline of some textile regions and the rise of others, most of them in the newer producing countries. It is thus appropriate to end this section with a comparison of the changing character of the traditional cotton area of Lancashire and the new and expanding textile industry of South Korea given in Case Study 11.2.

The emergence of high technology industries

Perhaps more than any of the selected industries so far considered, the new high technology industry demonstrates the shift in emphasis amongst the factors influencing the location of industry.

Whereas the longer established industries like iron and steel, and textiles have demonstrated something of the inadequacy of traditional location theory with its emphasis on such things as transport costs, raw material and market pulls, and availability of labour, it is the more recently developed ones — motor vehicles and especially the new high technology industries — which really expose the inappropriateness of this kind of explanatory framework. In its place we need something more comprehensive and flexible with the emphasis on such factors as agglomerative and deglomerative forces, and the behavioural influence at one scale of multinational corporations and governments and at the other the individual entrepreneur.

Given these changes and the greater complexity in the way these operate, it is not surprising that the geographical pattern of these newer industries is different from earlier ones. The three key but related elements now seem to be: deconcentration away from major industrial conurbations; the growth of new zones or centres in which industry though closely linked by communication is more loosely agglomerated; and the maintenance of linkages with major conurbations by a more efficient communication network allowing physical distances between market and industry to be stretched.

Characteristics

High technology industries are difficult to closely define but it is generally accepted that they include computers, micro-electronic components and other products associated with information technology. These industries have a larger than average proportion of highly skilled and highly educated personnel in professional, scientific and engineering posts (around 25% of the total as opposed to 5% for

11:2 SOUTH LANCASHIRE AND SOUTH KOREA

Decline and growth in the textile industry

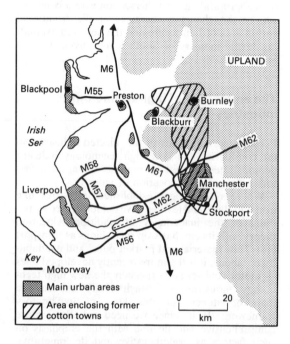

Key
— Motorway
▓ Main urban areas
▨ Area enclosing former cotton towns

0   20
km

DECLINE AND REORGANISATION OF THE SOUTH LANCASHIRE COTTON INDUSTRY

1 Declining importance

In the 1900s South Lancs was the leading world producer and exporter (with 60% of world trade) — employing 600 000. Now the region is only a minor producer employing 25 000 — decline especially steep since the 1970s.

What is left is still regionally concentrated but now dominated by a few producers and in integrated works with a heavy emphasis on artificial fibres. (Previously many smaller producers with a tendency to specialise in one branch of the cotton industry.) Towns such as Oldham, Rochdale, Burnley and Bolton have now lost most of their cotton industry — many old mills divided into small light industrial and service units — ∴ employment diversified.

Some new large integrated works opened up in the new towns e.g. Courtaulds at Skelmersdale, but recent economic depression led to closure of this and other newer works — thus continued rationalisation plus a move into new industrial fibres.

1971-1981 — output declined by a further 30% in

UK as a whole (even more rapid in Lancs) and share of home market fell from 54% to 30%.

2 Initial locating factors and their residual influences

(a) From the 17th Century — existence of cottage woollen and linen industry offered a skill basis, local water power from upland streams and later local coal, soft water and high humidity to aid processes e.g. dyeing and spinning, local chemicals for bleaching.
Canal and later rail transport network together with port proximity to aid import of raw cotton and export of finished products via Manchester and Liverpool — also export across Pennines and through Hull.

(b) Residual influences — skilled labour pool, associated supportive trades, Manchester the centre of merchanting, entrepreneurship and innovative skills, capital investment in plant etc.

(c) Present influences — excellent motorway network and infrastructure plus government support subsidies and incentives.

3 Decline due to —

(a) Home market static in demand volume.
(b) Increased competition from lower cost overseas producers.
(c) Failure to reorganise industry sufficiently quickly to take advantage of new artificial fibres, technological advances, and integration into large units to gain economies of scale.
(d) Failure to cope with changing fashions and markets especially for casual wear.
(e) Traditional separation of processes e.g. spinning, weaving, finishing made the necessary integration difficult.
(f) Government aid proved a mixed blessing — the Cotton Board along with large corporation I.C.I. (Viyella), Courtaulds and Tootal encouraged amalgamation and vertical linkage of processes plus marketing. But only partially successful as government still aiding older small firms. Tariff protection also shielded inefficient producers too long.
(g) Lacked flexibility and design flair in casual wear compared to German, Italian, American and Japanese competitors.

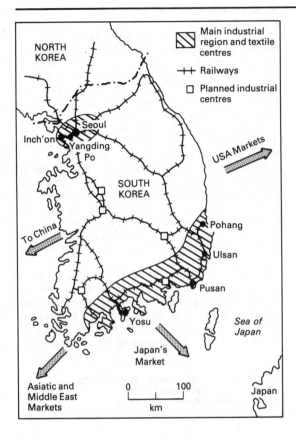

There is increasing competition in the cheaper fabric sector from Hong Kong, Taiwan, Sri Lanka and China ∴ South Korea needs to concentrate more on the better quality end of the market.

2 Factors favouring growth

(a) Need to develop exports to pay for much needed food, raw materials and capital goods in the 1950s and following the Korean war.

(b) Access to raw cotton from neighbouring Asiatic countries e.g. China and increasing supplies of artificial fibre from its own fast growing petro-chemical industry.

(c) Adequate pool of skilled, adaptable and modestly paid labour.

(d) Well positioned for access to expanding markets overseas.

(e) Government subsidies and support available as part of national development plans in which iron and steel, shipbuilding, heavy chemicals and textiles were seen as the basis.

(f) Combination of large foreign investment and technological 'knowhow' from overseas — especially the U.S.A. and Japan.

(g) Advantage of new large scale production units offering economies of scale.

3 South Korea however is vulnerable

(a) Being heavily dependent on the casual wear and household wear markets now increasingly the targets of other Asiatic producers. Needs to diversify into unwoven textiles for industrial and domestic use.

(b) Currency is linked to the volatile U.S. dollar — vulnerable to exchange value fluctuations.

AN EXPANDING TEXTILE REGION — SOUTH KOREA

1 Increasing importance

Third in world production and second as a textile exporter with increasing emphasis on finished products rather than semi-finished fibre. Textiles account for 30% of South Korea's exports by value and still rising. Its main markets are U.S.A., Japan, the remainder of Asia, the Middle East and EEC though here restricted by quota. Market potential is good.

Textiles employ 25% of South Korea's workforce and the industry is organised into large units. The basis of the industry is cotton allied to artificial fibres. There is increasing investment in technology to maintain its competitiveness.

Textile manufacture is concentrated in the main industrial regions but especially in Seoul e.g. here are the Cheli synthetic textile and Sunkyong companies.

Exercise

● The contrasting fortunes of the Lancashire region and South Korea as textile producers are not simply a matter of wage level differences. Discuss.

manufacturing as a whole). The rest of the work-force is largely unskilled, mainly female and concerned with assembly work. The employment structure thus shows a clear division and gap between the two sectors.

High technology industries are also identified by a high growth rate since the 1970s, at a time when most industry was stagnating and employment numbers declining. This growth rate, averaging 10%, and the future prospects of the industry have attracted a large amount of public interest and government financial support. In the United States, Japan and West European countries an expanding investment in high technology industry is increasingly seen as essential to the future economic well-being of a country. This is not only because of high technology's own potential for growth but also because of the effects of its application in other sectors of industry as well as the office and service sector. There were also initially high hopes that employment opportunities in this sector might offset losses in other areas; but whilst some opportunities exist they are insufficient to compensate for job losses. Moreover in the future more application of high technology in other areas may well further hasten job losses.

Structure and organisation

The computer, micro-electronic and allied industries making up this growing sector exhibit a dual structure and organisation in that whilst a few multinational corporations such as IBM (International Business Machines) hold a virtual monopoly of the larger hardware end of the industry such as production of computer frames, there is a vast range of small support businesses. In addition a constant spawning of new seedbed firms occurs, arising from further innovations and breakthroughs in the industry. This applies not only to specialised and ancillary equipment but also to the software side, for example the design and production of programmes to be used with the equipment for different purposes. Because it is an infant industry with rapid growth and change, there is a rapid turnover of small businesses — new ones coming in, some going bankrupt and mergers occurring.

However, whilst many of the small businesses may represent individual entrepreneurship, further studies increasingly show that many are either closely linked to the large multinationals which control the heavier end of the industry or are financially backed by large corporations which see these small

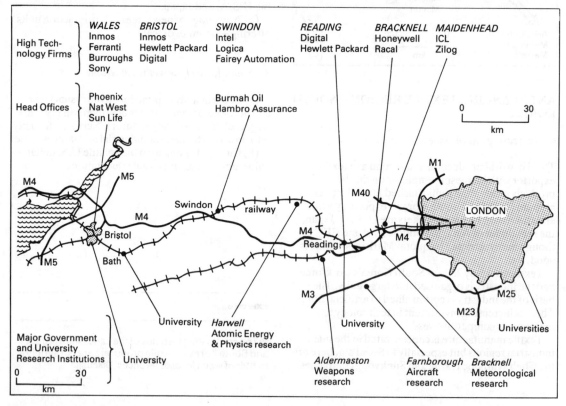

Fig. 11.10   The M4 growth corridor — high technology, government and university research centres and head offices

concerns as a way into this expanding sector of the economy.

Locational pattern

The locational pattern of high technology industry tends to be distinctive. Though it exhibits high regional concentration, the form of distribution within a region and its overall locational pattern lies outside both large conurbations and established industrial regions to which however it still has close contact and communication links.

In the United Kingdom major growth has been concentrated in Berkshire as part of a corridor either side of the M4 motorway, between London and Bristol (see Fig. 11.10). Within this it is the smaller free-standing urban centres such as Newbury and Reading which have attracted high technology firms, a feature also characteristic of new office location. Other centres include Cambridge in East Anglia and Stirling in Scotland. In the United States by far the largest concentration is in California, in what has become known as Silicon Valley and which is acknowledged as the birth place of information high technology. But there are other centres including a corridor of growth along Route 126 in Massachusetts in the North East and around Houston in Texas.

The crucial locating factor seems to be the presence of scientific and technological know-how in an area and the entrepreneurial drive of individuals involved to capitalise on this. In the case of the M4 corridor part of this arose among research and other staff at universities such as Reading and especially at Government Research Establishments in Aldermaston, Farnborough and Bracknell who saw commercial applications for the scientific processes and technologies employed in research projects. Individuals therefore left and set themselves up to produce electronic equipment and programme material.

A further allied factor was that the area attracted business concerns supplying back up support to the government research units and also those anxious to recruit highly trained staff. These included branches of American and Japanese corporations already involved in high technology production and which saw the M4 corridor as a convenient location for branch plants. This was not only because it offered a pool of highly skilled people but also access to further technological innovations which might be going on in the area, as well as a good jumping off point for penetrating EEC markets. As a result of this kind of process nearly 60% of the technology firms in the M4 corridor have been established since 1977.

The catalyst therefore is the existence of research and innovative skills which once utilised attract further growth leading to agglomerative economies. But a pleasant environment, space for development and excellent communications as general factors attracting all kinds of economic growth including offices and services are also contributory influences. The most outstanding case of this kind of locational growth is certainly that of Silicon Valley in California. The following Case Study of it highlights not only the complex set of interrelated factors at work but also something of the way growth occurs.

11:3 SILICON VALLEY, CALIFORNIA

High technology industry

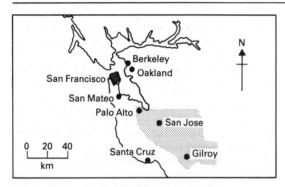

Location of Silicon Valley

Development has spread from Palo Alto inland — includes micro-chip production, micro-processors, integrated circuits, computer software products. Also associated research institutions and offices.

Factors favouring growth

Developed from research originally by Frederick Terman at Stanford University and later linked to the Hewlett Packard Electronic works, which was rapidly expanded during World War II.

Location and growth further encouraged by presence of innovators, research facilities, entrepreneurs and trained salesmen.

Firms attracted by prestige name which Silicon Valley gaining.

Until recently plentiful sites and pleasant environment.

Access to West coast coloured labour — Hispanic, Vietnamese to work on assembly etc. of products.

Fast communication network link to San Francisco and other West coast conurbations and by air etc. to the Midwest, South and East coast.

Diseconomies and business fluctuations emerging now due to over rapid expansion, lack of space, rising labour costs, increasing housing costs, motor vehicle pollution and social reactions to these.

Some dispersion occurring e.g. Apple Computers with 20 buildings in Silicon Valley now have branch plants in Texas, Singapore, Ireland etc.

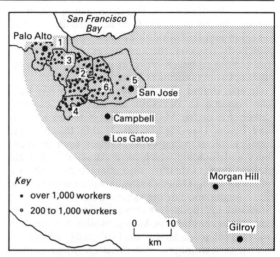

Silicon Valley in Santa Clara county

COMPANIES EMPLOYING MORE THAN 1000

1   PALO ALTO
Ford Aerospace &
  Communications
  Corp./Western
  Development
  Laboratories Division
Hewlett-Packard Co.
  Varian Associates
Watkins-Johnson Co.

2   SUNNYVALE
Advanced Micro
  Devices Inc.
Amdahl Corp.
Atari Inc.
Itek Corp/ Applied
  Technology
Lockheed Missiles &
  Space Co.Inc.
Monolithic Memories
  Inc.
National Semiconductor
  Corp.
Shugart Associates
Sigentics Corp.
Verbatim Corp.

3   MOUNTAIN VIEW
Acurex Corp.
Fairchild Camera &
  Instrument Corp.
General Telephone &
  Electronics

Corp/Western
  Division
Spectra-Physics Inc.

4   CUPERTINO
Four-Phase Systems Incs.
Hewlett-Packard Co.
  (4 divisions)
ISS/Sperry Univac
Intersil Inc.
Litronix Inc.
Measurex Corp.
Plantronics Inc.
Tymshare Inc.

5   SAN JOSE
International Business
  Machines
  Corp./General
  Products Divisions
Qume Corp.

6   SANTA CLARA
American Microsystems
  Inc.
Hewlett-Packard
  CO./Santa Clara
  Division
Intel Corp.
Memorex Corp.
National Semiconductor
  Corp.
Rolm Corp.
Silconix Inc.

12 De-industrialisation and Newly Industrialising Countries

Whilst the developed world is concerned about the relative declining importance of industry in the economy and deepening unemployment, industrialisation is gathering pace amongst developing countries. The more forward of them are now being grouped together as the newly industrialising countries (NICs). These now have a number of advantages in respect of certain basic industries such as iron and steel. Thus at a simple level this shift in favour of the NICs for certain industries can be explained as arising from the law of comparative advantage — areas tend to produce those items in which they have the greatest ratio advantage over other areas, but in reality both the change in the level and pace of industrialisation from one part of the world to another and its causes are much more complex.

De-industrialisation in the developed world

Amongst developed countries industry once the engine room of economic growth, is now being dis-placed by service-led growth. In the UK for example in 1980, manufacturing contributed 24% of the nation's output of goods and services as against nearly 40% in 1960. It had an even smaller proportion of the employed workforce. Three and a half million jobs have been lost in manufacturing over the last 20 years, most of them since 1970. Though the recent world recession accounts for some of these losses, much of it represents a long term change in the structure of the economy which has important spatial and social repercussions.

This process of de-industrialisation, strictly defined as an absolute loss of jobs in industrial activities, is not uniform across the range of manufacturing nor at the same rate in every region. It tends to be both regionally and industry selective. The greatest losses have hitherto occurred in the staple industries, partly as we have seen earlier because these have lost markets to new competitors, but also because in an effort to modernise and compete, new labour saving technologies have been introduced. In the UK for example employment in textiles such as

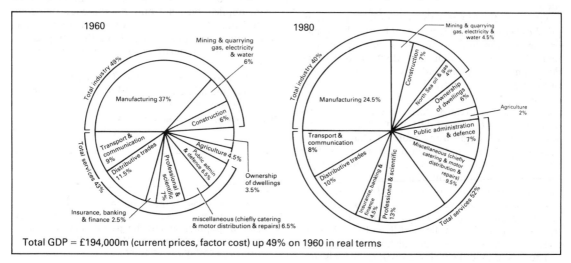

Fig. 12.1   *Change in the United Kingdom economy, 1960–80*

115

clothing and leather has declined since 1951, in ship building and engineering from 1956, and this has been followed by losses in iron and steel and heavy chemicals. All of these are concentrated in older industrial areas associated with the coalfields. Now however for similar reasons unemployment is selectively being felt on a long term basis in certain later established industries, found mainly in the Midlands and the South East, notably in the motor vehicle industry and its ancillaries.

These losses are only partially being offset by expansion in the service and new growth industries as these mature industrial nations move into the new industrial revolution — that of high technology and associated developments centring on computing and microprocessing, telecommunications and bio-engineering. This is because much of these new kinds of activity involves automation and therefore a low ratio of labour input to capital investment is required.

This shift to service led growth and high technology industry has important spatial implications. Whilst most of the service activity and established industry will remain in large conurbations, much of the new growth has been decentralised away from these, as well as away from older industrial regions such as the North East.

These decentralisation trends have only partially been offset by government intervention and incentives in an effort to maintain a sufficient level of economic activity in older industrial and inner urban areas. The new growth zones for high technology industry such as the M4 corridor in the U.K. and Silicon Valley, California can basically be seen as further expression of this decentralisation trend. These have been reinforced by a shift of office location in the service sector to the periphery of cities and growth areas in these more rural environments.

Studies of the M4 growth corridor have for example shown that office development has made a greater contribution here to the expansion of employment than the new industry. Much of this office development represents either wholesale relocation of businesses from central London or the hiving off of the large routine office area to new locations leaving only the prestige part and directors' offices in the city. For the larger part of the office complex, which is increasingly using more mechanised data processing, storage and retrieval systems, more floor space is required and this can be more cheaply obtained outside the central locations. Also labour and living costs tend to be lower and the more rural environment attractive. But the improvement in communication is also an important factor allowing for rapid and efficient links still with established centres but now over greater distances.

The loss of manufacturing growth to NICs is not, however, without some compensations. Advanced industrial countries can profitably sell their expertise and technology to the NICs and multinational corporations are responsible for a substantial part of the investment needed to finance industrial growth in the developing world. Hence loss of overseas earnings from a decline in some kinds of manufacturing, are more than compensated for by service and investment returns from abroad which are counted in the balance of trade returns as invisible earnings. Furthermore, whilst de-industrialisation is an important feature of developed countries, these still do remain by far the most important industrial nations measured by volume and value of manufacturing output and are likely to remain so in the foreseeable future.

Industrialisation in the developing world

The Newly Industrialising Countries

The rate of manufacturing growth amongst countries in the developing world (Fig. 12.2) is very variable. Some like the smaller central African states such as Uganda and Andean Latin American countries, like Bolivia, have had little growth whilst others, such as Brazil, Mexico and South Korea, have experienced so much growth that they are now significant exporters of manufactured goods, these making up about third of all exports by value. Overall the developing countries have experienced a manufacturing growth rate of between 6%–10% annually since the 1960s, more than twice that of established industrial nations. Even so, their contribution to total world manufacturing output remains modest, around 9% in 1977.

The important feature, however, is that this contribution continues to rise and this will have significant implications, not only for the countries concerned but also for patterns of world trade; some developing countries already have the competitive edge over older industrial countries in certain manufactures.

In the early 1970s a number of international organisations, including the World Bank, began to identify what were termed Newly Industrialising Countries (NICs) showing not only a rapid growth in

Exercises

1 Attempt to classify the countries in Fig. 12.2 into three groups on the basis of potential home market size (by population) and the growth rates shown.
2 Suggest some reasons why the growth rate varies from one country to another.

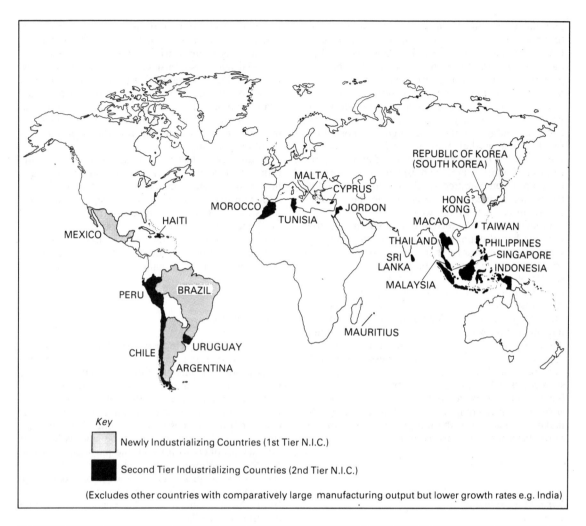

Key
Newly Industrializing Countries (1st Tier N.I.C.)

Second Tier Industrializing Countries (2nd Tier N.I.C.)

(Excludes other countries with comparatively large manufacturing output but lower growth rates e.g. India)

Growth Rates % of Manufacturing

First Tier NIC	1970–80	Population (mills)	Second Tier[1] NIC	1970–80	Population (mills)
Argentina	1.0	28	Chile	−0.5	11
	(Falkland War)		Haiti	7.1	5
Brazil	10.3	121	Peru	3.2	17
Mexico	5.9	72	Uruguay	4.1	3
Hong Kong	9.3	5	Indonesia	12.8	148
South Korea	16.6	39	Malaysia	11.8	15
Singapore	9.6	3	Philippines	7.2	50
Taiwan	6–10%*	17	Sri Lanka	1.9	15
* estimate			Thailand	10.6	48
			Morocco	5.8	21
			Tunisia	11.2	7

1 Later industrialising than the First Tier

Fig. 12.2   1st and 2nd tier NICs

manufacturing but also a need to export manufactured goods. Now a second wave of such countries is being identified as their industrialisation gathers pace. However, these have been identified by growth rate (in particular by increasing exports) and not by total volume or value of manufactured goods. There are other countries such as India and China which have a much greater volume of output but because their growth rate is not high and most of it is for the home market, they do not figure in the list. Useful therefore though categories of Newly Industrialising Countries are, we must widen our horizons if we are to fully appreciate the contribution industrialisation is making to the economies and lives of people in the developing world.

Indeed it must take recognition too of the fact that in a number of countries much the highest employment in manufacturing is in the informal sector of small businesses run on family lines in the backstreets of cities and villages. Unlike production in factories run by governments or large private firms, the statistics for this informal sector do not appear in official figures for manufacturing output and employment. For example in India whilst 5 million are employed in the organised sector, four times that number are employed in small businesses using little technology and capital investment. Their output of such goods as food, clothing, footwear, small implements and now more sophisticated goods such as small electrical equipment and household goods, makes a major contribution to the needs of the domestic market in these countries.

Types of manufacturing

Small businesses

This informal sector of manufacturing is in fact the longest established one, since most developing countries have always had small craft industries in villages and cities to supply everyday needs. Also certain specialist crafts such as metal working and pottery making have had a market in neighbouring countries too.

Whilst some of this indigenous craft was lost due to the cheap import of substitute goods during colonial times, a lot survived particularly in the rural areas. With political independence, increasing population numbers and rising demand, there has been a revival of small business, but most of it is now centred in the towns. Some governments recognising this as an important source of goods at basic prices the people can afford and an important supplier of jobs to the many flocking into the cities, are now giving official financial support and protection to it. India, for example, has encouraged the growth

of co-operatives to help these small family concerns and under the small industries development organisation has set up district centres offering technical, financial and other business advice to small firms. Under its Development Plans the manufacture of six hundred products is exclusively reserved for small firms. Significantly these now include more sophisticated products such as electronic and light engineering products as well as the traditional products of food and clothing etc.

Small scale industry has many advantages — the ratio of employed to capital investment is much higher than in large scale industry, increasing labour opportunities but using minimum capital. Also products can be tailored to meet the needs of limited local markets and output can be flexible to suit changes in demand. This sector is therefore seen as increasingly important today in the diversification of the economy of developing countries.

Processing for export

The other sector of industry which is of long standing is that of processing or semi-processing of primary products from agriculture, mining and forestry ready for export. Some processing is needed either because of the perishable nature of the product in its raw state or because its reduction in bulk makes for cheaper transport costs. The extent of this processing sector depends on the type and volume of primary products with which the particular colonial territory is endowed. Most countries have a narrow range of such products often with one being the dominant, for example, copper from Zambia, sugar from the Caribbean islands, cocoa and certain minerals from Ghana.

Since independence, states in the developing world have tried to reduce dependence on this narrow range of exports because such exports are subject to fluctuating world demand and frequently controlled by foreign owned multinational companies. But since these exports earn much needed foreign currency and form an important sector in the economy, the processing of primary products for exports remains very important as for example in the case of Kenya and Peru. However, where feasible, governments are now demanding that an increasing proportion of primary products are fully processed before export. This therefore puts them into the category of manufactured products, raises their export value and provides more revenue and employment in the producing country. Brazil, for example, now smelts a significant proportion of its own iron-ore to make iron and steel, Ghana has its own aluminium industry, using locally mined bauxite, and Malaysia increasingly more of its own rubber products factories.

Import substitution and capital intensive industries

Apart from the further development of small scale industry and the extension of some processing into manufacturing, developing countries have sought to widen their industrial base sufficiently so as to be less dependent on foreign imports of manufactured goods. They have also seen further industrialisation as a way of modernising the country and given it status in the eyes of the outside world. But there have been serious problems — insufficient finance, technical know-how, suitable labour skills and inability to compete with foreign produced manufactures in some areas. Early efforts at industrialisation placed over-emphasis on developing capital industries, such as iron and steel and heavy engineering or production of modern durable consumer goods which only a limited and more affluent sector of the population could afford. This diverted finance and expertise away from economically more viable and important areas in the economy such as agriculture and small scale industry.

Nevertheless important strides in these other areas of industry have been made by some countries notably Brazil, Mexico, India and some South East Asian countries, such as Taiwan and Korea. In nearly every case, however, development has relied heavily on government support, foreign technology and investment, frequently from the kind of large multinational corporations of which the newly independent states in the world are politically so critical. This newer industrial growth can be broadly divided into import substitution light industries and heavy capital industry.

As regards light industry, this tends to be centred on consumer goods such as foods, drinks, tobacco, textiles and clothing, the manufacture of which does not require complex technology and is labour intensive relative to the amount of capital invested. Much of it is in branch plants established by foreign companies attracted by lower labour costs, weak union organisation of labour and expanding markets. Textiles have particularly been seen as one of the ways of extending manufacturing. But as for other products much depends on the size of the home market available and the potential for export. It is therefore not surprising that import substitution industries have expanded most in countries with large populations, for example India, Brazil and Nigeria. But many developing countries have less than 10 million population and this is a serious handicap to any significant industrialisation.

Where light industries have developed they have by a process of cumulative causation attracted other industrial growth and been able to expand to gain more economies of scale. This has attracted more investment, raised the quality of products whilst maintaining prices at a competitive level. Particularly important it has given a base for growing exports

to other countries. The range of consumer goods is now being extended in the most successful countries to include durable consumers such as motor vehicle assembly and electrical goods as in Brazil and South East Asian countries such as Singapore, Philippines, Taiwan and South Korea.

Whilst most countries have tried to develop heavy basic industries under the protection and direct involvement of governments including provision of strong tariff protection, only a few countries have done this successfully. In most countries insufficient raw materials, power resources, finance and the limited size of the home market have meant that these industries have operated at a continuous loss whatever their prestige value.

Where home markets are large, the country has important raw materials of its own or can import these cheaply and is well enough on the road to industrialisation to have sufficient support infrastructure and skilled manpower, capital intensive industries have been established successfully — ranging from iron and steel, to other metals, chemicals and heavy engineering. India has for example an important iron and steel industry centred on the Damodar valley where iron-ore, coal, and hydro-electric power are available. The Middle East countries are developing important petro-chemical industries based on plentiful oil supplies and finance gained from export of oil, whilst South Korea has been in a position to import raw materials to add to its own to make it a significant iron and steel, shipbuilding and marine engineering producer.

Unfortunately, in the case of a number of these industrialising nations the recent world recession and over-extension of foreign borrowing have led them into massive balance of payment problems and foreign debt. This has brought inflation and economic disruption at home and a serious reappraisal of the role of industrialisation in the economy — Nigeria, Brazil, Mexico, Argentina are some of the nations with massive debt problems. Perhaps out of the hard realism which these countries have to face may come more securely based policies which take into account more the capacity and needs of the domestic home market and the necessity of putting economic viability before political expediency.

The location of manufacturing

When we consider the pattern of industry in these countries its most dominant feature is its concentration into a few centres (see Fig. 12.3a). The largest concentrations of population have attracted the most industry. These are the centres offering the largest markets, and they have advantages arising from cumulative causation and agglomeration effects. Where coastally situated they have the added advantage of an export point which attracted

119

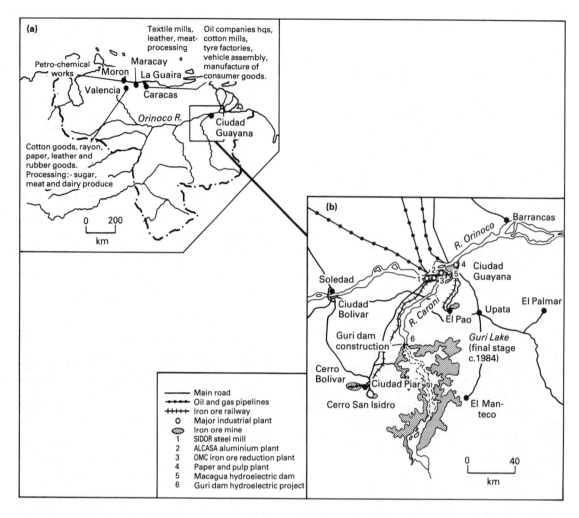

Fig. 12.3 (a) *Ciudad Guayana in relation to other major industrial centres in Venezuela*
(b) *The new growth centre*

earlier processing industries and the growth of an infrastructure.

Large ports and capital cities are particularly attractive locations to manufacturing. However there are other centres based on a narrow and more specialist range of factors, in particular the presence or access to raw material and power. Examples include the petro-chemical industry located at oil refining centres which have access to local oil supplies, e.g. at Maracaibo in Venezuela and copper smelting at Kitwe in Zambia.

However in longer established industrial regions such as South East Brazil the process of deconcentration or dispersion, so important in advanced countries, is beginning to take place. The reasons are similar to those in the developed world e.g. increasing diseconomies where industry is heavily concentrated and government directives both to relieve pressure on heavily congested regions and to generate alternative growth centres in areas requiring more employment opportunities.

Much dispersion tends to be only to the edge of cities with such features as industrial trading estates and greenfield site factories becoming common, as for instance, on the edge of Sao Paulo in Brazil and Singapore. But new growth poles are also evident in most of the NICs. A notable example is Ciudad Guayana in Venezuela (Fig. 12.3b) where access to iron-ore, bauxite, local timber and hydro-electric power potential together with navigable river access provided a good basis for industrial development. This it is hoped will aid general growth in the southern part of the country and reduce pressure on Caracas and other centres in the North.

13   The Basis of Agriculture

Whilst the geographer is centrally concerned with the distribution of different kinds of farming, including why and where these are changing, he has also been drawn into related and more fundamental issues. One of these is whether sufficient food can be made available for the continuously growing world population. This involves amongst other things, examining how different kinds of farming can be made productive, particularly those in tropical regions. Other questions are concerned with whether such increases can be achieved without damaging the environment or the fabric of society in rural areas.

Consideration of such issues brings us to the very basis of farming and it is this we need to explore before looking at particular types of farming.

The farming system

A systems approach to agriculture has steadily gained in popularity over recent years. This is partly because it highlights inter-relationships touching on some of the important issues to do with agriculture. But it is also because central to systems is the idea of process and change, which is so fundamental to our understanding of farming patterns today. Except for the simple system for subsistence agriculture (Fig. 13.1) in which the farmer is growing for the needs of himself and his family, it is important to see farming as composed of two linked parts or subsystems (Fig. 13.2). There is the production subsystem, the group or groups of farms, and the marketing subsystem

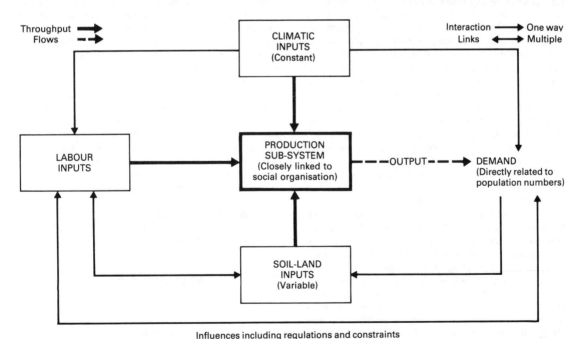

Fig. 13.1   A simple subsistence farming system

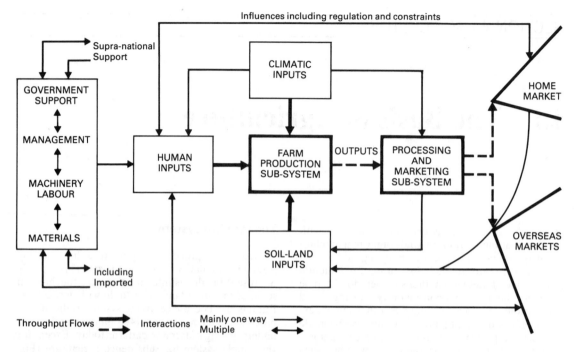

Fig. 13.2 *The complex commercial farming system*

responsible for processing and packing and marketing the produce. This may be controlled by the farmer or company running the farm but more often it is run separately by some marketing organisation.

Since production and marketing subsystems are usually separate, adequate transport links are required between them as well as between the marketing organisation and the ultimate consumer of the farm produce. In addition to the movement of produce to market there is also the movement into farms of inputs or resources that are needed in growing crops or rearing livestock. Some come direct from the natural environment — climate, soil and land inputs. Others are human inputs, some of which involve transport of materials to the farm as well as on the farm itself e.g. fertilizers, labour, machinery etc. Efficient and cost effective transport is therefore another part of the total farming system. So we can see a farming system consists of much more than the farm or farms on which the food or agricultural raw materials are produced. It is also to do with efficient marketing and transport facilities.

Apart from providing us with a more comprehensive view of agriculture at any given time, a systems context is valuable because it emphasises the movements, processes and inter-relationships through which one part of any farming is affected by and affects the rest. Change and the reasons for change are summarised in Fig. 13.3a,b of the old cotton belt of the South in the United States.

Assessing its efficiency

Until recently, the developed world has been inclined to measure the efficiency of any production and marketing system in terms of its financial profitability — that is the amount by which input costs including production, transport, processing and other marketing costs, are exceeded by the revenue gained by selling the produce output — but this is at best a partial measure of the system's efficiency. It does not give an adequate measure of environmental costs, for example the extent to which farming practice maintains or increases soil fertility to provide an adequate input from the soil in the future. Nor does it necessarily highlight some other ways in which more food could be obtained from the system to meet the needs of society in any area. Yet these are matters of central importance from which we can gain some understanding if we take the trouble to move beyond simply a monetary or straight economic assessment of a system.

An assessment along ecological lines

Energy flows and food chains

Using an ecological approach, inputs and outputs from a man-made agricultural system can be measured like any natural eco-system in terms of the

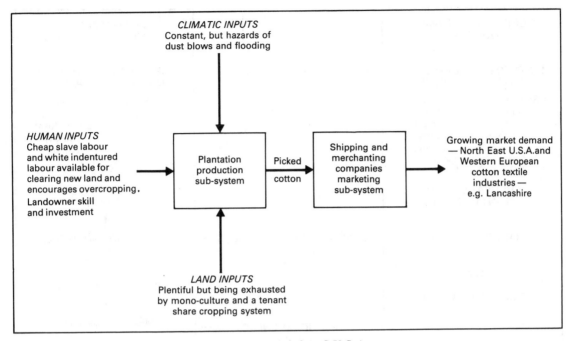

Fig. 13.3   (a) Forces for change e.g. in the old cotton belt in S U.S.A.

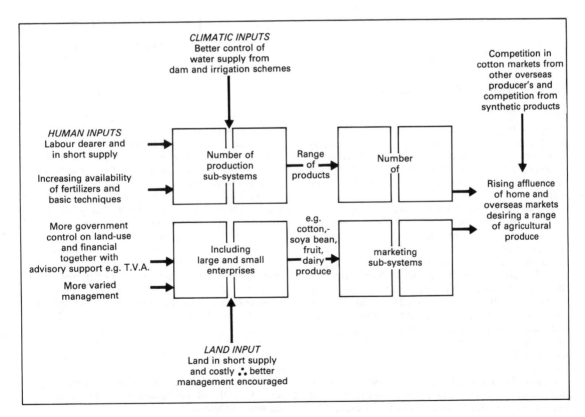

Fig. 13.3   (b) Current forces for diversified agriculture in S U.S.A.

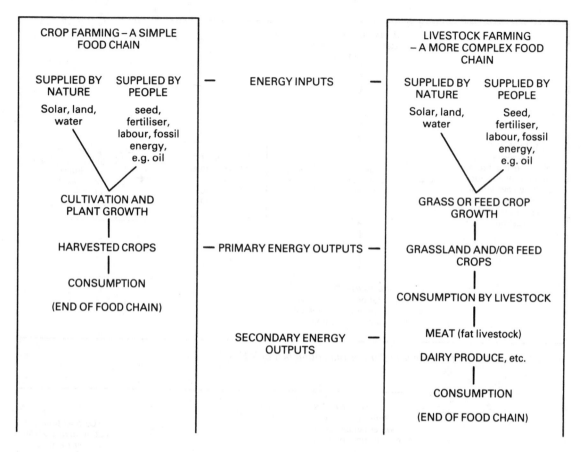

Fig. 13.4   *Two food chains compared*

energy flows passing through it. Inputs can be measured in terms of solar and people supplied energy and output measured in millions of calories. (However it is not only the calorific value of the food product which is important, but also its nutritional value.)

The through puts of energy can be seen as food chains. Different types of farming are represented by different food chains. One kind of food chain is that for arable farming in which crops are grown to be directly consumed. Livestock farming is represented by different and longer food chains, in which the crops or grasses which are grown are first eaten by livestock which in turn provide the produce for human consumption. Arable farming thus has only one stage in the food chain while livestock or pastoral farming has two (see Fig. 13.4). We can thus view the different kinds of farming as a series of food chains.

One of the interesting and important features of this sort of approach is that the relative efficiency of two or more farming systems can be measured by comparing for each food chain, the amount of ener-

gy output with the amount of energy input required to produce that output. Inevitably as energy flows through the food chain some of it is lost in a variety of ways, but the loss is greater for some types of food chains than others. In the case of food chain A in Fig. 13.4 where tillage crops are produced for human consumption much of the energy remains as output because there is only one stage in the food chain. But in the case of food chain B for livestock farming, there are two stages in the chain and there is therefore a greater chance that energy will be lost as it passes through each stage. The above can be illustrated from a comparison done between the growing of potatoes, the food chain A example, and the fattening of cattle for beef, food chain B example.

Apart from emphasising the much greater efficiency of crop farming over livestock farming, regarding systems as food chains also highlights where energy losses occur in the total farming process. It can therefore indicate ways of making farming more efficient.

Frequently when considering the food needs of

people in the developing world, emphasis is put on the need to develop higher yielding strains of crops or breeds of livestock and in the need to increase inputs of fertilizers and in some cases more machinery. Whilst these may be of benefit they are difficult and costly to implement. But as we can see from the two examples of food chains given, much more of the energy input would be saved and therefore the amount of food effectively increased if greater attention was given to more efficient methods of harvesting, storing and processing agricultural products. Since the latter could be achieved relatively cheaply, the benefits to the poorer parts of the developing world would be significant.

However, any assessment must not only take account of the percentage of energy balance emerging at the end of the food chain, but also its nutritional value. Meat and fish are on the whole richer in protein than food crops and this partly explains why there is so much livestock farming despite its apparent inefficiency in terms of large inputs needed relative to the output of energy produced. But certain crops are also relatively rich in protein and therefore can to some extent substitute for meat and fish. These have traditionally included pulses such as peas and beans, which have the added advantage of restoring nitrogen content to the soil when used in crop rotation. More recently increasing attention has been given to the soya bean plant. Its acreage has been increased rapidly in areas such as the

Southern United States and the more humid parts of the Steppes in the Soviet Union and China. Also a number of agricultural research institutions have been established in the tropics to develop other high yielding strains of protein rich pulses and cereals.

Unfortunately scientific advances like these and other changes in the kind of food eaten in the developing world are hindered by conservative market demand — traditional food being preferred or more acceptable for cultural and religious reasons. The relationship between people's food needs and the kind of agriculture developed to meet them are thus complex.

There is still yet another dimension to this question of efficiency which needs considering. This is the effect that pressures for increasing food supplies and agricultural raw materials have on what might be termed the health of the environment. If the land is not kept in good heart, yields can rapidly decline.

Efficiency and the environmental impact

The effects the demand for food and agricultural raw materials have on the environment can firstly be illustrated by examining the nutrient flows within any farming system. The nutrient output consumed as human food is only one of a number of nutrient flows within an agrosystem. (Fig. 13.5)

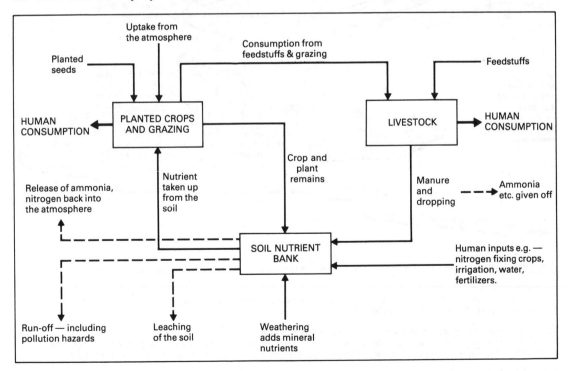

Fig. 13.5 Simple nutrient flows in an agro-system

1. *CAUSES* — Poor farming and other detrimental land use practices accelerate natural processes of erosion by wind and water in climatically vulnerable areas and places of steep terrain. Soil erosion increases at a rate exceeding that at which natural processes and human inputs can renew the soil structure and cover

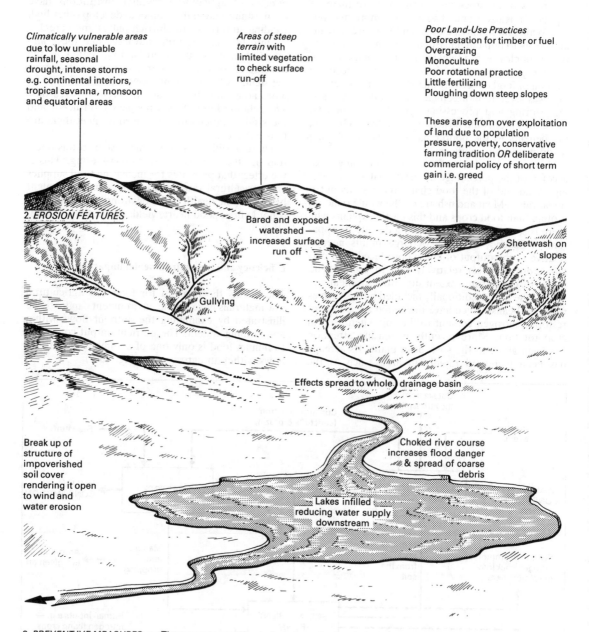

Climatically vulnerable areas due to low unreliable rainfall, seasonal drought, intense storms e.g. continental interiors, tropical savanna, monsoon and equatorial areas

Areas of steep terrain with limited vegetation to check surface run-off

Poor Land-Use Practices
Deforestation for timber or fuel
Overgrazing
Monoculture
Poor rotational practice
Little fertilizing
Ploughing down steep slopes

These arise from over exploitation of land due to population pressure, poverty, conservative farming tradition *OR* deliberate commercial policy of short term gain i.e. greed

2. *EROSION FEATURES*

Bared and exposed watershed — increased surface run off

Sheetwash on slopes

Gullying

Effects spread to whole drainage basin

Break up of structure of impoverished soil cover rendering it open to wind and water erosion

Choked river course increases flood danger & spread of coarse debris

Lakes infilled reducing water supply downstream

3. *PREVENTIVE MEASURES* — These must cover the whole drainage basin as misuse in one area affects the whole basin.

(a) *Direct measures*
Afforestation, control of livestock numbers, responsible cultivation practices e.g. adequate humus inputs, windbreaks, good drainage, suitable rotation, diversified farming.

(b) *These are not likely to occur without more comprehensive measures*
Advisory and education services to disseminate good practices, adequate finance provision, responsible population policies, alternate employment to reduce pressure on the land, conservation legislation especially to protect watershed areas.

Fig. 13.6 Soil erosion

126

Nutrient flows are brought into farming systems both through nature's own activities and by people's — such as manuring and application of fertilizers. These nutrients are mainly held in the soil as a nutrient bank. The nutrient bank is also renewed from plant remains left in the field after harvesting and from livestock droppings. Nutrients can also be taken directly from the atmosphere by plants; legume plants for example are able to fix nitrogen from the atmosphere.

Nutrients are lost out of the system, not only by direct output in the form of harvested crops and livestock produced, but also through natural processes such as the leaching out of nutrients through water percolating down through the soil and surface run off. Nutrients are also lost through other surface processes breaking down and removing the soil itself along with the nutrients contained. Just as good farming practice can reduce this loss, bad farming practices can accelerate and in extreme cases lead to soil erosion by wind blow and sheet and gully erosion by water run off (Fig. 13.6). We should therefore also assess any farming according to how well it maintains and builds up the soil nutrient bank, since this is an essential requisite for the soil's fertility and yield, and therefore the efficiency of any farming undertaken.

There are many examples of the results of bad farming practice which in areas with difficult climate conditions such as low and uncertain rainfall, seasonal drought or excessive rainfall lead to severe soil erosion and loss of nutrients at a rate nature is unable to replace. Overcropping and overgrazing where too little is put into the soil and too much taken out are common causes. In the old cotton belt of the Southern United States, for example, a series of exceptionally dry years combined with poor farming practices under the share cropping system led to the now well-known Dust Bowl phenomenon. In some areas it totally destroyed the soil's fertility. In tropical regions where torrential rains of the hot wet season alternate with a hot dry season when wind blow can be a potent erosion force, soil erosion is also a severe problem. This is especially so where there is pressure of population, ignorance or poverty or commercial greed. For example overgrazing by the cattle of the Masai round water-holes in East Africa has led to breakdown of the soil and widespread gully erosion around the water-holes. Also widespread clearance of land and mono-culture by Europeans, as for example in the coffee lands of South East Brazil and other tropical regions, have had equally disastrous results.

The effects of these kinds of bad farming practices are now clearly recognised and measures have been taken to remedy them. These include more diversification of agriculture and the adoption of multi-purpose schemes such as that under the Tennessee Valley Authority in the United States.

However, in modern farming practice there are less obvious but also equally serious ways in which the nutrient bank and the environment in general can be harmed. Overuse of fertilizers and insecticides whilst over the short term increasing yields, can lead to harmful chemicals being carried off in solution and with it some of the soil nutrients. These enter lakes and water courses creating widespread pollution hazards. Overuse of insecticides can also have detrimental effects on wildlife and through contamination of food, human health. Thus even wider environmental issues are opened up as indicated in the Case Study of the Gezira Scheme in the Sudan (p. 128).

A better understanding of nutrient cycles and overall ecological conditions will encourage better farming practices which will maintain and even improve agricultural productivity. But more than this, it can also improve the land drainage, soil and other environmental resources upon which agriculture ultimately depends now and for the future.

A classification of agricultural regions based on farming systems

In order to study the distribution of different kinds of farming, it is necessary to identify them. There are a number of existing classifications, one of the most well-known being that by Whittlesey, which is based on five criteria. These are: crop and livestock combinations, methods employed, intensity of use of labour–capital–organisation, method of disposal of farm products and finally the kinds of buildings and structures necessary to carry on the agricultural activities. On this basis he produces 13 divisions of world farming.

Though now somewhat dated Whittlesey's classification has proved useful. But it is not a sufficiently genetic classification i.e. one leading to some identification of the factors indicating why one area has a different kind of farming from another. However, if we extend the basis of classification along the systems approach line this enables us to see that the character of any farming is determined by the demand for its output and the kinds of physical and human inputs needed to use that output (Fig. 13.7).

Output demand

The demand factor is the most influential because without the demand there would be no agriculture. This must therefore form the basis of a world classification of farming types. The simplest kind of demand is a subsistence one in which the farmer and his family consume their own produce, except for any surplus which may be sold locally to provide

13:1   THE GEZIRA, SUDAN

A two million hectare irrigation scheme

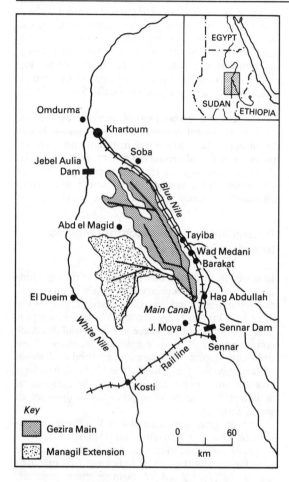

The Irrigation Scheme in the Gezira Plain

Key
- Gezira Main
- Managil Extension

0   60
km

THE SCHEME

The scheme was begun in 1922 to increase supplies of long staple cotton for the UK textile industry. There was wholesale clearance of large forest areas in the Southern Gezira and the Blue Nile valley. Initially (1926) 50 000ha of crops were put under irrigation. Since then the area has been steadily extended, including the Managil South West Extension. In 1980 the scheme covered 840 000 ha.

Perhaps its most positive benefit is that over the years the fine long staple cotton has brought in much needed foreign exchange revenue.

Problems and detrimental effects

1   To maintain yeilds fertilizer and technical inputs have had to be increased not only raising costs but also causing 'panning' in the soil and increasing drainage problems.

2   Application of insecticides including D.D.T. has led to water pollution and poisoning of fish including species in the Nile and Lake Nubia further downstream.

3   One pest has been replaced by another. Spraying for example has eradicated the American bollworm but its eradication allowed the spread of whitefly.

4   Flooding of lagoons behind the dam has provided more breeding grounds for disease carrying snails and mosquitoes. Schistomasas disease carried by snails and transmission of malaria are perennial problems. In 1972 schistomasas disease affected 60% of the population.

5   Adversely affected the basic economy and culture of the local people. There has been too much emphasis on export crops with little research into raising food output. The Sudan is now a net importer of food. The promised material prosperity has not come. The family as a social unit has been disrupted and the younger element has emigrated to the towns of Khartoum and Omdurman.

Exercise

● What lessons can be learnt from the Gezira Scheme for future irrigation and agricultural projects in the Tropics? Is there any evidence of the adoption of a more balanced approach?

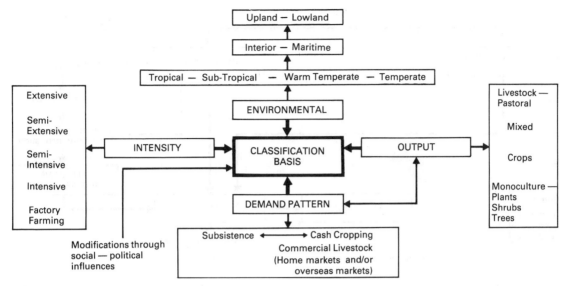

Fig. 13.1   A classification basis for farming systems

cash to meet other household needs and commitments such as payment of taxes and family debts. The other kind of demand is the commercial one in which farming is essentially geared to production for sale on the market i.e. cash farming. By its very nature it involves separating the production side from the marketing side, the two frequently being run by separate business concerns, though in plantation farming a business corporation may have overall control from growing the crop to marketing the produce.

Human input factors — intensive and extensive farming

Just as the demand side has led to the basic division of farming types into subsistence farming on the one hand and commercial farming on the other, consideration of the human side leads to a further subdivision within each of these two groups. This is on the basis of the intensity with which these human inputs are applied — leading to the well-known division into intensive and extensive farming.

Intensive farming is defined by the ratio of labour, capital and other inputs to the available land area. The simplest form is intensive subsistence rice farming in South East Asia, where large amounts of labour energy are invested on small plots to obtain as high a yield as possible. More complex are the commercial intensive systems such as market gardening in which a high amount of technology, fertilizers etc., and labour are invested per unit of land area to obtain maximum yields.

At the other end of the scale, extensive farming

occurs where land is sufficiently plentiful for the producer to think in terms of overall returns across his whole land holding and not primarily in terms of yield per unit area. Because of the amount of land at his disposal he will instead concentrate on keeping his cost per unit area as low as possible. Moderate or low yields may result, but if the total unit acreage is large, overall profits can be high. This is the case with sheep ranching in areas such as central Queensland. Extensive grain farming on prairie lands in the United States and Canada is similar, except that capital inputs will be higher by way of fertilizers and the use of machinery etc. It is more difficult to find examples of extensive subsistence agriculture. But shifting agriculture may be termed as extensive despite the fact that only part of the tribal territory is cleared for cultivation at any one time. The amount of labour input is low and so too relatively are yields.

Social and political influences

The intervention of government and other institutions is becoming increasingly important in agriculture as in other spheres. It is of course strongest in socialist countries such as the Soviet Union, China, Cuba and Tanzania. Policies adopted towards agriculture depend not only upon the kind of political ideology prevailing in a country but also upon the attitudes and values held by different societies about the relative national importance of farming. These can influence both the input and output sides of farming systems. For example on the input side grant aid and tax concessions to farmers on purchase

129

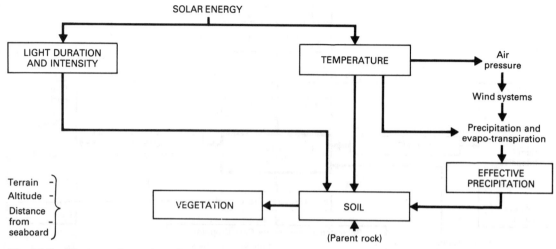

Fig. 13.8   *The interrelationship of ecological influences*

of machinery and other capital inputs encourages more mechanisation and lower labour inputs, whilst price support schemes as a guaranteed price for the produce whatever happens to the market price encourages farmers to maintain or even expand output. In this country, both policies have been influential in maintaining for example the hill farming in marginal areas such as the Welsh Uplands and the Lake District, when under a free market economy such farming would most likely have been uneconomic.

We cannot however leave this question of social and political influences without some word about the opposite end of the spectrum from government interference, namely personal preferences. The strongest personal preference element paradoxically seems to be in marginal farming areas. It is for example epitomised in the hill farmer of upland areas in Western Europe and in a different way by the subsistence cultivators of tropical lands.

Physical inputs — climate, soil and vegetation

Climatic influences seriously limit the type of agriculture which can be carried on in particular parts of the world. For this reason there is a broad similarity between patterns on a climatic map of the world and one showing the different types of agriculture. The same remains true at a more regional level, for example in the United States.

The prime moving force influencing other climatic factors affecting agriculture is solar energy. This determines the daily duration and intensity of insolation received, the temperature regime and wind systems. Combined with these, solar energy also influences the amount of precipitation and evapo-

transpiration in any locality and thus its effective precipitation. (Refer to Fig. 13.8.)

This importance of solar energy and precipitation is further increased when we recognise that they in turn play a dominant role in influencing the character of the soil and vegetation, which also affect the type of agriculture that can be practised in any given locality. Whilst vegetation is of minor importance as a factor once the land has been cleared for farming, the one exception being livestock grazing on natural pasture when of course vegetation plays a primary role, soil is a directly important factor. Apart from river alluvium and wind borne loess, the main zonal soils of the world are largely determined by climatic conditions and therefore by incorporating an index of climate in our classification we are also covering the effect of soil type.

The resulting classification

Following on from the above identification of factors affecting types and patterns of farming the matrix into which the different farming systems has been placed (Fig. 13.9) has as its frame side the type of output from the system together with the type of food chain to which it is related. Across the top are broad environmental divisions based on latitude belts. Within this outer frame have been inserted the scale of inputs ranging from intensive through to extensive input combinations. Finally, within the matrix boxes a subdivision into subsistence systems (*) and commercial systems has been made.

It is of course a simplification of the systems actually existing. All classifications are bound to be generalisations omitting some of the less important and more localised types. But an attempt has been made to cover the main regional types.

Fig. 13.9 A classification of farming systems

	TEMPERATE		WARM TEMPERATE to SUB-TROPICAL		TROPICAL	
	Extensive	Intensive	Extensive	Intensive	Extensive	Intensive
LIVESTOCK (Chain B)	SHEEP (Wool) C. Australia CATTLE (Beef) W. U.S.A. Pampas	DAIRYING New Zealand, Denmark, Netherlands, U.K., S.E. Australia FACTORY FARMING (Pigs, Poultry, Dairying) W. Europe, U.S.A. UPLAND SHEEP (Meat) S. New Zealand	SHEEP (Wool) S.W. & S.E. Australia, Veld – S. Africa CATTLE Texas – New Mexico	DAIRYING N. Japan, S.E. U.S.A., S.W. Australia FACTORY FARMING Poultry Dairying e.g. California SHEEP & GOATS Mediterranean	CATTLE (Beef, Hides) N.E. Brazil, Amazonia, Orinocco Lowlands, Queensland – Australia	DAIRYING Kenya, Zimbabwe
					*NOMADIC PASTORALISM – Sahara, Savanna – Africa	
	*NOMADIC REINDEER HERDING Finland		*NOMADIC PASTORALISM – N. Africa, Middle East			
MIXED (Livestock & Tillage) (Chains A & B)	MIXED W. European Lowlands, St Lawrence Lowland, S.E. Australia, Tasmania, Corn belt – U.S.A.		MIXED (Cotton, Tobacco with Livestock) S.E. U.S.A. (Wheat, Leys and Sheep) S. Australia, S. Brazil, C. Chile, Budapest Lowlands		MIXED (Maize, Millet, Legumes, Cattle) C. Africa, C. Brazil, Uruguay	
	*PEASANT SMALLHOLDINGS C. Europe, Appalachians		*PEASANT SMALLHOLDINGS S. Europe – Cereal Olives, Fruit, Sheep, Goats		SEMI-SUBSISTENCE Food crops, Livestock Cash crop e.g. Coffee E. Africa, Andes	
TILLAGE CROPS (Chain A)	ARABLE (Cereals, Roots) W. Europe Lowlands e.g. Fenlands	HORTICULTURE Netherlands, E. Coast U.S.A. MKT GARDENING Netherlands, E. Coast U.S.A., Urban Europe			MAIZE, TOBACCO, COTTON, FRUIT Zimbabwe, S. Brazil *SHIFTING AGRICULTURE Upland S.E. Asia C.W. Africa, Amazon	RICE Thailand, Burma, Japan WHEAT (irrigated) N. Punjab SEDENTARY HOE (Millet etc, Rice & Veg) S. China
					BUSH FALLOW C. Africa	
MONOCULTURE Plants, Trees, Shrubs (Chain A)	GRAIN Prairies, Pampas, U.S.S.R. Steppes	FRUIT (e.g. Cider Apples) U.K. VITICULTURE France	GRAIN Prairies, Veld – S. Africa, Steppe	RICE S. U.S.A. COTTON S. U.S.S.R.	PLANTATIONS (Coastal & accessible inland areas) (Sisal, Sugar, Pineapple, Rubber, Cacao, Palm Oil, Coconut, Bananas, Coffee, Tea, Cotton	*RICE Monsoon Asia

*SUBSISTENCE ORIENTATED

14   Von Thunen's 'Isolated State' Theory

ITS RELEVANCE TO FARMING SYSTEMS AND REGIONAL PATTERNS

So far we have been concerned to explore the nature of agriculture in its wider world context. But much of agricultural geography has been concerned with patterns on a regional and more localised scale. It would of course be feasible and useful to discuss these within the kind of comprehensive framework developed in the last chapter in which economic forces were seen as only one of a group of influences affecting the character and pattern of farming. But much of the literature centres on an essentially economic approach rooted in Von Thunen's 'Isolated State' theory which is concerned with how land-use patterns change with distance from a centrally located market.

For this reason it is worth exploring the kind of contribution this initially more narrowly based approach can make to both our understanding of different kinds of farming systems and patterns of land-use change at the regional level.

Von Thunen's land-use theory has been prominent in agricultural geography literature since the mid-1950s. It particularly helps to highlight how changes in supply and demand relative to cost and price variations, are reflected in spatial changes in land-use within the area serving a market.

The theory

Johanne Henrich Von Thunen lived in Germany from 1783 until 1850 and is noted for the first theory on the location of agricultural production. This was partly based on his studies of the work of economists such as Adam Smith and Albrecht Thaer and partly on his experience of owning and running his own landed estate of Tellow near Rostock in Mecklenburg from 1810 until his death. Thus his theory was both rooted in ideas from the classic economic theory of his day and worked out using data gained from running his own estate, including cost accounting over many years.

Assumptions underlying the theory

At the centre of Von Thunen's theory is the concept of the 'Isolierte Staat' — the idea of an isolated state in which there is only one market i.e. the central city and around it an extensive plain of tillable land of uniform physical character. The market is served by one mode of transport — horse and cart. The farmers occupying the land supply the central city and adjust their resources so as to meet any changes in demand.

Thunen made these assumptions to hold constant a number of the factors which normally contribute to the diversity of farming at a regional level, such as changes in soil fertility. But though holding these constant in order to focus attention on what he considered the most important variables affecting the locational pattern of agricultural production, he still clearly recognised that in the reality of any situation the varying effects of these other factors would also need to be taken into account. Assumptions would ultimately have to be relaxed to allow these factors some part in an explanation. Thus though adopting a narrower initial base than that outlined in the previous chapter, it is in fact nearer in spirit to this approach than first appears.

The other important thing to note is that he assumed farmers would respond to changes in the market situation. His was not the static theory some writers would have us believe. On the contrary, one of the greatest values of Von Thunen's work is not his visual presentation of concentric rings of different land-use round the central market (Fig. 14.1) but the fact that changes in market demand will bring ripples of change throughout the pattern of farming around the market as well as in the nature of the farming system characteristic of each zone of land-use. This he illustrated in a number of ways — the most commonly quoted being the effects of a secondary market introduced into a region and of another form of transport, namely water transport in addition to the horse and cart.

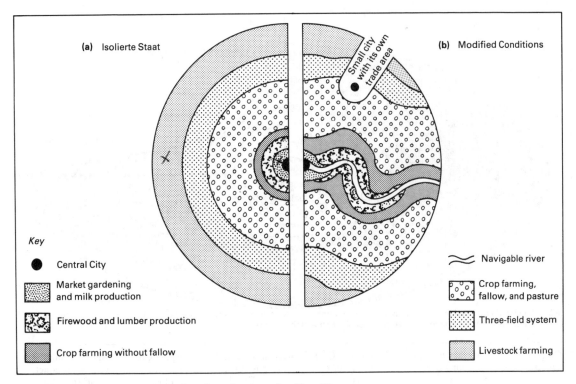

Key

● Central City

Market gardening
and milk production

Firewood and lumber production

Crop farming without fallow

(a) Isolierte Staat

(b) Modified Conditions

Small city with its own trade area

≈ Navigable river

Crop farming,
fallow, and pasture

Three-field system

Livestock farming

Fig. 14.1   The location of agricultural production after Von Thunen

But much greater in importance is Thunen's discussion of how the agland i.e. the cultivated land and its zones of land-use, would be extended as increasing population in the central city forced up the demand for agricultural foods. Change lies at the heart of Thunen's theory and it is this which makes his work of direct relevance to current discussions on farming patterns and systems.

Principles of his theory

The central relationships Thunen emphasised were to do with three variables (factors) — distance of farms from the market, the price received by farmers for their products and economic rent.

The relationship between *distance and market price* is in essence a simple one. The price a farmer obtained for any unit of his product was equal to its price at the market minus the cost of transporting it to the market. *Thus the nearer the farmer was to the market the greater his returns from the sale of his produce.* These high returns from land near the market and the greater competition for such land raising its price, encouraged farmers to make the most use of the land, thus land-use tended to be the most intensive near the market and decreased in intensity with distance away from it. A further factor leading to less intensive use of land away from the

market was that as transport costs increased with distance, so farmers could not afford to put the other amounts of inputs into farming which were necessary to give higher yields.

The other factor of *economic rent* was concerned with returns which could be obtained by putting land to a particular use. The return or economic rent could be calculated by subtracting production and transport costs from the revenue obtained from selling the produce at the market.

Formula: $V - (E + T) = P$

Where V is the value or revenue from the product, E is the production cost and T transport cost, whilst P is the net return profit or economic rent.

Since the market revenue or price on any product varied as did production and transport costs so would the returns or economic rent. Thus a farmer out to make maximum profits would choose that crop or combination of agricultural produce which would give the best economic rent.

But for any one crop or other produce, the economic rent gain on it would fall with distance from the market because whilst other costs and the price at the market remained constant, transport costs would rise. There would be diminishing returns with distance, until a point would be reached when it was not worth using the land for that crop. The margins of cultivation would have been reached. This is illustrated in Fig. 14.2 for certain sample crops.

133

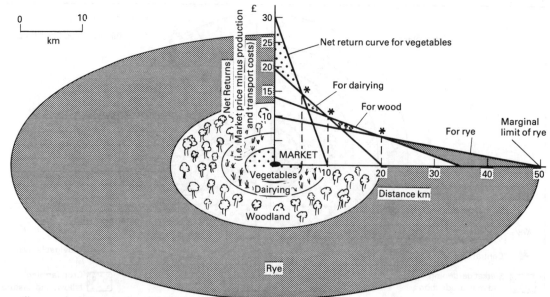

Note * Point of intersection of the two net revenue curves indicates the distance from the market at which it is profitable to change land use in favour of that product giving the higher return.

Crop or Product	Market Revenue or Price (V)	Production Cost per Hectare (E)	Return without Transport Cost (V–E)	Transport Cost per km (T)	Marginal limit of crop or product (km from the market)
Vegetables	60	30	30	3.00	10
Dairying	45	25	20	1.00	20
Wood	24	10	14	0.40	35
Rye	15	5	10	0.20	50

Fig. 14.2   Declining returns (economic rent) with distance from market for selected land uses

Patterns of land-use round the market

As we have seen, the pattern of land-use was dependent on the relative returns which each agricultural product could command with distance from the market. At any particular distance those agricultural products giving the highest returns would relegate other usages to an outer zone. This process can be represented graphically and diagrammatically by taking successive examples of products and land-use zones nearest the market. (Fig. 14.2)

When we look at the zonation in more detail we note that these are not only distinguished by differences in what is produced but also by the system under which production occurs. Different combinations of inputs were used and different kinds of crop rotations adopted both to maximise returns and maintain the land in a state of good fertility.

Exercise

With reference to Fig. 14.2 what would be the effect on mariginal crop/product limits given a) a 10% rise in market revenue whilst costs remained unchanged, and b) a tax of 20% on transport charges?

The scale of farming also had changed, becoming more extensive with distance from the market. This was because to compensate for increased transport costs, not only those of getting produce to market but also cost of transport for inputs to the farm such as seed, fertilizer and labour, the farmer had to cut down on the amount of some inputs purchased. This inevitably led to lower yields per unit of area of land farmed. But the farmer could still maintain his overall profit by farming more land. This was possible because land was both cheaper and more plentiful away from the market — hence farms were larger.

The main features of each zone starting with that nearest the market were as follows (refer to Fig 14.1):

1 *Intensive dairying and market gardening* — fresh milk and vegetables are required constantly in the city. Given their perishability and the slow means of cartage they had to be produced close to the market. Prices therefore had to be high enough to make it profitable for farmers close to the market to go in for dairying and market gardening rather than any other land-use. Thus in effect dairying and fresh vegetable production gave the highest returns and therefore yielded the highest economic rent.

2 In Thunen's time *wood* was also needed constantly for fuel, building and other purposes. Silviculture for wood production then occupied the second zone because of this need and because of the cost of transporting such a bulky good. Also silviculture yielded a higher rent, since trees produce a high bulk of product for each unit of land occupied.

3 Beyond the woodland lay three zones in which *rye* from which bread was made was one of the most important crops.

The difference between the three zones lay in the system under which rye and associated crops such as flax were cultivated. To offset distance cost and maximise returns the type of crop rotation varied and the intensive land-use declined from the nearer to the outer of the three zones. Thus an intensive arable zone with a six fold rotation, no fallow and stall fed cattle, was followed by a less intensive arable zone with some fallow and then ultimately an extensive three field system with more land given over each year to fallow and more pasture.

4 Finally at the outermost edge of the cultivated land came an area of *livestock farming*. Here the distance was so great that even the most extensive and cost saving method of rye production could not yield a sufficiently high rent to make it worthwhile transporting it to market. Instead it was produced on the farm to feed livestock and the animal products were marketed. Livestock for meat was sent on the hoof thus saving transport costs, while such products as cheese and butter were small in bulk and therefore relatively cheap to transport compared to the favourable price received for them on the market.

However, apart from some appreciation of the way zonation occurred the other important point to note is that the extent and location of the zones changed over time. Demand for any agricultural product varied and hence the price changed. Also costs varied, thus economic rent changed for one product as against another. Therefore as today a farmer at any one location would respond by changing to that crop or combination of agricultural products which would give the highest returns. Thus the limit of each zonation would fluctuate over time.

Overall what generally happened over a period of time was that the margins of farming were pushed outward. For as population increased, demand for food and other agricultural produce rose, pushing up market prices, making it profitable and necessary to extend the margins of farming. More land was brought under cultivation — the agland (farmed area) was extended and the limits of each zone in it also pushed outwards as rippling effects of rising demand made themselves felt through the entire farming area.

Eventually there would come a point where all the needs of a region's population could not be met from the land around and some agricultural produce had to be imported. Thus in effect the outer limit of the agland was extended to take in land beyond the state. Hence some writers have seen present zonations at a much larger scale as a reflection of the continuing influence of the basic principles which Thunen outlined in his theory. For example the extensive wheatlands of the prairies of North America are seen as part of the outer zone of agriculture serving West European markets.

The value of Thunen's work

Times and methods of farming have changed but some of the important principles recognised by Thunen remain. It matters not that we can no longer really recognise concentric zonation around a central market except in the simplest of farming economies — usually those under subsistence agriculture in the tropics and in some Mediterranean lands (see Chapter 15). As Thunen himself pointed out, even in his day there were modifying influences — a number of markets had to be served not one, transport methods and accessibility varied and outside competition made inroads into the potential markets threatening home produce. Physical variations also interrupt the postulated ideal zonation of land-use. Thus today we should not expect a simple zonation pattern in any region but only some semblance towards one (Fig. 14.3).

Distance from market does still influence the relative location of different crops and particular agricultural products. There is still for example a tendency for liquid milk production and market gardening to be dominant only where there is quick access to markets, albeit that technological advances have distorted the actual location pattern giving locations both physically close to the market and others further away. Extensive farming of non-perishable crops such as grain is mainly carried out

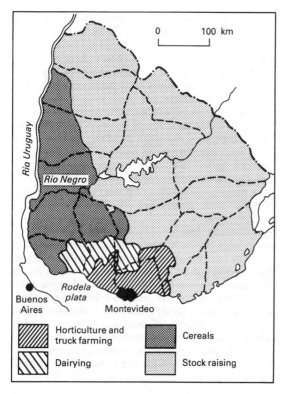

Scale: 0 — 100 km

Rio Uruguay

Rio Negro

Rodela
plata

Buenos
Aires

Montevideo

| Horticulture and truck farming | Cereals |
| Dairying | Stock raising |

Fig. 14.3 Land use in Uruguay (after Griffin)

at a further distance from markets. Whilst some cereal growing it is true does take place in Western Europe for example, the bulk of the grain supplies come from extensive producers like those of the American prairies.

Further, as Thunen indicated, any particular crop can still be grown under different farming systems with the production inputs including land being altered to compensate for other increased costs. For example as we have just seen, wheat is intensively cultivated under a mixed arable system in the lowlands of Western Europe such as East Anglia with high yields per unit area, whereas the same crop is grown under a mono-culture system and much more extensively in the poorer lands of the continental interiors. Here lower yields are compensated for by lower production costs especially labour and by much larger size of farm holding. Again the keeping of beef cattle can be done under a more intensive mixed system including some stall feeding as in the

north east United States and English Midlands, or under extensive ranching as in Queensland, and on the pampas of South America, where the farming system is very different. In each case the different producers are reacting in the most appropriate way to general market conditions as well as to the economic and physical conditions of the particular region in which they find themselves.

Moreover just as in Thunen's time changes in market demand brought changes in methods and the overall pattern of farming, so this is evident today. As we have seen Thunen demonstrated quite clearly that as population rose the growth in demand could only be met in two ways. First the yields could be increased on existing agricultural lands by improvements in farming and secondly new land could be taken in with successive zones of cultivation being pushed progressively outwards. Both are very much in evidence today prompted by rapidly rising demand. In the developing world this comes from a sheer increase in the number of mouths to be fed as in India and China, whilst in the developed world it is prompted by rising affluence.

The forwardness of Thunen's thinking is even further emphasised if we conclude with some brief observations on the second and much less publicised part of his text 'The Isolated State'. For though social and political influences are more important today than in the 19th century, Thunen in Part 2 of his writing, centres on such issues. He discussed for example how a natural (just) wage could be arrived at and made the point that capital spent on working class education is repaid at ample interest by the workers' higher productivity. He brings in other current issues in farming such as the effects of increased taxation and of competition from imports. Thus Thunen not only saw man as economic man making rational decisions in response to changes in supply and demand, but also as part of society and subject to its social and political influences.

Above all Von Thunen recognised change as a fundamental fact of life; he lived like us in a period of change. These were part of wider changes which had been going on for some time, part of a modernisation process which continues to the present, both in the developed and developing world. Change in systems and patterns of farming are part of this process. Thus the work of Von Thunen in its wider and more dynamic interpretation can also help to shed some light on the different systems of farming discussed more fully in the remainder of this section on agriculture.

15 Tropical Farming Systems

Subsistence farming

Shifting agriculture

Despite its declining importance it was estimated in 1970 that approximately 200 million people were still dependent on some form of shifting agriculture. As Fig. 15.1 shows it is practised extensively in the tropics taking up about one third of the world's cultivable soils. The systems vary from one continent to another and within one continent from region to region. It is most widespread in Africa where it is commonly called Chitimene. In South East Asia the term Swidden is used to distinguish it from sedentary rice agriculture. In Latin America shifting agriculture also takes place under different regional names, e.g. Milpa in Mexico and Roca in Brazil.

Characteristics

Before rising population pressures and increasing shortage of land combined to force on most shifting agriculturalists some modification in the system they practised, shifting agriculture in its classical form was extremely well adapted to the environmental conditions in which it took place. Following clearance of a small area of tribal territory and its use for a number of years, the clearing and settlement were abandoned for a long period, somewhere in the region of 20 years, to allow the natural regeneration of vegetation and a restoration of fertility before the soil was used again.

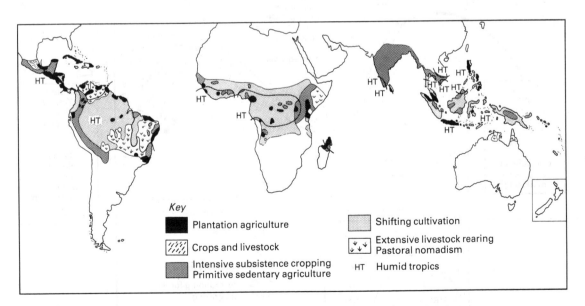

Fig. 15.1   *Land use patterns in the humid tropics*

15:1 NEW GUINEA HIGHLANDS

The Chimbu agricultural system

Illustrated from part of the Chimbu Territory held by the Naregu Tribe

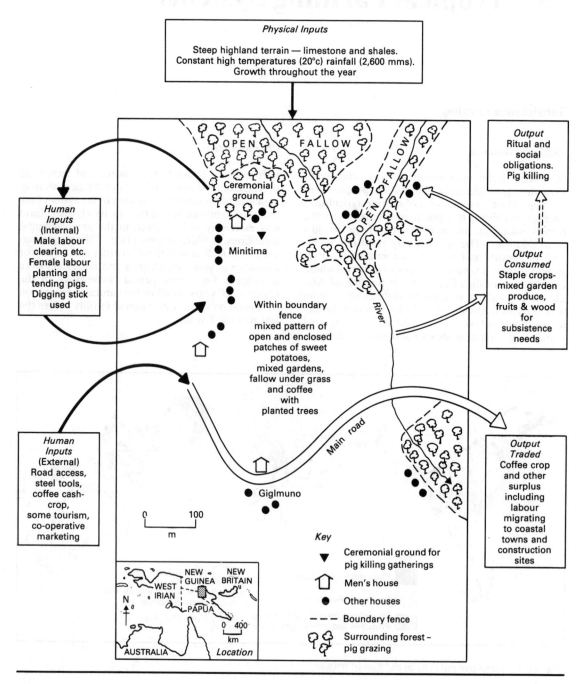

Physical Inputs

Steep highland terrain — limestone and shales.
Constant high temperatures (20°c) rainfall (2,600 mms).
Growth throughout the year

Human Inputs (Internal)
Male labour clearing etc. Female labour planting and tending pigs. Digging stick used

Human Inputs (External)
Road access, steel tools, coffee cash-crop, some tourism, co-operative marketing

OPEN FALLOW

Ceremonial ground

Minitima

OPEN FALLOW

River

Within boundary fence mixed pattern of open and enclosed patches of sweet potatoes, mixed gardens, fallow under grass and coffee with planted trees

Main road

Giglmuno

0 100
m

Output
Ritual and social obligations. Pig killing

Output Consumed
Staple crops- mixed garden produce, fruits & wood for subsistence needs

Output Traded
Coffee crop and other surplus including labour migrating to coastal towns and construction sites

Location

NEW GUINEA   NEW BRITAIN
WEST IRIAN
PAPUA
0 400
km
AUSTRALIA

Key

▼ Ceremonial ground for pig killing gatherings

⌂ Men's house

● Other houses

--- Boundary fence

Surrounding forest - pig grazing

MAIN ECONOMIC AND SOCIAL CHARACTERISTICS

Land and food crops
Land is held communally but cultivated by individual families on a 6-8 year cycle followed by fallow. Mixed 'garden' — intercropping of staple foods of yam and cassava with taro beans, green veg. and sugar cane — supplemented by bananas and other tree fruits.

Dominance of the pig killing cycle in their culture and way of life
800 pigs are grazed and fattened for periodic ceremonial gathering kills and to meet social obligations. Pig production is the fundamental basis of interpersonal and group relations.

A. TRADITIONAL FEATURES

Traditional tension between food and pig production as pig population encroaches on crop land.

Competition — for land between food and cash crops.

INCREASING PRESSURES AND TENSIONS

Incompatability of the traditional way of life with an imported money economy and outside job opportunities.

Increased medical facilities caused rising population pressure from 100 to 200 per sq km. This is overtaxing land, shortening fallow period, soil exhaustion and erosion occurring.

B. EXTERNALLY INTRODUCED FEATURES

Introduction of a coffee cash crop and market sale of surplus food with outside advice and through an introduced cooperative system.

Additional income from entertaining tourists with tribal dances and other customs etc.

Yields were low and methods perhaps in economic terms inefficient, compared to other systems. But shifting agriculture supplemented by hunting and gathering was sufficient to maintain a small population given a plentiful supply of land.

The whole practice of shifting agriculture is closely bound up with the cultural traditions of a tribe and the individual groups practising it. Despite the low level of agriculture output achieved, much human energy and a substantial proportion of the output were regularly diverted to satisfy social obligations and towards the observance of tribal rituals. Any assessment therefore of shifting agriculture must have regard to this important fact. It was not simply a means of keeping alive, but also a way of life. No serious modification of it could take place without having repercussions on the culture of the people practising it.

Everywhere today however this traditional way of living is under threat. In some locations such as Thailand the practice of it has been made illegal because it is considered incompatible with other uses of the forest land where it is practised and detrimental to the environment. In other areas, outside influences and the increasing population numbers which have to be supported are drastically changing it both as an agricultural system and as a way of life. The incompatibility between a traditional way of life practised for centuries and the trappings of the 20th century with which it is now forcibly in contact, raise serious questions and dilemmas which should occupy the minds of geographers as well as others concerned and interested in the ways and rights of different peoples.

The Case Study of the Chimbu economy and culture in the New Guinea highlands highlights some of the features associated with this kind of subsistence agriculture and the problems associated with change.

Subsistence rice culture

The staple food grain of Monsoon Asia

Most of the population living in the wet tropics particularly in Monsoon Asia depend upon rice as their staple food crop. China and India with the world's largest populations, 1000 and 712 millions respectively, produce half of the world's rice which is used almost exclusively for home consumption. Rice is essentially a subsistence crop, at the basis of a farming system almost as ancient as shifting agriculture. Apart from internal domestic trade to meet needs in the rapidly growing towns, rice is commercially important only to Burma and Thailand in the tropics, though rice is also of some commercial importance to countries such as the U.S.A., Australia, France and Italy where it is grown under irriga-

tion. The main areas in the U.S.A. are the Gulf Coast and Southern California; in Australia the Murray-Murrumbidgee basin; in Italy the Valley of the Po and in France towards the mouth of the Rhone.

Japan has traditionally been seen as one of the main subsistence rice regions, but in Japan today rice is grown intensively increasingly using modern methods and mainly as a cash crop to be sold on the home market. The bulk of Japan's population is now urbanised, with approximately two thirds in the Industrial Pacific Belt centred on Tokyo, Kobe and Osaka. Only a small proportion of the rice grown is consumed on the farms.

Just as with shifting agriculture, rice farming systems vary from region to region, but the broad distinction is that between unirrigated upland rice, frequently grown as well by shifting agriculturalists in Monsoon Asia, and lowland rice or paddy which is grown under irrigation and gives a much higher yield. This is the rice which supports the high concentrations of rural population on the well watered alluvial valleys and coastal plains of India, China and other monsoon countries.

The many varieties of rice within each of these two broad divisions have been added to by the new hybrid varieties developed as part of the Green Revolution. New hybrids have not only complicated farming patterns in traditional areas such as the Ganges plain in India, but also extended the crop's climatic limits, since some of the new varieties require a shorter growing period and can withstand more severe conditions than established types of paddy. For example in Japan rice can be grown as far north as Hokkaido in temperate latitudes, whilst the shorter growing season required allows a more widespread use of multi-cropping. Thus both in terms of area under cultivation and total yields rice is more important than ever.

Characteristics of paddy farming systems

Paddy farming is an intensive system, farming units being small frequently under 1 hectare and fragmented into scattered strips, except where land reforms have led to some consolidation and rationalisation as in Japan and China. Labour inputs are high, a heavy dependence being placed on unpaid family labour, with limited hired help. In relation to this high labour intensity, capital inputs such as fertilizers and insecticides are limited. All these inputs are carefully regulated by the marked seasonal rhythm which holds sway over rice cultivation.

Climatic inputs are commonly and loosely generalised as those of a monsoon regime, that is high temperatures and a marked seasonal incidence of rainfall. But wherever temperatures exceed 20°C in the growing season and there is an abundant supply of moisture, rice can be grown; as is shown for example by the increasing area under rice in the equatorial coastlands of West Africa and Brazil. The length of growing season needed varies with the types of rice ranging from three to eight months.

Though alluvial lowlands such as the Mekong River Basin in Vietnam are eminently suitable, rice is reasonably tolerant of soil conditions. As long as the soil is moisture retentive it will grow in both medium and heavy soils where the land is naturally level or has been terraced to allow flooding of paddy fields in the growing season and the general control of the water supply.

These physical conditions combined with a high labour input per unit of cultivated area underlie the intensive nature of the system. Yields from each unit area under rice vary considerably. It is much higher in the more mechanised rice growing areas outside the tropics such as the Gulf Coast of the U.S.A. than in the traditional rice lowlands of South East Asia. This is generally because more advanced countries make use of larger amounts of capital inputs like fertilizers and herbicides. These more scientific methods help to give yields as much as 8 to 10 times those in subsistence rice areas. But the more widespread use of new hybrid varieties together with more capital inputs is markedly improving yields.

Impact of the Green Revolution

One of the major problems in the tropics is the increasing pressure population growth is bringing on food supplies. Because the amount of new land which can be brought under cultivation is severely limited, strenuous efforts have been made to find new strains of cereals, especially rice and maize which will mature in a shorter time and give much higher yields than traditional varieties. Though pioneered initially by American researchers in Mexico to improve yields of wheat and maize, the 'Green Revolution' as it is called has come to be particularly associated with improving rice yields in Monsoon Asia. In the 1960s the International Rice Research Institute (I.R.R.A.) was set up in the Philippines under the auspices of the World Food and Agricultural Organisation.

Its most widespread impact has been in India and Pakistan, but the term 'Green Revolution' has also come to be associated with the adoption of any new techniques and crop varieties in the tropical world. For example it covers improvements in countries like Japan and China which have not been part of the F.A.O. programme.

In respect of subsistence rice farming, two important aspects of the Green Revolution need to be noted. Firstly because of the nature of the new high yielding varieties of rice, their use has far reaching consequences for not only farming methods, but also the social structure of rice communities. Secondly whilst in some areas it can dramatically improve yields it is really only the more prosperous farmers who could afford to adopt the new strains. Traditional rice growing still persists among the mass of poorer rice farmers who paradoxically need most of all to increase their farm yields. Thus contrasts are heightened rather than reduced. Farmers using the new strains must adopt a whole package of measures such as addition of artificial fertilizers, a carefully controlled water supply and the use of insecticides. Earlier efforts to diffuse the new innovations across the whole community have petered out in many areas.

In the 1960s, where the new hybrid strains were used the result was little short of spectacular. The total planted rose from 49 000 hectares in 1965 to 16 million hectares in 1973, mainly in Pakistan, India, Sri Lanka. Yields were on average 50% higher than those for traditional varieties. But as Dr. Chandler director of R.I.I.A. warned, the new hybrids were only 'miraculous in so far as they could be protected from disease, received appropriate amounts of fertilizer, carefully controlled irrigation water and adequate drainage'.

Apart from cost being a limiting factor, these conditions could only be met where areas had irrigation and adequate drainage facilities. Areas were unsuitable where rice was dependent on natural rainfall or on limited watering from small village tanks. Moreover fragmented holdings had to be rationalised and this meant in effect land reform measures from which the richer farmers benefited most because they had influence in the community and the money to buy out poorer farmers. Thus despite the funded aid and technical help fed in by organisations such as U.S.A.I.D. (United States Agency for International Development) the Green Revolution has brought with it serious economic and social problems, raising yields overall but not benefiting enough those in real need.

Ingrid Palmer in her study of the 'Green Revolution' for the United Nations Research Institute for Social Development points to the break up of the old communal farming and village system in many of the areas affected by it. Moreover she claims too much attention has been given to improving cereal yields which are high in carbohydrates and not enough to improving crops rich in protein such as peas, beans and other pulses. Yet ironically the diet of most people in the tropics is seriously lacking in protein content.

Moreover Palmer and others claim that the real problem is not an overall shortage of food but the difficulty of distributing the right balance of food to where it is needed. There is not the infrastructure required to do this. Finance should be made available to improve distribution and marketing methods

15:2 BANGLADESH

Rice culture

Rice is the dominant crop in all the farming systems except shifting subsistence and tea areas in the Chittagong Hills. There are three main seasonal crops of rice — aman, aus and boro.

Though mainly a subsistence crop there are cash sales to help meet debts, social obligations and buy

essentials. The amount of other cash cropping depends on physical conditions, size of holding and tenancy conditions — land let out on a share crop basis by absentee landlords may have significant cash cropping.

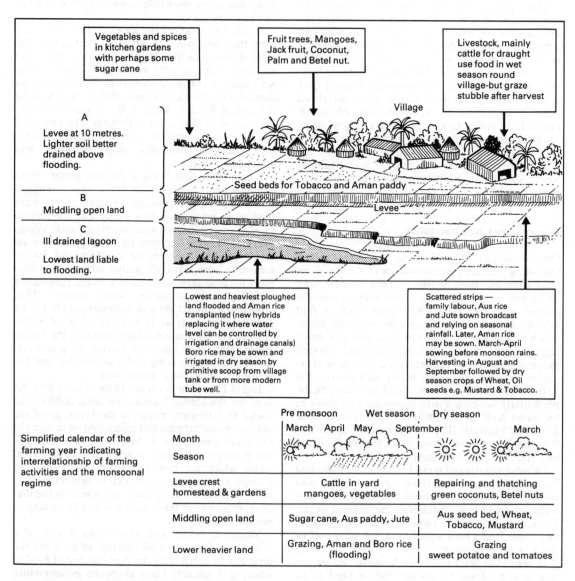

Agriculture in a village on the Lower Delta Region

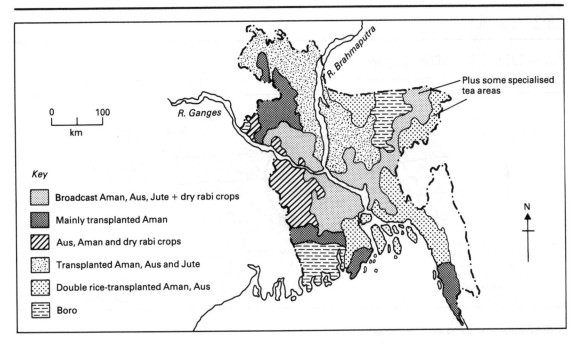

Agricultural regions

Key

- Broadcast Aman, Aus, Jute + dry rabi crops
- Mainly transplanted Aman
- Aus, Aman and dry rabi crops
- Transplanted Aman, Aus and Jute
- Double rice-transplanted Aman, Aus
- Boro

Plus some specialised tea areas

R. Brahmaputra

R. Ganges

0   100
km

N

AREA AND PRODUCTION 1973-78 (annual av.)		
Rice Type	Area (000 ha)	Production (000 tonnes)
Aman	5705	6923
Aus	3219	3049
Boro	1062	2163

THE NEED TO INCREASE AGRICULTURAL OUTPUT

Bangladesh is a low income country basically dependent on agriculture. It has a population of 95 million at a crude density of 650 per sq km and an annual average increase in population of 2.1%

WAYS OF INCREASING OUTPUT

1 Green Revolution — introduced new high yielding varieties and better techniques.

2 Consolidation of land holdings and land reform needed to benefit from new methods.

3 Poorer farmers need access — at present they have insufficient finance and education. Richer farmers hold the power at village level and 'corner' benefits for themselves.

4 Water supplies vital — government concentrated on redistributing available surface water and flood control including incursions of saline water in the lower delta. Only a quarter of the land can be irrigated in the dry season. Extension would effectively increase the acreage cropped — diesel pumping of groundwater could irrigate 1 million more hectares. Better canal distribution of river water needed e.g. Ganges — Kabadak scheme will irrigate 90 000 ha in the Kush district. Tube wells to tap groundwater on hill margins e.g. in northern district of Dinajpur could enable double rice cropping.

5 Adequate drainage needed as without it intensification of irrigation produces hard panning, increased soil salinity and declining yields.

Exercise

● Why is rice the staple crop of Bangladesh and what are the problems associated with expanding output?

15:3 NIGERIA

Fulani pastoralism, a changing way of life

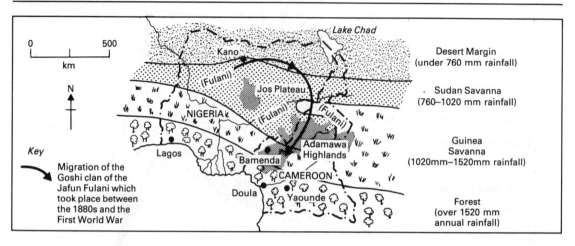

Cattle Fulani in Nigeria and Cameroon

Map labels: Lake Chad; Kano; (Fulani); Jos Plateau; NIGERIA; (Fulani); (Fulani); (Fulani); Adamawa Highlands; Lagos; Bamenda; CAMEROON; Doula; Yaounde

Desert Margin (under 760 mm rainfall)

Sudan Savanna (760–1020 mm rainfall)

Guinea Savanna (1020mm–1520mm rainfall)

Forest (over 1520 mm annual rainfall)

Key

Migration of the Goshi clan of the Jafun Fulani which took place between the 1880s and the First World War

BASIC CHARACTERISTICS OF FULANI PASTORALISM

The Fulani pastoralists' way of life and wealth are based on livestock. They have traditionally migrated seasonally with herds of cattle, also sheep and goats. The general direction has been Eastward across the Savanna and after harvest and with the onset of the dry season Southward away from the drier Savanna and onto stubble land in search of pasture. In exchange for use of the Hausa people's farmland, the fertility of the soil was annually renewed by the manure droppings of the livestock. The relationship was thus mutually beneficial to the two groups.

To supplement the staple diet based on milk, the Fulani sold butter etc. in the local markets in exchange for corn, rice, tea and coffee.

Periodic drought e.g. in 1983, and rinderpest could decimate herds and now increasing population pressure and the extension of farmland under irrigation has so reduced the opportunities for migration that apart from the Bororo, most Fulani are semi or permanently settled, growing crops as well as keeping livestock.

THE CHANGING ECONOMY AND WAY OF LIFE OF THE GOSHI — FULANI, NORTHERN CAMEROONS

The Goshi — a clan of the Jafun Fulani adopted a settled way of life earlier than most groups.

Originating from the Kano region they had by the 1920s settled in the Bamenda Grasslands, living alongside farming groups. Migration of livestock was limited to short distance moves.

The Goshi have had links with Europeans from this time with veterinary and cattle control officers advising on stock and grazing. After the Second World War strong support and encouragement from Cameroon government and external agencies e.g. World Bank to improve breeds, pasture and grow fodder for dry season. The ultimate aim as elsewhere was to settle the Fulani on cattle ranches to produce beef etc. for a growing population and urban market.

The Goshi people have increasingly been drawn into a moneyed economy — grazing cattle for rich urban based owners, regularly marketing cattle in the commercial centre and port of Doula. Cement dwellings are replacing traditional ones. The more wealthy own vehicles, cash purchases are made e.g. of imported tinned food and clothing.

There has also been some drift of Fulani youth to the towns.

Exercise

● Discuss the prospects in tropical areas, for increasing the supply of meat and other livestock produce by improving methods in existing livestock areas and opening up new lands.

and to help the poorer farmers improve their own output by educating them in such things as more efficient use of traditional methods and better storage of harvest surpluses. Also the increase in demand needs to be checked by further encouraging methods of population control. Surprisingly India, one of the countries with the most serious population problem, has had a total surplus of rice. Yet because of the shortcomings in the pricing system, distribution and marketing, millions still go hungry.

There are signs that the initial euphoria associated with the 'Green Revolution' has given way to a more balanced appraisal of its effects and the recognition of the need for more comprehensive measures of benefit to the poorest sectors of the populations in developing countries. Attention too has turned towards ways of improving agriculture in the semi-arid tropics, thus increasing the area under cultivation.

Rice growing in Bangladesh

Bangladesh is one of the most densely populated countries with 93 million people and an annual growth rate of 2.5% per annum. The importance of rice in the country's economy and as the basic food of most of the population is shown in Case Study 15.2 on p. 142. The main characteristics of the rice farming system are summarised and ways of improving output, including control of essential water supplies, are also indicated.

Pastoral nomadism and semi-nomadism

Though of declining importance, pastoral nomadism is still significant in the semi-humid tropics where conditions are unfavourable to crop growing. The classic definition of the term nomadism is that by Richthofen (1908).

Nomadism occurs in desert, savanna and steppeland regions when the whole tribe migrates with the herd according to marked seasonal variations in rainfall and in search of the basic fodder requirements of cattle, sheep, goats and camels. Individual families own no land, but the territory is held communally by the group. No cultivation of crops is undertaken, the group depending on what their livestock can provide apart from some occasional barter.

Such a definition would fit the old way of life of the Bedouin nomads on the Sahara fringes, the Khirghiz of the Asiatic Steppe and the Masai of the East African Plateau land. But in these and other cases, external influences and pressures are leading to a breakdown of this traditional way of life. For example, migration across national frontiers like those of the Fulbe or Fulani of West Africa (see Case Study 15.3 opposite) has been made illegal. Nomads have been encouraged to adopt a more settled way of life, advice and financial help being given to improve livestock, grazing and the growing of crops. Pure nomadism as described by Richthofen no longer exists as there are hardly any nomads who do not have some relationship with agriculture.

Tropical commercial farming

The character of tropical cash crop farming has changed substantially in the post-colonial period. Previously most of it was under European control to supply export markets in Western Europe and other parts of the developed world. But much of it is now under the control of the indigenous peoples with an increasing proportion of the agricultural output being absorbed within the tropics as populations increase, incomes rise and more and more people move into the towns.

Nationalisation and land reform measures have led to increasingly more land being taken from Europeans and returned to the local people. Some of this is still organised on plantation lines, much of it is linked to co-operatives or farmed as small cash crop holdings. But we begin this section by looking briefly at commercial livestock farming in the tropics, which still remains largely in the hands of white landowners or controlled by foreign companies in association with the governments concerned.

Commercial livestock farming

In tropical areas experiencing savanna conditions and where Europeans have settled, livestock farming has become important, for example beef rearing in North Australia. The Llanos area of the Orinocco Plains in Venezuela and Colombia, a region where strenuous efforts are being made to re-establish cattle ranching as part of a more general attempt to assist rural development and bring about a more balanced population distribution, is looked at in detail in the following Case Study.

The market for livestock produce is likely to be increasingly found within the tropics. Population and demand are growing here, whilst in the West, tropical livestock produce has to compete with much greater supplies from temperate farming areas. These have the advantage of more suitable environmental conditions and better proximity to markets in the industrialised countries. There is the further problem for tropical producers that some countries, in particular EEC members, are adopting more protective tariff and quota measures to help home livestock producers.

15:4 VENEZUELA

Beef rearing and fattening on the Llanos

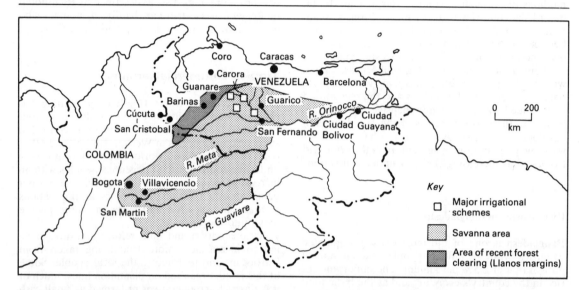

The Venezuelan and Colombia Llanos, a beef cattle and rearing region

Environmental conditions

Savanna but rainfall reliability and length of wet season vary — most favoured is the foot zone of Northern Highlands where cattle can be fattened.

African grasses introduced in the colonial period giving good pasture in belt 300-400 km wide along Orinocco and tributaries.

Recent improvements

(Part of general effort to diffuse growth). Pasture and fodder for dry season improved by well sinking and irrigation schemes extending fattening areas — main one in NW Llanos — Guarico government project 100 000 ha.

—Flood control on lower riverine plains.

—Control of malaria and cattle diseases.

—Improvement of herds by introducing more disease resistant Brahmin and San Gertrudis cattle stock.

Communication network

Communication especially by road greatly improved linking the region to markets in the North and the new industrial regions of the East.

Re-activation of historical pastoral economy

Long been cattle trade to Northern cities and export trade in hides and live cattle to West Indies with demand in plantation economy there. But Llanos pastoral economy collapsed early this century following Civil War.

Reactivated after Second World War to reduce population pressures in North and over-concentration on oil etc. in the North. Overall regional planning policy to expand agriculture, exploit minerals and develop industry on Lower Orinocco.

Italians, Spanish and also Venezuelan peasants encouraged to settle under regional development schemes.

Markets rapidly expanding.

In industrialised North — Caracas etc. and in new industrial centres on Llanos itself e.g. Cuidad Bolivar — further growth anticipated but limited export trade success as yet.

Exercise

● Discuss the factors for and against extension of livestock farming in the tropics.

Cash cropping in the tropics

Cash cropping in the tropics and sub-tropics is usually associated with plantations but plantation agriculture has declined relatively and absolutely, since the Second World War. It is being replaced by an extension of cash crop farming on native small holdings and medium sized enterprises, under the control of local people with strong government support. This can be illustrated from Malaysia, where rubber production was once dominated by European owned and managed plantations. Most rubber now comes from the small holding sector and even in the reduced estate sector most estates are owned and managed by non-Europeans.

	Malaysian Rubber Industry			
	Estate Sector		Small Holdings Sector	
	1970	1979	1970	1979
(Area 1000 hectares)	679	558	1334	1474
Production (1000 tonnes)	631	643	638	943

Source: *Standard Bank Review* p. 5. December 1980.

Apart from the political unpopularity of European managed plantations in countries now free from colonial rule there are other reasons why cash farming is coming to be more fully associated with native farming systems — peasant farmers increasingly need a cash income as they are drawn into a money economy and there is a growing domestic market to be served. For example of the shift towards cash crop farming in the humid savanna belt of West Africa, Burnham writes: 'The popularity of high yielding crops such as manioc, maize and yams in the lightly to moderately populated humid savanna zone is not simply a matter of adequately provisioning the producer societies with food. Increasingly over the last few decades these food crops have been produced in surplus for the national market.' Integration of the traditional farming system into the market economy and wider definition of what is meant by cash cropping to include the cash sale of staple food crops are both important.

Whilst the demand overseas for tropical foods and agricultural raw materials may fluctuate and competition for these markets has been intensified, it is still very substantial. Moreover many tropical countries continue to rely heavily on earnings from agricultural exports to advanced industrial countries and the newly industrialising countries of the tropics to pay for their essential imports. Thus whilst home markets may be increasingly important, cash farmers, whatever the organisational system under which they operate, will have to continue to compete in these overseas markets with plantation crops produced under European management.

Though there are a variety of agricultural holdings producing cash crops in the tropics ranging from the small native holding to plantations, here we concentrate on two main types.

Plantation cash cropping

Despite its declining contribution, the plantation system still remains important. Plantations were initially established to supply developed countries with certain luxury foods and beverages and raw materials which could only be produced under tropical conditions but which established farming systems were unable to produce in sufficient quantity or of a consistently high quality. As they needed large areas of land, yet accessibility to shipment points, plantations were established on thinly settled islands and coastal locations.

The classic definition of a plantation is that by Waibel (1933): 'The plantation is a large scale agricultural and industrial enterprise producing high value vegetable products, usually under the management of Europeans; and involving great investment in labour and capital equipment.' It may be added that plantations were usually mono-culture i.e. producing only one crop, so as to gain benefits from specialisation and large scale operations. The amount of processing of the crop before shipment varied with the crop, bananas clearly requiring no processing whilst rubber requires a considerable amount, as does sugar.

However, today the character of plantations has changed. Cultivation methods have been developed to take account of the need to maintain soil fertility and there has in many cases been some diversification of cropping patterns. Cocoa and oil palm are now intercropped in Ghana and Nigeria for example whilst, in the states of Parana and Sao Paulo in Brazil, livestock farming is associated with some coffee fazendas.

Larger plantations characteristically include facilities for the workers and their families such as schooling and medical facilities. In addition most have a garden patch on which to grow staple food crops and in order to keep their workers many owners allow some cash cropping to supplement plantation wages. In some areas this helps maintain a labour supply which might otherwise be attracted by higher wages in the city as for example in Malaysia.

But the value of the plantation system as opposed to smaller systems under non-European control has been a subject of considerable debate in recent years. The pros and cons are summarised in Fig. 15.2 and on balance it seems that essentially for social and political reasons, the plantation system

ADVANTAGES	DISADVANTAGES
High quality products due to better management and more scientific methods	Much of revenue goes out of the country
	Unfair competition for small holders wanting to develop cash farming, especially as much of the marketing system is controlled by the multinationals
Of a scale to meet rising demands in advanced countries for tropical agricultural products	
Opened up new areas and aided overall development	Initially overexploited and exhausted land under mono-culture
Provision of infrastructure including communication and port outlets	Reliance of region on export of narrow range of agricultural products, neglect of basic food crops and economic dependency on importing countries
Some diffusion of new techniques, encouragement of cash crop farming in area around	Disruptive and divisive of indigenous social system — leading to a dual system, firstly of areas under some plantation/western orientated system based on money income, with import of other ethnic labour e.g. negroes and secondly other usually remoter areas under old subsistence systems and a traditional culture
Cash income for workers encourages local market economy	

Fig. 15.2 The plantation system — for and against

will continue to decline though its final demise is a long way off as is illustrated from the study below of the place of transnational companies in the plantation system.

The role of transnationals in the banana industry

It is rather indicative of expanding food consumption in the tropical regions themselves that of the 39 million metric tonnes of bananas produced just over one fifth (7.1 million) enters world trade. Banana exports come mainly from certain Latin American –

Caribbean countries which are heavily dependent on this trade.

But this trade and the plantations on which the bananas are produced are controlled by three large American transnationals.

Efforts have been made by the governments of some of the main producing companies to gain a larger control of the production and trade in bananas. A union of Banana Exporting Countries (Ubec) has been set up and the Banana Multinational Marketing Company (Comunbanana) was established in 1977 with the aim of opening up markets in Eastern Europe. But the expertise and financial

Company	Owning plantations in	Workers	Commercial activities
Castle & Cook Incorp. operating as *Standard Fruit & Steamship Co.* centred on Hawaii	Panama, Costa Rica, Honduras, Liberia, Brazil	20 000 full time & 12 000 seasonal workers	Fresh foods (one third is bananas) Processed foods and manufacturing
Del Monte Corp. (Taken over by R.J. Reynolds)	Mainly Costa Rica, Guatemala 65 000 acres in all	43 000 full time up to 33 000 seasonal	Processed food and fresh fruit. Land and sea transport. Institutional services
United Brands Company merger of A.M.K. Corporation and United Fruit Co. Fyffe and Chiquita brands	Costa Rica and other Central American countries	52 000 agricultural workers	Mainly processing and sale of food and fruit (Subsidiary companies in Canada, UK, Japan, Holland, Italy)

Fig. 15.3 Multinational corporations in the banana industry

148

backing lies with the multinationals and the countries are simply not in a strong enough position economically to adopt a more radical policy against the multinationals. Despite creaming off much of the revenue, these do provide much needed export earnings for these small Central American and Caribbean republics, as well as employment to many who would otherwise be without work. It is a situation which is in varying degrees common amongst agricultural exporting countries in the tropics.

Cash cropping under a small holding system

Cash cropping in association with subsistence agriculture is often regarded as a recent phenomenon but in fact it has a long history under a variety of traditional systems. These range from some form of rotational fallowing of plots round a settlement to permanent plot cultivation. For example in the savanna belt of West Africa cotton and groundnuts are characteristic cash crops within a rotational fallowing system. Jute is an important cash crop in the settled intensive farming system of peasant cultivation in the delta region of Bangladesh. Tree crops such as oil palm have long provided additional income to small holders in the rain forest belts of both Africa and South East Asia.

In contrast to plantations most small holdings on which some cash crops are grown are usually under 5 hectares and rely mainly on family labour, hiring of labour placing a considerable burden on the farmer who has little spare finance to pay for it. Nevertheless there are in every region richer farmers or landlords who either rely on hired labour or let out part of their holdings under some tenancy or share cropping arrangement.

However despite the increasing variety of systems under which small scale cash cropping takes place many writers have commented on the prevalence of a common pattern akin to the infield and outfield system at one time present over much of peasant Europe. There is a circular arrangement to land-use around a village or small holding, with the intensity of cultivation declining with distance for reasons similar to those outlined by Thunen in his 'Isolated State'. The village or farm is the place where produce must be brought from off the land and inputs of labour and fertilizer also have to be got out from the village or farm to the land where it is needed. Consequently the nearest land, including house gardens, is the most intensively cultivated and kept fertile by the addition of waste material and dung from the settlement. Then there is a second zone further away which is less intensively cultivated because of the greater time required to get to and from it. Occasionally the land may be manured by putting cattle on it following harvesting. Then on the outer

fringes scattered clearings may be periodically made in the bush or forest and cultivated more extensively on a rotational bush fallow basis. After it has been cropped for a number of years it is allowed to return to bush so that natural processes may restore its fertility.

This zonation has been shown by Hocking and Thomson for the village of Poka in the forest belt of South West Nigeria (Fig. 15.4). Here the permanent cultivation of tree crops is combined with food and cash cropping farming on the various belts of land around the settlement. There is also some hunting and collecting in the forest beyond the zones of cultivation.

The advantages and disadvantages of this type of cash crop farming are summarised in Fig. 15.5.

Having discussed some of the characteristics of plantation and native cash crop farming and indicated some of the arguments for and against each, we look at the changing role of each for one type of product — rubber, given in Case Study 15.5 (p. 154, 155) on Malaysia.

The effects of political and social reform — Cuban sugar

An increasing area of the world is under socialist and communist governments, in which the state has control of the economic system. Instead of a free market economy, a command economy operates in which political policies and ideologies are dominant forces, frequently overriding economic considerations. This is so in the Eastern Bloc countries, in China and a number of countries in the tropical world such as Cuba, Tanzania and Angola.

Politics and a switch in export markets

Cuba, one of the world's leading producers of canesugar, was the first developing country, apart from China, to successfully establish a Communist regime when Fidel Del Castro was swept to power in the 1959 revolution. This occurred, despite its closeness to the United States which had strong financial and economic interests in Cuba, completely dominating production and trade in sugar, the main-stay of the economy. Sugar still dominates Cuba's exports accounting for over 80% by value. But the market for it is no longer the United States and Western Europe, but other Communist countries — in particular the Soviet Union (see Fig. 15.6). This change has little to do with economics, it is a result of politics. The United States broke off diplomatic and trading relations, whilst the Soviet Union and other Eastern Bloc countries offered every support. Whatever the fluctuations in world demand and prices for cane sugar, the Eastern Communist Bloc led by the Soviet Union guarantees Cuba a market for its sugar

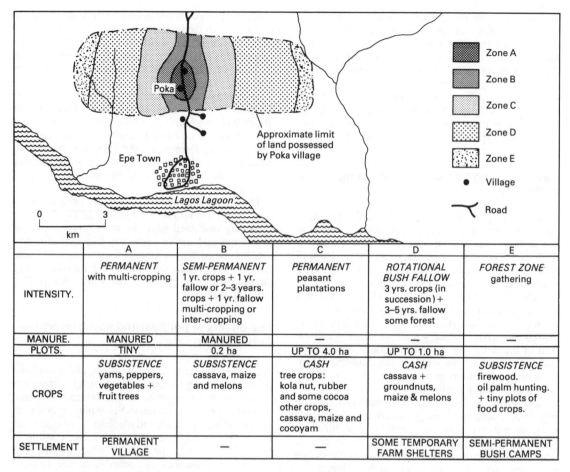

	A	B	C	D	E
INTENSITY.	*PERMANENT* with multi-cropping	*SEMI-PERMANENT* 1 yr. crops + 1 yr. fallow or 2–3 years. crops + 1 yr. fallow multi-cropping or inter-cropping	*PERMANENT* peasant plantations	*ROTATIONAL BUSH FALLOW* 3 yrs. crops (in succession) + 3–5 yrs. fallow some forest	*FOREST ZONE* gathering
MANURE.	MANURED	MANURED	—	—	—
PLOTS.	TINY	0.2 ha	UP TO 4.0 ha	UP TO 1.0 ha	
CROPS	*SUBSISTENCE* yams, peppers, vegetables + fruit trees	*SUBSISTENCE* cassava, maize and melons	*CASH* tree crops: kola nut, rubber and some cocoa other crops, cassava, maize and cocoyam	*CASH* cassava + groundnuts, maize & melons	*SUBSISTENCE* firewood. oil palm hunting. + tiny plots of food crops.
SETTLEMENT	PERMANENT VILLAGE	—	—	SOME TEMPORARY FARM SHELTERS	SEMI-PERMANENT BUSH CAMPS

Fig. 15.4   *Land use round Poka, SW Nigeria*

ADVANTAGES	DISADVANTAGES
Integrated with the general agricultural economy	Yields and quality generally lower
Utilises traditional farming methods, together with some modernisation. The emphasis is on family labour	Supplies are less reliable as farmers switch according to market prices
Provides a much needed cash income and helps to integrate rural and urban sectors of the economy and society	Some neglect of basic food crops therefore necessitating some import of these
Adaptable and flexible: can withstand market fluctuations better than plantations being able to switch more between food and cash crops	Uneven and dispersed distribution of small holdings makes provision of marketing and other infrastructure difficult and expensive. Diffusion of new techniques also difficult
Better adapted to tropical environmental conditions	Until recently government neglected needed support for agriculture in favour of industrialisation

Fig. 15.5   *Small holding cash crop farming — for and against*

	Sugar	Fisheries	Beverages	Tobacco	Nickel	(mills of Cuban Pesos) Others	Total
Market economies	687.9	98.3	26.8	54.1	56.3	106.0	1029.4
Socialist U.S.S.R.	2446.2	—	—	2.2	253.7	145.1	2867.4
Other socialist countries	146.7	—	1.6	—	2.3	—	150.6
Total	3300.8	98.3	28.4	56.3	312.3	251.1	4047.2

Source: National Bank of Cuba

Fig. 15.6   The relative importance of sugar to the economy (export trade by value), 1981

at a price way above the prevailing world market price. In 1976, for example, the Soviet Union subsidised Cuban sugar production to the extent of paying five times the world market price. This was part of a political policy aimed at maintaining a Communist presence close to the United States and of supporting Cuba's influence in Africa, especially in Angola. Whilst relations have improved with the United States and Cuba is now attempting to develop more trade with non-Communist countries, Cuba's economy remains overwhelmingly dependent on the country's Communist allies.

Land reform and other changes affecting sugar production

Before the revolution sugar production was organised under a plantation system run by American companies. But as part of the radical land reforms ushered in by the Communist revolution, plantations were abolished and along with them American capitalism. They were replaced by state collective farms in which sugar continued to be combined with cattle production.

There are today 622 state farms, large enterprises with 1000 to 1500 hectares under cultivation. Originally the farms were run as co-operatives (cooperativistas) the workers collectively owning the farm and sharing in the profits. But fears of declining production in 1962 led the state to take over and run the farms. The state therefore produces about three quarters of Cuba's sugar. The rest is grown by small peasant farmers, many of whom got their land when the plantations (latifundia) were broken up under the agricultural reform programme following the revolution. Paradoxically the small farmers are now being pressurised into giving up their peasant holdings and into joining state farm enterprises.

The state farms (grangas estatales) are now grouped on a geographical basis into 70 agrupac-

cones, each of which control about 7 state farms and is responsible for implementing government plans to increase sugar output by nationalising the use of labour and machines. Labour shortages in 1963 led to some use of Russian produced harvesting machines but these are costly and therefore most of the sugar-cane is still cut by hand.

In addition to this radical re-organisation there have been marked changes in the provision for the workers. Most are now housed in specially constructed rural towns (communidades rurales) and are provided with food, educational and other social facilities. The four storey concrete blocks of flats contrast strongly with the traditional timber and thatch homes of peasant farmers. Secondary education is open to all. Moreover the workers who travel out to the state farms are guaranteed continuous employment at a higher rate of pay than the returns obtained under the old share cropping system developed on the latifundias.

Persistent features in the system

Despite these radical changes, there is much that persists from the old system, partly because of insufficient money to alter some methods of production and also because of the nature of cane-sugar. This determines the distribution of sugar growing over the island as well as methods of cultivation and processing for export.

The distribution of sugar-cane growing remains much as it was before the 1959 revolution because of the physical requirements of the crop.

Large areas of flat land are required with a residual loam soil developed on karst (limestone) to ensure adequate drainage but also some moisture retention. Thus though most of Cuba has the consistently high temperatures of between 22°–28°C together with the 7–9 humid months with 1000–1500 mm of rainfall needed to grow sugar without irrigation, followed by a dry harvesting period, only certain parts have the necessary extent of flat land and soils. These are in the Occidente, Las Villas and Camaguey regions which also enjoy good coastal access for export of the sugar (Fig. 15.7). Where ground conditions abruptly change, sugar-cane growing gives way to some other pattern of production. Thus in the Camaguey plains where the red Mantazos loam of the karst gives way to igneous soils which are less well drained, there is a sharp change from sugar growing to permanent pasture for cattle.

Methods of production are much the same as before the revolution. Sugar-cane growing is still dominated by large enterprises and methods on the state farm are in many ways similar to those on the latifundia it has replaced. The land is still used under the old rotation system. The rectangular and uni-form fields of sugar-cane are interspersed with fallow pasture on which beef cattle graze and bounded by railway tracks on which the wagons run, taking the raw cane to the centrally located processing factory. Despite an increased use of machinery including mechanical loading on to trailers, sugar production is still labour intensive because much of the harvesting which takes place in the dry season still has to be done by hand and the sugar factories are heavy users of labour.

In the diagram summarising the system under which cane-sugar is grown and produced, we can see how these persistent factors combine with the new facets introduced as a result of the political and social revolution of 1959 (Fig. 15.8).

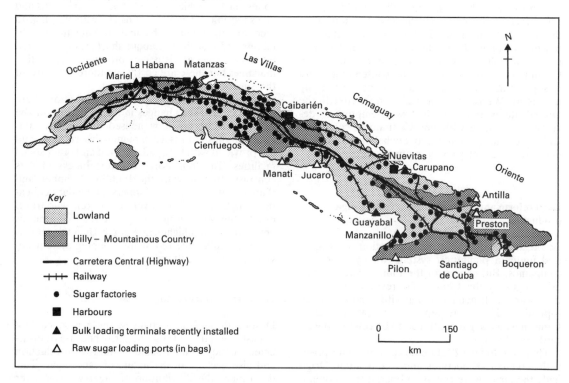

Fig. 15.7   Sugar producing centres in Cuba relative to terrain and communications

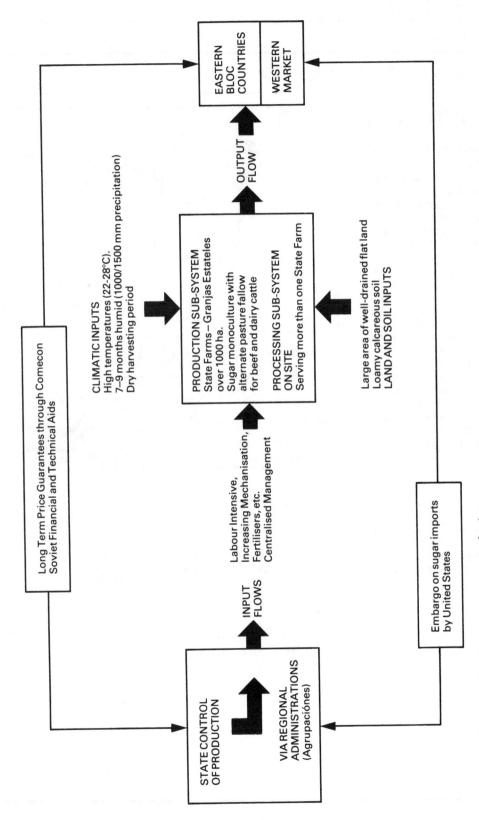

Fig. 15.8 The system for Cuban sugar cane production

153

15:5 MALAYSIA

Distribution and production of natural rubber

A FACTORS FAVOURING MALAYSIA

HUMAN INPUTS

1   Historic and continuing British colonial interest — finance, entrepreneurship and expertise including research. But also now includes local Chinese and Malaysian investment

2   Labour. Use of imported Tamils and Chinese together with indigenous Malaysians

3   Infrastructure and port outlets. These already established by the British for tin mining sector.

4   Government stimulus to production especially for small holdings. Cooperation in Assoc. of Natural Rubber Producers to help keep world share of the market despite competition from synthetic rubber.

OUTPUT—MARKETS

UK and rest of EEC, U.S.A. and Japan — helped by technological advances in the uses or rubber e.g. tyres, tubing.

PHYSICAL INPUTS

1   Climate. Constantly high temperatures 25°-30°C. Seasonally well distributed rainfall especially in the West, of 2500mm +.

2   Land. Initially plentiful. Undulating coastal land favoured as good drainage is needed. Tolerant of a variety of soils.

SHARE OF WORLD PRODUCTION
1982 ('000 tonnes)

Malaysia	1550
Indonesia	990
Thailand	540

B   CHANGING ROLE OF PLANTATIONS IN RUBBER PRODUCTION
(relative to non-European owned medium and small scale cash crop holdings)

60% now comes from holdings of 40 ha or less

1   Holdings come partly from government division and sell off of former foreign plantations and partly from land resettlement schemes by the government through FELDA (Federal Land Development Authority).

2   Rubber is the most important cash crop on family holdings. Usual Felda scheme is to clear land and allocate to Malays small holdings each of which has ⅔ under subsistence crops e.g. rice, veg, etc. Government also provided loans, infrastructure and marketing facilities. By 1973 there were 67 schemes covering 290 000 ha.
(The government also has its own large block planting schemes run by Felda.)

3   Chinese and Indians have more medium sized holdings and use hired labour.

Plantations have a reduced share due to pressure from the Malaysian government

1   Plantations are still significant employing 200 000 workers directly and indirectly e.g. in transporting and shipping of rubber through Kelang and Penang.

2   Plantations are still largely monoculture. The largest input costs are land preparation and in the 5-7 years wait for new trees to produce, also in buildings etc. and rising labour costs tapping the latex.

3   But costs per unit of latex are falling due to higher yielding strains of rubber e.g. RRIM 700 and through the use of tree stimulants.
(Plantation companies aid the small holding sector by disseminating research findings etc.)

4   The British company of Harrison and Crossfields with 92 000 ha of plantations was one of the biggest owners but an increasing acreage of plantations is under Asian ownership.

Exercise

● With reference to Malaysian rubber production compare and contrast the role of plantations and small holdings in the agricultural economy of a country.

16 Temperate Farming Systems

It is the developed countries which mainly make up the temperate lands (Fig. 16.1). Here the most striking feature about agriculture as indicated in Fig. 16.2 is its small contribution to the national wealth compared to the industrial and service sectors in the economy. This is so even for countries such as Canada and Australia which we so readily visualise as countries of wide open spaces with extensive wheat fields and grazing lands.

But before dismissing agriculture as unimportant it must be realised that there are other yardsticks by which we can assess its worth, as the following newspaper extract shows.

BRITAIN MUST DO MORE TO FEED IT-SELF, SAYS WALKER

Britain, now more self-sufficient in food than ever before, still needs to do more to cut imports, the Agriculture Minister, Mr Peter Walker said yesterday.

In the last year, Britain's self-sufficiency in those products which can be grown in the UK has increased from 70 per cent to 75 per cent.

'In spite of many difficulties facing the industry, this is clearly a success story, and the achievements of our agriculture and food industries provide a

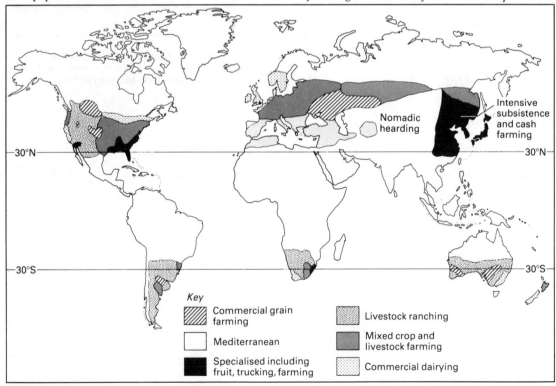

Fig. 16.1   Types of temperate farming systems

	Agriculture	Industry	Services
United Kingdom	2	33	65
Japan	4	42	54
U.S.A.	3	33	64
Canada	4	29	67
Australia	6	35	59
Average for all Industrialised Countries	3	36	61

Source: World Bank Development Report (1984)

Fig. 16.2   Percentage contribution of different sectors to national income

model for the rest of our economy to follow,' he adds.

Mr Walker made his remarks during a press briefing.

Britain, he said, still imported £3,000 million worth of food which could be grown 'and the potential for our food exports is very large indeed.'

The latest ministry figures show that UK farmers and fishermen produce just over half of all the food consumed in Britain. In 1970 Britain was only 47 per cent self-sufficient.

Today's home production is worth £6,200 million out of the total UK food bill of £11,500 million.

'Remarkable progress has been made,' added Mr Walker. But more progress would bring greater prosperity and more jobs.

The Guardian 2.11.81

Food is a basic necessity and the more a country can produce for itself the more secure it feels and the less it has to pay out of its precious export earnings on food imports.

Farming on the urban fringe

One of the problems facing agriculturalists in the heavily populated industrial countries is the loss of good farming land due to continued urban sprawl. The expansion of urban areas into the countryside has brought more problems than opportunities. This is contrary to Thunen's expectations of highest returns on land closest to the market; nor do we find his simple zonation of market gardening followed by dairying (and then silviculture).

Instead, as the example of Ranstaadt indicates in Fig. 16.3, the land-use is very mixed. The area around the city is an unstable shadow or fringe zone, which moves outwards as urban pressures successfully result in the incorporation of more and more land into the city. There is an intermingling of land-use, involving an irregular transition from farm to non-farm land. It is also characterised by land speculation, with land values fluctuating and ownership changing. Agricultural land also falls into disuse under urban pressures and financial speculation on its change to urban use.

Because building land is so much more valuable than agricultural land, it is not surprising that given the continued pressure for expansion of large cities, agricultural landowners have sold out to the urban developer and speculator. But it is less easy to appreciate why much land on the urban fringe is falling into disuse, in particular land trapped within the urban fringe.

The reasons are summarised in Fig. 16.4. Despite the more light hearted side of some of the comments, the issues raised are important ones.

Types

Some of those usually associated with land close to an urban market have declined in importance. These include market gardening and horticulture. This is due to a variety of reasons — increased fencing costs, damage to crops from trespassers and vandalism, labour problems with alternative better paid factory jobs usually being available, increased competition with cheaper fruit and vegetables brought in from elsewhere. Some of these difficulties have also led to a decline of pastoral farming on moorland areas close to industrial cities such as Manchester, Leeds and Sheffield.

However intensive livestock production under cover and in conditions similar to factory assembly line production has increased. Factory farming is helping to meet the rising demand for meat, poultry and eggs from supermarket chains, and it makes the most of sites which are expensive and costly to maintain. There is also greater security where stock can be housed behind locked doors. In addition the latest production techniques including quality control can be applied indoors to make the most economic use of the labour which is employed and ensure the combination of steady production and high quality needed today.

Factory farming now covers a range of activities — broiler chicken rearing, battery hen production, deep litter method of pig production, calf rearing for veal and fully automatic dairies with stall feeding all the year round. All these activities have expanded in this and other industrialised countries. For example, a survey on the outer western fringe of London showed that the number of poultry reared under battery conditions increased by just over a third between 1968 and 1971 and there was a similar expansion in pig rearing. In the United States it is estimated that 200 000 dairy cows are kept within the Los Angeles Metropolitan area and stall fed from feed brought in e.g. peanuts and citrus waste.

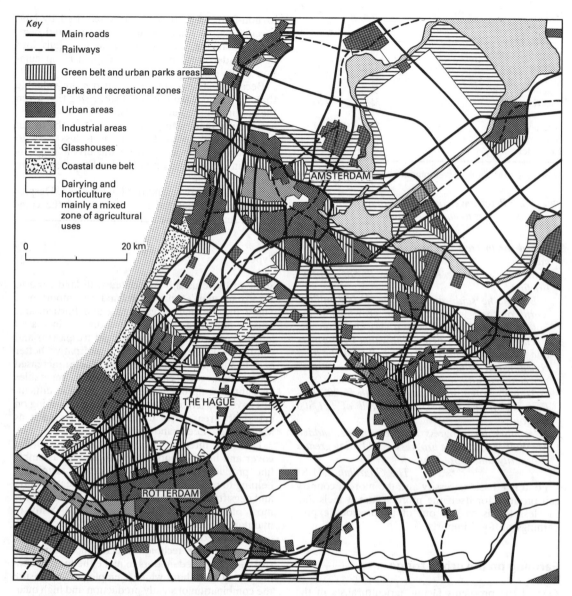

Key
— Main roads
- - - Railways

▥ Green belt and urban parks areas
▤ Parks and recreational zones
▦ Urban areas
▨ Industrial areas
▤ Glasshouses
▨ Coastal dune belt
☐ Dairying and horticulture mainly a mixed zone of agricultural uses

0   20 km

AMSTERDAM

THE HAGUE

ROTTERDAM

Fig. 16.3   Ranstaadt region of the Netherlands (Proposed pattern of land use, AD 2000)

Some dairying, market gardening and soft fruit growing are still done on open land, especially in those parts of the fringe further away from built up areas and where physical conditions are suitable. Examples include the Central and Imperial valleys of California with proximity to San Francisco and Los Angeles. Here alluvial bottom land, a Mediterranean climate and irrigation facilities all favour intensive production for urban markets. This is also the case with the Lower Rhone valley in France just above Marseilles, a city of over one million.

Market gardening, horticulture and fruit growing: its changing character

Market gardening, or truck farming as it is known in the United States, is concerned with the intensive cultivation of vegetables, fruit and flowers on open land. Horticulture has tended to be used as a term for even more intensive growing of these under nursery conditions, where much of the land is under greenhouse or some other protective cover such as cloche and polythene sheeting. However, the distinction between the two terms has tended to dis-

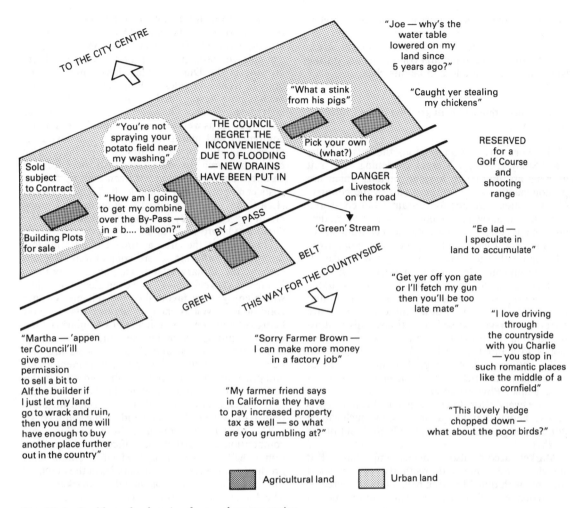

Fig. 16.4   Problems for farming from urban expansion

appear. More and more market gardeners have intensified cultivation by making use of a similar method to those in nurseries, whilst increasingly more vegetables are being grown under open field systems on arable farms under contracts with canning and freezing firms.

Here market gardening will be used as a general term to cover all the various systems under which vegetables, fruit and flowers are produced using intensive methods. Moreover what is said about these is also applicable to orchard fruit growing.

Market gardening, apart from factory farming, is probably the most intensive type of cultivation with a very high ratio of inputs to each land unit area utilised and a high value output. It has generally been noted for being very labour intensive and it still is when compared with other kinds of agriculture. But in absolute terms the amount of labour used has declined, partly because labour has become in-

creasingly expensive but also because of the use of labour saving technology, such as roto-cultivators, automatic sprinklers and harvesting machines. The whole market gardening scene has become increasingly capital intensive and it is this rather than labour intensity which is the most outstanding feature of the industry today.

It is not simply a matter of labour saving devices, but the introduction of other costly inputs such as polythene and other cover to extend the growing season, oil-heating of greenhouses, and a much greater amount and variety of fertilizer and other conditioning media to improve soil conditions. There is also much more capital invested in processing, packaging and marketing the crops to provide as high and consistent a quality as possible.

Thus the character of market gardening is changing. This is in response to a variety of influences. These include expanding markets for quick frozen

159

produce, other technological advances, higher labour costs and increasing competition from overseas, such as Mediterranean and tropical areas where natural environmental conditions are on the whole more favourable and labour cheaper.

Market gardening and fruit growing in the United Kingdom

Throughout this section refer to the maps in the Case Study (p. 162). Market gardening and fruit growing are limited to lowland regions which are predominantly in the southern half of the country. Growing areas are not too distant from coast and estuaries, so allowing oceanic influences to moderate climatic conditions. Despite the increasing introduction of artificial ways of protecting crops from adverse weather and extending the growing season, climatic influences remain very important. The mild winters and early springs, together with reliable rainfall experienced in areas such as Cornwall and the Vale of Evesham are still significant. So too are terrain, drainage and soil conditions. This is illustrated from the presence of fruit growing on lower slopes to avoid the frost pockets which occur in valley bottoms in late spring; also intensive market gardening on the rich peat fens around the Wash is an example. Physical conditions remain important because every effort to create artificial conditions is costly; there is therefore a limit to how much can be done, if the grower is not to price himself out of the market.

Market access also remains important. But speedier and improved methods of transport together with quick freezing have allowed a greater dispersion of market gardening and fruit production away from traditional areas to other areas with favourable environments such as those on the south coast and in Somerset.

But a more dispersed distribution is also due to the trend for some vegetables such as peas, early carrots, brassicas and runner beans to be grown as field crops in areas such as East Anglia. Here various companies offer growing contracts to farmers, together with an assured price for the product which is then quick frozen or canned by the companies. Frequently the freezing and canning plants are located on the coast so that fish products may be similarly processed, again making for economies of scale. The swing away from intensive market garden growing of some crops to open field growing has also been favoured by improvements in freezing and marketing techniques as well as the greatly increased demand for frozen products with most households now having a deep freeze as well as a fridge.

Despite these dispersion trends, the fact remains that certain concentrations of market gardening persist, even though technological developments have reduced some of the advantages these locations initially enjoyed. These concentrations include for example rhubarb growing round Leeds, raspberry growing in the Dundee area, cherry orchards and hops in Kent and cider orchards in Herefordshire. Such regions have gained a reputation for a particular type of produce, have accumulated experience and expertise as well as invested capital in buildings, equipment and marketing outlets — all favouring the continuation of each particular speciality in an established area. In some cases also some form of co-operative organisation has been built up to keep costs competitive. For example the Nursery Trades (Lea Valley) Ltd. was initially set up to serve growers in the Lea Valley but now has members as far afield as Oxford and Suffolk.

However, at the present time United Kingdom growers are suffering severe competition. Regions such as the Canary Islands (tomatoes), Southern France (early vegetables), and even Kenya (orchids) which enjoy more favourable and reliable weather conditions as well as cheaper labour costs, are now being offered cheaper freight rates to market their produce through shops and supermarket chains in this country. French and Dutch growers are also being more heavily subsidised by government grants and price support arrangements than growers in this country. For example Dutch glasshouse growers have lower heating costs than their opposite numbers in the Vale of Evesham and on the south coast.

The harder times resulting from this increased competition are further intensified by overproduction in the EEC as a whole, producing a glut of some produce such as tomatoes and apples at the height of the season and a consequent fall in market price. The lot of English growers is also not made any easier by the stricter EEC regulations being introduced on the kind and type of produce which can be grown, so as to standardise market quality and reduce the spread of disease.

Thus, the area under intensive market gardening and fruit orchards is for a variety of reasons steadily being reduced and the trend is likely to continue.

Truck farming and fruit growing in Mediterranean and sub-tropical areas

Though there is not the space here to deal with these kinds of region in any detail some comment is needed because of the increasingly important contribution these regions make to world production.

Where countries reach continental proportions as, for example, the United States, the Soviet Union and Australia, the sheer distance to market becomes an important cost factor. To some extent this is offset by the improved methods of transport and technological developments such as refrigeration which have already been mentioned in connection with the United Kingdom. But what offsets market distance costs are the particularly favourable climatic conditions enjoyed by such areas compared with those in the United Kingdom and other areas of Western Europe. The major fruit and truck farming regions in warm temperate to sub-tropical latitudes enjoy a constantly warm and sunny climate and have irrigation facilities to ensure water through the growing season. Such for example is the case with Florida and California in the United States, the Black Sea regions of the Soviet Union and the Murray-Murrumbidgee valley of South Australia.

Dairying: an intensive form of pastoral farming

This covers farming in which the main activity is the production of liquid milk either to be sold as such in urban markets or processed for sale as cream, butter, cheese and dried milk products (Fig. 16.5). Like market gardening it is usually regarded as intensive in nature, there being a high ratio of inputs — capital, labour, fertilizer etc. — to each unit area farmed and an emphasis on obtaining maximum yield per head of dairy cattle kept. But as with market gardening, the degree of intensity varies — from a factory type system in which dairy cattle are stall fed all the year round (as in the vicinity of large

cities such as Los Angeles or increasingly in old traushumance regions like Switzerland and Norway), to an all the year round open grazing system in regions such as North Island, New Zealand where holdings reach an average size of 250 hectares.

The locational pattern of dairying also has some similarity with that for market gardening since it is influenced to an important extent by similar conditions. Liquid milk production, like fresh vegetables and fruit needs to be within easy reach of large urban markets but as we have seen this can be either immediately in the vicinity of urban centres (in which case holdings tend to be particularly intensive in character) or a few hours away. Greater London receives its liquid milk from as far away as the West Country as well as from nearer areas such as North Essex and the Vale of Oxford.

As in Von Thunen's day where dairying takes place beyond daily freight distance of markets the liquid milk has to be processed into some form that will keep, be in market demand, as well as stand the cost of transport e.g. butter and cheese. In the case of Western European markets producing regions of this kind include nearer ones such as Denmark, the Netherlands, Austria and Switzerland (supplying the large population of industrial regions) and also distant ones such as New Zealand and South East Australia which may be as much as 30 days in shipping distance from West European markets. Yet refrigeration and other technical developments still allow them a share in this market.

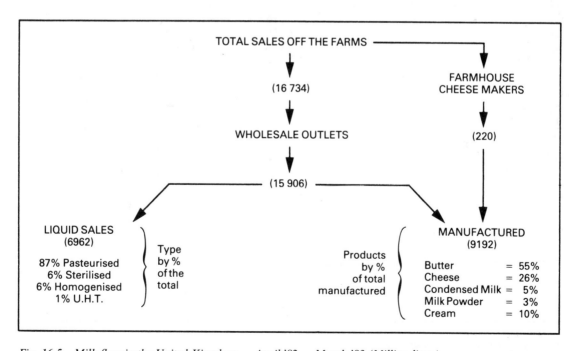

Fig. 16.5   Milk flow in the United Kingdom — April '82 — March '83 (Million litres)

161

16:1 UNITED KINGDOM

Market gardening and horticulture

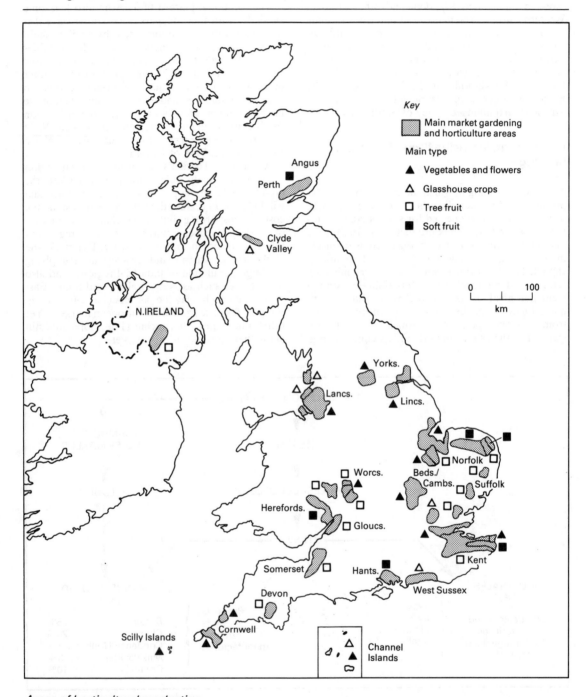

Key

- Main market gardening and horticulture areas

Main type

- ▲ Vegetables and flowers
- △ Glasshouse crops
- ☐ Tree fruit
- ■ Soft fruit

Angus
Perth
Clyde Valley
N.IRELAND
Yorks.
Lancs.
Lincs.
Norfolk
Worcs.
Beds./ Cambs.
Suffolk
Herefords.
Gloucs.
Kent
Somerset
Hants.
West Sussex
Devon
Cornwell
Scilly Islands
Channel Islands

0   100
km

Areas of horticultural production

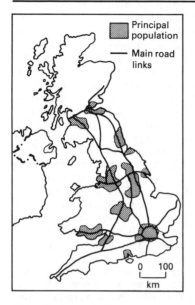

Principal population concentrations and some main road links

HUMAN AND ECONOMIC FACTORS

Historical Accumulation of Expertise and Investment for specialist crops

Extent of Government Support

Growing and Marketing Associations

Market Demand and Proximity — for salad veg., fruit and flower products

FACTORS AFFECTING THE DISTRIBUTION OF MARKET GARDENING AND FRUIT PRODUCTION

Technological Developments in freezing, transport etc. protective covering seed, fertilizer and water supply control

Mild Damp Weather favouring early growth and maturing of crops

Average to Above Average Days of Sunshine

Level or Undulating Terrain but above frost pockets

Well Drained Light to Medium soils

PHYSICAL FACTORS

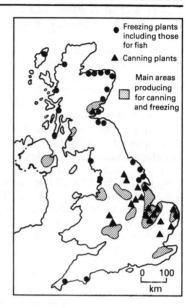

Freezing, canning areas

Competition from continental and overseas suppliers

Exercise

● From considering the regional distribution of horticulture including fruit growing, is it possible to identify for any one region the most significant factor(s) responsible for its importance?

Sunshine

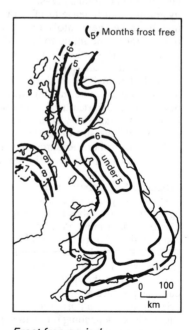

Frost free period

Government intervention — EEC legislation with particular reference to dairy products

Increasingly however as with other forms of farming, government intervention is significantly affecting the pattern of production and trade in dairy products and it would seem appropriate at this point to say something about this. (Though particularly discussed here in a dairying context it is important to bear in mind that government policies at national and supra-national level are not limited to dairying but affect cereals, fruit, market garden produce and root crops such as sugar beet etc.)

Policies within the EEC concern us here. EEC legislation formulated since the Treaty of Rome (1958) is gradually replacing legislation by individual member countries. The treaty laid down guidelines for a Common Agricultural Policy (C.A.P.) the main objectives being:

1 To increase agricultural productivity;
2 Ensure for agricultural workers a standard of living comparable with other workers;
3 Stabilisation of markets for agricultural produce;
4 Ensure adequate supplies of agricultural produce at reasonable prices to the consumers.

General policies to achieve this include free trade between member countries so far as possible and common levels of support for producers.

Action under these general policies has brought a marked alteration in the organisation of farming in Western Europe. Uneconomic producers, particularly those in marginal areas, have been encouraged by grants either to leave farming or rationalise holdings to make them into larger and more efficient units. Grants amounting to 25% of costs have been paid. Under this rationalisation, new methods such as greater mechanisation in dairying including for example herringbone milking parlours, automatic feeding and machine milking, have resulted in the number of the agricultural workforce being halved in the EEC since 1958, from 18 million to 9 million, and the average size of holdings increased.

There are other measures of which perhaps the most significant have been the stabilisation of markets and guarantee of prices for most agricultural products. Since there is as yet no common EEC currency a 'green rate' has been established for agriculture to establish price support for farmers. The EEC determine on the basis of the 'green rate' the guaranteed price for a product, and according to the market price in the individual countries relative to this will, if need be, step in and 'top up' the market price to the appropriate amount. When agricultural produce is traded across national boundaries in the EEC a border levy or subsidy is paid to the producer depending on relative prices either side of the national boundary.

Such measures have affected UK agriculture including dairying and on the whole have been more beneficial than the national measures previously ruling. For example the Milk Marketing Board which fixed the price of milk as uniform across the country at the farm gate thereby taking off the farmer the cost of transport and guaranteeing sales, guaranteed only the price of liquid milk. Whilst this helped producers particularly in the more distant hill margin areas, the Board did not guarantee the price of surplus as cheese or butter. However under EEC legislation there is now support, not only for liquid milk, but also for butter and skimmed milk (and therefore indirectly cheese). So much so that in 1983 subsidy of the EEC dairying industries accounted for a surprising 20% of the EEC's total budget.

In addition there has been support through the strong advertising and selling campaigns to consumers carried on by the Milk Marketing Board and other organisations on behalf of dairy farmers.

Despite this, consumption of liquid milk and other dairy produce, except cheese, has fallen in the EEC whilst production has expanded. There is therefore now a serious situation of overproduction. EEC support measures have led to inflated prices being paid to dairy farmers. There is therefore a growing stockpile of EEC butter and skimmed milk.

Recently a variety of measures have therefore had to be introduced to reduce dairy output in the EEC. Marginal dairy farmers have been given financial aid to help them move into other kinds of farming. In November 1983 a quota system was introduced limiting liquid milk output for each farm to about 10% below the usual output. Where the quota output is exceeded, penalties have been introduced. In addition a tax has been levied on dairy herds above a certain size, i.e. beyond about 15–20 head. However, it was generally agreed these measures do not go far enough and recently further measures have been taken to reduce the number of dairy cattle in an effort to bring production more in line with market demand.

Overproduction in the EEC has made it increasingly difficult for overseas dairy producers like New Zealand to maintain a share of the important West European market. Not only this, they are now also faced with competition in other markets from EEC members as they attempt to unload surplus production on to world markets.

Dairying in New Zealand

New Zealand is one of the world's most important dairying countries with 80% of its production concentrated on North Island. Its pre-eminence stems from the last part of the 19th century when the invention of refrigeration in 1882 and faster steamships brought the United Kingdom and other West European markets in its reach. Very favourable physical conditions, efficient production methods, together with strict government controls and support enable producers in this region to still maintain an important share of these traditional markets as well as penetrating new ones such as Japan where increased affluence and changing tastes have created a rapidly expanding market for dairy produce.

'Fieldview' is a typical dairy farm in New Zealand and may be used to illustrate the character of dairying in the North Island and the factors affecting it. (Refer to Case Study 16.2 on p. 166.)

Commercial cereal farming — wheat growing

Wheat is the dominant cereal in temperate lands and is also found in drier areas of Monsoon Asia such as Pakistan. Though generally associated with the interior steppe and prairie lands, wheat is grown under a variety of physical conditions and under both intensive and extensive systems. For example in East Anglia it is produced as part of a mixed arable system on farms averaging around 600 hectares in size whereas in the drier Soviet steppelands of Kazakhstan it was until recently commonly grown under mono-culture on state farms averaging 27 000 hectares in size.

One of the reasons why wheat is found under a variety of conditions is the widespread demand for it as a staple food. Another is the many kinds of wheat available, each tolerating differing environmental conditions. The two broad types are winter wheat and spring wheat. Winter sown wheat is favoured where conditions are milder but spring sown wheat has to be grown where winters are severe. Winter wheat is lower in gluten content than spring wheat and therefore the flour made from it is softer, whereas the high gluten content of winter wheat makes it ideal for bread. It is the spring wheat grown in the surplus producing interior continental regions of the old world which enters most into world trade.

Wheat production — the case of the Soviet Union

The Soviet Union is by far the most important wheat producing country. But it is not a major exporter since with a population of 270 million, most of what is produced is consumed at home. In certain years it is a net importer of hard spring wheat, and what export trade it has goes mainly to neighbouring Communist bloc countries.

A broad geographical division can be made between wheat growing lands in the west where winter wheat is grown with little surplus for other regions; and lands to the east of the Volga River, mainly in Siberia (Fig. 16.6), where spring wheat is grown under more extensive conditions and mainly for shipment back to the heavily populated industrial areas in the west.

Wheat growing areas coincide with the wooded steppelands and the Steppes proper, where an un-

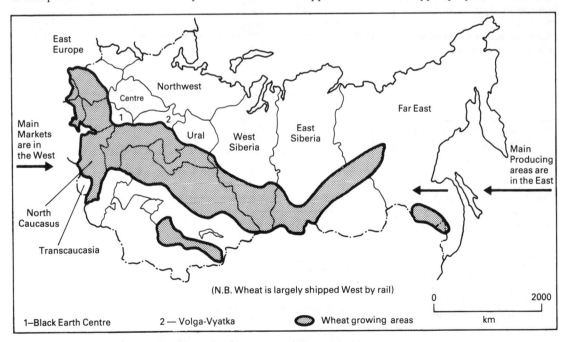

Fig. 16.6   Main wheat growing areas, U.S.S.R.

16:2 NEW ZEALAND

Dairy farming

CHARACTERISTICS AND FARM ORGANISATION

Cattle graze out all year

Rotational grazing using mobile electric fencing

Paddocks — heavy fertilizer input and pest sprayed. Two resown each year with rye grass

Other cropping — one fifth of paddocks shut off for hay and silage
Kale and soft turnips winter strip grazed. Barley for pig feed

Livestock — 90 Jersey herd — 50 000 gallon annual output sent to Rongotea butter plant. Return skim milk for intensive veal calf fattening together with 200 pork bacon pig fattening unit

Family farm of 150 ha subdivided into paddocks each with piped water

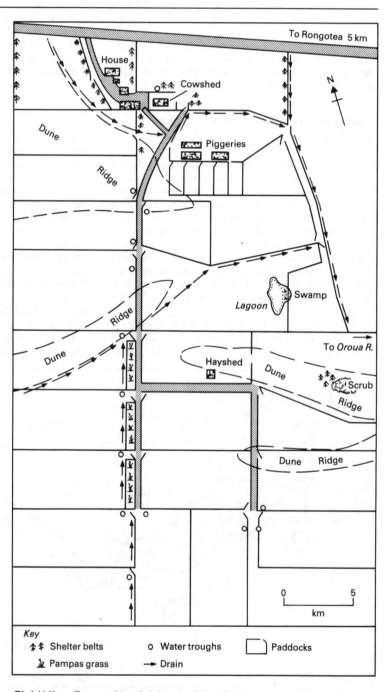

Key

↟ ↟ Shelter belts   o Water troughs   ☐ Paddocks

⇟ Pampas grass   → Drain

Field View Farm—North Island. New Zealand

FACTORS AFFECTING THE FARMING SYSTEM

HUMAN AND ECONOMIC INPUTS

Investment and expertise of family unit

Processing and marketing organisation — Manawatu Dairy Cooperative — giving economies of scale advantages and competitive strength. Butter, cheese, dried milk — mainly for export via Wellington

Dependent on export markets — EEC restrictions led to greater dependence on other markets e.g. Japan, U.S.A., though UK still significant

Government and research support —
Local — Palmerston University, Artificial Insemination Centre.
National — Herd Improvement Society, Dairy Research Institute.
Price and quality control — via Government's Dairy Products Prices Authority and Dairy Production and Marketing Board

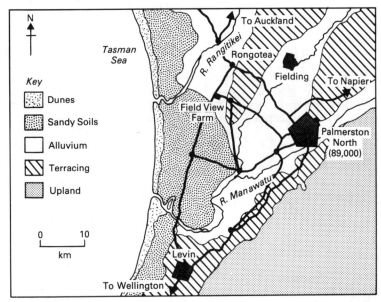

Location of Field View Farm, Manawatu area

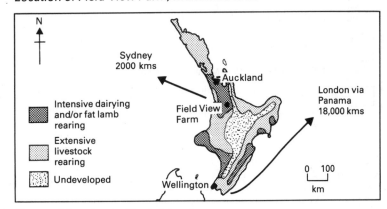

Types of farming in North Island

PHYSICAL INPUTS

Undulating terrain with gravel alluvial soils suitable for pasture

Climate — prevailing westerlies bring well distributed rainfall all the year

Mild winters and warm summers also help to ensure good outdoor grazing throughout the year

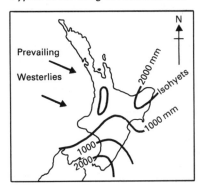

Climate of North Island

Exports still rising (NZ$ million)			
	1976	1980	1984
Meat	674	1326	1900
Wool	512	967	1104
Dairy products	473	810	1444

167

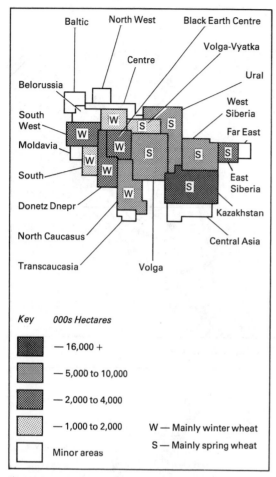

Fig. 16.7 Wheat growing by region

Key 000s Hectares

■ — 16,000 +

▨ — 5,000 to 10,000

▦ — 2,000 to 4,000

░ — 1,000 to 2,000   W — Mainly winter wheat

□ Minor areas   S — Mainly spring wheat

Regions labelled on map: Baltic, North West, Black Earth Centre, Volga-Vyatka, Centre, Ural, Belorussia, West Siberia, South West, Far East, Moldavia, East Siberia, South, Donetz Dnepr, Kazakhstan, North Caucasus, Central Asia, Transcaucasia, Volga

dulating terrain of well drained loamy chernozem soil favours cereal growing under mechanisation. These regions also provide the necessary climatic conditions. Wheat requires an average of 100 growing days to mature but further north in the continental interior where summer days are longer a fast maturing variety requiring as little as 60 days can be sown. The most favourable climate is in the west as here temperatures are higher, the growing season longer and precipitation more reliable (though falling off rapidly southward towards the Black Sea). Wheat requires an effective rainfall of between 380–760 mm including moist conditions for its germination and early growth, some precipitation to swell the wheat ears during the ripening period but a dry harvesting spell. Increasingly to the east these conditions are not met. The severe winters restrict production to spring grown wheat. Severe frost to the north limits growth in that direction and in the south and eastward rainfall is less reliable both in amount and incidence.

Already some indication has been given of a broad contrast between wheat growing in the west and that in the east and this needs taking further. In the west in regions such as the Ukraine, wheat growing developed earlier and the land is used more intensively, though still in large unit holdings — either a collective farm (kolkhoze) or a state farm (sovkhozy). The former, averaging 6000 hectares predominate in the west, being a form of co-operative owned by the 400 or so families who live on it but subject to production targets and marketing arrangements fixed by the state. A greater range of crops is grown with agriculture more diversified than further east. Pigs and cattle are also integrated into the farm system. This diversification has partly been a response to deteriorating soil conditions and declining yields up to the 1960s, due to too much concentration on winter wheat farming. But it is also partly due to a more diversified demand as urbanisation and industrialisation increased for example in the Ukraine as well as in the Moscow region. Nearly all the wheat grown is marketed within the main producing regions largely through the state system and the state run transport network.

To the east of the Volga conditions are markedly different with farming becoming increasingly extensive the further east one goes. Kazakhstan and West Siberia are now the great surplus producing regions upon which the industrialised regions are vitally dependent. But these regions have only been opened up under State Plans since 1954–1961, when the rising population and declining yields further west required a rapid increase in food output.

As a result the state initiated the now well-known 'virgin and idle lands campaign' to open up the fertile steppelands of Siberia. Several hundreds of thousands of volunteers from European Russia and other regions to the west were encouraged by the state to settle in these frontier regions to the east. The regions were divided up into huge state farms averaging 27 000 hectares and supporting 4000 people. These were highly mechanised and state financed with workers paid wages on piece rates. Output per worker is high but yields per unit area much lower than further west or on wheat growing areas of Western Europe. Initially despite the unreliability of climatic conditions, the rich virgin soil helped make wheat growing a success. But apart from fluctuations in yield, increasing problems have emerged including the need for increasing fertilizers

Exercise

Compare and contrast the systems under which wheat is grown to the west of the Volga in European Russia with that to the east in Siberia.

and other inputs to offset deteriorating soil conditions. Recently therefore determined efforts have been made to move away from the near monoculture (one crop growing) characteristic of much of the main wheat belt of the Kazakhstan and West Siberia to more diversified systems. This has included better crop rotation and more attention to livestock production, some areas on the climatic margins being returned to pastureland.

Thus despite being developed and organised under a different political condition wheat growing in the Soviet Union has undergone a similar change to that found on the prairie lands of Canada and the U.S.A. However though the area under wheat may decline this is likely to be compensated for by increased yields under better farming methods.

Marginal farming

It is not at all easy to see what is meant by marginal farming since it tends to be discussed both in economic and physical terms.

Economic margins of farming

Perhaps the most useful lead in is given by Von Thunen. For him marginal farming occurred on the outer periphery of the city state where, whatever the method of farming adopted, the farmer had difficulty in covering his costs and making a living. A lot of problems were associated with the long distance from the central market. Despite the farmer's efforts to compensate for increased transport costs by cutting down on other costs and farming extensively, there came a point where farming was no longer viable. Beyond this point the land was not worth farming. Today isolation from market remains an important factor in deciding the marginality or otherwise of farming.

But apart from the ultimate margin beyond which no kind of farming will occur, there are also economic margins to each kind of farming system, thereafter it will be replaced by another kind from which profits can be made. These and the outermost margin are not fixed, but change in response to changes in the circumstances controlling them.

Falling transport costs for example will clearly allow the outer economic margin of farming to be pushed further out still, with more land being taken in for farming, and each zone of farming being pushed outwards. A subsidy on some costs will have a similar effect. Rising revenue due to an increased demand and therefore rising prices, would also encourage farmers to move out to the margin and take in more land. This was the case for example with wheat farming in South Australia in 1880–1920. The opposite will occur if costs rise or prices fall.

Physical margins to farming

We have in effect already begun to touch on this other aspect of marginality for as demand for agricultural products increased so there was the temptation to push agriculture into regions with harsh physical conditions of one sort or another. Here remoteness combined to make the costs of farming high and return on investment in time, labour and money uncertain. Every continent has its physical margins for farming as we have already seen, not only in the case of wheat growing on the steppes of the U.S.S.R. but also in the tropical regions discussed earlier. Here on the periphery economic margin and physical margin fuse into a single concept of marginality.

We turn now to look at two types of extensive livestock farming in which the concept of margin is important in both an economic and physical sense.

Extensive livestock production in the continental interior

Because returns on extensive livestock production are lower than those from cereal growing, extensive livestock production has been forced into marginal regions where the rainfall is too low and unreliable for cereal growing. These are the semi-arid grasslands and steppe scrubland of the continental interiors, for example the High Plains of western North America and the drier pampas region of South America.

Uncertain physical conditions, relatively poor communication links to markets, yet an abundant supply of land dictate that the only profitable way to manage livestock ranching is along extensive lines. For example sheep ranches which concentrate on wool production are commonly 50 000 hectares to a million hectares in size with the latter running as many as 100 000 sheep at around 1 head per 10 hectares. Beef cattle ranches may extend from 6000 to 20 000 sq km. In the driest areas, such as the Basin Ranges of western U.S.A., there may be only 1 head of cattle for every 40 hectares. Returns per unit area are therefore low and in order for an enterprise to be profitable it has to be very large. Generally, the larger the better, with the limit decided by the area which can be effectively controlled under one management.

Labour and capital inputs per unit area are very low once the initial capital investment in fencing, water supplies and buildings has been made. Because quite a lot of the uncertainties have now been taken out of livestock ranching these large enterprises are guaranteed a profit but in the earlier years climatic hazards such as drought or an over severe winter frequently meant bankruptcy as for example during the 1930s, the famous Dustbowl era.

Beef and wool production are not limited to extensive pastoral systems. Indeed today more of both is produced on mixed farming systems in areas of more reliable rainfall and milder climatic conditions, for example beef fattening in the United States south and Mid West and wool production in New Zealand. Because of this increasing competition and an extension of irrigation and water supply schemes, the simple regional patterns of extensive livestock production have been changing since the 1950s. This can be illustrated from beef cattle fattening and rearing in the United States.

Before the 1950s the commonest situation was for cattle to be reared on the drier ranges of the Western Plains and taken east to the Corn Belt for fattening. But today many of the cattle are fattened on feed lots in the Western Plains itself or sent not only to the Mid West but also to California and the south. This is because fattening is not only associated with a diversification of agriculture in these regions but also with growing markets, as California and the south have become increasingly industrialised and have higher shares of the country's population.

The nature of the livestock industry and the conditions underlying it can be further illustrated from the Case Study (16.3) of Texas, one of the chief cattle regions of the United States

Marginal hill farming — an extensive form of pastoralism in the United Kingdom

About one third of Britain's agricultural land is in fact suitable only for hill farming. This is land defined by the Ministry of Agriculture as of such a nature as to be only fit for the rearing of livestock and not their fattening. The official size of holdings gives little indication of the amount of land actually needed to support the number of sheep necessary to make an upland farm viable, for the size given usually takes into account only the enclosed land which may be anything from 24 hectares up to 1000 hectares if it is run by an estate company. But in addition large areas of open moorland are used for summer grazing. The enclosed land is mainly used for permanent pasture on which to winter the stock and grow summer grass for silage. Because of the increasing costs of labour, little of the lower land is now used for winter feed crop growing such as kale, turnips and oats as was formerly the case.

At the present time these hill farms account for half of Britain's sheep population as well as a significant if minor number of its beef and dairy cattle. (The monthly milk cheque is one of the few sources of regular income which many of the small hill farmers have.) Their direct contribution to British farming is small, by value only about 7%. But hill farming remains important for two basic reasons.

Firstly it is still considered the most valuable way of using the upland margins of Britain, providing not only a vital income to isolated rural settlements but also helping to maintain the social viability of the communities at a time when depopulation of highland fringes theatens their existence. Secondly, upland farms are the main suppliers of sheep for fattening on lowland farms and provide some of the young cattle stock. They therefore make an important contribution to the success of the mixed farming system on neighbouring lowland areas such as those in the West Midlands and Central Scotland.

However, because of the many problems increasingly encountered, the number of hill farms is declining (refer to Case Study 16.4). Including those in Northern Ireland there were only 26 000 full-time hill farmers in Britain in the mid 1970s and numbers continue to fall. There were another 35 000 part-time farmers making up their income in a variety of ways. For example it is estimated that about one third of Lake District farms offer tourist facilities such as bed and breakfast and camping/caravan sites. Many hill farmers and others in the household take on outside jobs, either seasonally or through the year in such things as forestry and hotel work because the farm alone cannot provide a living.

Efforts have been made to improve the lot of hill farming. Ever since the Hill Farming Act of 1945, grants and subsidies have been available under which buildings and land have been improved, and price supports given. This has been continued under the auspices of the EEC through the European Fund for Regional Development. Most hope is seen through such measures as amalgamation of uneconomic holdings, improvement of moorland by drainage schemes, reseeding of permanent pastures, closer cooperation in the use of machinery and in marketing and an improved advisory and insurance service to avoid heavy financial loss during very hard winters.

It would seem that in the future here and elsewhere in Western Europe — such as the Alps and the South of Italy, where the nature of hill farming is different to that in this country — the trend is likely to be one of decline. It is becoming increasingly difficult for the EEC to finance its current agricultural budget and cutbacks are already occurring. As these bite deeper the lot of hill farming will become increasingly precarious.

16:3 TEXAS, UNITED STATES

Extensive cattle rearing and beef production

THE UNITED STATES BEEF FATTENING SYSTEM BASED
INITIALLY ON CATTLE REARING IN THE TEXAS HIGH PLAINS

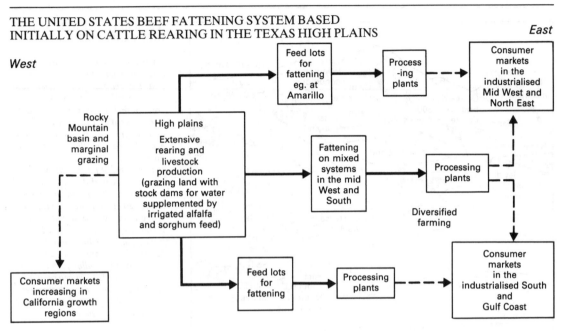

West · *East*

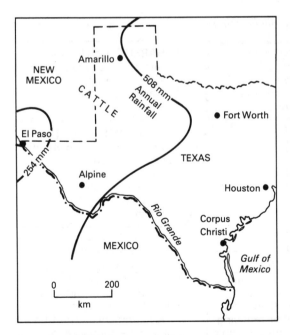

*Location of 06 Ranch near Alpine and of
Amarillo area*

A BEEF FATTENING LOT EXEMPLIFIED FROM AMARILLO AREA—TEXAS

5 million cattle coming off the High Plains to the West are fattened in feed yards with capacities from 1000 to 80 000 cattle each. Stock feed lots use sorghum feed — which is replacing wheat in marginal areas. Most sorghum growing requires irrigation especially in marginal areas — 728 000 ha planted. The feed yards both supply 14 regional processing and packing plants and ship a further 50-75 000 head weekly to mixed fattening systems further East.

REARING LIVESTOCK PRODUCTION ILLUSTRATED FROM THE 06 RANCH NORTH OF ALPINE—SOUTH WEST TEXAS

Ranch covers 350 sq km extending into Davis Mts. foothills. Cattle graze in traditional way but grazing improved by adding more waterholes.

Climate is one of extremes — floods, droughts, blizzards and tornadoes — 'softer' seasons are short.

Yearling steers and calves raised and sold by contract to company owning fattening lots in Oklahoma. Herds of British and mixed breeds including Brahma round up in the fall and shipped by rail.

Hill farming and its problems

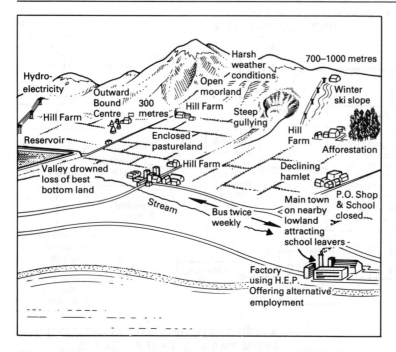

A FARMER'S VIEWPOINT ON HILL FARMING IN WALES

They were failing their owners because in general they were too small and the returns from sheep and cattle insufficient to maintain the costs of their improvement. I got to know several of them over the years and in almost every case their owners sold them as they got tired of them

I revisited the area last week. It looked as beautiful as it always had done to me. There has been some improvement on the better farms. Government grants and hill subsidies have provided the means for new buildings, reseeding and fencing. Many of the farms have been made bigger as the smaller farmers went out. Since the EEC sheep regulation came in, farmers are getting a reasonable reward for their labours. But it is no easy street.

Financial Times 13.11.81

Physical, Economic and Social Conditions Affecting Hill Farming

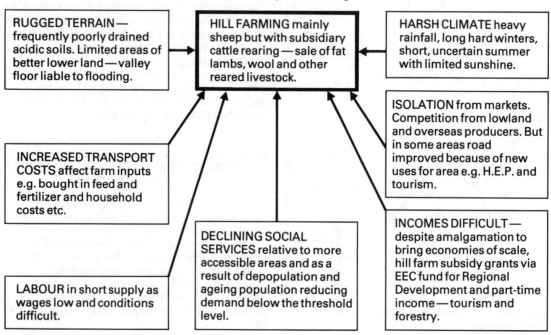

RUGGED TERRAIN — frequently poorly drained acidic soils. Limited areas of better lower land — valley floor liable to flooding.

HILL FARMING mainly sheep but with subsidiary cattle rearing — sale of fat lambs, wool and other reared livestock.

HARSH CLIMATE heavy rainfall, long hard winters, short, uncertain summer with limited sunshine.

INCREASED TRANSPORT COSTS affect farm inputs e.g. bought in feed and fertilizer and household costs etc.

ISOLATION from markets. Competition from lowland and overseas producers. But in some areas road improved because of new uses for area e.g. H.E.P. and tourism.

LABOUR in short supply as wages low and conditions difficult.

DECLINING SOCIAL SERVICES relative to more accessible areas and as a result of depopulation and ageing population reducing demand below the threshold level.

INCOMES DIFFICULT — despite amalgamation to bring economies of scale, hill farm subsidy grants via EEC fund for Regional Development and part-time income — tourism and forestry.

17   The Nature of Resources

QUESTIONS OF SUPPLY AND DEMAND

Resource is a term applicable to a wide range of environmental attributes which are of potential use to man either directly as an input to the agricultural or industrial economy or indirectly by exchanging the resource for monetary assets.
Cook, J.A. *Resource Assessment in Africa* (Geography 1979 No. 283 — Vol. 64, Part 2).

In an earlier section we dealt with those environmental attributes such as land area, soil quality and climate which can be considered as resource inputs for agriculture. Here we are concerned with those which are largely, but not exclusively, inputs into the industrial economy — minerals, power, water and forestry. It is convenient also to consider fisheries since these too need careful management.

Though a resource is defined as something of potential use to man, at any one point in time the essentially important resources are those which can be and are actually being used. These are but a small part of the total potential which exist in the environment. Many resource areas are as yet unexplored and unassessed. Many others though known to exist, cannot at present be used, either because they are not financially worthwhile or we have not the technology to make them viable. For example North Sea oil and gas resources were known to exist in large quantities over thirty years ago, but it is only since the 1970s that the rise in world prices and advances in technology have been such as to justify extraction of oil and gas in the very difficult physical conditions existing in the North Sea fields.

Resource shortage: concerns and effects

Despite the many resource discoveries being made and a continual advance in technology, one of the major features of postwar years has been the fear that because of population growth and the almost insatiable demand of modern consumer societies, demands would outstrip available world resources. Though some resources such as water are renewable most are regarded as non-renewable; they are considered finite and once used cannot be replaced. Concern grew following the publication in the early 1960s of 'Limits to Growth' by the Club of Rome, an international body of eminent people, and later because of the oil crisis of the 1970s: there was the real fear of a growing scarcity of certain essential resources, in particular energy resources. The 'energy crisis' as it is called, is familiar to us all and has been accompanied by rising energy costs.

Along with the threat of exhaustion of valuable resources has come an increasing concern for the environment. In the drive to raise material standards of living not only is it feared that resources are being used up too quickly, but also in the process of getting at these resources and using them, irreparable damage is being done to the environment. Extraction of coal and minerals leaves scars on the landscape, whilst the processing and consumption of them leads to pollution in rivers, in coastal areas, on the land and in the atmosphere. Thus the concern for proper resource management and conservation includes not only a careful monitoring of resource extraction but also this wider concern for the direct and indirect effects resource use can have on the environment. (Refer to Case Study 18.1 on p. 179.)

It is, however, important that we distinguish between the two issues, the one the worry about using up the world's resources too quickly, and the other about managing and protecting the environment. We shall here deal with the first issue and then later consider the wider issue of managing the environment as a whole.

Why the world will not run out of power and mineral resources

If necessity is the mother of invention, economic incentive is the midwife.
Resource and energy crises are nothing new. Throughout history man has at different periods faced them, and within the very crisis itself has been

173

not only the spur to its solution but also the beginnings of another phase of material progress. This was the very stuff out of which the Industrial Revolution was made.

Tapping more of the same resource and the development of alternatives

Towards the end of the 18th century the advanced economies of Western Europe, and in particular Britain, faced two major crises. One was the using up of available woodland which was the major source of building material as well as of the charcoal which provided their only means of smelting iron-ore. The other was the exhaustion of coal supplies since much of the surface coal had been used and due to flooding there was no way of extracting the coal at deeper levels. It is now a matter of history that the invention of the steam engine provided the power for the pumps and coal winding gear needed for deeper mining and that the invention of a way to process coal into coke provided an alternative fuel to charcoal for smelting the iron-ore. This in turn eased the demand on wood as a building material since iron could now also be used.

Thus further discoveries and technological breakthroughs can not only make available more of the same resource but can enable one resource to be replaced by another.

Recycling

More recently there is yet another way to, in effect, increase the quantity of resource, namely recycle the product made from it. We have seen this in the case of scrap replacing some iron-ore input in the steel industry. Recovery of waste is also in a sense recycling. Due to technological advances it is now possible to recover mineral content from the residue dumped from earlier mining operations, as is happening for example in areas of earlier lead and tin mining.

Factors affecting the exploitation and supply of resources

As we have seen, whilst resources are being used in increasing amounts there are a variety of ways in which a sufficient supply can be ensured. If this is so, then the question arises as to why there are periodic crises about the scarcity of resources. Much of it is to do with the way the price of a raw material changes relative to the supply and demand for it, and the level and cost of the technology needed to enable the resource to be extracted and distributed to the market. All these are important factors affecting the exploitation and supply of resources. Unfortunately

it takes time to respond to market changes in demand, and the problems of over-supply and recurrent shortage occur.

When a demand arises the first deposits of a resource to be exploited are those which are the least costly to extract, but in sufficient quantity and quality for it to be worthwhile. However, whilst demand may continue to rise it can increasingly only be met by extracting the less accessible parts of a deposit and therefore the more costly it is to extract. Unless companies have guarantees of a rise in price to cover increased extraction costs, a situation can arise where demand is expanding and yet supplies are diminishing, or at best are at a static level. Consequently a scarcity crisis arises.

In such a crisis situation, customers are then willing to pay higher prices for the resource and price rises occur. This triggers a variety of responses which resolve the crisis. Existing producers can cover the costs of the more difficult extraction at existing deposits but there is also the incentive to explore for other deposits and to develop technology to exploit hitherto inaccessible deposits. Further there is a search for substitute deposits. This and other reactions to the oil crisis of 1973 have occurred to such an extent that this is paradoxically partly the cause of the current glut in oil supplies which is depressing prices.

However, the broad mechanism outlined above is usually complicated by other factors. For instance in the case of oil supplies, member countries of O.P.E.C. deliberately conspired during the 1960s to curtail supplies and therefore cause a rise in prices. There was the further complication of the revolution in Iran which cut off one of the main sources of Middle East oil. Then also the world recession partly brought on by the 1973 oil crisis has led to a depressed demand for oil.

Whilst used to illustrate the almost cyclic scarcity to over-supply situation which periodically occurs in relation to many important resources, the above outline of the mechanics of the underlying process also illustrates the range of factors which interact to influence whether a resource body will be exploited or not (Fig. 17.1).

Hay's Location Theory

A number of attempts have been made to generalise the various situations under which a resource in any given area may or may not be utilised.

Hay's Location Theory for Mining Activity is seen as perhaps the most useful of these, since it allows for changing economic circumstances and is applicable to a range of resources in addition to those mined.

Hay's model has a number of merits — it not only takes account of the two major cost factors dif-

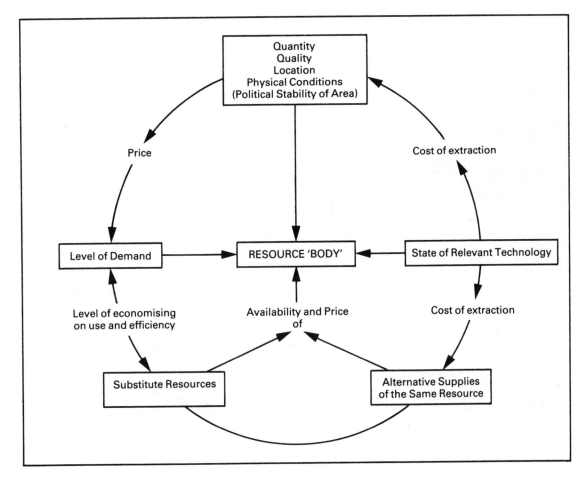

Fig. 17.1 Factors affecting the development of a particular resource 'body'

ferentiating between production and transport costs, but also takes into account the revenue factor. In turn these three will reflect important underlying factors. They are geological circumstances which will be reflected in production costs, break of bulk charge at a road/rail junction in the transport costs and competition from substitute materials reflected in the prevailing market price. Thus it is more than a cost/revenue model.

Further it is a dynamic model in that changes in production or transport costs as well as those suggested for market price can be accommodated by altering the relevant variable in the graphed relationship. However Hay does make an additional point not amenable to visual representation but an important one, namely that cost and price are not as factors independent of one another. For example if improved techniques reduce mining costs then mine producers will bring more output on the market for

sale and increased supply may depress the price and therefore the revenue obtained, if consuming industries do not need the increased output on the market.

What Hay's model does not include are the behavioural and political circumstances to which increasing attention is being paid. But this need not diminish the usefulness of the model, since these additional factors can be introduced into the analysis at a later stage.

Exercise

Using the information in Fig. 17.2 and the graph given in d), list by letter which mines are profitable at each of the effective price situations given in the table.

Interaction of cost and
price (revenue) factors
↓

A. Production Costs

1 *Nature of the mineral deposit*
Mineral content of the ore
Size of deposit
Seam thickness
Depth of overburden
Drainage conditions

2 *Human/economic influences*
Presence or absence of needed
infrastructure e.g. communications
power lines, water supply,
settlement facilities, shipment
facilities.

Cost of labour — wages etc.

Compensation to landowners etc.

Other environmental costs
e.g. protection against effluent
pollution.

Political e.g. taxes and royalties
to governments.

B. Transport Costs
Note — more complex than shown
as may e.g. include two
different kinds of transport and
break of bulk handling costs

C. Variable Market Price
Factor
(which producer as well as
consumer can influence)

Cost/revenue (price)
relationships indicate
which mine locations
are viable

Production cost and location of
mines A-Q relative to the market

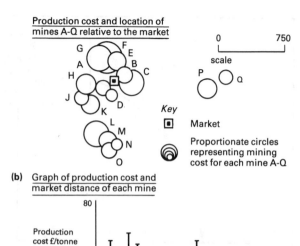

(b) Graph of production cost and
market distance of each mine

Production
cost £/tonne

80

■ Market

ABCD E F G H J K   L M N O P   Q

→ Distance from market → 1500 km
Transport costs for each mine

Production costs vary from one
mine to another

(c) Graph of transport cost & increase
with distance from market

Transport
cost £/tonne
per km

■ Market

→ Distance from market → 1500 km

Since distance to market varies
for each mine so will transport
costs

(d) Effective price revenue (market
price less transport) curves related
to production costs

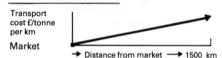

Effective
market
price and   25
£/tonne   20
Production   15
cost   10
£/tonne   5

■ Market   ABCD E F G H J K   L M N O P Q
             Market distance in km

Transport costs must be subtracted
from the market price to give the
effective price obtained.
In d) effective price/revenue curves
for different market situations
are set against the production cost
line *for each mine located* in diag. (a)
For a mine to be profitable the
production cost line must fall below
any given revenue curve

Effective revenue/cost situations
or price supply relationships in fig d.

= Price: £/tonne	5	10	15	20	25
→ Number of mines viable	2	5	8	13	16

Fig. 17.2   Hay's location theory for mining activity

18   Mineral Exploitation

Mineral deposits represent non-renewable resources, an important fact not only for industries dependent on them but also for the region in which mining occurs. Some regions thus have only a fleeting prosperity and once the mineral deposit is exhausted are abandoned. Ghost towns and old workings, as in the gold rush areas of Kalgoorlie (Australia) and the Yukon (Alaska), are all that remain of the short boom period.

However in other cases such may be the size of deposits and other favourable factors, for example availability of power and an accessible location, that mining leads to further development attracting lasting settlement. This in turn has further multiplier effects resulting in a region having a large and diversified economic base, with sufficient momentum to maintain growth, even after the initial mineral workings have been exhausted. For example the Rand gold mining area where mining began in the late 19th century is now one of the world's major industrial regions. At its heart lies Johannesburg, a large metropolis of 1.5 million people, where economic growth is likely to continue even when gold mining is no longer possible.

Factors affecting mineral development

Of the factors determining the fortunes or otherwise of mining areas some are geological such as the size and quality of the deposit, others economic such as its location relative to prospective markets and costs of development compared to alternative source areas. Yet others not covered in Hay's model outlined earlier, are political and social. Warren summarises it thus: 'The geography of mining is the response of an enterprise to the known geological facts, though conditioned by the availability of capital and labour, by political considerations, planning controls and very importantly by the legacy from past patterns'.

But this is not all — situations change as Warren's reference to past patterns implies. Thus, for example, a mineral deposit which at one point in time was not worth mining or which may have been abandoned because mining was no longer viable may at a later date be worth exploiting. Demand may have risen causing a rise in market price making it possible to cover higher mining costs or new techniques may have been developed reducing mining costs. For example, old tin mining areas in Cornwall have been re-opened as a result of such changes in circumstance.

Mineral classification

The classification by Blunden is useful to the geographer since it not only groups minerals according to their physical/chemical characteristics but also on the basis of their locational occurrence. His basic division is as follows:

a   Ubiquitous non-metallic minerals, e.g. gravel, limestone etc.
b   Localised non-metallic minerals, e.g. salt, potash, china-clay etc.
c   Non-ferrous metals, e.g. copper, bauxite, tin etc.
d   Ferrous metals, e.g. various kinds of iron-ore
e   Carbon and hydro-carbon fuels, e.g. oil, coal.

Ubiquitous non-metallic minerals

Materials used in the building and construction industry dominate this group. Minerals in this group include gravel and brick clays, which because of their widespread (ubiquitous) occurrence and low unit value, are unable to stand the cost of transport over any appreciable distance. Thus they tend to be exploited close to their markets and there are many workings where suitable outcrops of the parent materials occur. Depending to some extent on the size of the market served, workings tend to be on a small scale though some may be extensive as is the case for example with the brick clay workings at

177

Peterborough and Bedford serving the Midlands and Home Counties or the Lea Valley gravel workings, north of London.

Because workings are open-cast, large scale extraction may pose particular problems — stripping of over-burden and dumping of waste scars the landscape; pits are liable to flooding. In the case of brick making, atmospheric pollution may be caused and in general heavy lorries cause congestion and possibly some damage to local roads. However, increasingly tight planning controls and the growing influence exercised by environmental groups do today ensure not only the sympathetic location of extraction sites but also proper reclamation of worked over land. Indeed an eyesore may be turned into a community asset providing storage and recreational facilities. It is difficult for example to know what would happen to the mountains of waste created by modern living were not disused quarries and other kinds of pits available as dumping areas, the infill later being reclaimed as land for agriculture or light industrial building. On a much larger scale the old gravel workings along the flooded gravel pits of the Lea Valley for example have been linked by walkways and grassed areas to provide the Lea Valley Regional Park, a major recreational outlet for the population not only of Greater London but also the growing numbers in the commuter belt through which the park runs (Fig. 18.1).

Localised non-metallic minerals

Because they are so localised and less plentiful than those in the ubiquitous non-metal group, this group of minerals have a higher unit value than the ubiquitous class of minerals and can therefore stand the cost of transport over longer distances. In general they are the raw materials of more specialised industries. Potash and salt for example are used in branches of the chemical industry, whilst china-clay is an important ingredient in the finer side of the pottery industry and in paper making.

Whilst providing employment opportunities and prompting some infrastructure development in a region, together with limited ancillary activities, only in a few cases does the exploitation of localised non-metallic minerals provide the basis for sustained industrial growth. Much depends on other factors such as the availability of a plentiful water supply, power supplies and proximity to outlet points for the manufactured product. In the case of the chemical industries of Cheshire and Teesside, these other factors were present in that for example both are near coalfields and have close links to a sizeable home market as well as port outlets. The latter also allowed the import of other raw materials as the region's industries became more diversified. Consequently industrial growth did occur.

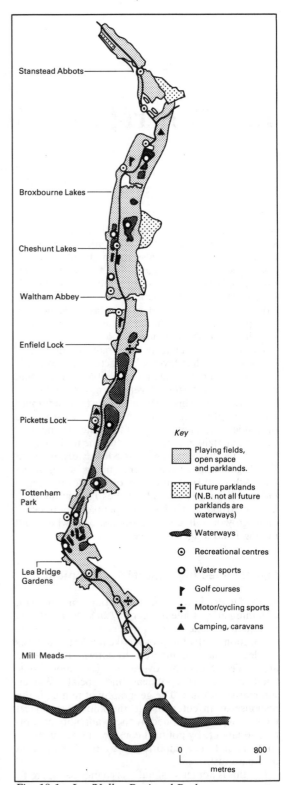

Key

	Playing fields, open space and parklands.
	Future parklands (N.B. not all future parklands are waterways)
	Waterways
	Recreational centres
	Water sports
	Golf courses
	Motor/cycling sports
	Camping, caravans

Fig. 18.1   Lea Valley Regional Park

18:1 LEE MOOR, DARTMOOR

Expansion plans for china clay working

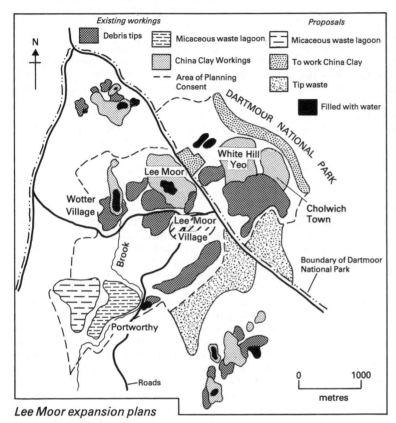

Lee Moor expansion plans

Legend:

Existing workings
- Debris tips
- China Clay Workings
- Area of Planning Consent
- Micaceous waste lagoon

Proposals
- Micaceous waste lagoon
- To work China Clay
- Tip waste
- Filled with water

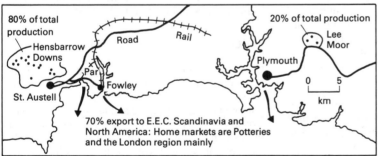

Location of Lee Moor relative to the main producing area— Hensbarrow Downs

80% of total production — Hensbarrow Downs — St. Austell — Par — Fowley

20% of total production — Lee Moor — Plymouth

70% export to E.E.C. Scandinavia and North America: Home markets are Potteries and the London region mainly

RESULT OF PLANNING APPLICATION AND OBJECTIONS — A COMPROMISE

The extension of workings was allowed but tipping was forbidden on a major part of the planned site in the National Park.
Since then the workings have been extended in a series of developments up to the mid 1980s.

THE PLAN

1 Extend present working from 900ft to 1000ft contour making available another 1.7 million tonnes of china clay.
2 Take another 237 ha for waste tipping and a slurry lake.

CLAIMED ADVANTAGES

1 Help meet a rising home and overseas demand projected to exceed current supplies.
2 Provide more jobs in a region short of employment.
3 Eventual reclamation of used area provides a leisure lake area which would reduce pressures on Dartmoor National Park.

OPPOSITION TO THE PLAN

1 Not from local resident population to whom china clay workings are part of their landscape heritage and a source of jobs.
2 Opposition came from environmental groups especially the Dartmoor Preservation Society and led by some influential people living in the region. Opposition mainly on grounds of damage to part of the Dartmoor National Park and danger hazard of slurry lakes especially to local children.

Exercise

● As part of a group evaluate the pros and cons of a local planning application for the extraction of some material or— establishment of a possibly obnoxious industry in an area known to you.

In contrast, exploitation of china-clay in Cornwall where there are no coalfield sites and no large market areas close to hand, whilst important to the region because of other limited employment opportunities, has not led to any appreciable industrial growth. The china-clay is either sent out by road to the Potteries of North Staffordshire or the paper works in the London region and elsewhere or exported from the ports of Par and Fowey.

Particularly with increasing demands in the paper industry where china-clay is used to give a sheen to paper, the china-clay industry since the 1930s has considerably expanded. Apart from large deposits in Georgia (U.S.A.) the Cornwall deposits are said to be the only major source of kaolin (china-clay). The large companies involved in working this deposit, including English Clays Lovering Pochin & Co. Ltd., which has also large undertakings in quarrying, transport, building and civil engineering, have thus initiated large scale schemes for extending the workings.

Because of the environmental implications of this, heightened as it is by the location of the main area of workings around St. Austell on the borders of the Dartmoor National Park, there has been widespread opposition to plans to extend workings. The case of the Lee Moor workings illustrate well the sort of compromise which is reached to reconcile economic needs with responsible management of an environment. (See Case Study 18.1, p. 179.)

Non-ferrous metals

This group includes a wide range of minerals from precious ones like gold, silver and uranium to important ones essential to modern industry such as tin, bauxite and copper. Whilst the United States and the Soviet Union have large deposits of most of these minerals, most other industrial countries are heavily dependent on imports, mainly from developing countries or Australia and Canada.

Supplies are sensitive to changes in the level of world prices and demand and there have been serious fluctuations in these since the 1960s. These have badly affected the economies of those countries such as Chile, Peru, Zaire and Zambia which are dependent upon a narrow range of exports in which metals figure prominently. For example copper from the Copper Belt makes up over 70% by value of Zaire and Zambia's exports.

Fluctuations on the world commodity market are due to a number of causes, including economic recession in importing countries, availability of more favourably priced substitute materials and the discovery and exploitation of new sources of a mineral. For example rich deposits of manganese and uranium are now being exploited in the small country of Gabon in Central Africa and further

exploratory survey has uncovered deposits of barytes, lead, zinc, copper as well as smaller deposits of gold and diamond. These and large ferrous deposits of iron-ore are also likely to be exploited once the railway is further extended inland from the coast.

Two important developments in this side of the mining industry have been the use of new techniques enabling a much larger scale of working including viable access to deposits of poorer mineral content hitherto considered uneconomic to mine, and more semi-processing of the mineral before export. Both have significant implications for the countries concerned. Whilst for example more mechanisation would reduce the demand for labour, the compensating larger scale of working does help to maintain the existing workforce and attracts ancillary activities such as power and maintenance services, giving a multiplier effect attracting more labour to the area. Increased processing of the mineral also generates more employment opportunities as well as raising the unit value of the mineral before export, thereby increasing not only the revenue to be gained by the producing country, but also providing much needed foreign exchange and capital for other developments in the economy. Some of these cumulative advantages are illustrated in Fig. 18.2.

Not surprisingly, as former colonial territories have gained independence, they have adopted measures to give them an important controlling stake in the country's resources and to raise the level of revenue earned by adopting a greater degree of processing before export. However there is a limit to how far this can go, as developing countries on the whole need the capital and expertise from foreign investment and the activities of the large multinational companies which tend to dominate export resource development in the newer countries, as for example in Namibia–South West Africa.

The Copper Belt in Zaire and Zambia

Though there are larger producers, the Copper Belt is the most important single district in the world for copper, contributing about 15% of the world's output, making Zaire and Zambia two of the major world exporters. It may be used as an example to indicate the conditions under which copper is mined and its impact on those economies where it is a principal source of export earnings (Case Study 18.2).

Ferrous metals

Iron is one of the most common minerals and most countries producing iron and steel also have iron-ore deposits of one kind or other. But as home resources have become depleted and iron and steel production

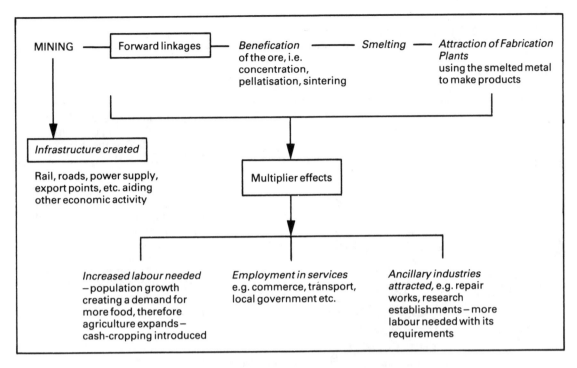

Fig. 18.2   Possible development effects of mineral exploitation

has expanded, iron has increasingly entered into world trade. Of the major industrial nations only the Soviet Union has sufficient domestic deposits, all others import large amounts of iron-ore. But though the United States is an important importer, its dependence on world trade is much less than Japan and the major West European producers such as Germany and the United Kingdom.

Trade in iron-ore has also increased because the development of bulk ore carriers has made it economic to transport iron-ore over longer distances. Also better mining and processing techniques have enabled the concentration of the ore by pelletisation or some other method reducing the amount of waste in iron-ore carried by these bulk carriers.

The leading exporters are those countries still in the process of industrialising and in which large workable deposits have recently been discovered. Indeed one of the outstanding features of the post-war iron and steel industry has been the rapidity with which certain countries such as Canada, Australia, Brazil and India have risen in the ranks of world production to become the foremost exporters e.g. both Australia and India are important suppliers to the Japanese iron and steel industries, whilst these together with Canada and Brazil also ship ore to the United States and Western Europe.

However, except where the ores are in relatively remote locations, the major exporters are also de-

veloping important iron and steel industries themselves. So unlike exports of non-ferrous metals, iron exports only represent a proportion of the iron-ore actually mined. Development of a domestic iron and steel industry is considered one of the major priorities when countries set out on the path to industrialisation. Thus as these countries industrialise, advanced countries which depend on iron imports must invest in further exploration for new supplies either with existing exporting countries or in other countries. For example Japan, the country most dependent on iron imports, has invested heavily in Brazil to uncover additional supplies to those already being exploited in the Minais Gerais region. Foreign investment has also been made in new regions such as the African countries of Gabon and Mauritania which have neither the capital nor home demand to exploit their own ore resources.

It is magnetite and haematite ores which mainly enter world trade, as these kinds of deposits contain sufficient iron content to make export worth while.

Both occur on a large scale and can be worked by open-cast methods. Magnetite has the highest iron content varying between 70% and 45%. That worked in Kiruna and Gallivare in North Sweden and exported via Narvik (Norway) and Lulea (Sweden) for example has a 60% iron content, whilst those in Mauritania at Fort Gourand in the Sahara and shipped out via Port Etienne are of 65% iron content.

181

18:2 ZAIRE AND ZAMBIA

Copper mining

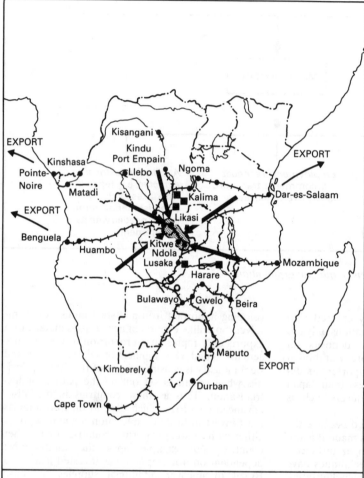

Position in World Copper Smelting Capacity (000 tonnes) 1982	
U.S.S.R.	1220
Chile	1046
U.S.A.	975
Japan	948
Zambia	581
Zaire	466
Canada	367
(But together with Chile Zambia and Zaire are leading exporters)	

Key

_·—·_	National boundary
─┼┼─	Railway
(shaded oval)	Copper belt
➔	Labour migration
■	H.E.P. sites
○	Coal

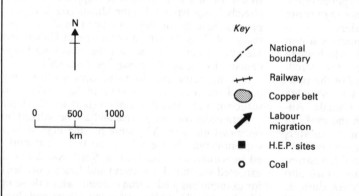

Towns (000s) ZAIRE — 1975		
Kinshasa	2242	} Copper belt
Lumbumbashi	481	
Kananga	377	
ZAMBIA — 1980		
Lusaka	641	
Kitwe	341	} Copper belt
Ndola	323	
Mufulina	150	

POLITICAL STABILITY
Needed not only in Zaire and
Zambia but also in
neighbouring states

LABOUR
Migrant labour not only from
areas in Zambia outside the
Copper Belt but also from
neighbouring Rwandi,
Burundi and Zimbabwe

OCCURRENCE
150 km axial belt of copper
mainly copper oxides in
Saba (Katanga) which are of
better quality and earlier
developed than the mainly
copper sulphides in Zambia

FACTORS AFFECTING
DEVELOPMENT

DEPENDENT ON FOREIGN
INVESTMENT, MINING
TECHNOLOGY AND
MANAGEMENT

POWER SUPPLIES
In Zaire from HEP schemes
on Lufira and Luataba Rivers

Zambia used to be
dependent on Hwange coal
(Zimbabwe) with a long rail
haul and from 1950s on its
share of Kariba HEP scheme.
Now also has developed its
own Kafue HEP scheme
and Mamba coal deposits

EXPORT MARKET DEMAND
Demand and price fluctuate
according to competition
and world economic
situation

PROBLEMS OF TRANSPORT
Copper semi-processed for
export to reduce volume and
raise export value

Problem of landlocked
situation and long costly rail
haul through neighbouring
states to coast

Before unrest bulk went
from Zaire via own rail and
river route and also by rail
through Angola to Benguela

Zambia exported via
Zimbabwe/Mozambique to
Benguela. Civil Wars led to
construction of alternative
Tanzam rail route to Dar es
Salaam, but rail and port still
of insufficient capacity

IMPACT ON EACH COUNTRY'S ECONOMY

Advantages — Copper Belt a growth centre — important export earning —
stimulated power and infrastructure development aiding other parts of the
economy. (But not brought much manufacturing.)

Disadvantages — Overconcentration to the neglect of agriculture and
development in other areas (new government developing Lusaka as a
counter growth pole). Over dependent on copper and foreign investment
— vulnerable to disruption in neighbouring countries and fluctuation on
world markets. Labour migrations disrupted tribal and family life.

Exercise

● Discuss some of the problems
arising from the exploitation of
one major non-ferrous metal.

18:3 PILBARA REGION, WESTERN AUSTRALIA

Iron ore mining

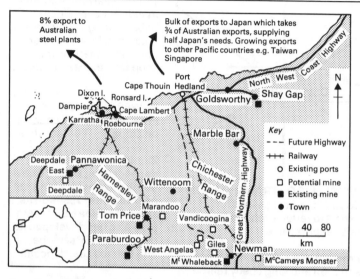

Location of Iron ore mining and associated development

A   IMPORTANCE

The Pilbara region supplies 90% of Australia's iron-ore output. But due to the recent world economic recession the region is working at under-capacity. It has a capacity of 100 million tonnes annual output but in 1983 produced 73 million tonnes.

The mining industry provides half the region's total employment.

B   A SOCIAL INJUSTICE PROBLEM HAS ARISEN

As in other cases when big business including multinationals begin to exploit a region, it can have unfortunate consequences for the indigenous population — in this case the territorial right of the Aboriginals and their way of life have been affected. But there are signs now of a more sympathetic awareness of this problem as in other cases e.g. S W Namibia (Africa).

C   FACTORS INFLUENCING EXPLOITATION

(a) Large scale iron-ore deposits were known about before World War II in the Hammersley and Ophthalmia ranges but they were too remote and expensive to mine compared to deposits elsewhere e.g. S E Brazil.

(b) Market demand and capital available in the 1950s when Japan became a major iron and steel producer urgently requiring increasing amounts of iron-ore. Mitsui Company along with Australian companies provided the huge financial outlay required.

(c) Infrastructure — power, communication network costly in this remote area. Of the £155 million invested by 1970 ⅔ was spent on infrastructure installations.

(d) Transport — aided by technological developments — bulk ocean ore carriers lowered sea transport costs, though rail haul to the coast is long. Again helped by bulk ore trains of 1700 tonnes capacity each. Benefication plants at mine site reduced waste in ore transported. Also some palletisation at port before export.
480 km rail link developed inland and deepwater ports at Port Hedland, Dampier etc.

(e) Water and power costly compared to elsewhere e.g. Labrador, Venezuela. Power based on imported oil and coal. North West offshore gasfield a possible future source of power.

(f) Labour — extremely costly (significant cost despite being a capital intensive industry). High wages and other incentives needed to attract labour to this remote area. Townships with amenities recently developed partly aided by tourism in this part of Western Australia.

Exercise

● To what extent does the development of iron-ore deposits in W Australia reflect the principles outlined in Hay's model for mineral exploitation?

But at present haematite ores with on average a lower iron content than magnetite enter most into world trade. For example the bulk of Brazil and Australia's deposits are of this kind. Because of their lower iron-ore content, the development of pelletisation methods to reduce the waste before shipment has been particularly important for the various kinds of haematite ore being exploited.

We now turn to a more detailed consideration of the geography of iron-ore mining through a study of the Pilbara region in Western Australia. Australia is now the world's major exporter of iron-ore and by volume of production exceeded only by the Soviet Union. The Pilbara area is Australia's main iron-ore region.

Mineral development — the case of Australia

The importance of mineral developments

Australia with only 15 million population is at present experiencing a boom in mineral production making it the fastest growing sector in the economy with a forecast rise of from 5% to 10% of the Gross National Product and a similar growth in export earnings over the next decade. Australia has rich mineral reserves and more are being discovered each year (Fig. 18.3).

At present Australia is one of the world's largest producers of iron-ore, bauxite, alumina and titanium. In addition it has 15% of the world's recoverable uranium, the main raw material for generating atomic energy and is a significant producer of nickel, lead, zinc, copper, manganese, tin, gold and silver.

Foreign investment by multinationals

Foreign based multinational companies have invested heavily in the development of Australian resources (Fig. 18.4). There are a number of reasons for this. It is partly because of the variety and size of mineral deposits available particularly in Western Australia and in Queensland. Australia is also a politically stable area and allied to the developed world so it is also unlikely to nationalise the assets of foreign companies. These advantages together with

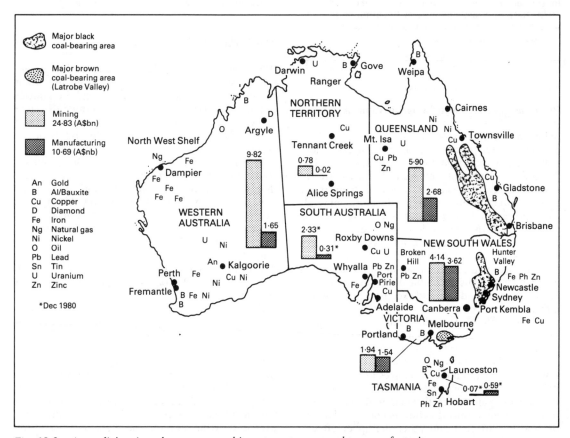

Fig. 18.3 Australia's mineral resources and investment compared to manufacturing

185

	UK	Other EEC	USA	Canada	Japan	Non EEC others	Total
1978–1979	311	88	554	−6	267	24	1238
1979–1980	374	444	359	81	308	327	1894
1980–1981	1211	351	763	33	676	627–721	4383

Source: Australian Bureau of Statistics

Fig. 18.4   Source of foreign investment into Australia, 1978–81 (A$ mill.)

the availability of high technology skills in the country, make it in many instances more attractive for investment than the developing countries located in less stable regions such as Africa and Latin America.

Exercise

Comment on the reasons for the increasing foreign investment in mining in Australia over the period 1978–1981. Suggest reasons why the amount of investment from the different sources shown has changed between 1978–1981.

Problems associated with foreign investment

Whilst this foreign investment in mining has helped to bring greater prosperity it has its dangers. There is the anxiety that large multinationals, such as Rio Tinto Zinc, may simply see Australia as a source of raw materials to meet the needs of their many manufacturing plants overseas. If more minerals were processed before export and more used as a basis for further expansion of manufacturing in Australia, this would appreciably benefit the economy and generate more job opportunities. There are the additional fears that outside interests would gain too much influence on the direction the Australian economy would take and exercise a neo-colonial influence.

A recent official Australian Survey has indicated that by more processing of mined minerals prior to export, the value of mineral export earnings could be increased by a surprising 700%. Further exploitation of mineral and power resources between 1981–85 it is estimated would directly provide 15 000 more jobs in mining and indirectly another 47 500 because of the additional infrastructure needs, ancillary industrial employment and other multiplier effects. This could be much greater with more use of minerals at home. At present for example whilst Australia provides 11% of the world's iron-ore it produces only 1% of its finished pig-iron and steel.

The government is adopting various policies to prevent overdependence on multinational corporations and encourage more processing and manufacturing. In the future any new mining and resource projects will only be permitted if 50% of the ownership of firms undertaking a project is in Australian hands. By this and other measures Australia hopes to retain better control of its own resources and foster industries which can utilise them.

Aboriginal rights

Whilst future mineral developments and manufacturing associated with these may to an important extent depend on economic factors and the policies of multinational companies and governments, there are other factors of an environmental and social nature. The largest is to do with the rights of the Aboriginals.

In Australia one of the most intractable problems is the fact that a number of the biggest mineral discoveries in Western Australia and Queensland have occurred on land reserved for the Aboriginals. For example some of the largest uranium deposits are in the Alligator River region including part of the Arnhem Land Reserve. Any exploitation not only affects the rights of the Aboriginal but in the case of uranium may well pose grave environmental risks, including the danger of polluted rainwater run-off.

Recently, the Australian Government under pressure from various groups including representatives of the Aboriginals have granted Land Rights over much of the Northern Territory to the Aboriginals, making it increasingly difficult for multinational companies to put into effect projects such as those at Pilbara. But it remains to be seen whether matters of social justice and protection of the environment will take precedence over the pressures exercised by big business and the economics of the market place.

19 Energy Resources

Despite the recent expansion in other energy supplies such as hydro-electricity and nuclear power,
the fossil fuels — coal and oil and gas — still supply
the bulk of the world's energy needs and are likely
to continue to do so for some time to come. It is
estimated that at current rates of usage present
known reserves of coal will last until the 22nd century and oil into the next century (Fig. 19.1).

Uneven distribution of energy resources

Much of South Asia, despite the many peoples living
there, is like the vast interiors of South America and
Africa, deficient in fossil energy, though in certain
parts this is compensated for to some extent by

useful hydro-electric potential. However, industrialised regions of the northern hemisphere and the
populated areas of Australia are comparatively well
off. They are as a group, rich in coal and uranium
and reasonably well off for oil, other large known oil
reserves being confined to the Middle East and
around the Caribbean.

It is not only, however, a matter of the global
distribution of reserves, but also the fact that as
energy prices have increased, so supplies have gravi-
tated even more to the rich industrial economies of
the northern hemisphere further exacerbating the
energy consumption gap between richer and poorer
nations. At present one quarter of the world's people enjoy 80% of the world's energy wealth (Fig.
19.2).

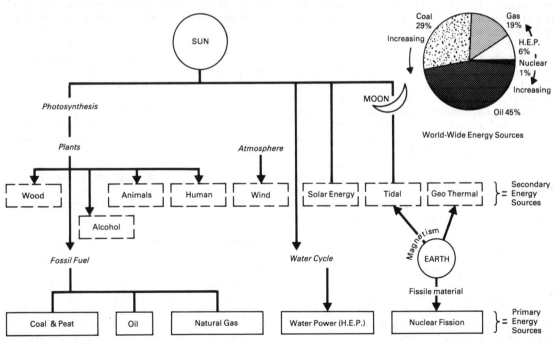

Fig. 19.1   Energy sources

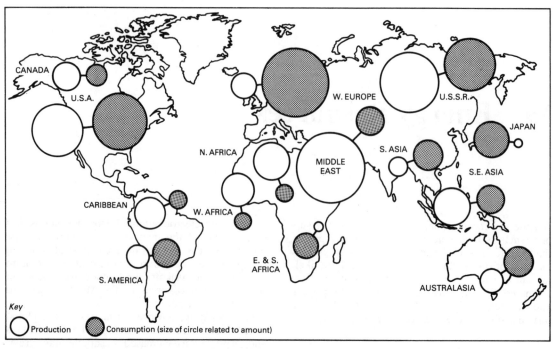

Fig. 19.2   Production and consumption of energy

Coal production

The present world pattern of production as can be seen from the table (Fig. 19.3) is also a good reflection of the location of known reserves. It can be seen that distribution is very uneven.

Though oil and coal are formed by similar processes of sedimentation and compression, coal reserves are more abundant than oil and gas reserves. Coal is a solid material and when formed remains in place. However, oil and gas are fluid and unless trapped by an overlying impermeable strata of rock will tend to migrate and escape over geological time. Thus whereas coal tends to occur as larger and more continuous deposits around the edge of uplands as in Western Europe, oil and gas occur in patches where suitable impermeable capping has trapped it within the sedimentation beds. This patchy occurrence also helps to explain why exploration and exploitation of gas and oilfields are generally a more expensive business than locating and working coal deposits.

Conditions affecting mining

Like oil, coal deposits vary in quality and mode of geological occurrence. This together with their location relative to markets greatly influences whether a deposit will be worked or not.

The easiest to work and therefore the cheapest to extract is that near the surface because it can be strip mined. Though costs have increased since it has become the responsibility of the mining operator to restore the landscape scarred by open-cast mining, it is still cheaper to work than deeper coal. Technological advances in machinery have also made it possible to work on a much larger scale. So open-cast mining is on the increase, particularly in the western United States where the Navajo mine near Farmington, New Mexico is one of the largest in the world.

The rest of the world's coal is extracted by shaft mining, but as the more accessible seams are worked out, these are at increasing depth making working more expensive. Most of the mining is now on the concealed part of coalfields with a consequent closure of old pits on the exposed field, loss of jobs and the decline of mining settlements. This is well exemplified by the eastward shift of coalmining on the fields along the eastern flank of the English Pennines (Fig. 19.4).

However even in the more difficult parts of the coalfield where seams are thin and faulted, coal may still be worth mining if it is of high quality, that is high in carbon/hydro-carbon content and low in impurities and moisture content. Thus anthracite with 95% carbon content and bituminous coals like coking and steam coal with 80% carbon are, for example, still being mined in South Wales despite difficult working conditions.

Coal Production ('000 metric tonnes)			
	1981	% of world total	Reserves 1977 (mill tonnes)
USSR	704 100	25.5	3 993 557
USA	686 340	24.9	2 285 763
China	600 000	21.8	1 011 000
Poland	163 520	5.9	45 741
UK	127 788	4.6	162 814
South Africa	127 584	4.6	44 339
India	123 012	4.5	80 953
Australia	100 872	3.7	111 865
West Germany	88 460	3.2	230 304

Fig. 19.3   World distribution of coalfields

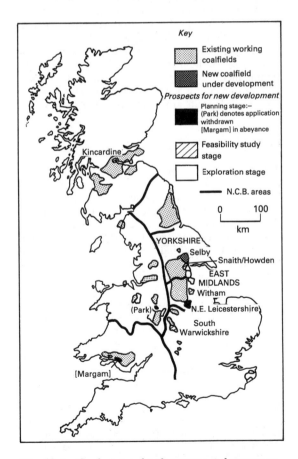

Fig. 19.4   Coalmining developments and prospects, 1981

Exercise

Discuss the distribution of coal production shown in Fig. 19.3 and indicate the kinds of factors which would influence the future use of the economic reserves shown in the third column.

Fortunately low grade coal such as brown coal and lignite also occur near the surface and if deposits are large and close enough to a market then they will be worked. Most low grade coal is consumed in thermal power stations. Lignite from the Tula field in the Kasnoyansk in Siberia is extracted to supply power to Moscow.

However as we have seen, it is not only factors like the quality of the coal, the geological conditions under which it is found and its location relative to market which determine whether a deposit will be developed. There are other factors such as the price of alternative coal supplies and that of competing fuels such as oil and gas. Cheap imported coal and North Sea oil and gas for example have severely affected the profitability of the coalmining industry in the United Kingdom. On the other hand the depletion of United States reserves of oil and gas and the rising price of imported oil during the first half of the 1970s have greatly stimulated the extension of coalmining in the west of the United States. The United States has nearly a quarter of the world's coal reserves and therefore it makes economic sense to develop them.

The revival of the United States coal industry

Contribution to energy requirements

Though coal has been mined in the United States from the early 18th century it was not until the 1880s that coal replaced wood as the major fuel source (Fig. 19.5). By the mid 1920s 70% of the United States fuel and energy needs were met from coal, but by the late 1940s it was overtaken by oil and gas as they were cheaper and easier to transport than coal. Now however production of coal is once again being expanded with a record 800 million tonnes being mined in 1980. Despite this output level, coal still supplies only about one fifth of United States energy requirements — a measure of the great expansion of energy requirements over the postwar years.

There are a number of reasons why coal output has doubled since 1960. One is the sheer growth in energy demand. Others are the uncertainties of the political situation in the Middle East, the major source of imported oil, and fears about future energy supplies. This led in 1974 to President Carter's Energy Plan in which he emphasised the need to expand home energy supplies, in particular a greater use of the country's plentiful coal reserves. This is now more feasible because the rise in oil and gas prices has left coal as a cheaper alternative and further mechanisation of open-cast coalmining has reduced the unit cost of extraction.

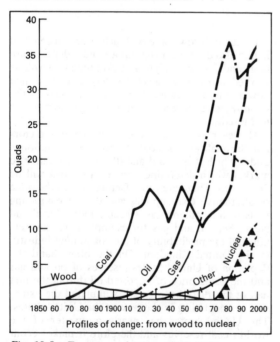

Fig. 19.5   Energy production, 1850–2000

Distribution of coal production

As can be seen from the map (Fig. 19.6) the coal resources are widely distributed. East of the Mississippi, most coal is obtained by underground mining whilst to the west, open-cast strip mining is more important. Apart from the general rise in production the most important changes have been the much greater reliance placed on open-cast mining in the areas west of the Mississippi and the increased importance of the low sulphur coal deposits in these areas. There has thus been some swing in emphasis away from the Appalachian Region, traditionally the most important producer. Appalachia however still retains its lead in total production.

Apart from the increased need for coal, the reasons for the greater exploitation of reserves by open-cast methods include important improvements in the size and efficiency of strip mining equipment. This has greatly increased the output per man day in open-cast areas to 28 tonnes, double the average for deep mining and an important factor in view of increasing wage costs for deep mining. Other factors include better labour relations in the newer western fields and fewer health hazards with strip mining. Anti-pollution laws, including the 1970 Clean Air Amendment Act, have favoured the use of low sulphur coals, the main type produced by open-cast mining methods, despite the fact that more is needed to produce the same energy, for many low sulphur coal deposits are relatively low in heat value.

Location of markets

The main markets for coal are thermal power stations, steel and metallurgical industries, but there has also been some resurgence in coal exports. This is likely to continue as Japan and some countries of Western Europe switch power stations from oil to coal burning and recovery from the world recession in the metallurgical industry increases the demand for coking coal abroad. At present United States coking coal can be imported more cheaply than coking coal can be mined in Western Europe; whilst Japan's own coal resources have been largely depleted. The level of exports will also depend on the extent of competition from other expanding coal exporters such as Canada, Australia and South Africa.

Exercise

Describe and account for the broad regional changes which have occurred in the distribution of coalmining in the U.S.A. since 1962.

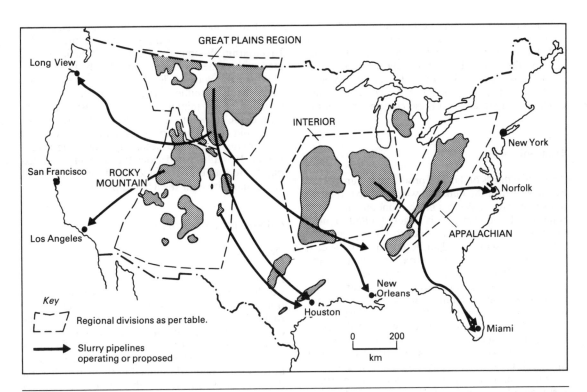

	1962	1965	1970	1975	1979	1981	% open-cast mined in 1979
Pennsylvania	65.3	80.3	80.5	84.1	92.5	82.0	52.0
Ohio	34.1	39.4	55.4	46.8	42.9	38.0	70.0
Virginia	29.5	34.1	35.0	35.5	35.0	41.0	29.0
West Virginia	118.5	149.2	144.1	109.3	111.6	125.0	18.0
Kentucky	69.2	85.8	125.3	143.6	142.5	158.0	55.0
Alabama	12.9	14.8	20.6	22.6	24.3	22.0	70.0
Total Appalachia	337.5	371.4	417.8	395.5	464.0	466.0	NA
Illinois	48.5	58.5	65.1	59.5	58.5	54.0	44.0
Indiana	15.7	15.6	22.3	25.1	27.9	28.0	97.0
Total Eastern Interior	67.2	113.2	140.2	141.0	NA	124.0	NA
Arizona			0.5	7.0	11.8	10.0	100.0
Colorado	3.4	4.8	6.0	8.2	18.0	18.0	56.0
Montana	0.4	0.4	3.4	22.0	32.9	38.0	100.0
New Mexico	0.7	3.2	7.4	8.8	12.9	18.0	95.0
North Dakota	2.7	2.7	5.5	8.5	14.6	17.0	100.0
Texas (started 1972)	—	—	—	11.0	25.6	37.0	100.0
Utah	4.3	5.0	4.7	7.0	12.2	16.0	0
Wyoming	2.6	3.3	7.2	23.8	75.0	106.0	99.0
Total Rocky Mountains and Great Plains		19.4	34.6	96.0	203.0	260.0	90.0
Total U.S.A.	422.1	512.0	603.0	655.0	771.7	824.0	60.0

Source: Davis J.M. *Shifts in U.S. Coal Production* Geography 1981

Fig. 19.6   U.S. coalfields

The bulk of home market demand in the United States is in the industrialised north east, together with the more recently industrialised Pacific coast belt and the south. Thus most long distance movement is associated with shipments from the interior fields including the Northern Great Plains and Rocky Mountain areas to these consuming regions.

Trans-shipment

About two thirds of the coal produced is transported by railway since the bulk and weight of coal relative to its unit value make this more economic than road transport. Road transport is largely limited to moving coal from the smaller mines to railway or water loading depots and to redistributing some of the coal shipments to the small industrial consumers at the other end. Because of the change in the pattern of production, coal is increasingly being carried on parts of the national rail network which were not designed for it. Consequently there are insufficient railroad handling facilities in the west, whilst ironically exhaustion of some older coalmines in the east, especially in Appalachia, has led to the closure of many rail lines traditionally associated with coal.

Water borne transport has also experienced a resurgence but as with the railways the pattern has changed. On the Great Lakes for example whereas most of the shipments were from Lake Erie ports serving the north eastern coalfields, now much is also shipped from Duluth-Superior at the western end of the Great Lakes to the east. Lake freighters have been enlarged to carry as much as 60 000 tonnes each thus making lake transport relatively cheaper. Other waterways, particularly those focusing on and including the Mississippi, have also been improved to take the increased coal movements from the interior fields.

A significant amount of coal is carried by combining rail and water transport, with for example rail important in the west where few waterways occur and then some of the coal being transferred to lake or waterway routes in the east where receiving centres border unloading points. There is an increasing export in coal from east coast ports such as Baltimore and South Atlantic ports which also have rail networks tapping the interior and eastern fields and also some from west coast ports to Japan. Overseas trade is likely to expand as U.S. coal is at present cheaper at points of delivery than home produced coal in the EEC and other developed countries.

Environmental concern for old and new mining areas

Public concern is at its most sensitive where coalmining is likely to be introduced into rural areas of outstanding natural beauty. This is illustrated from the development of open-cast mining in the Powder River basin, Wyoming, a region traditionally associated with cattle ranching. (Case Study 19.1)

Whilst this type of development may attract the most media attention, even more serious is the situation of old mining areas in the east: there not only is the question one of restoring worked over areas, but also of providing alternative employment to communities in the declining coalmining settlements. It is illustrated from the case of the Pittsburgh area, one of the oldest and most important coalmining areas in the United States.

Oil and petrochemicals

Occurrence

Petroleum occurs in porous sedimentary rocks which are interbedded with non-porous rocks, thus trapping the oil and associated gas. Gently folded rock providing anticlines in which the oil and gas concentrates, present the most favourable conditions and these occur in certain parts of the world such as the Middle East and in offshore basins such as those now being developed in the North Sea, on the edge of the Mexican Gulf and now off parts of South East Asia. Oil also occurs in the oil shales such as those in the Athabasca basin of Canada.

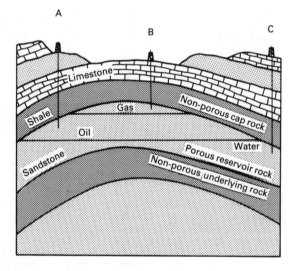

Fig. 19.7   Anticlinal oil trap

The importance of the oil industry

The dimensions of the oil industry are somewhat different to those of coal. Firstly, until recently, apart from the U.S.S.R., industrial countries have been particularly dependent on oil imports especially from the Middle East. Discovery of the vast North Sea oil and natural gas deposits have greatly reduced this for EEC countries. But the United States and Japan in particular will continue to depend heavily on imported oil though these countries are seeking to widen their sources for oil imports.

Secondly, whilst this dependency on imports and the dramatic rise in the price of oil have led to a search for alternative energy sources, there are two sectors of consumption in which oil must remain the major energy or raw material source for some years to come.

These are firstly for engine fuel (diesel oil, jet fuel and petrol) and secondly for feedstock for the petrochemical industry, the source of many products such as plastics, artificial fibres and various chemicals which like fuel oil are so vital to modern societies.

The oil crisis of the 1970s and its aftermath

In the early 1960s, the oil rich nations of the Middle East, the Caribbean and Nigeria formed O.P.E.C. (Organisation of Petroleum Exporting Countries). Its aim was to advance the interests of member countries by getting a greater share of oil profits from the international oil companies such as Shell which were developing the oil resources of these countries. The O.P.E.C. countries, since they controlled much of the world oil exports, were also able to force up the price of oil to their advantage but with a resultant energy crisis for importing countries.

Much discussion and controversy associated with the oil crisis of 1973 and its aftermath have centred on the problems it has created for the industrialised countries. However, the crisis has been even harder for developing nations, most of whom also rely on oil imports. Even before the oil crisis, these countries were heavily in debt having borrowed huge amounts to finance some imports and to finance various development schemes. Then came the oil crisis which severely hit them and not only because of the sudden rise in world oil prices. The economic recession which it helped to bring on, also drastically reduced overseas markets for the raw materials these developing countries exported leaving them with less money anyway to pay for oil imports.

There has now been a further twist on the international oil scene. Despite some fall off in production by O.P.E.C. countries, continued overproduction relative to the reduced demand for oil has led to a world glut and falling prices. This has now badly hit certain O.P.E.C. countries especially Nigeria and Venezuela. These countries had invested heavily in ambitious modernisation programmes, borrowing

huge sums from international banks and agencies against future oil revenues. But falling oil revenues have meant that these countries now have a serious debt crisis — so serious that Venezuela and Nigeria face bankruptcy. In an effort to restore oil price levels O.P.E.C. countries have accepted cuts in the output quota allowed them, but world oil prices are now also very much influenced by North Sea oil and alternative energy output. Thus wider agreement is necessary to achieve stabilisation of prices.

Production, trade and consumption

The case of the Soviet Union

In the concern for other parts of the world, and because the U.S.S.R. is not a major supplier or importer of oil on the open market, we are apt to forget that this country has been for a number of years the most important oil producing country (Fig. 19.8). Moreover, recent finds of oil and gas in the U.S.S.R. ensure that its position is likely to remain unchallenged in the foreseeable future.

Oil and gasfields in the Soviet Union are associated with the sedimentary basins stretching eastward from the Caspian Sea and into Siberia, with the latest developments lying astride the great Ob river system draining north into the Arctic. From 1870 to the end of the Second World War the major producing region was the Baku and North Caucasus field lying between the Caspian and Black Sea. But since then the centre of production has shifted eastwards, first to the Volga–Urals field which by the 1960s was providing three quarters of the oil production, and

Production '000 tonnes Leading Producers (1983)		Percentage of World Reserves (1977)
U.S.S.R.	618 000	11
U.S.A.	486 700	5
Saudi Arabia	246 000	21
Mexico	149 000	2
Iran	124 000	8
UK	114 500	2
China	105 000	3
Venezuela	97 500	2
Canada	76 500	—
Indonesia	63 000	2
Nigeria	60 000	3
Kuwait	54 000	14
Libya	52 000	5
Iraq	46 000	6

Source: Geographical Digest (1984)

Fig. 19.8 Production of oil and world reserves

19:1 THE POWDER RIVER BASIN, WYOMING

Open cast coalmining – a new energy frontier

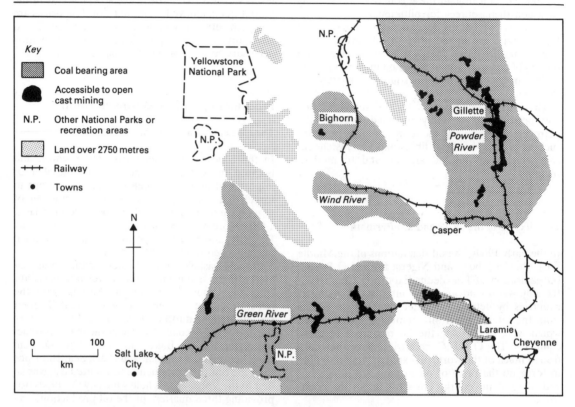

Key

▓	Coal bearing area
●	Accessible to open cast mining
N.P.	Other National Parks or recreation areas
░	Land over 2750 metres
+++	Railway
●	Towns

Location relative to other coal bearing areas in Wyoming

A ECONOMIC ASPECTS OF COAL EXPLOITATION

1 Expanding demand

In home markets mainly for power stations e.g. in the Houston growth area and Chicago. Export demand from Japan.

2 Favourable conditions

Huge reserves — 60 billion tonnes of bituminous reserves near the surface in the Powder River Basin alone — amenable to low cost mechanised open cast mining.

Low in sulphur content ∴ attractive to users under pressure to comply with clean air legislation.

3 Problems

Long market haul both to home markets and export points.

Coal is of lower calorific (heating) value than that of the main eastern coalfields.

Limited infrastructure and labour supplies, as Wyoming was until recently mainly cattle country.

In an area of special environmental attractions.

4 Development

Powder River Basin was developed from 1969. It had 12 strip mines by 1980 with a further 20 planned. Output rose from 7 million tonnes in 1970 to 80 million tonnes in 1980.

Labour attracted by high wages.

Coal is shipped by trains 1 km long each with a 12 000 tonnes capacity.

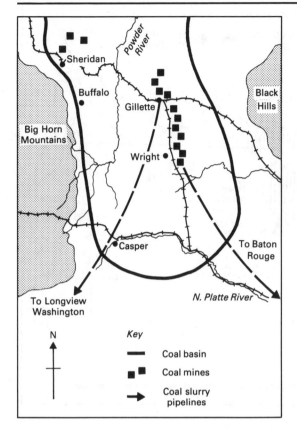

The Powder River Basin

B   SOCIAL AND ENVIRONMENTAL ISSUES

1   *Population pressure*

Labour influx caused by 41% rise in population between 1970-80 — severe pressure on limited amenities — housing, leisure facilities etc. Town of Gillette has grown e.g. from 4000 in 1969 to 14 000 in 1980. 'Boom frontier' conditions are causing the break up of the established cattle country rural communities.

2   *Environmental pressures on cattle country and the national parks*

Opposition from cattle ranchers and environmentalists as strip mining destroys large areas of grazing and creates soil heaps and slurry lakes. Legislation to ensure companies reclaim land but new land susceptible to erosion due to drought, severe winters and heavy grazing.

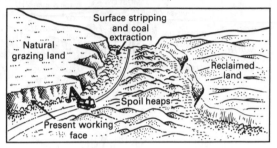

3   *Pollution hazard*

Hazard to water courses and the air including emissions of Texaco and Mobil plants near Buffalo which convert coal into synthetic fuel.

4   *Pressure on water supplies*

In a region where drought may occur there is pressure on water supplies. Heavy demand by increased population has already led to a falling water table. Further demand for slurry transport will add to the problems.

Exercise

● What are the problems associated with large scale open cast mining? Suggest ways in which these may be solved.

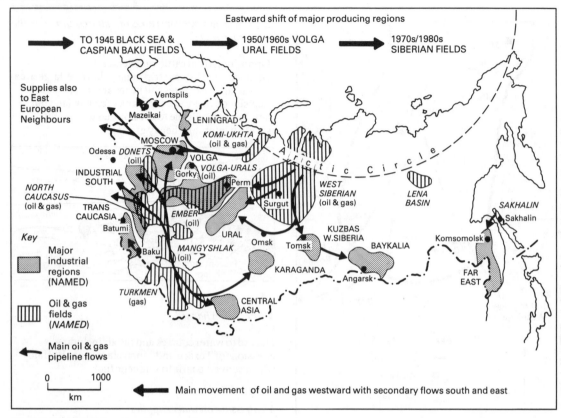

Eastward shift of major producing regions

TO 1945 BLACK SEA & CASPIAN BAKU FIELDS → 1950/1960s VOLGA URAL FIELDS → 1970s/1980s SIBERIAN FIELDS

Supplies also to East European Neighbours

Key

Major industrial regions (NAMED)

Oil & gas fields (NAMED)

Main oil & gas pipeline flows

0   1000
km

Main movement of oil and gas westward with secondary flows south and east

Fig. 19.9   U.S.S.R. oil and gas production

now an increasing amount is coming from the Western Siberian oilfield as well as much of the Soviet Union's natural gas output (Fig. 19.9).

Like the recent Alaskan development in the Prudhoe Bay area, the problem is that the Western Siberian oil and gasfields occur in a very harsh environment. This has made development so expensive that only since the rise in oil price and the threat of declining production in older fields has it taken place. The area is characterised by a sub-arctic climate, permafrost ground conditions and extensive bogs and swamps which hinder not only the extraction of the oil and gas, but also pipeline construction. Labour is expensive and in short supply and all requirements have to be brought in. Despite this, the two principal oil towns of Nizhnevartovsk and Surgut on the Ob now have populations of around 150 000 each and as the huge gasfield of Urengoy to the north is developed these will increase further.

Much of the industrial and domestic market lies in European Russia including the Moscow region but production is increasingly further away from this. Thus a very extensive network of pipelines has been constructed from the oil and gasfields to the consuming regions and extended further westward to serve

the increasing needs of the Soviet Union's communist neighbours in Eastern Europe. Whilst a substantial amount of oil is still transferred by rail and waterways such as the Black Sea, Caspian Sea and the Volga, pipelines are increasingly important since they provide a more flexible network which can be easily extended and following installation, maintenance costs are less. In addition to the main movement westward of oil and gas, pipelines have also been constructed northward from the recently developed Turkmen gasfield in the south and there are plans to extend the network eastward to the Pacific coast since the Sakhalin field is too small to serve regional needs here and there is a significant demand in Japan and other export markets.

However, apart from the substantial trade between the U.S.S.R. and its eastern bloc neighbours, by far the most significant development has been the agreement by Russia with certain West European countries to supply huge amounts of natural gas from its West Siberian field by a 5600 km projected pipeline right into the heart of the EEC. This is in addition to smaller lines already established.

Currently the bulk of West Europe's supply is from the declining Netherlands Groningen gasfield.

Whilst North Sea gasfields can to some extent fill the gap, it is estimated that Europe as a whole will need to import half its gas needs. The vast Siberian fields, containing an estimated third of the earth's known gas deposits, are seen as a logical source and despite the large distances involved the gas can be supplied more cheaply than from the offshore North Sea fields. In return for supplying gas principally to West Germany, France, Italy, Switzerland and Austria the Soviet Union would be able to utilise Western technology not only to develop her reserves but also the capacity power booster stations needed along the pipeline to transmit the gas over vast distances. Thus a number of construction and engineering companies in Western Europe would benefit by filling orders for pipes, turbines and other equipment.

Unfortunately the United States has not been favourably disposed towards the project, seeing this link up between the Soviet Union and N.A.T.O. countries as strategically undesirable. The Western European countries have responded by pointing out that Russia would still supply only in general 5% of their energy needs and the alternative is to import gas or oil more expensively from the O.P.E.C. countries of North Africa and the Middle East which is also politically less desirable. Thus the link up is likely to go ahead.

The Middle East producers — the case of Saudi Arabia

Despite the emergence of new major producers such as the United Kingdom, the Middle East oil countries, because of their huge reserves and established production capacity, are likely to continue to play a major role in the world trade in oil. Of these by far the most important producer is Saudi Arabia. In 1980 it provided 40% of O.P.E.C. output and is still the largest world producer next to the U.S.A. and the U.S.S.R. With its vast reserves of oil and gas it is likely to maintain its leading position over the next 30 years. But more than this it is now beginning to develop its own oil refining and petro-chemical industries and may therefore soon be an important competitor for a share of world trade in petrochemical products. (See Case Study 19.2.)

Amongst O.P.E.C. countries Saudi Arabia stands out as the country most appreciating the need to safeguard the long term future by attempting to moderate oil price demands within O.P.E.C., regulate supplies to steady world markets and maintain oil as a competitive source of energy for countries reliant on imports from the Middle East. Whilst Saudi has been affected by the recent fall in the demand for oil, it has sufficient production to finance its economy in contrast to other O.P.E.C. producers such as Nigeria, Venezuela and Libya.

North Sea oil and gas

Development

Because North Sea oil and gas finds are at the centre of one of the heartlands of the Western world, developments here have tended to overshadow equally important developments elsewhere. We have already mentioned those in the difficult cold lands of the North and in the Middle East, but the North Sea fields are but one of a group of offshore developments which are taking place around the world. There are others, for example around the Caribbean, off the coast of West Africa, in South East Asia and in particular off China where rapid economic advancement and a population of 1000 million are creating unprecedented energy demands.

It is likely that finds in these offshore regions will ultimately exceed those in the North Sea. The North Sea developments warrant attention partly because of their size and also because they illustrate the conditions under which offshore development takes place. They have had significant impact on the international trade in oil as well as on the energy programmes and economies of those Western European countries most directly involved, namely the United Kingdom, Norway and the Netherlands. (See Fig. 19.10, p. 200.)

Following the important discoveries in the late 1950s of a large gasfield near Groningen in the Netherlands (and smaller developments across the border in Germany) exploration was intensified offshore in the North Sea where gas and oil deposits were already known to exist. Despite the difficulties created by the uncertain sea and weather conditions, a number of major companies such as Shell sought exploration concessions. Gas was first exploited and piped ashore to Easington (Humberside) in 1967 and later Bacton (Norfolk) from the West Sole and Leman fields in the southern sector of the North Sea. These ashore supplies were linked into a national distribution network focused on the Canvey Island–Leeds axis and thus coal gas was replaced by natural gas.

Oil development then followed. The first was from the Ekofisk field in the Norwegian sector, the oil being pumped ashore at Teesside since to lay a pipeline to a terminal in Norway would have been very much more difficult and expensive. Other finds followed, the largest development being that of the Brentfield 160 km from Shetland and in a depth of about 150 m of water. This oil is piped ashore at Sullom Voe in the Shetlands where an oil complex has been developed. It is estimated that there are reserves to last well into the 20th century and probably other fields to be developed including off the west coast of Ireland.

Today the United Kingdom and Norway are self-

19:2 SAUDI ARABIA

Oil production

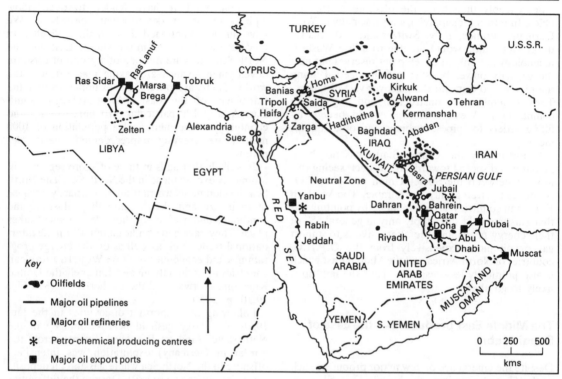

Middle East oil producing areas

SAUDI ARABIA OIL AND GAS

Oil and gas production and location

Developed since 1930 largely in association with U.S. companies. Now Saudi oil is produced as a joint venture under Aramco (Arab American Oil Co.). But the government controls production levels and further development of fields and refineries through the Petrobin Oil Co. and marketing through its Norbec organisation.

Only half of oilfields currently tapped, mainly on and offshore in the Persian Gulf. Largest fields are onshore — Ghawar and offshore — Safaniya. But most rapid expansion has been in natural gas to power Saudi's desalination (water) plants and provide feedstock for expanding petro-chemical industry. Export of liquified gas to Japan etc.

Saudi Arabia's Leading Position Amongst OPEC Producers

OPEC OIL PRODUCTION AGREEMENT (1983)

	New estimated maximum output (b/d)	Estimated production in early March (b/d)
Algeria	650 000	700 000
Ecuador	200 000	200 000
Gabon	150 000	150 000
Indonesia	1 300 000	1 450 000
Iran	1 200 000	1 200 000
Iraq	1 200 000	1 200 000
Kuwait	650 000	775 000
Libya	750 000	600 000
Nigeria	1 300 000	1 300 000
Qatar	300 000	350 000
Saudi Arabia	7 000 000	7 325 000
United Arab Emirates	1 000 000	1 250 000
Venezuela	1 500 000	1 700 000
Neutral Zone	300 000	250 000

DIRECTION OF OIL EXPORTS FROM SAUDI ARABIA
(millions of U.S. barrels)

	Crude	Refined	Crude	Refined	Crude	Refined
	1976		1978		1980	
North America	171	8	509	1	619	4
Latin America	490	8	139	3	127	2
Western Europe	1268	13	1092	15	1432	36
Middle East	83	1	94	1	98	1
Africa	31	4	13	2	43	1
Asia and Far East	860	100	928	102	1008	100
Oceania	33	5	34	2	46	2
Bunkers	—	63	—	47	—	31
TOTAL	2939	205	2812	178	3375	180

Transport and shipment

Until recently most was exported by bulk tanker via Persian Gulf (with the closure of Suez). The long haul and political instability in the Gulf prompted a pipeline across the country West to Yanbu and use of the reopened Suez route by smaller tankers. But still use of Cape route for bulk tankers and in exports to Japan.

Relation of the oil and gas sector to the remainder of the economy

Whilst remaining an important oil exporter at a time of threats of a world glut and depression of prices, Saudi is refining more oil and gas, as a basis for the country's own industrialisation. With foreign investors e.g. Japan, Saudi set up more petro-chemical complexes at Yanbu and Jubail to produce ethylene, caustic soda, polythene, nitrogen etc.

Oil revenue including returns on growing investment abroad provided revenue for infrastructure development, financed industry — iron and steel, consumer industries at Riyadh and Jeddah etc. But domestic market is limited (7 million population of which 2 million is still nomadic). Still strong disparities between few rich and many poor and regionally between rural interior and growth areas on coast.

Exercise

● Comment on the importance of oil and natural gas to the economy of Saudi Arabia.

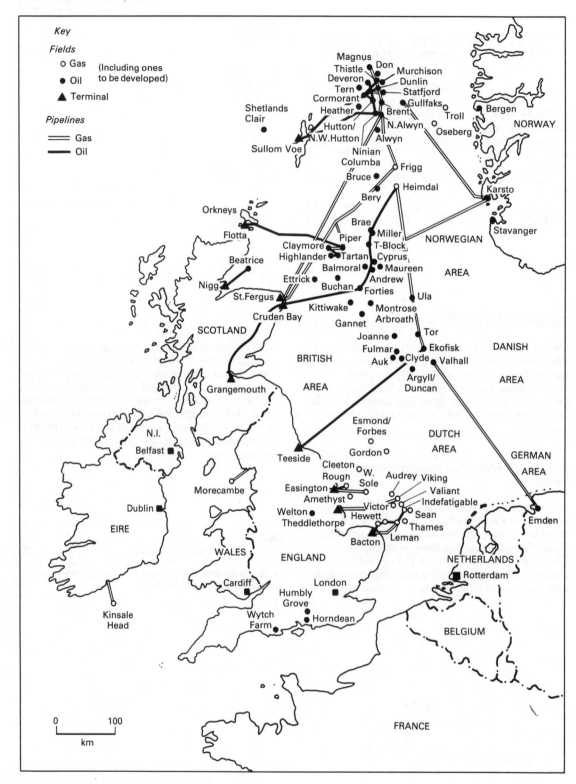

Fig. 19.10   North Sea oil and gas/fields

sufficient in gas and oil and have become net exporters chiefly to neighbouring Western European countries. In respect of the total energy scene North Sea oil and gas supplies about 12% of Western European energy needs but because of a crucial need for oil to ensure petroleum supplies and feedstock for the vital petro-chemical industry, its importance is greater than the percentage contribution alone suggests.

Factors influencing further development

Whilst North Sea oil and gas are expensive to exploit and further development in deeper waters poses technological problems these are not likely to be the major difficulties in the near future. The amount of annual investment needed is small compared to available investment funds in Western Europe. Technological developments are also more than keeping pace with North Sea needs and there is now a very good entrepreneurial back up, with an expanding number of companies specialising in the provision of the services and equipment needed. Furthermore governments are committed to expansion of North Sea oil and gas production both by direct involvement and by state support for oil companies working in the North Sea. The EEC as a corporate body is also providing investment funds and supporting the important research needed to keep Western European producers in the forefront. The United Kingdom and Norway and to a lesser extent the Netherlands are also dependent on the direct and indirect tax revenues brought in by the oil industry, not only to finance further development but also to provide finance for other sectors of the economy as well as parts of the social services, including unemployment benefits.

There are thus plenty of incentives for continued development of North Sea oil and gas and for extending it to other areas such as that off the west of Ireland. The pace of development and volume of production depends more on what happens to world oil prices and oil and gas developments elsewhere in the world: North Sea oil and gas are comparatively expensive to extract; the recent fall in world oil prices and a current glut in oil are disincentives. This contrasts greatly with the rise in price and shortage which were the major factors influencing North Sea development in the first place.

The other important constraints are political ones. There is for example disagreement between Western European governments about what should be the volume of output of North Sea oil and gas. Producers want to keep production down to ensure reserves last longer and prices are kept sufficiently high, whereas those countries without their own supplies are pressing for an expansion of output to reduce reliance on less certain overseas suppliers. Much will depend on the kind of price guarantees and assurances of a continued market that Western European consuming countries can give to producers.

The other area of controversy lies between the governments and the large multinational oil companies. Governments are attempting to tax away the

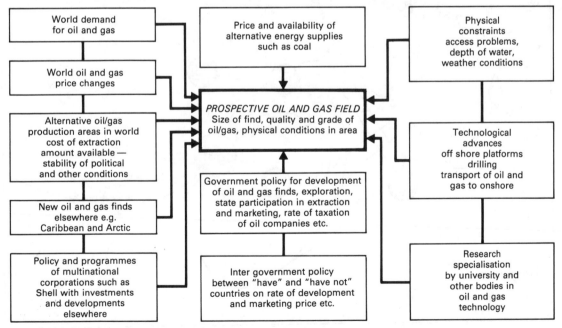

Fig. 19.11   Factors influencing North Sea oil and gas developments

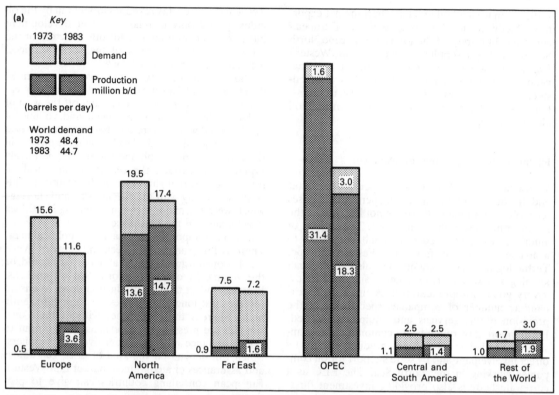

Fig. 19.12   (a) World oil demand and production, 1973 and 1983

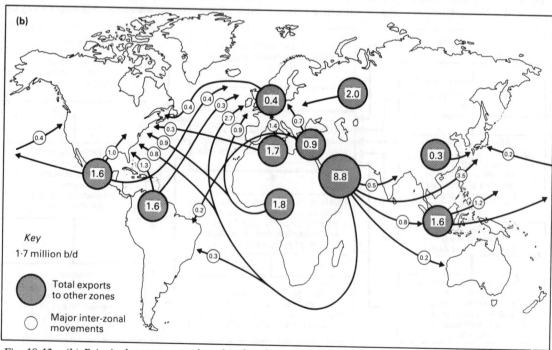

Fig. 19.12   (b) Principal movements of crude oil and products, 1984

above-normal profits oil companies are making out of North Sea production and this makes the return on investments less attractive for companies, encouraging them to invest in oil exploitation elsewhere. There is of course also the question of the extent to which governments will press for an expansion of coal output since some Western European countries such as the United Kingdom and Western Germany have very large coal reserves to provide an alternative energy supply.

World trade in oil

Whilst the Soviet Union is an important exporter of oil and gas to neighbouring East European countries and also now increasingly to Western Europe, international trade in oil is still dominated by the O.P.E.C. producers on the one hand and the needs of the advanced industrial countries on the other (Fig. 19.12).

Whilst Western European countries have to an important extent freed themselves from too much reliance on O.P.E.C. exporters, Japan and the United States will remain very much dependent on Middle East and Caribbean suppliers, despite strenuous efforts towards energy conservation and development of alternative energy sources. This is illustrated by the direction and volume of trade in oil (see Fig. 19.12).

However, it must also be noted that a number of developing countries as they increasingly seek to mature, will correspondingly need more oil and become increasingly dependent on O.P.E.C. supplies. Energy supplies are vital to any modernisation programme. Yet because of a relatively low Gross National Product, it is harder for developing countries to finance energy imports and investment in developing any alternative domestic resources, such as potential hydro-electric power which they might have. Thus trade in oil between exporting countries and developing countries is even more affected by price fluctuations like those which have occurred in the 1970s, than is trade to advanced industrial nations. Thus greater stability of price and a more coherent planning of future development of oil and gas reserves are as vital to the poorer nations as to

affluent nations, even though current needs in absolute terms are much less.

The petro-chemical industry and its location

Vast oil refining petro-chemical industries have developed based on the exploiting of crude oil and gas. These supply the modern world with a range of needs considered vital to modern living including not only fuels but also plastics, artificial fibres, a range of fertilizers and heavy chemicals, bitumen for road surfacing and a host of other products including protein foods.

Because so many derivatives are associated with oil refining it has proved more economic in the past to locate both refining and the petro-chemical industries at points of entry into the consuming countries. Hence most large ports such as Rotterdam, Antwerp and Southampton have an oil-refining and heavy chemicals sector. These are usually locationally distinct from other port activities and at a distance from any residential areas, because of the obnoxious character of petroleum refining and the heavy chemicals industry and also because of the potential risk associated with it. But there are other factors involved such as the need for large sites both for the plants and marshalling yards adjacent to them, the need for large water supplies and coastal access to dispose of treated effluent. Whilst the industry is capital intensive, a large financial outlay being needed to establish the plant and associated

Exercise

Using Figs 9.8 and 19.12 showing production by country in 1983 and world trade in oil, discuss the relationship between world demand and production for 1983. Indicate the reasons for any major changes shown between 1973 and 1983.

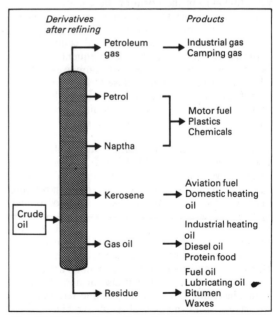

Fig. 19.13 *Products of crude oil refining*

infrastructure, it is not labour intensive and therefore access to labour is not a significant locational factor.

However, apart from the need of a coastal location where oil or natural gas can readily be brought ashore or imported, the industry does require access to a good communication network both by rail and road for the shipment of varied products to their distinctive markets. Road transport with the use of economic bulk carriers and the construction of a national motorway network in advanced countries has become increasingly important.

During the 1950s and 1960s as demand for oil and gas products expanded, and the size of ocean bulk oil carriers increased to over 100 000 tonnes, new deep-water coastal locations were sought outside of the established port complexes which either had not the necessary deep-water anchorages to accommodate bulk carriers, or the site space for large scale petro-chemical complexes. In some cases new sites were developed close by as at Marseilles and Rotterdam, further down the estuary, or a short way along the coast where both deep-water access and large sites were available on drained alluvial flats. But in a number of cases totally new sites were developed at some distance from established ports. In some, multiple usage was developed, iron and steel or aluminium smelting also being established at the same coastal site. In the United Kingdom, Teesside provides an example of the latter while Milford Haven in Pembrokeshire was an example of a one purpose development for oil-refining and petro-chemicals. In Japan Tsurusaki on the southern island of Kyushu is a multi-purpose development as is Ishikari in Southern Hokkaido in the north of the country.

However during the economic recession, which deepened at the end of the 1970s, the petrochemical industry in most advanced countries has suffered from over-capacity. Consequently a number of these new large specialist complexes such as Milford Haven are being closed. In contrast the oil-refining and petro-chemical industry has been expanded in some of the oil producing countries, since overall, higher prices can be gained from refined products than from the export of crude oil or national gas in liquified form. During the 1970s rising oil prices have enabled O.P.E.C. countries to finance developments in this field. Pressure has also been put on oil companies to invest more in refining in the producing countries. Also as state companies have been founded to share in the exploitation of oil and gas resources these have been financially supported by the state to process some of their own oil and gas production. Consequently oil and petrochemical complexes have been expanded not only at established export points but also at new shipment points including those for oil pipeline terminals, as we have seen in the case of Saudi Arabia.

Developments here are mirrored in other oil exporting countries such as Algeria, Mexico and Venezuela. However expansion is limited due to current world over-capacity in oil-refining and petrochemicals and by the limited markets available. Thus despite this trend towards more oil-refining in exporting countries, oil-refining and petro-chemicals measured by output remain overwhelmingly concentrated in the developed countries since these still provide the main markets. Also included among them are the U.S.S.R., the United States, the two largest producers, and also the United Kingdom and Norway, as they have now entered the premier league of oil and natural gas producers.

Water power

Though water power is one of the oldest sources of power the water wheel being in use in Roman times, the development of electricity generated directly from water power is a relatively recent one, the first hydro-electric power station being established at Niagara (Canada) in 1895. Today, despite the vast potential of hydro-electric power, it actually contributes to only a small proportion of the world's energy needs. However it is a very important source of energy for those parts of the world with few oil, gas and coal reserves. These include much of South America, Africa and parts of South East Asia, in other words most of the developing nations outside of the Caribbean and Middle East. In addition for some developed countries like Switzerland, Norway and Sweden it is the major energy source and for others like Italy, France and Japan a significant secondary source. However at a recent World Energy Conference the largest potential capacity was stated to be in China, the Soviet Union and the United States and certainly in terms of total present production the Soviet Union and the United States are the largest producers.

Energy from hydro-electricity has the advantage over energy based on coal, oil and natural gas in that it is based upon a renewable resource, though the problem of silting in reservoirs can effectively reduce the amount of water available. It is also a clean and highly efficient source of energy. Whereas oil and coal have an efficiency of only 30%, hydro-electricity is 80% to 90% efficient, efficiency being based on that proportion of input which can be effectively used as energy. However, per unit of output capital costs are much higher, hydro-electric schemes being very costly to install. For this reason, despite lower running costs, countries have only invested in schemes which have the best prospects.

Many of the world's largest potential sites are in remote and sparsely populated areas, for example on the upper reaches of the Amazon in South America. This not only raises the costs of the scheme, materials and labour being very costly to transport, but also effectively puts the potential site out of reach of market demand. However the distance over which electricity may be transmitted without too much loss in the process is being steadily expanded. Up to the 1960s it was only possible to transmit electricity economically over 300 km, whereas now it is 800 km. This technological advance has been an important factor in recent large scale hydro-electric schemes in some parts of Africa and Latin America. For example the Cabora-Bassa scheme on the lower Zambezi in Mozambique was set up not only to supply power to Mozambique but also to South Africa, which helped finance the scheme. Long distance transmission of energy is also contemplated for the Niger Dams project at Kainji, Jebba and Shiroro in Nigeria and for the largest single scheme in the world now nearing completion at Itaipu on the Parana River. This will supply one fifth of Brazil's electricity needs as well as much of that of neighbouring Paraguay.

Hydro-electric power schemes can basically be divided into two types, those on the one hand solely constructed to generate electricity and on the other, multi-purpose schemes which not only supply power but are also designed for additional purposes such as the control of seasonal flooding, provision of irrigation water and an aid to navigating by ensuring a consistent water level. In some cases lake or reservoir schemes can also lead to an expansion of fishing. This is especially important in tropical regions where much of the malnutrition amongst people is due to protein deficiencies. Both types of schemes can also provide an added tourist attraction.

Factors affecting development

Before considering examples of the different types of schemes it would be useful to summarise the factors affecting the development of hydro-electric power (Fig. 19.14). These factors are then explored more fully in a discussion of the different types of development which follow.

Large scale specialist and multi-purpose schemes

Turning to these larger schemes, whilst some of the major ones have been developed in North America and the Soviet Union, the greatest need is amongst developing countries and thus it is appropriate to consider an example from this part of the world.

Multi-purpose schemes in Africa

In Africa large scale developments are multi-purpose, particularly combining provision of irrigation water with increasing energy supplies. Since the rainfall over much of Africa is seasonal and unreliable and other energy supplies, with the exception

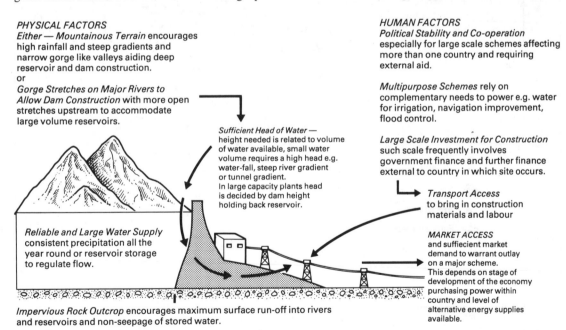

PHYSICAL FACTORS
Either — Mountainous Terrain encourages high rainfall and steep gradients and narrow gorge like valleys aiding deep reservoir and dam construction.
or
Gorge Stretches on Major Rivers to Allow Dam Construction with more open stretches upstream to accommodate large volume reservoirs.

Sufficient Head of Water — height needed is related to volume of water available, small water volume requires a high head e.g. water-fall, steep river gradient or tunnel gradient.
In large capacity plants head is decided by dam height holding back reservoir.

Reliable and Large Water Supply consistent precipitation all the year round or reservoir storage to regulate flow.

Impervious Rock Outcrop encourages maximum surface run-off into rivers and reservoirs and non-seepage of stored water.

HUMAN FACTORS
Political Stability and Co-operation especially for large scale schemes affecting more than one country and requiring external aid.

Multipurpose Schemes rely on complementary needs to power e.g. water for irrigation, navigation improvement, flood control.

Large Scale Investment for Construction such scale frequently involves government finance and further finance external to country in which site occurs.

Transport Access to bring in construction materials and labour

MARKET ACCESS and suffiecient market demand to warrant outlay on a major scheme. This depends on stage of development of the economy purchasing power within country and level of alternative energy supplies available.

(N.B. Some economic activities with a high electricity demand may be drawn to hydro-electric sites, e.g. electro-chemicals and eletro-metallurgical industries such as aluminium).

Fig. 19.14 Factors affecting the location and implementation of H.E.P. schemes

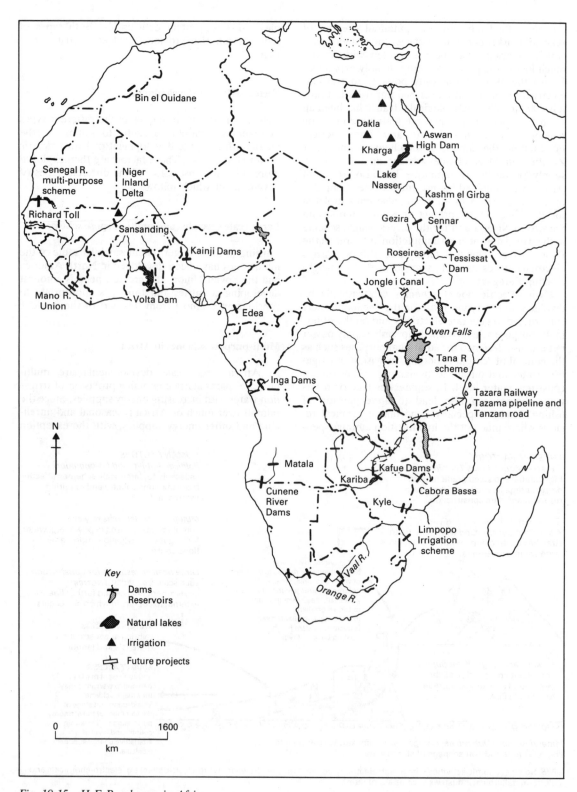

Fig. 19.15 H.E.P. schemes in Africa

of some coal in South Africa and Zimbabwe and oil in Nigeria and north of the Sahara, are in very short supply it was logical that the various countries should look to some of the major rivers flowing from the heart of the continent. Fortunately where these break through the high plateau rim suitable sites are available. Others occur where crystalline block uplands are encountered by rivers giving deep gorge sections.

As the map (Fig. 19.15) shows, a number of schemes have been developed in each of Africa's major rivers including the Nile, the Zambezi and the Niger. These have largely been externally financed and also much of the technical skills needed imported, since African countries have neither the capital nor the skills to undertake such large scale developments. For example most recently a hydro-electric and irrigation plant is to be developed in Angola on the Kwando River using Brazilian and Russian financial and technical aid. Whilst not the largest, the Aswan Dam project in Egypt (also involving the neighbouring parts of the Sudan) is one of the most well established schemes. It highlights both the advantages and problems which can result from the impact of these types of scheme on the economy and social conditions in the countries concerned (Case Study 19.3).

Thermal power

This is largely provided from coal fed power stations, oil having lost some of its importance during the 1970s. Except in countries like the Soviet Union with plentiful supplies of domestic oil, the rise in oil prices during this period encouraged the conversion of a number of coastally based oil-fired stations to utilisation of coal. This is continuing for example in the United Kingdom and the United States, despite a recent relative fall in oil prices, since coal reserves are estimated to have a much longer life than oil and natural gas.

Coal-fired stations are located close to coal supplies since this is a bulky material and in relation to its price, costly to transport. In contrast as we have seen the electricity generated can be economically transported over long distances and widely distributed via a national grid network. It therefore makes sense to locate power stations close to coalfields or at coastal locations where supplies can be cheaply imported. However, another critical locational factor is ample supplies of water for cooling purposes, hence power stations are located along major rivers (usually outside of built up areas to avoid pollution risks) or at coastal estuary sites. The availability of space is also important since power station complexes together with storage yards for coal stocks and freight marshalling facilities require large sites.

Such locational considerations are well illustrated from the concentration of power stations along the middle Trent Valley in the United Kingdom (Fig. 19.16). This contains the largest concentration of power stations in the country earning it the name of 'Kilowatt Valley'. Shuttle trains operate to bring coal from the Notts, York, Derby coalfield, the

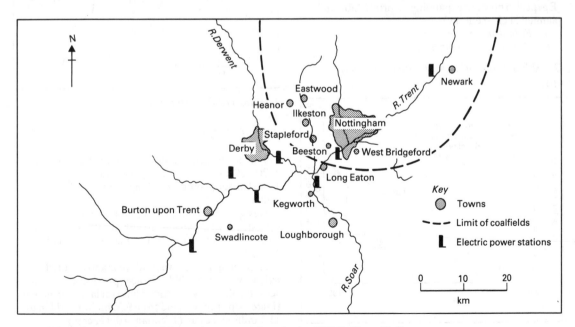

Fig. 19.16 Concentration of thermal power stations in the Middle Trent Valley

19:3 ASWAN DAM, EGYPT

A multi-purpose H.E.P. scheme

DEMAND FOR THE DAM

1 *Need for more food* — in a dry country requires extension of irrigation. Population growth (2.7% p.a.) has outstripped increase in agricultural productivity.

2 *Nile is the main source* of water, but fed by monsoon seasonal rainfall leading to 30% seasonal fluctuation in water available. Aswan Dam would pond back Nile in Lake Nasser, providing regular flow of water for irrigation all the year. Enable intensification of agriculture (double and treble cropping), Egypt negotiated to share Nile water with Sudan to the South (1970 Egypt was to have greater proportion). Irrigation area could be extended. (Recently embarked on reclamation and irrigation from bore holes in 'New Valley' area and centred on main oases in Sahara.)

3 *Control flooding hazard* — especially the seasonal flood damage to land and urban areas in lower Egypt.

4 *Power for industry* and rapidly expanding urban areas. Serious energy crisis 1960s dependent on oil and coal imports — Aswan dam a positive contribution to a solution. H.E.P. now provides 50% of energy needs. Bulk is transmitted to Cairo and lower Egypt but encouraged industry in lower Egypt e.g. fertilizers and chemicals at Aswan (Egypt also now has expanding oil production and planned nuclear energy).

5 *Fishing in Lake Nasser*

6 *Increased tourist attraction*

Growth of population and agricultural land in Egypt

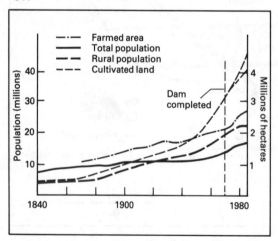

'It's significance rests not so much in its size as the contribution it makes towards a solution to the country's economic and social problems.'

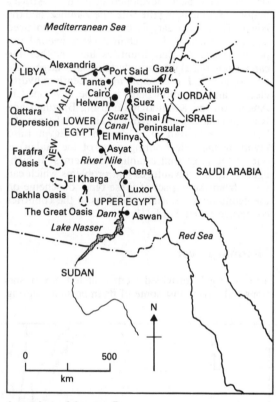

Location of Aswan Dam

THE SCHEME

On site of an earlier dam (1902) to control flooding. 1970 Aswan dam completed ponding 215 km long Lake Nasser behind extending back into Northern Sudan.

Designed to generate 10 million MW hours but operates at 70% capacity to link in with seasonally varied irrigation water requirements for agriculture (see graph).

Assured irrigation water all year and enabled irrigation of higher Nile terraces previously beyond seasonal flood water. Aided land reclamation in delta (increased cropped land from 9.3. million feddan to 11.1 million feddan (1 feddan = 0.42 acres).

PROBLEMS

Envisaged at the outset include:

Resettlement of Nubian people from drowned area.

Loss of Nile silt brought down under natural seasonal flooding to replenish soil fertility therefore need for more fertilizers.

Silting up of Lake Nasser would gradually reduce its capacity.

Loss of water by evaporation whilst stored in Lake Nasser.

Perennial irrigation increases salination of soil.

Less silting at Nile delta increases danger of marine erosion.

Drowning under lake of rich archaeological sites, cost of raising Abu Simbel site above flood.

Political problems of future agreement with Sudan contemplating own schemes e.g. Jonglei Project — reduce flow into Lake Nasser.

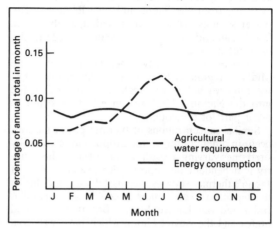

Patterns of agricultural water requirements and energy consumption

Ensuing Problems include:

Panning and salination of soil even more serious.

Intensified agriculture increased fertilizer and pesticide cost as no fallow period.

Constant water flow scouring Nile banks

No mineral silt ∴ reduced pilchard catch off coast near delta.

largest in the country. A plentiful supply of water is available from the Trent and its tributaries. The power stations are located immediately above the flood plain and as the map indicates outside of the main urban areas.

Some of the electricity generated is used in the Midlands region itself where a significant amount of the country's industry is located, but the bulk is fed into the National Grid and in effect exported to other parts of the country.

Similar concentrations of thermal power stations occur in other countries, the proportion of coastally sited ones varying according to the extent the country is dependent on imports. For example most of Japan's thermal stations are coastally located due to its dependence on imported coal from Australia, India and the United States. But in the United States and the Soviet Union which have vast coal reserves, riverside locations predominate. In Africa, in both South Africa and Zimbabwe the major coal-fired electricity generating stations have been erected on the coalfields. These are in the South East Transvaal and the neighbouring parts of the Orange Free State in South Africa and on the Wankie coalfield in Zimbabwe, which together with the power generated from the Kafue and Kariba hydro-electricity schemes on the Zambezi provides Zimbabwe with most of its energy needs.

Apart from the importance of thermal electricity to domestic users, one of the greatest benefits it has brought is to release industry from its tie to power supply locations, in particular coalfield sites. During the Industrial Revolution and up to the First World War, much of the United Kingdom's industry was drawn to coalfield sites or to waterside locations as in London along Thameside where coal could be cheaply brought by water. But during the interwar and postwar years, transmission of electricity has been one of the factors aiding the dispersion of industry and allowing a more flexible choice of site. However, the effect has varied from one industry to another depending on the relative importance of power to other inputs.

Nuclear power

The contribution of nuclear power to world energy supplies continues to rise from for example 8% in 1980 to 17% in 1985. But its future as a source of energy is uncertain. Expansion has slowed down compared to that originally forecast. Progress has also been very variable from one country to another.

Whilst in the Soviet Union and other Comecon countries it continues to be rapid, in the United States and Western Europe apart from France, nuclear programmes have been drastically revised downwards. Indeed in the United States which at present has the largest output of nuclear electricity, 37 nuclear reactors have been closed down since 1980 and plans for 15 new ones shelved indefinitely.

Whereas amongst developed countries there have been increasing reservations about the role nuclear energy will play, no such reservations exist amongst developing countries since these are anxious to increase their energy output and cut down costly oil imports. Unfortunately most are not in a financial position to develop a nuclear programme of their own and there is also opposition to nuclear know-how being put in the hands of some countries as it might be misused. However, some like South Korea, India and Pakistan are embarking on nuclear programmes and look forward to nuclear energy making a major contribution to their energy needs. South Korea for example at present relies on imported oil for half its needs but by the end of the century hopes to have two thirds of its energy requirements met from nuclear energy.

Advantages and disadvantages of developing nuclear energy

Uncertainties about the future of nuclear energy have arisen for a number of reasons. Some are to do with economics, but the central issue appears to be a wavering of public confidence. There are fears about how safe nuclear reactors are, following some breakdowns and the escape of radioactive matter into the atmosphere; in particular at the Chernobyl reactor in 1986 near Kiev in the U.S.S.R. Antinuclear demonstrations against the use of nuclear weapons have also heightened public emotions against the commercial use of nuclear energy. Because these are emotive issues it is difficult to obtain an objective view about the relative merits of nuclear energy, compared to the more traditional generation of electricity from coal and oil fuelled power stations.

The arguments in favour of developing more nuclear energy must be set within the context of the total energy scene. In the foreseeable future (not withstanding short term fluctuations), world energy needs will continue to rise, particularly amongst the newly industrialising countries. Oil and coal at present provide the bulk of world energy needs but these are finite resources and it is therefore unlikely they can be sufficiently further utilised to meet expanding requirements. For example even with a planned doubling of output from coal-fired power stations, the developed countries in the west will have a shortfall of energy unless nuclear energy's share of output can be increased to 30% of the total. It is unlikely that further gas and oil supplies could be made available to meet the shortfall. Also other alternative new energy sources such as geo-thermal, wind and solar power whilst significant in particular instances could not be sufficiently developed to cover additional needs. But there is no shortage of uranium which is the main resource base for nuclear energy, nor of manufacturing capacity for building the reactors and other processing plants needed. It seems then that further nuclear energy will be needed and that there is the capacity there for expansion.

Apart from anticipated needs there is also the question of relative costs. Whilst construction costs are greater per unit of production for nuclear power stations, running costs though variable from one region to another, are generally lower than for oil and coal-powered thermal stations. In France for example nuclear electricity costs only one third and in the U.S.A. only half that of oil. Where coal is abundant and therefore relatively cheap, savings are not so great but on the whole nuclear electricity is still cheaper.

However beyond these broad economic advantages, there are questions to do with safety and possible detrimental effects to the environment. Opponents of nuclear reactors have made much of these aspects, but in reality nuclear reactors have as good a safety record so far, as conventional power stations. They are also less detrimental to the environment. Since nuclear stations require less fuel per unit of electricity produced the associated pollution from dirt, transportation of materials and storage is reduced and less pollutants such as CO_2 and SO_2 are emitted into the atmosphere. However, disposal of waste is a more serious problem because of its radioactive nature and this is therefore one of the crucial areas of controversy. Opponents to the setting up of further nuclear reactors range from environmental groups such as 'Friends of the Earth' and anti-nuclear groups like C.N.D., to local authorities and political groups. These groups oppose nuclear reactors for two basic reasons — one economic and the other that of public safety.

They question the economic need for further nuclear power in the West claiming that forecasts of future needs are over optimistic. For since the oil crisis of 1973 and the world economic recession the rise in demand for electricity has slowed down to such an extent that any additional needs can be met from conventional sources. Also such is the delay between planning and building a nuclear reactor that costs escalate making it more and not less costly to build than a conventional oil or coal-fired station. In the United States the time between planning and building is 6 years and because of lengthy planning enquiries is likely to be longer in the future.

As regards the safety factor most arguments focus on the possibility of accidents during processing and the danger of radioactive contamination from waste products. Since a number of stages are involved from treating the uranium raw base to the production of electricity, the danger of accidents, it is claimed, is increased.

Whilst there are different kinds of reactor, the latest being a Fast Breeder Reactor, processing and production stages are basically similar. In the case of the United Kingdom uranium is imported.

Uranium is imported as a crude oxide (yellow cake) from Australia, Africa and North America to the British Nuclear Fuels plant at Springfields (Lancashire) where it is purified. These purified elements are fed into the reactor in the form of rods which make up the core and provide power for several years either by a gas-cooled or heavy water processing system. The used rods can then be replaced without shutting down the reactor and the used fuel cells transferred to a reprocessing plant. Here reusable uranium and plutonium can be separated out leaving a residue of radioactive fission products. At each stage of processing a safety risk is also involved when transporting radioactive material. The critical problem is what to do with the waste. At present it is generally incorporated into steel clad glass boxes and stored at Windscale in Cumbria, but it is planned to sink much of it out at sea. There is a strong public fear that despite elaborate precautions some contamination will occur in transit or at the point of disposal endangering health and polluting the environment. The General Electricity Board in the UK and other authorities involved in nuclear energy programmes claim the stringent safety precautions taken are sufficient safeguard.

The Sizewell enquiry

The controversy over the future of nuclear energy programmes and the arguments for and against it have been starkly highlighted in the public enquiry into the Central Electricity Generating Board's (C.E.G.B.) plan to build an additional nuclear reactor at Sizewell on the Suffolk coast. It also raises the whole issue of how objective such enquiries can be, since the C.E.G.B. has been able to spend £5 million on preparing its case and advocating it through the media. The C.E.G.B. is thus accused of swamping the enquiry with money and propaganda and making the result a foregone conclusion (Case Study 19.4).

The Layfield Report (January 26 1987) recommended that 'not withstanding health and economic reservations, the building of a second reactor sizewell B should go ahead'.

The location and siting of nuclear power stations

The prime factors in the location of nuclear power stations are ones of safety, location near an abundant supply of water and an expanse of level site. As the location map for Japan and South Korea (Fig. 19.17) shows, coastal sites well away from any

211

19:4   SIZEWELL, SUFFOLK

The nuclear power expansion controversy

**CASE AGAINST
ANOTHER REACTOR
BEING BUILT AT
SIZEWELL**

Objectors include 'Friends of the Earth', Town and Country Planning Association, some unions including NUM, Campaign for Nuclear Disarmament
These points put forward by 'Friends of the Earth' are representative of the general case.

On safety and environmental grounds

1 *Any failure* could create a very dangerous release of radiation and highly active waste is poisonous. Threat is too great — near disaster 1970 at Three Mile Island (USA).
2 *Overlaps with nuclear warfare* weapons — claim plutonium produced has been used in U.S.A. military programme and technology advance 'spin' off into military sphere.
3 *Health hazard* in countries where uranium raw material mined.
4 *C.E.G.B.* — autocratic in approach and using public money to finance its case.

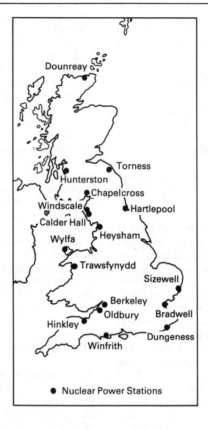

• Nuclear Power Stations

MAGNOX stations	Date of commissioning	Nett capability
		MW sent out
Calder Hall	1956	200
Chapelcross	1958	200
Berkeley	1962	276
Bradwell	1963	250
Dungnss.'A'	1965	410
Hinkley P. 'A'	1965	430
Huntrstn.'A'	1964	300
Oldbury	1967	416
Sizewell 'A'	1966	420
Trawsfynydd	1965	390
Wylfa	1971	840

AGR stations		Nominal capacity MW
Windscale	1962	33
Hinkley P. 'B'	1976	1320
Huntrstn.'B'	1976	1320
Dungnss. 'B'	1980	1200
Hartlepool	1981	1320
Heysham 'A'	1981	1320
Heysham 'B'	Late 1980s	1320
Torness	Late 1980s	1320

Other stations		Gross capacity MW
SGHWR, Winfrith	1967	100
PFR, Dounreay	1975	250

On economic grounds

1 *Government and C.E.G.B. overestimated future demand* — this could be met more cheaply by more efficient use of current energy output (i.e. energy conservation) and using spare capacity already available — more cost effective than new nuclear investment.
2 *Invest in alternative renewable energy sources* — solar heating, wind etc., and use of organic refuse and forestry waste etc. to make gas and liquid fuels.
Commons Select Committee indicated past nuclear investment had had low productivity — contrary to C.E.G.B. claims.
Nuclear plants are in too large a unit, smaller sized plants using other forms of energy would be more flexible.

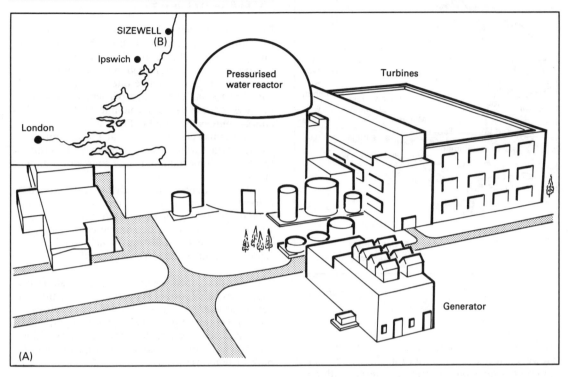

Layout of the established plant (A) and position of possible future Sizewell (B)

CASE FOR — PUT BY THE
C.E.G.B. FOR A P.W.R.
REACTOR — STATION
B (AT THE ENQUIRY
1983-84)

General

1   *Cheap* — nuclear is the
cheapest electricity to produce,
especially by a P.W.R.
Reactor.

2   *Safe* — nuclear power is
safe, no member of the public
has ever been killed or injured
by radiation leaks or
contamination since first built
in 1957. (There will in any case
be close monitoring to ensure
safety and no contamination in
air, on ground, or in water) —
regular checks for 40 km
around.

3   *Clean* — no unsightly
emissions waste carefully
disposed.

4   *Experience* — shown by
landscaping and care of wildlife
at Sizewell. As elsewhere can
be harmonious with nature. No
objections from Nature
Conservancy.

*In favour of the Sizewell
location*

1   *Transmission lines* for
Sizewell A has capacity to take
output from the proposed B
reactor.

2   *Close to main market* in
the South East.

3   *C.E.G.B. already own
the land* for the site

4   *Close to the sea* therefore
access to cooling water — 1000
million galls a day needed. As
drawn and returned to sea no
cooling towers needed.

5   *Sizewell A has good
production record* and no
objection from the local
community.

6   *Benefits to Sizewell*
3000 jobs on construction and
400 jobs in running and support
activities.
C.E.G.B. will help pay for
Saxmunden by-pass and better
access roads of benefit to whole
community.
Sizewell A brought more
prosperity to Sizewell and
therefore anticipated B will
add more amenities.

Exercise

● Assume that you have to
locate one of the following in the
United Kingdom, *either* a
nuclear power station *or* a new
multi-million tonne coalmine.
● Which locality would you
choose for the enterprise? Give
a carefully reasoned argument
for your choice including a
supporting sketch map.

Fig. 19.17   Distribution of nuclear power stations, Japan and S Korea, 1981

population concentration are the most favoured. However, the location pattern in the Soviet Union and other Comecon countries is different with most stations established at an inland location. Because of the scale of distance involved in the Soviet Union compared with say Japan or the United Kingdom the sites in the Soviet Union are some way from centres of population. Also they are still on waterside locations. Though important the safety factor is not so stringent as in capitalist countries and stations are now being built to specifically provide heating and power to particular cities, for example Minsk and Volgograd; distance from cities is not such a crucial issue in Comecon countries.

Apart from specific schemes to supply power to particular areas as in the Soviet case, electricity generated from nuclear reactors is fed into national grid networks. Thus provided reactors are within economic link to the grid, markets have only limited influence on the siting of reactors. Also, though dispersal of exhausted reactor fuel presents a problem its small volume makes it possible to transport it over considerable distances usually by rail at off peak periods, and this reduces the risks of accident.

The general pattern of location is unlikely to change in the near future, partly because existing locational factors are likely to remain and there is the tendency to locate new reactors adjacent to an old one, as in the case of Sizewell and outline expansion plans for other sites such as Hinkley Point (Somerset). This is because agglomerative advantages can be gained from utilising an established infrastructure and ancillary support services.

Other energy sources

Because of the limited resources of coal and oil in the world and reservations about the expansion of nuclear energy, the search for alternative energy sources has been intensified both at international and national level. Possible ones such as wind, tide and direct solar energy are particularly important because if these can be economically harnessed as energy sources they are limitless. While the location of geothermal energy sites is at present much restricted, with further research this may too ultimately prove an important and large source of untapped energy.

All these sources are already being developed on a local scale but it is only recently with further technological developments that there has been widespread interest in the commercial feasibility of setting up larger installations which could make a significant contribution to energy needs at a regional level.

Whilst developed countries see these alternative sources as an important supplement to existing conventional energy sources, developing countries see these as central sources of energy which particularly at a rural level can replace the use of traditional fuels such as firewood and dung which supply the bulk of domestic needs.

Direct solar energy

Solar heaters have been used for a long time in sunny climates to supply hot water and central heating for buildings. Now their use is being extended into more temperate areas as a summer supplement for other sources of energy. For example an increasing number of Japanese houses have solar heating panels in the roof. But until recently there have been formidable technical and financial obstacles to developing direct solar energy on any larger scale.

However, a number of pilot schemes have now been in operation over a number of years which clearly indicate that solar energy is a commercial alternative to other sources. One of the most encouraging developments has been that related to the production of photovoltaic devices or solar cells. These are made of wafers of crystalline material such as silicon, to which two metal contacts are fastened and through which electricity is passed when the cells are exposed to sunlight. The American Solar Technology Associated Research Co. at Aurora in New York State, has recently managed to develop a simple and efficient micro-corduroy photovoltaic cell which can produce energy at a cost of 70 cents a watt, which is less than the nuclear energy equivalent. In Southern California the Arco Solar Co. have installed a 1 MW capacity plant which is feeding electricity to consumers via the main grid network. In Saudi Arabia a pilot scheme set up in 1981 to supply electricity to three villages in a remote area has proved a success.

It seems that direct solar energy will be extended in the near future in suitable climatic areas. Whilst it may make a significant supplementary contribution to energy needs in developed regions which already have a well established energy network based on conventional sources of power, its most important contribution is likely to be made in developing countries. The long periods of intense sunshine enjoyed in tropical countries favour its development and the shortage of other energy sources in many areas makes it highly necessary.

Wind energy

Wind was one of the earliest sources of power used and over the centuries it has served a variety of purposes such as threshing and grinding corn, powering a drive wheel for pumping up water and since the 20th century for providing and driving a generator for electricity to homes. It has been widely used in more remote rural areas where other forms of electrification are not available, especially in Australia and the U.S.A. There is now much research into its use on a wider scale not only in developing countries but also in developed countries such as the United Kingdom and Sweden. Whilst some new wind generators are sophisticated and costly, machinery for harnessing the wind can be simply built at a modest cost and this is particularly important for poorer rural areas of the world.

On a small scale the main advances have been in producing small wind machines of light weight which can be easily erected. These have generating capacities of 5 kW to 100 kW. For example the Intermediate Technology Development Group investigating ways of providing simple energy generators and other machinery for the developing countries, have designed a machine with a rotor diameter of about 7 m and of improved operating efficiency. This is now being manufactured in Kenya at a modest cost for use in agricultural areas. One of the problems of depending on wind as a primary energy source is that of wind variability from day to day. Storage batteries for the current generated will greatly improve the reliability of wind power. Furthermore their use is being extended into such things as providing electricity for production of fertilizers, aerating ponds on fish farms and desalination of seawater.

Apart from its increasing potential for small scale needs, much more expenditure and research is going on into the contribution it can make to multi-energy systems not only for use in isolated and island communities but also as an additional energy supply to national grid systems. Outside of open plains, high-land and coastal sites provide useful locations, being more exposed to the wind than sheltered sites. The Italian government have already embarked on the development of wind energy farms. The one at Fiume Santo on the north west Sardinian coast consists of ten aero-generators. Energy farms like this one can be used to supply power to a particular district or supply electricity into the general grid.

In the United Kingdom, development of wind energy is part of the Department of Energy's alternative energy programme (Fig. 19.18). Large wind turbines are being designed with capacities ranging from 10 kW to 5 MW (5000 kW). The one at Carmarthen Bay, installed in 1982, has a capacity of 200 kW and is sited adjacent to Burry Point power station, hence supplementing the supplies of electricity generated there. It is hoped that ultimately wind generators could produce as much as 15% of the National Grid requirement.

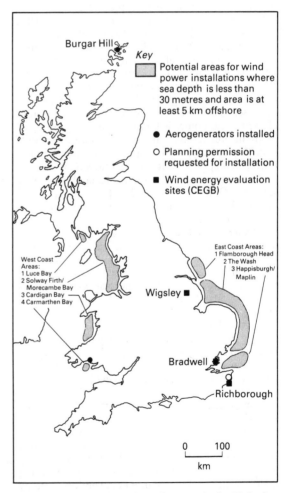

Fig. 19.18   Location of wind energy in the United Kingdom

215

Geothermal energy

Geothermal energy is the natural heat of the earth's crust stored in rock and water within the earth. This energy can be extracted via natural channels in the earth's crust or by drilling wells to tap concentrations of steam at high pressures and at depths shallow enough to be economically justified. The steam is led out through pipes and can either be used directly for heating purposes or to drive electricity generating turbines so providing a source of power.

Geothermal fields are fairly widespread in the world, most notably near the surface in areas of earthquake and volcanic action. Large fields, however, have also been found at much greater depths underlying the thick layers of sedimentary rocks across continental areas and the ocean floor. It is estimated for example that one third of the Soviet Union is underlain by exploitable geothermal energy. Generally it is at a depth of more than 20 km making it uneconomical to exploit at present.

Fracture zones in unstable areas of the earth's crust such as around the Pacific edge and the Mediterranean, New Zealand and the Rift Valley area of East Africa, allow steam and water to circulate carrying some of the earth's heat to the surface. Where it is available, the simplest and cheapest use of geothermal energy has been for direct heating purposes. The steam can be led directly into pipes either to heat domestic houses or for the growing of crops in greenhouses. It was first utilised in 1904 near Pisa in Italy, a noted area of volcanic activity. Later, geothermal heat was developed on a local scale in areas as far apart as Iceland and New Zealand. One of its great advantages is that direct heating by geothermal energy is half the cost of oil-fired heating.

Because of high capital costs and the technological problems involved, world interest in geothermal energy as a power source was negligible until the 1950s when intensive exploration activities then led to the commissioning of geothermal power stations in New Zealand, Japan, the USA and later in Iceland.

A United Nations Conference on New Sources of Energy in 1961 helped to further publicise the benefits and possibilities of using geothermal energy as a reliable source of energy. Since then a number of countries including the United Kingdom have been actively involved in developing geothermal programmes. In developed countries geothermal sources are likely to remain a very secondary source of energy, but in some developing countries where the shortage is chronic, utilisation of geothermal supplies may well help to meet the short term energy gap, until larger capital intensive schemes using hydro-electricity or some other conventional energy source can be developed.

Kenya is a case in point. Currently most of its

Source	Capacity (MW)
Hydro-electricity	309
Steam (coal)	120
Diesel oil	49
Gas turbine	30
Geothermal	(45 MW planned for 1985)
Total	508

Fig. 19.19   Electricity capacity, Kenya, 1982

energy needs are met from hydro-electricity, with steam and oil-fired thermal stations using imported coal and oil providing most of the remainder (Fig. 19.19). As demand rises the only short term way of meeting extra needs is either by costly import of more oil or from geothermal sources. Fortunately Kenya lies across the East African Rift Valley volcanic zone and it has been possible to economically tap supplies near the surface in the Olkaria area where underground water from Lake Naivasha to the north percolates along surface layers into the heat zone.

The World Bank provided half the capital cost to develop the first generator driven by geothermal steam. This has a capacity of 15 MW and two more are now being developed. Within the next decade 15% of Kenya's energy supplies are planned to come from geothermal energy, since further suitable areas have already been proven in the Menengai Crater area, around Lake Bogoria, Baringo and Magadi as well as to the south of Lake Turkana. Although capital costs are more than twice that of oil-fired stations, not only are operating costs very much lower but the life of geothermal stations is much greater.

Energy transition in the developing countries

The energy problems of the industrialised nations, serious though they are, pale in comparison to those facing most of the world's developing countries. The 'energy crisis' of the rich countries may merely be the initial trauma of converting to a leaner, but adequate and certainly healthier energy diet. But for most developing countries, the existing energy situation is more one of debilitatingly inadequate nutrition, virtually a condition of energy starvation.
Smith, V. & Knowland, K. *Energy in the Developing World* (O.U.P.) 1980

The energy crisis

Apart from oil rich nations, most of the developing countries are chronically short of commercial energy supplies both for domestic needs, industry and the rural sector. Yet if these countries are to achieve economic and social progress an adequate energy supply is a basic necessity.

At present whilst richer nations are consuming commercial energy at an average rate of 5 tonnes of coal equivalent per head, consumption amongst the poorer nations is barely 0.25 tonne equivalent.

This low consumption reflects a number of disturbing facets about developing nations. On the supply side, a number of the poorer nations are not well endowed with energy resources. Apart from limited hydro-electricity potential this applies for example to much of sub-Sahara Africa. Where there is potential there is insufficient finance and technical know-how available to develop it.

Consequently there is heavy reliance on imported oil not only to provide electricity but also for the transport system of a country. Since the 1970s the rising price of oil has placed an increasing strain on oil importing countries as a whole, but particularly on the poorer nations given these have the greatest problem in paying the energy bill. The steep rise in oil prices came at a time of world recession when in any case export of the agricultural goods and other raw materials needed to pay for all imports was becoming increasingly difficult and had a most serious effect on the economic stability of these countries. Without the continuance of international aid and loans a number such as Bangladesh, Uganda and Tanzania would be bankrupt.

The demand for commercial energy however is also low compared to demand in developed countries. This partly reflects low levels of industrialisation in the developing countries and the backwardness of agriculture. Most of the energy needed for agriculture must be supplied by human labour and draught animals. Also the low demand for commercial energy reflects the fact that for domestic needs most people rely not on commercial energy sources such as gas and electricity, but on traditional supplies — wood fuel, farm waste and animal dung. In 1980 those traditional sources of energy made up over 30% of China's energy supplies and 50% of India's. In some African countries wood and animal dung contributed as much as 90% of all energy needs.

Nor are these simply the main sources for rural populations. The increasing urban sector is also chiefly dependent on wood fuel for cooking and heating. As populations continue to rise more firewood is being burnt than can be replenished. Consequently much woodland is disappearing. Increasing amounts of animal dung are also being burnt in an effort to meet requirements.

As a result of the destruction of woodland and the diversion of much needed animal dung to maintain soil fertility, serious environmental problems are arising. More of the land is open to soil erosion and the increased seasonal flooding in the south of Bangladesh, for example, is being attributed to the more rapid surface run-off of water now that much of the woodland has been cleared on watershed areas.

Towards solutions

It is only over the last decade that developing nations have attempted to formulate comprehensive energy policies and intensify the search for exploitable home energy sources in order to lower their dependency on imported oil and cut down on the use of wood and animal dung.

In some appropriately endowed regions hydroelectric schemes have been developed with outside financial and technical aid. Mozambique for example has linked up with South Africa as well as other developed countries outside of Africa, to develop the Caborra Bassa Dam on the lower Zambezi. Generally most emphasis is being placed on exploration for oil and gas and coal reserves. Oil and gas reserves are the most significant, since oil supplies half as much energy again as its coal equivalent, is easily stored and is more versatile in the uses to which it can be put. However, whilst important discoveries are being made, especially in shallow offshore waters, for example off Thailand and Malaysia in South East Asia, costs of development are very high. Also many poorer countries simply have not the infrastructure network needed to enable supplies to be used across the country as a whole, especially in the rural areas, where the main need is likely to be. Useful though oil discoveries may be both directly to the economy and indirectly as an export earner, other sources of energy are obviously required such as the uses of wind generators and simple direct solar heating devices. Considerable research is also going on into the treatment of farm waste and animal dung to produce gas which can be used for domestic heating and cooking, and yet leave the residue suitable for spreading on the land to maintain soil fertility.

Probably however the greatest contribution may be made through devising more efficient ways of using traditional fuels; at present most cooking is done on open fires which is very wasteful of precious wood fuel. Widespread efforts are being made to replant areas with species of quick growing timber, including the eucalyptus, as a means of replenishing depleted forest and woodland sources. Again all this depends on finance, basic technical skill and persuading the indigenous population to change traditional habits.

What is clear is that any energy programme has to be a comprehensive one based on diversity of energy sources, recognising not only the growing need of commercial energy for developing industry and services in the urban sector but most important of all ways of solving the crisis now affecting much of the rural sector. A successful development programme overall is inseparably linked to a viable energy programme. Yet so variable is the situation from one nation to another, that a common energy programme is not feasible.

20 Fishing, Forestry and Water

Fishing

Whilst not comparable with agriculture in terms of yield of food, marine and to a lesser extent freshwater fishing remains an important source of protein. This is particularly so for developing countries where fish already provide something like 20% of protein needs. In addition to its importance as a direct food supply many smaller fish, and other organisms such as krill from the southern oceans are industrially processed for animal feed and agricultural fertilizer.

Over recent years advances in fish farming or mari-culture have attracted considerable public attention but for the foreseeable future the bulk of the demand must be met from conventional fisheries, in the main established fishing grounds.

It is thus vital that the fishing stocks of these grounds are carefully managed to ensure maximum future yields. This requires an idea of market demands in relation to the fishing stock which it is economically viable to take. It also requires a knowledge of the physical and ecological conditions under which the various kinds of fish and associated life forms live and reproduce. Whilst freshwater fishing is locally and even regionally important, particularly in the vicinity of large freshwater bodies such as the Rift Valley lakes like Lake Victoria in Africa and in ponded areas in South East Asia, the vast bulk of the fish eaten or processed into animal feed comes from the ocean. Thus much of the discussion must centre on marine fishing.

Conditions affecting the level of fishing

Different parts of the ocean vary in their productivity (Fig. 20.1). Ecologically the richest areas occur where upwellings of deep water happen along the margins of continents such as that off the Peruvian coast and along parts of the Iceland–Faroes ridge. Here are nutrient rich areas with plentiful phytoplankton (plant life) on which the zooplankton (mi-

nute animals) feed and which in turn support the fish at higher levels in the food chain. The most important fishing grounds are to be found along the continental shelf where the water is at depths of 200 m or less, allowing for light and oxygen to penetrate. These conditions along with nutrients partly carried by rivers and derived from the nearby land, again encourage an abundance of plankton and therefore plentiful supplies of fish.

Productivity is lowest in the ocean deeps and also comparatively low in tropical waters where a thermolayer occurs between the warm surface water and the cold deeps, inhibiting the functioning of the nutrient cycle. Though somewhat higher in the temperate and sub-polar waters there are marked seasonal variations in productivity.

Any major expansion of world fishing grounds is likely to be around the continental shelf including areas of upwelling waters. However, attention is also increasingly being focused on economic methods of fishing the deeper oceans for new species of fish and smaller livestock such as krill in the southern oceans.

Influences on fish stocks in the oceans

Interruption of the food chain

It is usual to divide marine life into pelagic life, which lives off the floor of the ocean, mainly in the surface layers of the oceans, and benthos life such as flat fish and crustaceans which live on the ocean bottom, principally the floor of the continental shelf. Herring is a typical pelagic fish, whilst cod and plaice are the commonest benthos fish. Each is supported by a food chain (Fig. 20.2) and any interruption of the food chain can have serious consequences. This can occur either as a result of natural events or human activity.

A change in physical conditions may for example drastically reduce the amount of phytoplankton and in turn the zooplankton upon which fish feed. Dur-

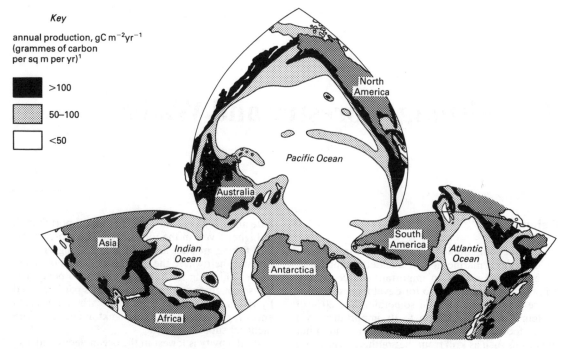

Key

annual production, $gC\,m^{-2}yr^{-1}$
(grammes of carbon
per sq m per yr)[1]

■ >100

▨ 50–100

□ <50

Fig. 20.1   Global distribution of primary marine production

ing medieval times a change in temperature conditions in the Baltic brought about a disastrous reduction in the plankton available to herring and therefore the stock of herring upon which the Baltic and Low Countries depended. More recently the once abundant anchovy off the Peruvian coast have been markedly reduced due to a change in the current flows affecting the upwelling and mixing of cold water with warmer surface waters and therefore the amount of plankton available to anchovy.

Changes in the conditions offshore have also been brought about by pollution especially off heavily populated coast areas such as those of Western Europe and California. This has directly affected the fish population as well as producing physical conditions detrimental to the plankton life on which fish feed.

Overfishing

Overfishing is even more serious since this reduces the amount of fish left to carry on the reproductive cycle essential to the level of future fish stocks in the ocean. The amount of fishing should not be determined by the total number of fish available i.e. by the standard crop, but by the rates of reproduction amongst the various fished stock. The production of fish potentially exploitable by people depends on a level of fishing which not only allows for maximum

reproduction, but also provides conditions which encourage fish to mature to the best marketable size.

Unfortunately major fishing nations including Japan, the U.S.S.R. and Peru have paid more attention to the economics of market demand than to the need to leave sufficient fish for maximum reproduction levels to be maintained. Where overfishing is combined with a change in the natural conditions affecting fish population, the results can be very serious. This is well illustrated from the fluctuating fortunes of the Peruvian fishing industry. This was rapidly developed after the Second World War to make Peru one of the world's leading fishing nations by the 1960s — only to be followed by a catastrophic decline from which the country is only now steadily recovering (Case Study 20.1).

But the nations which are causing the gravest concern are Japan and the U.S.S.R. Japan is at present the world's leading fishing nation, closely followed by the U.S.S.R. Both nations have important fishing grounds within their own limits, allowing onshore and deepwater fishing. But overfishing has occurred for a variety of reasons. It is partly, as we have already seen, due to increasing population raising market demand. It is also partly the availability of capital to invest in modern methods of fishing, including the building of factory ships and advanced radar and sonar techniques for locating shoals of fish.

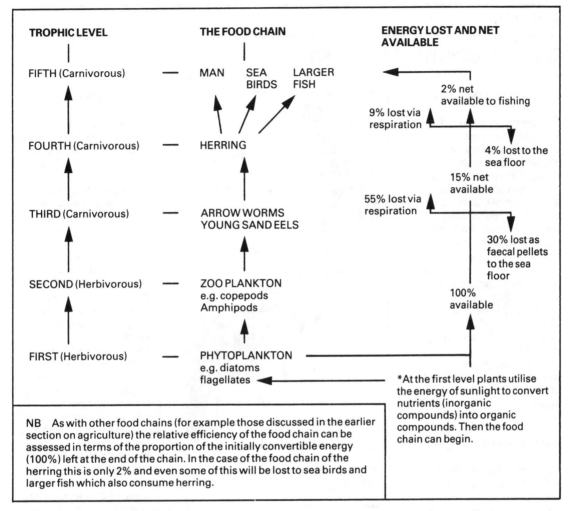

Fig. 20.2   *Food chain for the herring*

Both Japan and the U.S.S.R. have now also made a major penetration of other fishing grounds ranging from those of the north east Atlantic and north west Pacific to the tropical waters of the Indian Ocean and the southern oceans around Antarctica. This has increased the problem of overfishing in the north east Atlantic and north west Pacific, since countries bordering and traditionally fishing these areas had already been expanding their activities. Not surprisingly these countries vigorously oppose the aggressive fishing policies of Japan and the U.S.S.R. Countries have not only jealously guarded their own territorial waters but have tried to control fishing for 320 km off their coasts by creating Economic Exclusion Zones (E.E.Z.s). As the number of declarations increased, so that part of the old Law of the Sea allowing freedom of access to fish the oceans has become less and less meaningful. For these and

other reasons, the United Nations has sought to implement a new Law of the Sea, covering not only fishing but such things as access to marine minerals etc.

The United Nations

A new 'Law of the Sea' was agreed in 1982 by United Nations member states. Under this a coastal state is responsible for determining the allowable catch within its E.E.Z. and for its management and development. When a nation is not able to harvest the entire catch then it is required to give access to other countries by agreement, as has happened for EEC countries.

A World Fisheries Conference under the auspices of the Food and Agricultural Organisation (F.A.O.)

20:1 PERU

Changing conditions in the fishing industry

PHYSICAL CONDITIONS

Continental shelf extending for 150 km off the coast.

Upwellings of water occasioned by the cool Humbolt current made the area rich in nutrients and therefore in plankton which normally supports many species of fish in abundance but especially anchovy and tuna.

1971-2 disastrous extension of warm water 'El Nino' from the North brought conditions alien to plankton therefore rapid fall off in fish numbers. This contributed to a depression in Peru's fishing industry.

Favourable physical conditions now returned but other incursions of El Nino are likely.

IMPORTANCE

Government rationalised industry in 1973 but after rationalisation and reorganisation it was handed back to private enterprise. Now modest recovery 500 ships in the fleet — still mainly on anchovy catch.

Fish is an important source of protein in a country with limited livestock.

Fish meal and other fish based fertilizers are important for increasing productivity in agriculture.

An important export earner — leading export by value in the early 1970s.

40 000 people employed directly in fishing and fish processing — contributed to rising prosperity along the coast.

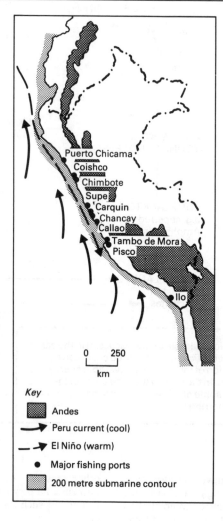

Key

- Andes
- Peru current (cool)
- El Niño (warm)
- Major fishing ports
- 200 metre submarine contour

0   250
km

Puerto Chicama
Coishco
Chimbote
Supe
Carquin
Chancay
Callao
Tambo de Mora
Pisco
Ilo

HUMAN CONDITIONS

Peru developed into one of the world's leading fishing nations from the 1950s largely on the basis of abundance of fish offshore, absence of controls on fishing, a rising demand overseas for fish meal and nitrate fertilizer, decline in competition due to overfishing e.g. off United States Pacific coast, and foreign investment in the fishing fleet and processing plants onshore.

The catch reached a record 9 million tonnes in 1954 and remained at a high level until the mid 1970s.

Overfishing by Peru and other nations, including indiscriminate catching of young stock by seine netting to process for fish meal and fertilizer contributed to a rapid decline in the industry through the late 1970s.

Peru has now taken measures to build up stocks through stricter regulations, including a 2-3 month closed season and trying to enforce a 320 km offshore limit against foreign fleets e.g. of Japan.

followed, in which the whole issue of global management and development of fish stocks was discussed. Out of this has come by consensus, an action programme involving planning, management and development of fisheries, development of aquaculture, international trade in fish and fish products and promoting fisheries to alleviate undernutritionment amongst the world's peoples. But the difficulties associated with implementing a successful policy for managing and increasing fishing stocks can be seen from efforts by EEC countries to achieve an acceptable policy relative to the North Sea and north east Atlantic fishing grounds which come within their joint E.E.Z. zone.

EEC fishing policy

Any change in regulations is related to predictions about future fishing stock, and is itself based on information from fish catches and other related economic factors such as market and price changes. Consequently any new regulations usually come too late to be effective. This can be illustrated from the case of the North Sea herring industry.

In general when fishing stocks are plentiful there is a good catch per unit effort and therefore a good return on capital investment. This encourages further investment, including larger scale operations, new and better methods of catching which lead to overfishing, and the depletion of young fish recruitments to the stock which form the basis of further breeding, as in the case of vacuum type fishing. The result is a rapid fall off of catch in relation to unit effort. This triggers off too late the passing of new regulations in an effort to raise sustainable yields.

Such was the fall off in North Sea herring stock that regulations made in 1971 to establish quotas amongst the different countries fishing the North Sea herring at 500 000 tonnes had to be revised in 1975 to 250 000 tonnes. Finally herring fishing was barred entirely for a few seasons. Yet estimates based on ecological measurements show that if the right conservation measures were employed at the right time, the effective sustainable catch is probably 750 000 tonnes.

Despite these difficulties the EEC members have continued to work towards a Common Fisheries Policy. In line with the U.N. Law of the Sea guidelines and the agreed programme arising from the 1982 World Fisheries Conference, the EEC Policy finally agreed in 1983, refers to waters within 320 km of the coastline of member countries (their E.E.Z. zone). There are two parts to this Common Fisheries Policy — one covers the structure of the fishing industry itself and the other the marketing of fish. But, instead of being complementary to one another there are contradictions between the two.

On the structural side the policy aims to ensure rational use of the resources of the sea, conserve resources, avoid discrimination between fishermen of different member states and prevent over capitalisation of the industry. The EEC has attempted to achieve these aims by setting quotas of catch for member states based on past performances, closing the fisheries once the Total Allowable Catch has . been reached, setting a minimum net mesh size and limiting the use of certain modern methods of catching, as well as setting up closed seasons for such fish as herring and plaice. Since EEC members such as the UK, Holland and Denmark need to fish also outside territorial waters, this has meant negotiating levels of mutual access with non EEC members, for example Greenland and Norway. Canada also allows some fishing in its waters in exchange for access to some of its own fish products into the EEC market. Developing countries have on the whole been excluded from the European 'pond'.

However, whilst all these structural measures are designed to raise the level of sustainable yields and conserve resources, much of the associated marketing policy ironically works against this. The fishermen of each nation are brought into 'Producer Organisations' which ensure marketing standards in size and freshness of fish offered for sale. In return the EEC guarantees a market price, intervening to subsidise the Producer Organisations if market price falls below a certain level. It also buys up excess stocks of cod, haddock and shrimps to take them off the market into cold storage and therefore keep up market price levels. The fishermen are therefore being given the incentive to overfish since the market price is to some extent guaranteed.

Recently efforts have been made to reduce catching capacity of fishing fleets, for example by not guaranteeing the price for more than 20% of the total catch. So far these efforts have been unsuccessful. Too many fishermen are still being attracted. For example, when herring fishing was allowed to be resumed for a brief season in 1982 after a total ban from 1977, the Danes exceeded their official quota of the catch by 1000%. Thus contradictory aspects of official policy are further compounded by EEC nations refusing to keep to quotas. There is also the continued unlawful incursions of non EEC fishing fleets into EEC waters.

Prospects for increasing world fish supplies

Apart from the action of EEC fishing nations and those of other developed countries such as Japan, additional pressure on the world's fishstock is coming from countries in the tropical world. It is clear that demand in some developing countries is beginning to expand rapidly as fish is an important source of protein. India and China figure prominently in world production levels and a number of other developing countries, such as North and South Korea, are creeping up the rankings.

At present there is little hope of extending fishing in the conventional fishing regions, and the greatest potential probably lies in responsible expansion of fishing of the suitable but lesser used waters of the south west Atlantic, and north west Indian Ocean. It is also estimated that some 15 million more tonnes might be added by harvesting other kinds of fish and marine life. Already some hitherto little marketed fish, for example those related to cod at the top of the food chain such as coley etc., are being exploited, and are becoming common on the fish sales counters at supermarkets. As regards the deepwater high seas resources, catch costs would be high thus only high value fish such as tuna will be worth exploiting.

Smaller organisms down the food chain, including zooplankton are now being successfully exploited. These occur earlier in the food chain therefore they provide higher productivity fishing as less of the primary productivity energy has been lost. The Russians and the Japanese have developed large suction retrieval and processing methods enabling midwater trawling of lantern fish and shrimps for example which congregate in large shoals at several hundred metres down. With the decline in the whale population in the Southern Ocean and waters around Antarctica the krill plankton on which whales feed has increased so much that it is now economic to harvest them. This is currently being done at the rate of 10 million tonnes a year and it could be up to 50 million tonnes. Careful management, however, is needed as krill are the food for a variety of marine life in these waters.

These smaller marine species are largely processed into livestock feed for chickens, pigs and cattle and therefore indirectly add an important extra source of protein to world diets. This could be particularly important in the future in helping solve protein deficiencies amongst the poorer countries. Apart from extending the range of harvesting to a greater variety, the other way of increasing fish, shellfish and other marine life, including edible seaweed and other plants, is by fish farming or mari-culture.

Fish farming or mari-culture

This has long been practised by Indonesia, Vietnam and other countries in South East Asia where milkfish and mullet are kept in coastal ponds linked by channels to open water. Freshwater carp reared in ponds have also been an important source of protein in China. Since fish are subject to more stress and variable conditions under artificial rearing the number of species which can be kept in this way is limited.

Japan and other South East Asian countries are developing marine polyculture especially on low wetland coasts with access to tidal water. Mangrove swamp areas offer particularly nutritious environs due to the rapid decomposition of plant life under tropical conditions. Here a variety of fish and shellfish are being reared in the same ponds. It is estimated that in wetland regions, including South East Asia where animal protein is in limited supply, something like 10–20 million tonnes of fish protein could be produced in this way.

Inland waters also offer important opportunities. In Africa for example a variety of fish farming schemes are under way including an expansion of shrimp fishing on Lake Kariba. In advanced countries mari-culture has largely been limited to high value fish which will quickly mature, including salmon, sea and freshwater trout. Intensive feeding and careful control of conditions have so hastened the maturing process that trout, once a high priced delicacy, are now as cheap as common sea fish such as cod and plaice. In suitable estuary sites oyster and mussel beds are also being established.

Conclusion

Mari-culture and harvesting of fish under natural conditions are not entirely separate activities. Small fry can be caught under natural conditions and introduced into other enclosed areas to be reared under fish farming conditions. Similarly efforts have been made to release artificially reared young fry into open water in an effort to increase fish stocks. This has so far had only limited success. What is probably more important is that the rearing of species under farming conditions will provide more understanding of the life cycles and food chain–web dependencies of different species. This will enable a better management of existing ocean fish stock through more relevant regulations etc. Ultimately, much will depend on co-operation between nations as the fishing fleets range even more widely in search of the harvest of the oceans.

Forestry

Though there are important woodland areas in middle latitudes and locally important forestry industries exist such as those in the Black Forest of Germany or the eucalyptus woodlands of Australia, the main forest belts are those of the humid tropics in the equatorial and monsoon regions and those of the cold temperate high latitudes in Northern Canada and Eurasia (Fig. 20.3) Important extensions of these occur in lower latitudes where mountainous

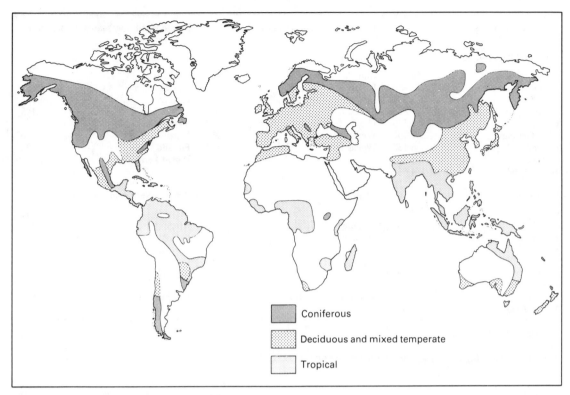

Coniferous

Deciduous and mixed temperate

Tropical

Fig. 20.3   Main forest areas of the world

terrain experiences similar climatic conditions to that of the northlands.

Because of the extensive need for paper and other timber products in industrial countries, we have been led to think of forested areas principally as sources for such products. Until recently this has led not only to over-exploitation of forests but also insufficient concern for the other uses of such areas, in particular as human and animal habitats. The contribution of forested areas to the oxygen balance of the earth's atmosphere and their effects on world climate have also been insufficiently understood. Now with a wakening realisation to the destruction of many forested areas, particularly in the tropics, and the wider issues involved in proper management of forest lands, more attention is being given to the conflicting demands made on the world's forest reserves and the replenishment of this important resource.

Softwood coniferous forest belts

Distribution

The present distribution of coniferous forest is largely controlled by climatic factors (including altitude)

and patterns of past exploitation. Coniferous evergreen species are able to withstand cold and drought, are adapted to a short growing season and can survive on poor sandy soils such as those of coastal dune lands. This explains the location of certain large tracts such as those of the sandy areas of the southern United States. The main commercial species are pines, firs and spruces but within these groups certain species are favoured because of certain qualities such as quick growth, straightness of trunk and use either as timber or pulp (poorer trees being used for the latter). Amongst the commonly known ones are the white pine, the Douglas fir and the Norwegian spruce. In the southern hemisphere the Parana pine of Latin America is particularly important, though as a supplier of softwood this is rapidly being ousted by planted eucalyptus tree tracts.

Unlike the deciduous woodland and tree species in the tropical rainforest, conifers occur in essentially pure stands with little undergrowth clutter, thus making exploitation of them easier. Increasingly today many of these pure stands, particularly along the earlier exploited southern margins of the coniferous belt in Eurasia and North America, are a result of replanting programmes initiated to bolster the world's depleting reserves of softwood timber.

Paper ('000s tonnes)		Wood pulp ('000s tonnes)		Round wood (logs, sawn timber etc.) mills m^3	
Paper and Paperboard		Mechanical		Coniferous	
U.S.A.	59 457	Canada	7 510	U.S.S.R.	298
Japan	17 913	U.S.A.	4 160	U.S.A.	253
Canada	13 390	Finland	2 485	Canada	123
China	8 804	Sweden	1 901	China	105
U.S.S.R.	8 733	U.S.S.R.	1 729	Sweden	42
West Germany	7 796	West Germany	1 210	Brazil	36
Finland	6 135	**World Total**	26 412	Finland	36
Sweden	6 132			**World Total**	1 172
World Total	174 862				
Newsprint		**Chemical**		**Broadleaved** (mainly tropical)	
Canada	8 625	U.S.A.	36 859	India	211
U.S.A.	4 135	Canada	11 789	Brazil	170
Japan	2 575	Sweden	6 267	U.S.A.	159
Finland	703	U.S.S.R.	6 005	Indonesia	150
Sweden	1 605	Japan	5 910	China	119
China	1 498	Finland	4 349	Nigeria	96
U.S.S.R.	1 354	Brazil	3 000	Vietnam	66
Norway	691	**World Total (mills m)**	86 859	**World Total**	1 868
World Total	26 563				

Source: Philips Digest 1984

Fig. 20.4   Leading countries for major timber products, 1981

Exploitation

Until the late 19th century most of the use of timber was localised to supply building and other construction needs as well as fuel and power from wood burning steam engines. But as the Old World became increasingly urbanised and industrialised, an insatiable demand occurred for timber products further afield. Initially it was for timber but during the interwar years this was overtaken by the great demand for pulp for paper making and later also pulp for artificial textile fibres and timber for composite building materials such as ply and chipboard. This is clearly indicated in the recent comparative figures for the production of the latter products compared to the relatively small amount of timber products as shown in Fig. 20.4.

In considering the location of the industries associated with the softwood forest areas, we must clearly distinguish between lumbering which is concerned with the felling and transport of logs, and the location of different processing industries. These can be divided into two groups: a) wood for the construction and building industries; and b) the pulping industry together with its further stage industries using the pulp as raw material input — paper and paperboard making, chipboard and other composite material and artificial fibres from wood cellulose for the textile industry. Whilst the construction and building sector has stagnated in the

Exercise

Substituting a country's rank order in each table (Fig. 20.4) for production amount, sum up for each country its rank positions in the tables. Using these, list the countries featured in order of their overall importance as timber producers.

Try to assess the reasons for the order of importance, referring to such factors as market demand and area under forests.

face of the world recession and competition from other construction and building materials, the pulp related industries have continued to expand and today exercise a dominant influence throughout the forestry industry as a whole.

Timber extraction

Like other sectors, this is today increasingly capital intensive with large scale mechanisation replacing much of the hand labour earlier required. Most of the felling and transport of lumber is still concentrated in the winter months, because the frost-bound ground facilitates the transport of logs to assembly points either by main rail and road routes or waterway float routes. But increasingly logging vehicles are being constructed which can cope with the softer ground conditions occasioned in summer over the permanent perma-frost layer below the surface. Thus lumbering is becoming an all the year round activity.

Most of the easily accessible forest areas have already been exploited and therefore extraction of timber is becoming more costly not only because of higher transport costs but also because in the more difficult areas harsher conditions reduce the quality of the timber stands. Though extensive reafforestation has occurred in more accessible areas giving good quality stands, the cost of doing this has also increased costs, as for example in sandy areas of the southern United States. Increasingly, to reduce costs, the practice is one of clear felling of whole stands (rather than selective felling) and an associated programme of replanting to ensure a steady future supply of timber. Thus in all the major producing countries there is a movement towards a situation of 'tree farming' rather than exploitation.

Location of industry

Because of the bulky nature of timber and its comparatively low unit cost, the first processing stages are located close to the lumbering regions. But other locational factors are important — power for the milling and pulping of timber, large amounts of water and access to markets. Waterside sites with hydro-electric facilities are particularly favoured locations, as is evidenced by the large number of plants found on fall-line situations behind which occur the forested shield plateaux and, in front, either navigable lake or river routes, as for example along the margins of the Canadian Shield in the Great Lakes region of Canada/USA and the Baltic Shield in Sweden (Fig. 20.5) and Finland. Here the fall-line comes close to navigable river estuaries and the coast. Other locations occur at the foot of mountainous upland into which coastal inlets have penetrated, as in British Columbia and Washington/Oregon in western North America.

Until recently whether the paperboard and cellulose fibre industries using pulp were also located in the timber producing regions largely depended on the size of the home market and the nearness of other markets. In the case of the USA/Canada the size of the United States market favoured large integrated plants in which linkage of pulp using industries to the pulping mills (as for instance in the case of the Thunder Bay works on the shores of Lake Superior in Ontario) provided important economies of scale, including the use of waste products as fuel to reduce power costs.

Today the trend is generally towards location of all processes in the timber producing countries and the closure of many of the small mills in timber

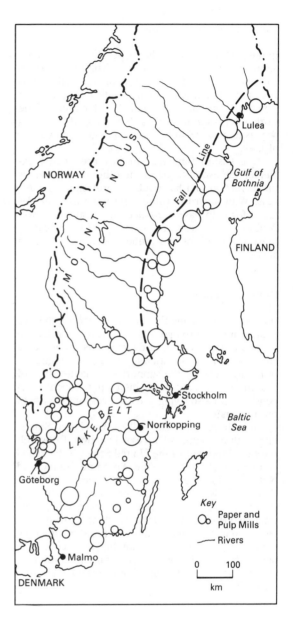

Fig. 20.5   Swedish paper and board industry

importing countries such as the United Kingdom. This has largely been caused by energy saving and other technological changes, which require heavy capital investment and large scale comprehensive production units able to produce the economies of scale needed to benefit from these changes. This shift is seen for example in the expansion of production of paper products such as newsprint, wrapping and packaging board in Finland and Sweden to serve the UK market and as a corollary the closure of branch plants in this country.

Management and conservation

In the past conservation has generally been synonymous with the preservation of existing forest lands and the wildlife dependent upon it. Today it is generally recognised that not only is any area of woodland constantly changing, but that much of the world's forested areas must be managed in such a way as to provide an increasing amount and variety of uses.

More leisure time has for instance greatly expanded the use of forested and other national areas for recreation and has made its provision big business. With regard to present resource use, the demand for pulp based products, it is estimated, will double in the next fifty years, putting increasing pressure on raising the timber yields in any given areas.

Forest preservation

As a way of resolving the difficulty between the two main groups of protagonists — conservationists and commercial users — most countries have adopted a common policy of identifying certain forest lands as primarily areas for the support and maintenance of wildlife and the natural habitat upon which it depends, whilst also trying to ensure responsible use of the remainder.

As far back as the early 1900s the United States, largely through the initiative of Theodore Roosevelt the then President of the United States, established National Parks such as the Yosemite Valley and National Monument Parks in the western United States. Finland today also has a comprehensive programme of nature reserves covering approximately one million hectares, much of it forest land. But even in protected areas some use is made of the woodland as a resource, notably as recreational areas, though this has to be carefully monitored to prevent detrimental effects both to the habitat and its wildlife.

Management of other forest areas

Outside of preservation areas, forest lands managed for commercial purposes under public or private ownership are still subject to legislation to give some protection to wildlife. In addition timber stands on watershed areas are protected from wholesale felling or clearance from other uses such as overgrazing which kills young saplings as well as destroying most of the undergrowth. If this did happen the resultant increased water run-off could lead to serious soil erosion in the way much of the Appalachian region was affected around the turn of the century.

In respect of timber extraction, in all major timber producing countries of the northern hemisphere the emphasis is on farming the timber rather than exploiting the forest land. In Finland timber is seen as a rotation crop with the government carefully overseeing the amount of timber felled and cut to ensure this is balanced against replanting and does not exceed market demand. As land is cut over it is being drained, ploughed, enriched with fertilizer to ensure the best conditions for the planting of young trees. Moreover these have been carefully selected from the most suitable species and nurtured until strong enough to be moved to their planting situations. Advisory services ensure careful management until the trees are mature enough for felling. Clear felling over limited tracts is today the most usual method as this not only increases timber yields but allows easier replanting cycles. Thus with improved management methods of the kind outlined it is estimated that Finland has doubled its timber yields without reducing the country's forest stock and the story is the same for most other producers.

In the United States, clear felling is more difficult because much of the commercial timber is on upland watershed land. Whether clear felling occurs or not depends on factors such as the age and composition of the trees, the slope of the land, type of soil, the amount and intensity of rainfall and the species and type of wildlife affected. In many locations only selected fellings are possible, but such has been the progress in forest management that it is estimated that the United States, at present dependent on a third of its needs being supplied by Canada, could within the next ten years be self-sufficient in timber and even a net exporter.

Acid rain

One of the most difficult problems affecting all kinds of woodland today is air pollution, particularly in countries with a large industrial base. In Central Europe for example acid rain, caused by sulphurous and other fumes swept up and carried in the wind bringing precipitation to forest lands, is having such a serious effect that it is estimated that about a quarter of woodland in West Germany is damaged beyond recovery. This is a far more important problem than ground pollution from water contaminated by effluent from timber mills or other industrial usages in and close to forest lands. Solution of this more widespread problem clearly requires legislation of a much more comprehensive nature than that directly concerned with the forest land itself. But as recent controversy over attempts to get the Central Electricity Generating Board in the United Kingdom to control emission of pollutants from its power stations indicate, such legislation is also difficult to enforce in practice.

More effective use of timber

Responsible management of timber resources does not end with the forest lands themselves. It must also be concerned with the efficient use of the timber once it is cut. Thus, in the case of timber needed for the construction industries much of the sawn timber output is being replaced by reconstituted timber resulting from the grinding up of whole trees to reduce waste and then the use of powerful glues to reconstitute and remould them to the consumer's needs. More effective recycling programmes for waste paper and other products are also important to enable the re-use of resources. Thus management of forest resources cannot simply be concerned only with the forest lands themselves but must also include efficient processing methods and re-use of timber and paper products where feasible.

Tropical forests

Natural conditions affecting exploitation

There are important differences between softwood coniferous forests and the tropical forests of monsoon and equatorial lands. Tropical forests are dominated by hardwoods and there is a much greater variety of species with few pure stands of any one particular type of tree. This makes extraction of commercial timber difficult.

Like the variety of species found, the greater amount of undergrowth including creepers found in tropical forests is larger than in coniferous forests despite the difficulty of light penetrating through over head canopy layers of leaves. This is a result of the hot and humid conditions together with a constant rotting organic layer in the soil favouring prolific growth except during dry spells.

Commercial exploitation of some of the most sought after hardwoods such as teak, ebony and mahogany is hindered not only by the fact that species are scattered throughout a forest tract, but by a number of other conditions. Felling and transportation to assembly points for larger distance shipments is made difficult by the close packing of trees and secondary growth. Conditions under foot are frequently swampy and much of the forest lands are away from any natural access routes such as navigable rivers. The hot humid climate also reduces the efficiency of labour and is detrimental to the health of people who work and live in remote logging areas away from medical and other amenities. It is thus not surprising that until relatively recently commercial exploitation of tropical forest lands has been very limited, taking place mainly where access to navigable coasts and rivers or road/rail transport was available.

Land clearance and domestic fuel demand

Whereas coniferous forest management has been centrally concerned with over-exploitation of the timber for commercial purposes without sufficient regard for other uses, future supplies and the effect on wildlife, in most tropical regions the biggest problem has been the destruction of many areas to meet local domestic needs for agricultural or grazing land. As populations have increased more and more land has been cleared. Overgrazing in marginal areas of the forest as in West Africa and Latin America led to the continual pushing back of forest margins.

Perhaps the greatest loss however has come through the use of wood as the major fuel in all tropical areas where woodland occurs (Fig. 20.6). It is estimated that in any one year nearly half of all the trees felled are to meet basic needs of cooking and heating in homes. Along with crop residue and cattle dung, firewood and charcoal meet something like 70% of Bangladesh's total energy needs and in rural India 85% of people's needs. In Nigeria and

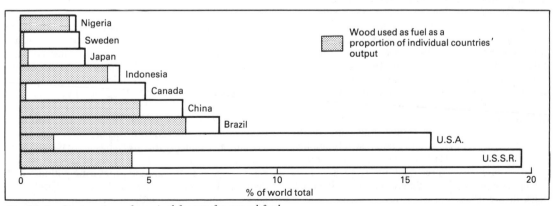

Fig. 20.6   Destruction of tropical forests for wood fuel

229

Tanzania consumption of firewood is estimated at 1 to 1.5 tonnes per person per year.

Apart from the harm done through forest destruction, reliance on firewood is time consuming of human labour, since wood has to be fetched at increasing distances from the village. Also, for those unable to obtain their own wood for heating and cooking it becomes increasingly expensive taking up to a quarter of a family's basic income in many parts of Africa.

Increasing exploitation for export

Whilst wood may also be used commercially as a fuel for rail transport and such things as local iron and salt making, increasingly tropical woods are being felled for export to developed countries. Though Brazil and India are important producers, the leading exporters are Indonesia, Malaysia and Nigeria and the main importers are Japan followed by the EEC and the United States.

Because of the growing world demand for tropical timber and the increasing attention given to the possibility of setting up plantations to supply pulp for paper and allied industries, strenuous efforts are being made to ensure future supplies and the regulating of world trade and prices. The impetus is coming from Japan to obtain an International Commodity Agreement (I.C.A.) which will help to stabilise prices and ensure sufficient future supplies. Malaysia for example is worried that her timber stocks will be depleted as logging exceeds reafforestation. The main problem at present is getting sufficient co-ordination between consumers and producers to ensure that logging and reafforestation programmes can be arranged. Insufficient investment funds for replanting programmes is the main stumbling block. The World Bank estimate that something like 2 million hectares of replanting must take place over the next 5–10 years. Tree plantations rather than replacement of felled timber in existing forest areas, are favoured as newly developed quick maturing species can then be planted, effectively raising yield over selective planting of traditional tree species by as much as 30 fold. At present most of the timber comes from selective felling of mature trees in mixed tropical forests.

The other major task is to promote more timber processing in the producer countries. At present something like 80% of exports is of sawn timber with the processing and finishing taking place in importing countries. This reduces the value of the timber to the producer country and restricts employment opportunities. It is thus likely that any International Commodity Agreement for tropical timber will include the condition that more processing takes place in the producing countries.

This is the case in Indonesia where under the country's second and third Five Year Plans not only has considerable expansion of lumbering taken place, but increasing numbers of factories have been established at the ports to produce plywoods and veneers. Most of the industry is concentrated on the island of Kalimantan, since the heavily populated islands such as Java and Bali have been largely cleared of rain forest (Case Study 20.2).

Other resources from tropical forests

Unlike coniferous forest areas where the main accent is on the value of the forest for timber or pulp, the tropical forests are a rich resource for many other products needed in a modern world, some of them not readily associated with tropical areas. It is estimated that a quarter of the medication issued on prescription in modern societies owes its origin to materials which come from plants or animals of tropical rain forests. Plants, roots and insects contain properties which are now commercially used in the treatment of cancer, leukaemia and various nervous disorders.

Besides this, specialist materials from tropical forests contribute to industry in a variety of ways. Latex, gums, camphor, resins, dyes and oils come from forest lands and plantations in South East Asia, West Africa and Latin America.

Hence any discussion about future use of tropical forests must take account of a multitude of uses to which forest and associated plants can be put, as well as ecological and other considerations.

Reconciling demand and conservation

Today the world is faced by two major and to some extent conflicting dilemmas in relation to tropical rain forests. On the one hand there is the need to make them produce more timber for local and export needs and on the other, the need for proper conservation and management of forests in the interests of humanity as a whole.

Whilst the needs of overseas markets are quite different from those of local populations increasingly desperate for wood for basic heating and cooking needs, the solution to both appears to be the establishment of woodland plantations of single species, since reliance on the natural regeneration of already exploited natural rain forest is unrealistic both in terms of the scale of demand and the length of time it takes for regeneration to occur.

Planting of eucalyptus trees has increasingly been seen as a solution, though in more arid areas the cassias tree is more suitable, maturing within 5 or 6 years. India, like other countries such as Zimbabwe and Zambia, is faced with an increasing shortage of wood at a time when population and demand con-

20:2 INDONESIA

Timber production

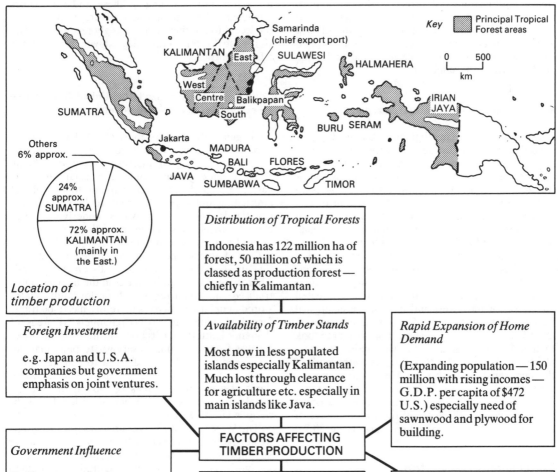

Location of timber production

Others 6% approx.

24% approx. SUMATRA

72% approx. KALIMANTAN (mainly in the East.)

Distribution of Tropical Forests

Indonesia has 122 million ha of forest, 50 million of which is classed as production forest — chiefly in Kalimantan.

Availability of Timber Stands

Most now in less populated islands especially Kalimantan. Much lost through clearance for agriculture etc. especially in main islands like Java.

Rapid Expansion of Home Demand

(Expanding population — 150 million with rising incomes — G.D.P. per capita of $472 U.S.) especially need of sawnwood and plywood for building.

Foreign Investment

e.g. Japan and U.S.A. companies but government emphasis on joint ventures.

FACTORS AFFECTING TIMBER PRODUCTION

Government Influence

Deliberate emphasis on expansion especially in 2nd and 3rd 5 Year Plans for national development.
    Control of foreign investment.
    Awareness of need to conserve and replant timber areas — much stronger measures enforced to prevent overcutting.
    Encouraging more processing before export to raise value of timber and increase foreign earnings.

Technology and Changes in Production

Traditional methods replaced by mechanisation.
    Dramatic rise in timber production 14 million m^3 (1971) to 32 million m^3 (1980) mainly from Meranti and Iquan species.
    Market shift from sawn logs to plywood and processed timber. Leading world plywood producer, 40% of world output.

Rising Overseas Demand

Especially in Japan and newly industrialising countries of South East Asia e.g. Taiwan. These took most of log exports. Plywood exports mainly to U.S.A., West Europe and Japan — 60% of timber products exported.

tinue to increase. Consequently afforestation programmes have been increasingly concerned with encouraging the planting of quick maturing species, in particular the eucalyptus tree which is indigenous to Australasia.

There is however considerable debate today at village and institutional level on the wisdom of relying too much on mono-culture of eucalyptus over wide areas. Attention is now being turned back to agro-forestry in which trees can be intercropped with field crops, thus allowing food and fuel to be produced from the same land.

Still wider issues — the case of Amazonia

Wider issues still are highlighted in the much publicised discussions on the future of the Amazon rain forests. A succession of controversial government measures have been passed since the 1950s to encourage exploitation of many other resources in addition to timber. Large areas of the rain forests are being cleared with serious consequences which are likely to be felt far beyond Amazonia and which will be very difficult to reverse. Up to the 1950s, incursion into the rain forest whilst bringing about a considerable reduction in the numbers of Indians through the spread of disease and disruption of their traditional ways of life, had not seriously affected the extent of the forest and its delicate ecological balance. But exploitation of its resources has escalated as the Brazilian government has begun to look to the Amazon region as the last major resource frontier and safety valve to the overcrowded lands of the impoverished north east. Multinational investment companies overseas have added to the pressures as better technology and improved transport bring the potentially rich and diverse resources of the Amazon forest within economic grasp (Fig. 20.7).

Water supply and control

Water, like food and shelter, is one of the most basic human necessities. Amongst simpler societies obtaining water or controlling it requires a constant physical effort and therefore it is appreciated as a precious commodity. Amongst advanced industrial societies a constant supply of water is usually taken for granted — a matter of simply turning on a tap. But such has been the rise in demand for water in most developed countries with the expansion of domestic and industrial usage, as well as for agriculture now that modern sprinklers and other equipment are available, that even amongst modern societies anxieties are being expressed about demand outstripping supplies. Danger of existing supplies being polluted is another worry, with greater industrialisation and use of chemicals in agriculture.

Given the finance and knowledge, people can do much to manage water supplies but ultimately they are dependent upon the rate at which water is supplied and replenished by nature through the hydrological cycle and the drainage basin systems via which it is distributed (Fig. 20.8). Thus the need for a full understanding of these and the factors influencing them in various ways from one part of the world to another is increasingly recognised. The European Water Charter lays down standards for EEC countries.

Control and use of water in the United Kingdom — an example of a developed country

As is generally the case most of the United Kingdom's water supply is taken from the surface waters of rivers and lakes, but increasing attention is being given to underground aquifers, especially in south eastern England where the scarpland topography of alternating outcrops of porous rocks such as the chalklands and of impervious underlying softer clays, provide favourable conditions for underground water to accumulate.

One of the problems in the United Kingdom is that most of the precipitation falls on the uplands whereas the greatest demand is in the heavily industrialised and urban regions of the lowlands. Water stored in upland reservoirs therefore has to be transferred by pipe and surface channels to areas of demand. Until the 1960s however most of the transfer was from individual reservoirs to particular demand centres, making it difficult to transfer water away from areas with a surplus to those where demand was either increasing too rapidly for the usual supply to meet it or where occasional drought periods cut back this supply.

The Water Act of 1973 set up new larger Regional Water Authorities to co-ordinate and control water supplies as well as manage associated features such as industrial waste disposal, pollution and flood control together with inland fisheries and water recreation. Britain today has a far more integrated and flexible system of water supply (Fig. 20.9).

Since demand still continues to outstrip supply some major problems remain and conflicts of interest in the use of surface water continue to occur. There is the question of flood control, not only from occasional excessive rainfall but also tidal incursions such as that affecting many eastern coastal areas in 1953 and again in 1969 and 1976.

Ensuring a supply of water

There are two ways in which water shortages may be met. These are to make better use of the water already available and secondly to build more storage

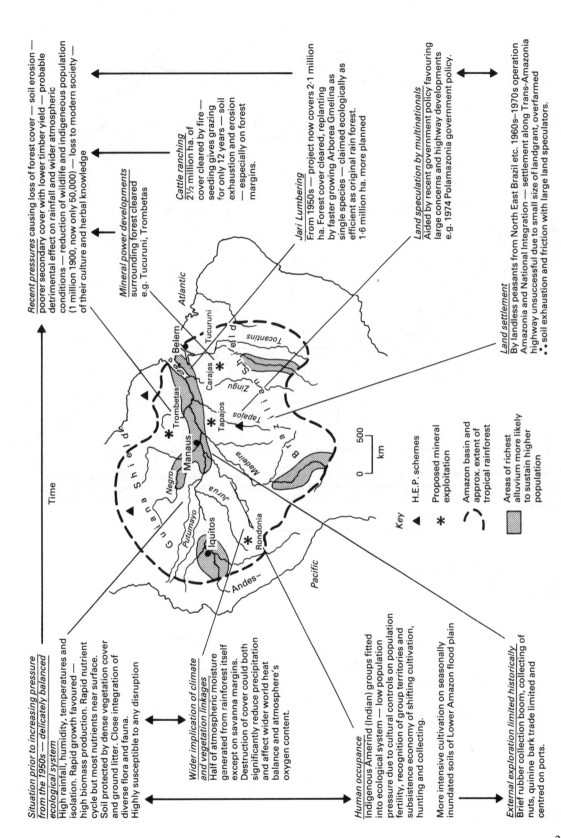

Fig. 20.7 Pressures on the Amazon rain forest

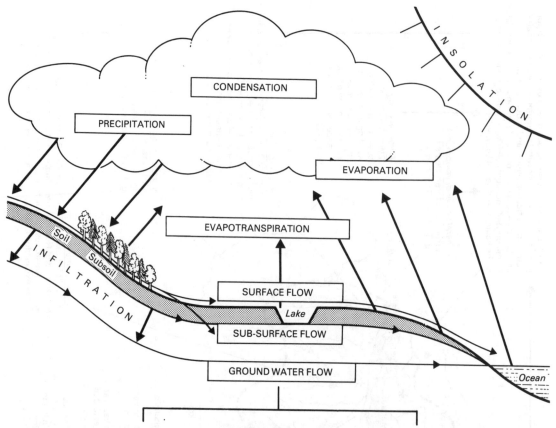

CONDENSATION

INSOLATION

PRECIPITATION

EVAPORATION

Soil

Subsoil

INFILTRATION

EVAPOTRANSPIRATION

SURFACE FLOW

Lake

SUB-SURFACE FLOW

GROUND WATER FLOW

Ocean

The throughput of water in the cycle is determined not only by physical conditions such as amounts and seasonal intensity of precipitation, evaporation rates, as well as vegetation cover, soil and geological conditions acting as storage elements, but also by storage of water in reservoirs and the amount and time of abstraction of water for various usages — agriculture, industrial and domestic.

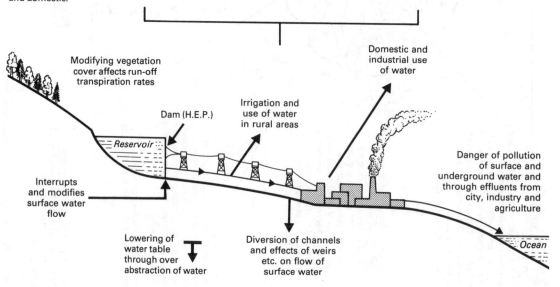

Modifying vegetation cover affects run-off transpiration rates

Domestic and industrial use of water

Dam (H.E.P.)

Irrigation and use of water in rural areas

Reservoir

Danger of pollution of surface and underground water and through effluents from city, industry and agriculture

Interrupts and modifies surface water flow

Ocean

Lowering of water table through over abstraction of water

Diversion of channels and effects of weirs etc. on flow of surface water

Fig. 20.8 Hydrological cycle

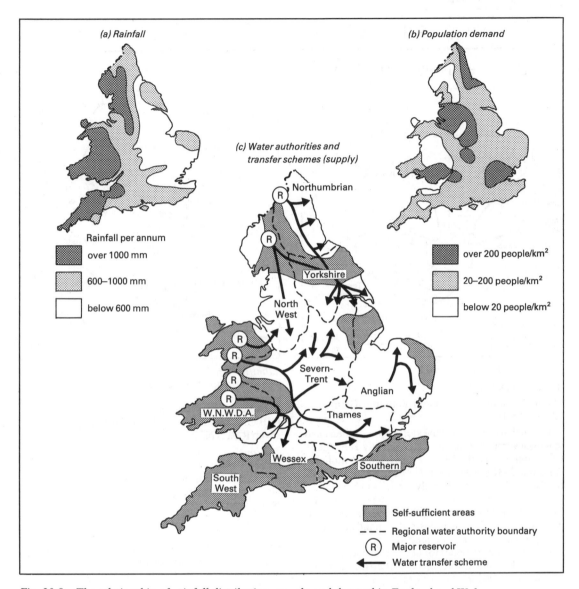

Fig. 20.9 The relationship of rainfall distribution, supply and demand in England and Wales

reservoirs to meet an anticipated continued increase in demand.

At present it is estimated by the National Water Council that one quarter of all water fed into the supply system does not reach the consumer because of leakages in the system through faulty piping and other causes. Steps are being taken to prevent losses but repair work is costly and perhaps easier ways would be to re-use water and by better price control monitor the use of water, especially for low value uses such as cleaning cars and bathing. Whilst considerable steps have already been taken to re-use water in industry only in Sweden has it been seriously attempted for domestic usage. Here bath water is recycled for flushing toilets and sewage water purified for re-use. Apart from the one district of Malvern, domestic water supplies in England and Wales are subject to a flat rate charge irrespective of how much is used in a home. Since at present this pricing is below the cost of obtaining new supplies and a significant proportion of domestic water is wastefully used, it would seem appropriate to measure consumption and charge accordingly. The various water authorities are now carefully considering switching to this system.

On the question of increasing reservoir capacities,

20:3 KIELDER WATER, N.E. ENGLAND

The Kielder Forest multipurpose scheme

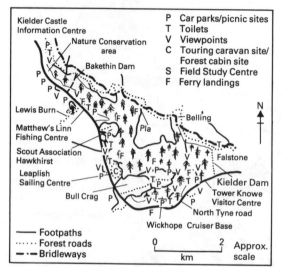

Kielder Castle
Information Centre
Nature Conservation
area
Bakethin Dam
Lewis Burn
Matthew's Linn
Fishing Centre
Scout Association
Hawkhirst
Leaplish
Sailing Centre
Bull Crag
Belling
Pla
Falstone
Kielder Dam
Tower Knowe
Visitor Centre
North Tyne road
Wickhope Cruiser Base

P Car parks/picnic sites
T Toilets
V Viewpoints
C Touring caravan site/
   Forest cabin site
S Field Study Centre
F Ferry landings

—— Footpaths
····· Forest roads
—·— Bridleways

0   2
   km
Approx.
scale

The Kielder Forest Scheme

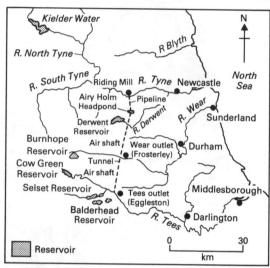

Kielder Water
R. North Tyne
R. South Tyne
Riding Mill
Airy Holm
Headpond
Derwent
Reservoir
Burnhope
Reservoir
Cow Green
Reservoir
Selset Reservoir
Balderhead
Reservoir
R Blyth
R. Tyne Newcastle
Pipeline
R. Derwent
R. Wear
Air shaft
Wear outlet
(Frosterley)
Tunnel
Air shaft
Tees outlet
(Eggleston)
R. Tees
North
Sea
Sunderland
Durham
Middlesborough
Darlington

▨ Reservoir

0   30
     km

Linking Kielder Water into the Northumbrian Water Authority catchment area

REASONS FOR IT

(National context — estimated doubling of demand 1970 — 2000)

  1   1960s to 1980s — of the storage water then used ⅔ to industry in the North East especially Teesside. I.C.I. and steelworks demand rose from 140 million gallons to 203 between 1961-71 and was estimated to be 370 in 1981. Existing supply capacity in North East was only 257. But because of economic recession this extra demand has not materialised. Population needs gone up by only 2% and industrial demand has fallen ∴ at present Kielder is not needed.)

  2   Guarantee supplies for decades ahead which it was thought would attract much needed industry to North East — water seen as a vital part of region's infrastructure.

  3   Regulate water within the Tyne basin taking the top off flooding and improving summer flow of the Tyne.

  4   Environmental opposition to a large number of small dams, encouraged Water Authority to look to a major reservoir in an upland area.

  5   Provide leisure facilities in association with the Forestry Commission which controlled forests around.

  6   Finance available. Financial Aid of £167 million needed. £36 million was available from the EEC Regional Fund and £26 million from the British Government (European Investment Bank was willing to loan remainder at a low rate of interest).

FEATURES OF THE SCHEME

(NB One of the National Water Board's planned seven Reservoirs)

1 *Aim*

Is to shift water from the high rainfall areas near the Scottish Border's to the large industrial centres in the North East.

2 *Location*

Following public enquiries to ensure safeguards for existing population and environment, two dams built in remote North Tyne Valley 35 km North of Hexham.

3. *Multipurpose*

  (a) Reservoir includes wild life Nature Reserve at upper end of lake.
  (b) 10 year leisure programme incorporated for lake and forest area around including boating, fishing and £¾ million outdoor centre at Hawkhirst Peninsula.

4 *Link into general catchment area*

56 km to Riding Mill where adjustment well and pumping station controls flow into Wear and Tees catchment area — thus integrated into the main drainage basin flows.

considerable expansion has taken place since the 1960s, particularly as EEC funds are available for this purpose. The building of more reservoirs has also been encouraged by a demand for recreational facilities which water areas can supply — boating, angling and in the surrounding area walking, picnicking and other family pursuits (Case Study 20.3).

However in some areas both reservoir building and other features of multi-purpose schemes are opposed by environmental lobbies anxious to preserve the vegetation and wildlife of an unspoilt area and also by farmers in lowland areas where agricultural land is valuable. But it has been demonstrated in both upland and lowland areas that careful planning and consultation with interested parties can lead to successful schemes, for example the Kielder Forest Reservoir in the Cheviots, and Rutland Water in the East Midlands.

One of the biggest problems in estimating future needs is correctly forecasting trend factors such as population growth in an area, the rise in real incomes (which affects the purchase of consumer durables such as washing machines and cars), and future expansion of industry. Economic recession over the 1970s in Britain as in other developed countries has brought a slowing down in the growth of demand for water, so much so that recently constructed reservoirs such as Kielder Water are not likely to be fully utilised in the near future. Currently the policy is to investigate other ways of making better use of existing resources rather than go in for new capital expenditure on further schemes.

Control of flooding

Abnormally heavy rainfall is the major cause of flooding on a world scale, most notably in monsoonal areas. In such countries as Bangladesh and China a combination of physical factors and the dense concentration of people on the rice alluvial flood plains which are particularly liable to serious flooding, has brought disasters with a huge loss of life. Whilst in England localised flooding does occur both in the west where the heaviest precipitation occurs and on the lowlands if rapid snow melt occurs when the ground underneath is still frozen, the most widespread flooding has come from North Sea surges (Fig. 20.10). These are most destructive where the surge inland at high tide is confined to estuaries and holds back river flow so that flooding occurs not only along tidal stretches but also inland on lowlying land adjacent to the lower swollen river reaches. The effects of such flooding have become widespread as lowland around the North Sea is gradually sinking relative to normal sea level, due to isostatic adjustment following the last ice age. High tide at London Bridge for example has been rising by about 0.73 m a decade.

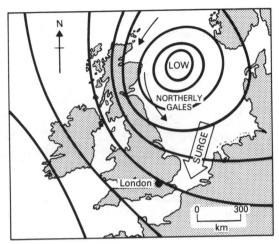

Fig. 20.10   Conditions leading to tidal flood (Cyclonic winds built up a tidal surge in the North Sea which funnelled with increasing intensity into the narrows between England and the Low Countries causing a storm surge and flooding along the east coast and the Dutch and Belgian coastline.)

Consequently sea defences and river embanking has been carried on throughout historical times both here and across the North Sea, most notably in Holland. Until the recent construction of the Thames Barrier, completed in 1983, much of Central London and boroughs lying east of this along Thameside were still liable to serious flooding at least once every 50 years, which if allowed to occur in 2030 would have left over one million more people homeless.

The Thames Barrier cost £730 million, but it is considered a small price compared with the estimated £3.5 billion flooding would have caused in damage to property and disruption of transport and other services. Now the flood barriers can be put in place at any time a high tidal surge is likely to cause undue flooding (Fig. 20.11).

Problems of water supply and control in developing countries

Because much of the developing world lies within the tropics where the extremes of drought and over abundant rainfall are most widespread, water supply and control are much greater problems than in developed countries. The problem is further intensified when we realise that the bulk of the world's population lies within the tropics and that there are serious shortages of both financial capital and technical know-how needed to ensure a better management of water.

237

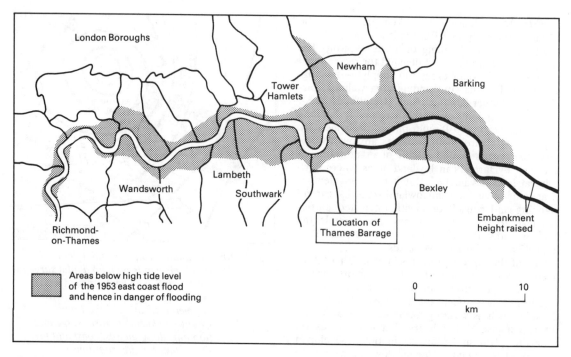

Fig. 20.11   The Thames Barrier

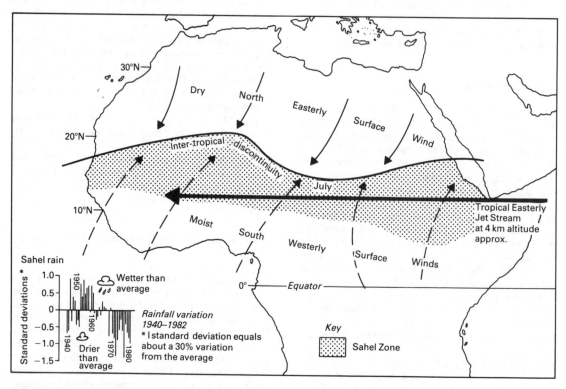

Fig. 20.12   Weather situation in the Sahel in July (within the rainy season)

Water supply

Problems of drought have recently been brought into world-wide focus by a succession of years of abnormally low rainfall in Africa. Whilst its effect has been most catastrophic along desert margins (Fig. 20.12) where rainfall is always uncertain, it has also been serious for savanna regions. These also depend upon hot season rainfall to provide enough water supply to last them through the dry season. Crop failure, loss of livestock and hunger have thus been features of life from West Africa down to the Cape in South Africa for most peoples depending on subsistence agriculture.

Efforts are being intensified with support from international agencies such as the World Bank to provide a more assured water supply. This is all the more imperative as population increase and economic development occurs leading to an upward trend in demand for the foreseeable future. In the worst hit areas such as the Sahel stretching along the southern margin of the Sahara from West Africa to the Sudan, well digging is part of a more comprehensive programme to rehabilitate the population. Efforts are being made to produce integrated supply schemes, an example of which is given in the following Case Study (20.4) of the State of Kano in Nigeria lying south of the Sahel belt proper.

To the west of Kano crystalline and impervious rock outcrops make surface storage schemes feasible, but in the east porous aquifer bearing rocks receiving groundwater from an easterly water flow mean that wells and boreholes are needed to reach this groundwater.

In some areas the scheme includes provision for flood control, hydro-electric power supplies, irrigation of land downstream from reservoirs and adjacent to well supplies, as well as further opportunities for fishing.

Problems of flooding and measures to combat it

Whilst in some coastal areas of the tropics typhoons and tidal surges may cause considerable flood damage, the most widespread flooding is associated with abnormally heavy rainfall in monsoonal regions. This may be illustrated from the Huang Ho or Yellow River basin in North China where catastrophic floods with widespread loss have occurred since as early as 600 BC. As population has increased and the land been intensively cultivated the problem has become progressively more serious. Only recently has a comprehensive conservation and flood control system been adopted for the whole basin (Case Study 20.5).

20:4 KANO REGION, NIGERIA

Water supply problems and schemes

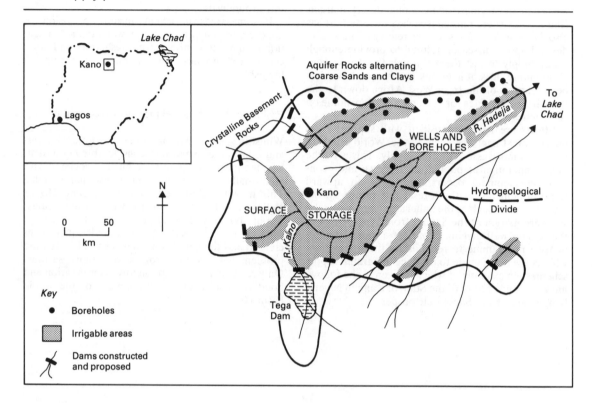

PROBLEMS

1   Too little and uncertain water supplies. Dry season marked — October to late May. Uncertain rainfall in wet season — high evaporation rates 1970s — rainfall 60% or less of mean annual precipitation of approx. 800 mm.

2   Expanding economy and population. More irrigation, domestic and industrial water needed.

3   Problems associated with bore holes and wells. Limited supplies plus inequitable distribution — villages near towns and towns favoured.

4   Problems associated with dam and surface storage scheme:
  (a) Costs high,
  (b) High evaporation rates,
  (c) Silting with seasonal flooding,
  (d) Displacement of villages and loss of common land rights,
  (e) Training peasants in new methods of agriculture associated with irrigation etc.,
  (f) Waterborne disease could be increased.

MAIN WATER SUPPLY SCHEME

Tega Dam and Reservoir

Dam at mouth of Kano gorge — impermeable crystalline rock base — deep water high volume to surface area reducing evaporation loss. Dam 50 m high and 6 km wide creating lake 40 km long.

Multipurpose

1   Supply domestic and industrial water to Kano.
2   Drive 20 000 kW HEP station to supply power.
3   Control seasonal flooding.
4   Enabling reclamation and irrigation of 500 000 ha downstream to enable double cropping — cereals and vegetables.
5   Fish farming.
6   Control of seasonal flooding will aid communications.

20:5   THE YELLOW RIVER BASIN, CHINA

Yellow River Basin and Hwang Ho Conservancy Scheme

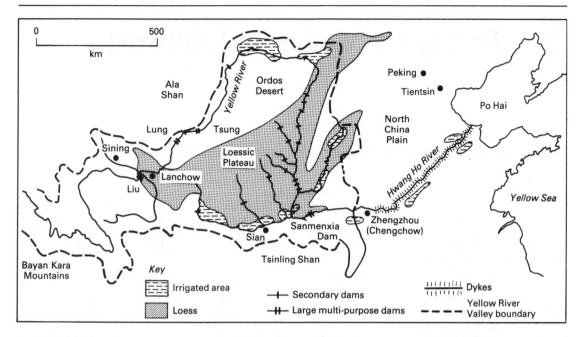

A   THE PROBLEM

Abnormal heavy seasonal monsoon rainfall over the basin.

Loess area subject to rapid run-off and erosion.

Heavy sediment load chokes river and successive floodings raise bed above flood-plain increasing risk of flooding and river course change.

Densely populated as rich rice growing area therefore effect of flood disaster heightened.

B   1953 MULTI-PURPOSE PLAN

Partial solution to control river and provide dry season irrigation together with H.E.P. centred on Sanmenxia Dam and reservoir, with tributary dams upriver and dyke (banks) down river.

Insufficient control of river in the loess section and watershed summit led to rapid silting of reservoir and continued flooding.

C   SINCE 1960s

Embarked on a comprehensive and integrated conservation and water control system for the whole basin. It was realised that the drainage basin is a total system with happenings in one part affecting the rest of the basin. In addition therefore to further measures of river control, the authorities embarked on widespread soil conservation including reduction of soil erosion and surface run-off on land in the basin. (By 1975 soil erosion reduced by 25% — a hopeful sign.)

Exercise

● With reference to examples comment on the statement that ensuring an adequate supply of water requires not only adequate knowledge of changes in demand but also a full appreciation of the way in which the hydrological cycle operates in any given region.

21   Transport Modes and Networks

Their central and changing importance

Transport routes and networks along with the ways used to transport goods, people and information along them are fundamental to the functioning of society. Over time people in any one place have come to increasingly depend on the world outside not only for a variety of goods and services, but also for the exchange of ideas and information. Decisions and happenings in the world around and conveyed by a variety of communication means, influence people's lives wherever they are. Thus communication, including transportation, has not only an important place in geographical studies for itself, but also because it is interdependent with all other aspects of human geography.

In Section 2 the role of transport networks in the city and the different kinds of movement along these were discussed. Here the wider world, national and regional links are considered.

It is often said that transport creates 'utilities of place' in that one of its prime functions is to move surplus raw materials and goods from one place to where there is a need for them, so increasing their value and encouraging more economic activity. As time has progressed areas have increasingly specialised on those types of economic activity for which they have been most suited, relying on the sale of their surplus in that specialised production and activity to pay for goods and services brought in from outside. This increasing specialisation and dependence on other areas has only been possible because of continuously improving means of transport and communications. Demand has led to better communication methods but as these have been established, in turn specialisation by area and exchange have been encouraged.

Today however much of the exchange is not only in the form of raw materials and goods but also in people and services. We have only to note the role of London and New York as financial centres and the intricate telex-satellite, telephone and cable links linking these centres constantly to every corner of the globe to realise this. But the intensity of exchange of information and services within a country between one part and another is no less important.

Whatever the scale of these many and varied links, faster and cheaper means of transport and communication have led to what is known as space-time convergence. In terms of time and cost of contact places in the world have come closer together — the globe has become smaller — so much so that the world is sometimes today described as the 'global village'. Events taking place in different parts of the world can for example be conveyed by satellite and shown on living room televisions as they happen. Again people and air freight can be conveyed over night from London to the other side of the world.

Space-time convergence is particularly well illustrated by considering how the journey time has been shortened between London and Edinburgh as a result of technological improvements in transport since the mid 18th century.

It is technological changes which have brought about this space-time convergence, in particular those occurring since the 1960s such as jet air travel and advanced telecommunications.

London to Edinburgh (629 km) 1754–1969		
Date	Mode	Time
1754	Coach	10 days
1776	Stage coach	4 days
1836	Mail coach	42 hrs 53 mins
1854	Steam train	11 hrs 25 mins
1914	Steam train	8 hrs 15 mins
1955	Steam train	6 hrs 30 mins
1967	Diesel train	5 hrs 27 mins
1969	High speed train	4 hrs 37 mins

Source: Janelle 1969

Fig. 21.1   An example of space-time convergence

Competition between different modes of transport has also as a result been intensified. On land, road transport has gained over rail. At an international level air travel has begun to replace ocean shipping for passenger travel and some specialist freighting, though carrying of bulk freightage is still by sea transport because of its relative cheapness.

Transport on land

Travel and freight by road

Movement by road is increasingly becoming the most important form of land transport (Fig. 21.2). This is largely a reflection of its convenience and flexibility, compared to rail and inland waterway transport. No other form of transport can offer a service directly from point of origin to destination. People and freight carried by rail, for example, have initially to be got to the railway station and then at the other end complete their journey from the station or depot by road. Part of the convenience of road transport is due to the comprehensive road network available, whilst the rapid expansion of motorways has provided the basic framework linking major cities (Fig. 21.3). These feed into the rest of the network giving direct access by road to almost every house and place of business whether it be a farm, office, warehouse or factory.

Furthermore road transport is also the most flexible mode of transport in terms of the amount of goods or passengers carried. The largest juggernaut lorries are capable of carrying loads of 40 tonnes and motorway buses over 50 passengers, but there are also small vans available to carry a few hundredweight of freight and it is common to see cars containing only one person.

Technological changes which have contributed to this increased flexibility have also been most important in speeding up road transport and yet at the same time improving on fuel economy. Saving of time helps to reduce costs in terms of man hours needed to complete a journey and releases the vehi-

cle in a quicker time for further work. But it is also additionally beneficial in that quicker transport has extended the area which can be covered from one distribution point in a given time. The number of depots is being reduced and they are increasingly placed near motorway junctions to take further advantage of time savings, as for example in the case of the M1–M62 motorway exchanges near Leeds and Manchester. These are larger depots and therefore also enable economies of scale to occur by handling more goods with a given amount of labour and equipment.

Rail transport

However, whilst the greatest expansion has taken place in road transport, considerable developments have also occurred to help maintain the competitiveness of the railways for certain kinds of freighting. Ironically in most developed countries this has partly been achieved by reducing the rail network, with the closure of many branch lines and improvement of the trackway between major cities and between industrial areas. In the United Kingdom the Beeching Report of 1963 led to the first postwar major rationalisation of the network to help make it more commercially viable. More recently still the Serpell Report (1983) has recommended further rationalisation.

Back in 1963 the Beeching (Reshaping) Report contained evidence that one half of the then existing route mileage carried only 4% of the total passenger miles traffic. Twenty years on, despite the restrictions in the network following the Beeching Report, the Serpell Report shows British Rail is still losing passenger freight, and operations are therefore unprofitable.

The Beeching Report recommended other changes to improve the viability and competitiveness of the main trunk network. Faster diesel locomotives were developed, and electrification extended out along the main lines to keep pace with the extension of the commuting area taking place around the larger cities. For on the passenger side it was the suburban lines and main regional commuting lines such as the London to Brighton line which carried the bulk of the passenger traffic and were therefore the lines most viable.

The greatest developments have occurred to take further advantage of those kinds of freight for which rail has always been preferred to road, namely heavy bulk materials and products, such as coal and iron-ore. Units of wagons can be assembled and specialist bulk handling sidings set up near raw material sources, factories and power stations. Freightliner trains and freightliner depots have been perhaps the most notable developments (Fig. 21.4).

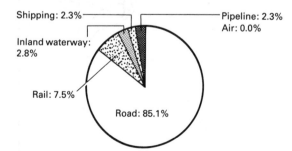

Fig. 21.2   Domestic traffic/goods transport within the EEC (million tonnes), 1981

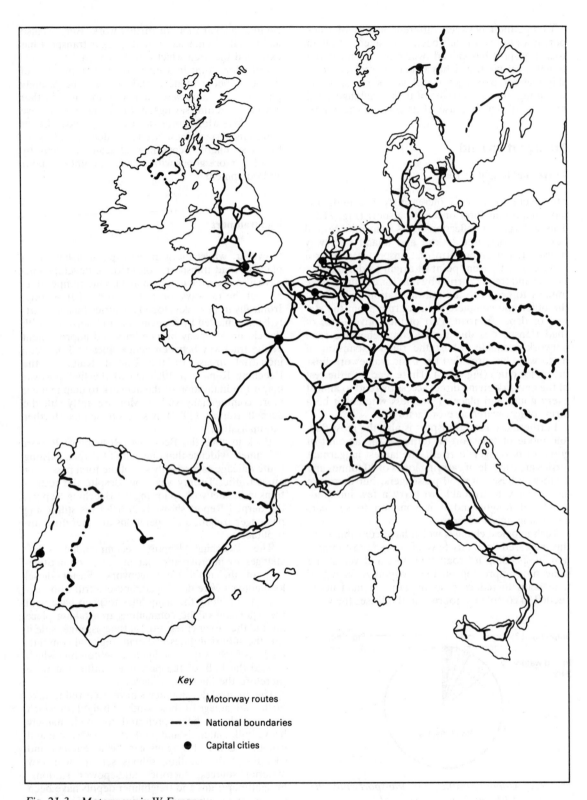

Fig. 21.3   Motorways in W Europe

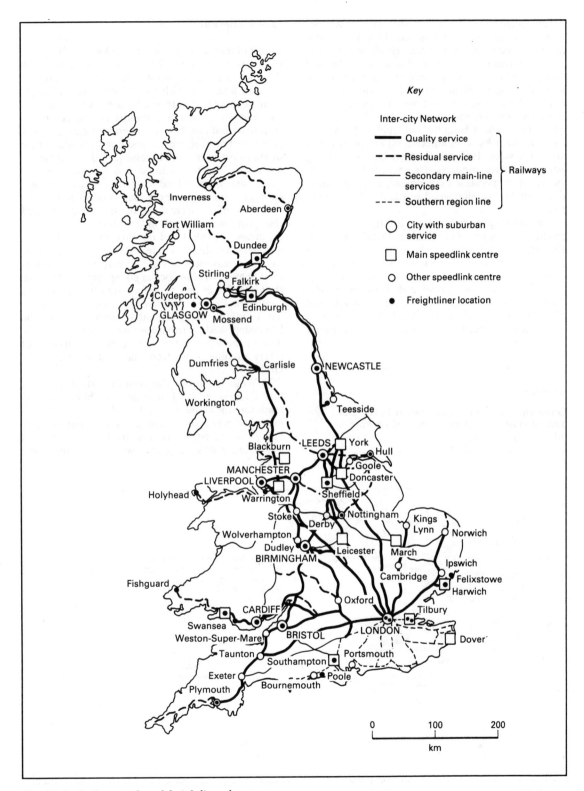

Fig. 21.4   Rail network and freightliner depots

The freightliner system in this and other developed countries, including the U.S.A., is also closely linked with the container revolution, whereby large containers of standard size can be loaded with packed freight at an assembly depot and transshipped using mechanical handling equipment. It can thus be transferred from one mode of transport to another quickly and cheaply, either from a lorry onto a rail truck or from the rail truck or lorry onto a ship at the dock. Containerisation has particularly expanded since 1965 for by then cost savings by using containers, progressively exceeded the investment cost in specialised equipment, and the sidings which are first of all needed to handle the containers.

The advantages of containers are that they allow quicker turn rounds of rail wagons, lorries, ships and aircraft, so enabling them to be used more frequently in a given time. The amount of labour needed to handle goods is also reduced and there is less loss through breakage and possible theft of goods. Because goods are transhipped more quickly and efficiently containerisation also reduced the amount of warehousing needed for stock to meet customer orders.

Exercise

Comment on the rail network pattern in Fig. 21.4 indicating what you think are the main factors influencing it.

Inland waterways

Whilst of minor importance in the United Kingdom, inland waterways in Western Europe and North America are an important part of the transport network linking in with the rail network and at the point of shipment with sea links between countries (see Fig. 21.6). Water transport is slow compared with road and rail, but very useful for carrying bulk cargo such as coal, timber and grain for which time of transport is not of the essence. Because waterways cost less to maintain and running costs of barges and other inland shipping are less, this is a cheaper form of transport than road or rail.

Just as efforts have been made to improve land transport, schemes are in hand in a number of countries to extend and improve the inland waterway network. In the United States one of the most significant advances was the opening of the St Lawrence Seaway to allow ocean going shipping to reach the Great Lakes and, therefore, into the heart of the continent. Less spectacular but also of importance has been the improvement of navigation on the Mississippi and its tributaries which, ever since the days of the white settlers, have been an important artery running south from the Mid West into the Gulf.

In Western Europe the most important system is that focused on the Rhine since its hinterland extends into the Benelux countries, France, West Germany and Switzerland (Fig. 21.5). It is used to carry bulky raw materials, non-perishable foodstuffs, and low value goods. Together with its linking canal

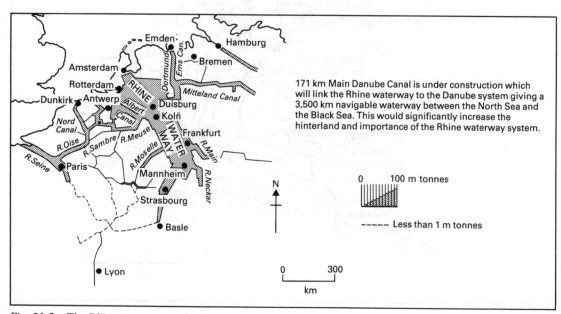

171 km Main Danube Canal is under construction which will link the Rhine waterway to the Danube system giving a 3,500 km navigable waterway between the North Sea and the Black Sea. This would significantly increase the hinterland and importance of the Rhine waterway system.

Fig. 21.5   The Rhine waterway and its links

Comparative Freight Totals (million tonne-km)

	Railway	Road	Inland Waterway
West Germany	56 300	93 700	44 100
France	66 700	89 100	10 300
Netherlands	2 900	16 600	28 400
Belgium	7 100	9 900	5 400

Fig. 21.6

systems and navigable tributaries the Rhine water-way is one of the world's major transport networks. Its importance to bordering countries is to some extent indicated by the comparative freight totals given in Fig. 21.6, though waterway transport is not limited solely to the Rhine system.

The Rhine waterway with its tributary rivers the Moselle, Main, Necker, Sambre, Meuse, Scheldt and linking canals has at its outlet to the North Sea, the major world port of Rotterdam. In addition major river ports have been established on the Rhine itself, which have attracted industries reliant on raw materials imported via the waterway and using also the road and rail links which follow the valley routes along which the waterways flow. Industries are diverse and include iron and steel, heavy engineering, oil refining, petro-chemicals, chemicals, paper, textiles and food processing.

But the importance of the Rhine waterway stretches further afield since on the one hand the Rhine–Main Danube Canal links it into the Danube waterway which flows into the Black Sea, and on the other hand the Rhine-Marne Canal links it into the Rhone river way which flows into the Mediterranean.

The significance of inland water transport has been increased not only by the deepening and widening and the building of more canal links, but also by improvements in the freight carriers themselves. Trains of barges drawn by modern high power diesel tugs have a greatly increased carrying capacity compared to the older type river barges. The main stretches of the waterway are capable now of carrying barges of 1500 tonne capacity.

Pipelines

For transport of gases and liquids, pipelines offer the least cost method. For example water is transferred by this method and much of the crude oil and lighter petroleum products are pumped through pipelines. Natural gas can only be transported by

pipeline overland. As dependence on water, oil and gas supplies increase, so the pipeline network, like the grids for electricity, are extended (Fig. 21.7). Apart from their importance in better populated areas, pipelines are also proving essential to convey oil and gas from extraction areas in remote locations to the consumption points in urban and industrial regions as in the case of the oil and gas pipeline system in Canada which brings supplies from producing fields in the far north including Alaska to the populated area around the Great Lakes and St Lawrence.

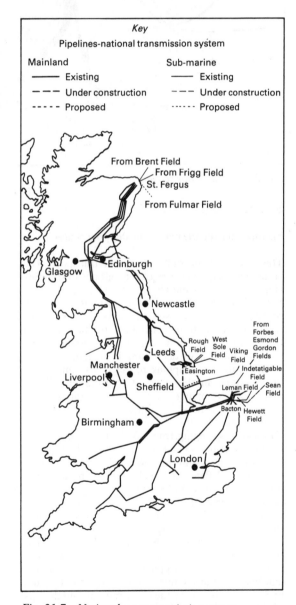

Fig. 21.7   National gas transmission system

247

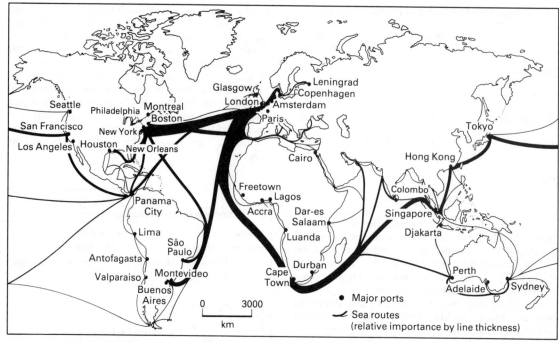

Fig. 21.8   The major sea lanes

Sea transport

Factors affecting the pattern of shipping routes

This is one of the oldest forms of transport. The volume and flow patterns of sea and ocean shipping (Fig. 21.8) are essentially a reflection of the locations of supply and demand for raw materials, semi-processed and processed products and manufactured goods. (With increasing competition from air traffic, passenger traffic except on cross-ferry and coastal routes, is of decreasing importance.)

The pattern of shipping routes is also influenced by variations in the physical environment. Technological developments whilst overcoming some of the limitations imposed by physical constraints, have also heightened others. For instance modern large bulk carriers ranging from 80 000 to the largest oil tanker at over 200 000 tonnes, can only berth at deepwater ports and are too large to pass through the Suez and Panama Canals. Hence these mainly use the Cape of Good Hope route.

The influence of basic physical constraints is also evident from the direction of the world's major shipping routes. Shipping avoids the severe weather and icy conditions of high latitudes. The shape and position of the major land masses are also significant. For example shipping moving between Japan and Western Europe must pass through the Panama or Suez Canals or take the Cape route round the tips of Africa and South America.

The configuration of coastlines is also important in funnelling ocean going traffic into particular sea lanes such as the English Channel passage, and in limiting the locations suitable for ports. Deep estuaries leading into highly developed and populous regions are particularly favoured, but some of the largest bulk carriers have to off load at more remote locations giving deepwater anchorage. The cargo then has to be moved along the coast to consuming areas. For example until its recent closure, bulk oil tankers had to berth in the deepwater inlet of Milford Haven, South Wales and oil and by-products from the refinery there were then moved by pipeline or shipped along the coast to consuming centres in industrial areas such as Cardiff and Neath.

In addition to the development of bulk carriers, the other important technological development of recent times has been the widespread adoption of containerisation and roll-on roll-off facilities. Containerisation of cargo into containers of standard size has enabled much of the handling to be done mechanically with a consequent saving of labour. Break of bulk en route is also avoided because cargo can be assembled at inland depots as well as at the ports, containers being transferred to shipping and, at the other end of the sea journey, back onto lorry or rail before being finally unpacked at the destination.

Roll-on roll-off facilities perform a similar function; road vehicles together with their loads can be

248

driven onto the ship or cross-channel ferry and then driven off at the end of the sea journey. This is an increasingly important component of cross-channel freighting between the United Kingdom and other EEC countries. It is also important for other short sea crossings for example between Germany and the Scandinavian countries. There is even a cross Atlantic link with barges coming down the Great Lakes in Canada/USA being transferred to ocean carriers and then being mechanically unloaded at Rotterdam/Europoorts to carry on the journey up the Rhine waterway with cargoes such as coal, iron-ore and grain.

Such recent developments are but the latest in a series of technological developments which have transformed the nature and volume of ocean going traffic. Earlier there was the advent for example of refrigeration enabling meat, fruit and dairy produce to be shipped from the other side of the globe to developed countries in the northern hemisphere. There was also the change from wind to steam and then to diesel propulsion which has increased the speed of ocean transport and together with improvements in materials and design made it less vulnerable to adverse weather conditions.

Port development

All these developments along with the economic advancement of countries and therefore the increased amount of trade, have had a substantial impact on sea terminals, ports and harbours. As the size of shipping and volume of traffic have increased and technological developments have occurred so the nature of port facilities has had to change. Many small ports without the natural and man-made facilities needed for modern shipping have declined and traffic is being concentrated in fewer ports, including some new specialised deepwater ports serving particular industries or other activities. These include for example the deepwater berth at Hunterston in West Scotland serving the Ravenscraig steel works.

In older port areas on large estuaries, or with large harbourage, there has been a gradual extension of dock facilities downstream as more specialised handling facilities, more dock space and deep anchorages have been required. In some cases as in the Port of London this has meant the abandonment of older outdated wharfage upstream. On the Thames, Hays Wharf and other docks have now been abandoned, awaiting redevelopment as part of the London Dockland Enterprise Zone and a number of the trades, including container handling, are centred downstream at Tilbury. However some trade has been lost to the fast expanding port of Felixstowe further north on the Suffolk coast.

Across the channel Rotterdam's extension including Europoort on the Rhine outlet, illustrates well the stages of development which occur over time of ports serving a thriving hinterland and having to be adapted to meet the changing character of ocean shipping. Such changes are to be found in many parts of the world and Bird (1963) in his study of United Kingdom seaports has postulated a model of port growth — 'Anyport' — within the context of which the development of particular ports such as that of Rotterdam/Europoort or Tokoradi (Ghana) can be studied. (Case Study 21.1)

Coastal trade

Whilst most of the discussion on ports and shipping is centred on overseas trade in raw materials, food and other goods, it must not be forgotten that for most nations having a coastline, coastwise trade and short passage to neighbouring countries are of considerable importance. Ferry and small ship traffic is mainly concerned with freighting, but because of its economic cost passenger transport remains significant. Indeed for certain crossings, because of increased affluence and mobility, it has increased. For example there is the growing tourist trade between the United Kingdom and the continent as well as within Western Europe itself with many taking their own cars by ferry over the different channel crossings. (Fig. 21.9)

As regards coastal traffic one of the countries where this has always been important is Japan. The mountainous inland makes land communication difficult and though there is now a good network by rail, road and air, coastal shipping remains significant. Some measure of the size and importance of coastal shipping is indicated by the fact that in the mid-1970s just over half of all the freight shipped from one part of the archipelago to another went by sea, as against 35% by road and 14% by rail. As would be expected the shipping is mainly used for low value bulk cargoes such as coal and coke, lumber, minerals and paper pulp shipped from ports of origin such as in Northern Kyushu and Hokkaido to industrial centres in the main island of Honshu. But a significant amount also includes entrepôt trade i.e. goods brought in from overseas to major ports such as Yokohama and redistributed to other points along the coast.

In the developing world ferry, coastal and sea transport, measured by volume is not as important as in developed countries. But relative to needs it is even more important in some areas because it may provide the only major kind of transport apart from expensive air travel which is beyond the reach of the mass of the population, and too expensive for the transfer of all but high value goods. This applies for example to the peoples and economies of the South Pacific as well as to peoples living around the major lake shores such as Lake Victoria in East Africa.

21:1 EUROPOORT, ROTTERDAM AND TAKORADI, GHANA

Port development in relation to the 'Anyport' concept

STAGES IN THE DEVELOPMENT OF 'ANYPORT'

1 Primitive port — at a place on the estuary where a harbour can be easily built adjacent to firm ground on which the town develops.

2 Marginal quay extension — need and establishment of quays begins to outstrip town growth.

3 Marginal quay elaboration — pressure for growth but area contained by building short jetties and cutting of small docks (hithes) into the banks.

4 Dock elaboration — wet docks are built further downstream where water is deeper and more space available onshore to which road and rail connections are built. Thus increased size of ships and greater volume can be met.

5 Simple lineal quayage — dock quays need to be modified and extended to accommodate larger vessels.

6 Specialised quayage — needed for particular bulk cargoes as well as for container and roll-on roll-off traffic.

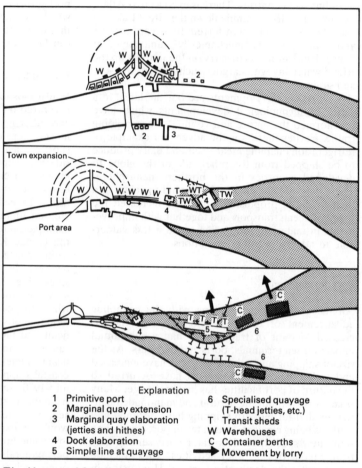

Explanation			
1	Primitive port	6	Specialised quayage (T-head jetties, etc.)
2	Marginal quay extension	T	Transit sheds
3	Marginal quay elaboration (jetties and hithes)	W	Warehouses
4	Dock elaboration	C	Container berths
5	Simple line at quayage	→	Movement by lorry

The 'Anyport' Concept

THE DEVELOPMENT OF TWO MAJOR PORTS

A *Rotterdam — Europoort*

1 Originally a medieval fishing village. But by the 18th Century with increasing Dutch overseas development it had become an important port.

2 1872 — a new waterway had to be cut to accommodate larger vessels. Importance increased with development of hinterland including the Ruhr and Lorraine. Docks were developed on the South bank at Waalhaven etc.

3 Trade boosted by EEC formation in 1958 and bulk/container traffic especially increased oil trade. New channel and Europoort-Botlek Development.

4 Most recent development reclamation for industrial sites and quays at Maasvlakte. Upper harbour modified to take container traffic.

5 Present situation — leading world port with waterway as well as fast rail and road links through hinterland. Important entrepôt trade (redistribution to other ports). One of world's leading industrial complexes — heavy industrial petro-chemicals and food processing, brewing etc. Pollution, congestion problems etc.

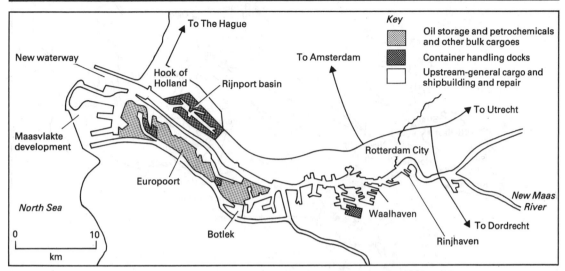

Rotterdam—Europoort

B   Takoradi — Ghana

1   1928 — artificial harbour at Takoradi to replace nearby Sekondi port which could not cope with Ghana's expanded trade and increased size of shipping.

2   Postwar — harbour deepened and expanded with more wharves to handle special as well as general cargo. Further expansion stimulated by improving communication network including trunk road system, which extended hinterland.

Trade includes export of timber, food products — cocoa and minerals — manganese etc. Import of capital equipment, oil, foodstuffs etc. Limited industry at the port.

Exercise

● To what extent does the development of Rotterdam-Europoort fit the 'Anyport' model? Why is Takoradi's development more limited than that of the European port?

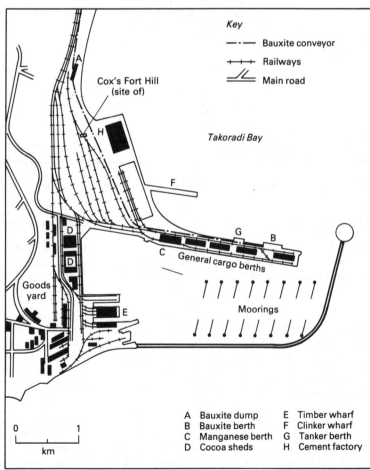

Key
— · — · —   Bauxite conveyor
+ + + +   Railways
/ /   Main road

A Bauxite dump	E Timber wharf
B Bauxite berth	F Clinker wharf
C Manganese berth	G Tanker berth
D Cocoa sheds	H Cement factory

Takoradi Port

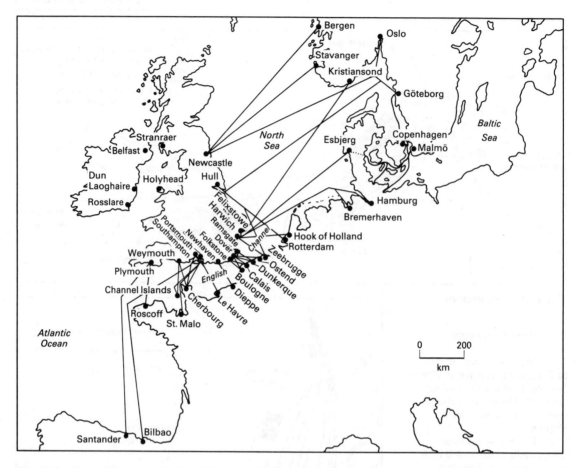

Fig. 21.9   Ferry links across the Irish Sea, English Channel and North Sea

Air transport

The world-wide growth in air traffic both at an international level and within regions, for the conveyance of passengers and certain kinds of bulk high value freight has greatly accelerated during the post-war years. Between 1972–1982 it has been growing at an annual average rate of 9.6% and in excess of this in Europe, North America and the Far East, which have the greatest share of air traffic.

This expansion is largely a reflection of the general economic growth underlying the demand for transport and the increased affluence of peoples in the developed countries and higher income groups elsewhere. But as is the case for other kinds of transport, it is also partly due to technological developments. These have not only greatly speeded up movement by air, but also increased the carrying capacity of aircraft, as for example illustrated in the latest jumbo jets. Associated with this have been increased technical facilities in navigation, ground control and airport infrastructure.

Constraints on routes

The outstanding advantages of air travel are its speed, the vast distances which can be covered, its directness and the improved accessibility it gives to remote and difficult locations. There is, however, not quite the freedom of the air, for movement has to be along designated flight corridors and countries place political restrictions on their air space, as indicated by the fate of the South Korean airliner in 1983 which, whilst on a scheduled flight from Anchorage to Seoul, strayed over Soviet air space.

Routes are not now so constrained by adverse physical conditions as they were, as jet aircraft fly at stratosphere levels above the atmosphere's weather. However it still seriously affects thousands of light aircraft which provide vital links to small and remote communities in different parts of the world. Also all aircraft, despite modern radar and other devices, are affected by weather conditions in the vicinity of take-off and landing points — fog, for example, remains a hazard.

Airport location

Modern airports are not only very costly to build and maintain, but require a very large area of land. The advent of larger, faster jet aircraft like the jumbo jet, has limited the number of sites available for large airports. Runways now need to be over 3000 m long and more are needed as the volume of air traffic continues to increase. Large areas too are needed for infrastructure facilities such as arrival and departure terminals, customs warehouses, maintenance hangars etc.

Airports not only need large areas of land but furthermore such areas must be at locations having good access to the main population centres which generate the demand for air traffic (Fig. 21.10). Yet increasing environmental concern particularly associated with the noise jet aircraft make on approach routes and when taking off or landing, puts further constraints on available sites. The tendency now is to locate airports at an increasing distance from the major population centres yet linked to them by fast connecting communication ser-

vices as illustrated by Birmingham International Airport (Fig. 21.11).

There is the suggestion of Maplin on the Essex coast or Stansted further north, as the location for a third London airport. In this particular case the lobby of the agricultural sector and those concerned with preserving the rural environment, together with the cost advantages of extending the existing airports of Heathrow and Gatwick which already have the basic infrastructure needed, may prevent it happening. However the debate continues — in 1984 a Parliamentary Commission recommended the extension of Stansted in Essex.

Limitations and expanding use

Despite its advantages of speed and linking locations at great distances from one another, air transport is limited in the volume of passenger and freight traffic it can carry, because it remains the most expensive form of transport. Aircraft have a small pay load capacity relative to their total weight and the fuel

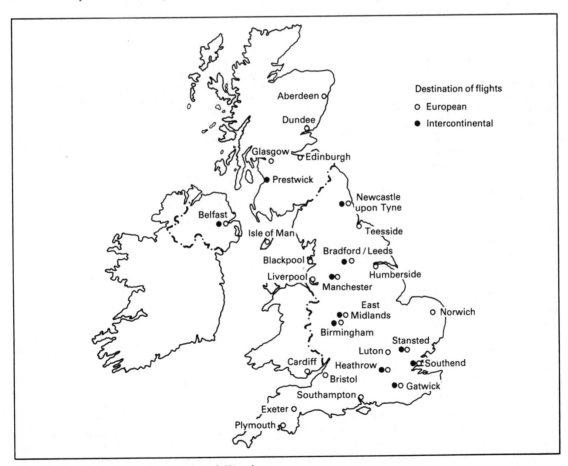

Fig. 21.10   Main air services in United Kingdom

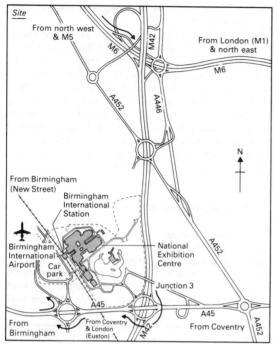

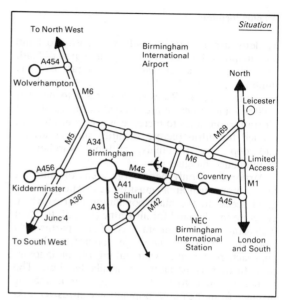

Fig. 21.11   *Location and accessibility for Birmingham's international airport*

carried and therefore to the costs involved. Aircraft also have a high depreciation cost and a high operating expenditure. They are, therefore, generally used by passengers who wish to economise on time and can afford the comparatively high fares. However, intense competition between airlines on the busiest routes, including rapidly expanding tourist charter flight lines, has resulted in falling fares. This has particularly stimulated further expansion of demand from the tourist trade. However, it has also resulted in highly complex air fare structures, with business executives paying far more than passengers on Apex, Stand-by, or Charter flight rates.

Freighting by air is also increasing. Though it currently represents only 2% of all traffic freight, from 1950–1970 there was a tenfold increase in the amount of freight carried by air and on the busiest route of all across the North Atlantic, a twenty-five-fold increase. Air transport is suitable for the carriage of commodities with a low bulk yet high value. These include such things as postal mail, parcels, spare machine and vehicle parts, high value electrical equipment and high value livestock such as race horses, as well as increasing trade in high priced out of season fruits and cut flowers. Orchids and carnations for example are flown from Kenya to the United States and Western Europe at out of season periods.

Trade and traffic are expanding for a number of reasons. The greatly increased level of economic activity and standard of living amongst wealthy nations have provided a greatly increased demand. At the same time technological developments in the

design of aircraft and increasing competition amongst airlines have made air freighting more economic. However many airlines are operating at a loss partly due to increased capital and maintenance costs and because they are partly maintained for social and political reasons.

Some developing nations have adopted a protectionist attitude subsidising unprofitable infant airlines to enable them to get established because a sound airline network is seen as vital to the future of the country. Air Zimbabwe is a case in point. Whilst it does operate on international routes for example Harare to Gatwick (London), the government sees the development of an internal air network as necessary to co-ordinate the different regions of Zimbabwe and a way of linking more remote communities. This is even more so for countries like Brazil, in which even greater distances are involved, as well as some very difficult terrain to be surmounted.

At the smaller end of the market, the development of the helicopter has captured the attention of the public with the role it plays in such ventures as North Sea oil operations. But of much greater significance is the further development and improvement of light aircraft, including the small jet executive and other specialised aircraft. For regions with very difficult terrain, scattered communities and poor land communications, these aircraft run largely by small operators or business companies are essential to the economic and social life of the region concerned as for example in the Canadian Northlands and the tropical forest lands of Central and South America.

Conveying and exchanging information

Telecommunications and the information revolution

Through the postal, telephone, telegraph and radio services we have long been accustomed to a transportation network which can convey the ideas and information on the basis of which many transactions and decisions are undertaken. The development of telecommunications is now bringing a dramatic increase in the scale and speed of these exchanges.

The nature of telecommunications

In telecommunications three major devices are involved — the telephone, the television and the computer. The computer is the key. It is needed to integrate these three kinds of devices, or any combination of two of them, into a powerful communication system.

One of the most commonly used link-up systems is teleprocessing. Small computers or terminals in the office or home can be linked via telephone lines to a mainframe computer or storage data bank containing the desired information. The information obtained can then be displayed on a television screen and if need be put on a computer printout.

More recently video-telephone links are coming into use making it possible for tele-conferences to be held amongst a group of people without their having to travel in person to a conference.

Whilst the link up directly through the computer or via computer terminals has created an entirely new type of communication system, what is even more revolutionary are the developments occurring within this system. These will not only improve the speed and reliability of information communications, but are already bringing down costs, making it possible, desirable and indeed essential for businesses and other organisations to use telecommunications systems. New designs and materials are also making the equipment much more compact, enabling it to be fitted into offices.

Computers themselves have become smaller and include faster and more powerful integrated circuits enabling much more data to be stored and handled. Computer graphic facilities have already greatly increased the usefulness of output data, whilst the current development of computers which have voice recognition and production will widen their scope further. Again for instance advances concerned with the telephone include the use of fibre optic wires made of very fine glass thread through which information can be transmitted by light impulse. This together with the development of satellite transmission has enabled the cheap transfer of audio, visual and data information over any distance.

Spatial implications of telecommunications

As yet the full implications of these developments are not realised but already some of the spatial effects are. The most outstanding one is that of spatial convergence. The speed at which information, transactions and exchange of ideas can now take place has brought output and receiving areas much closer together. This is evident at many different scale levels including office link ups, telex shopping and banking from home, to communication over national networks and on a full global scale.

But the effect is not simply of space convergence but also of greatly increasing the volume of exchange which can take place along telecommunication networks. The first Early Bird Communication Satellite sent up in 1965 for example could accommodate at any one time 240 international telephone calls, but British Aerospace are now developing a big space satellite to take 200 000 simultaneous calls and which can also be used to relay television pictures.

Systems are also comprehensive in coverage. For instance the International Maritime Satellite Organisation (Inmarsat) developed a new world system for maritime communications in 1982. Satellite coverage of the Atlantic, Pacific and Indian Oceans links ships at sea with land bases (Fig. 21.12). Once linked to one of the earth stations, an operator there can connect the ship to any telephone subscriber whether on the national or international network. Whilst this is useful in emergencies, its greatest use is in the normal directing of maritime traffic by shipping offices — ships can be rerouted to pick up cargo etc.

Apart from its influence on economic geography telecommunication has an important part to play in fostering better international relations and aiding the less fortunate areas of the world.

Two current illustrations are the use international agencies are making of telecommunications to convey information of food shipments to relief centres in famine areas, and the important information being gained on weather photographs and information from space satellites. This enables early warning of abnormal weather such as typhoons and hurricanes, as in the case of the recent typhoon and tidal wave which hit the coast of Bangladesh. It is also an aid to identifying factors which cause the recurring patterns of drought in Africa — information relayed by telecommunications and other means is being collated at the AGRHYMET centre in Niamey (Niger).

The importance of telecommunications and the information sector

Apart from the effects already outlined the information sector of which telecommunications is a central part is the most rapidly expanding sector in advanced economies. It has become the largest contributor to national income and employment. For example in the United States it contributes a surprising 42% of the national income and 32% of the employment.

Indirectly it will also affect other sectors of the economy. The shorter working hours and fewer employment opportunities generated by increased automation including telecommunication advances, bring increased leisure time and earlier retirement. Already these trends have led for example to a boom in leisure time activities and increased travel.

Whilst the major advances in telecommunications have been made by the richer developed nations, it would be wrong to assume that these new information systems will play a minor role in developing countries. Most for example are intent on setting up an efficient internal telecommunication network, especially where distances are great and other means of communication limited.

Developing countries are looking to these new communication media as a way of diffusing ideas and information more rapidly. This will speed up not only economic development but also help educational and other social programmes. In the next chapter we shall be looking at this whole question of communications and development.

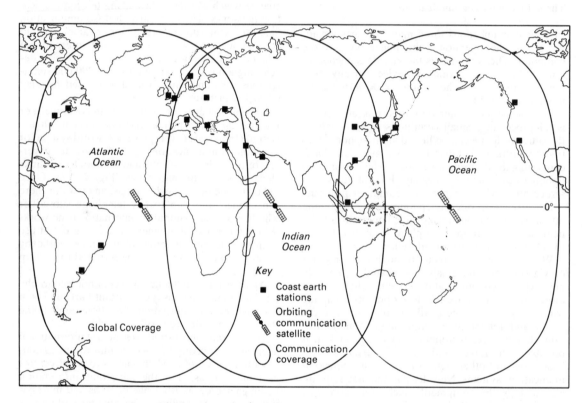

Fig. 21.12   A maritime world telecommunications system

256

22 Transport — Communications and Development

The importance of an adequate integrated transport and communications network to a country's economic, social and political life is indicated by the percentage of national income spent on transport. This is estimated variously from 20–40%. Investment in transport is regarded as a priority not only at government levels but also by the general public.

As a country develops and specialisation and diversification becomes a feature of the economy, so the need for transport is increased. For example, in its formative years the industrial revolution in Western Europe was accompanied by a revolution in transport with development of a canal and then an increasingly dense rail network.

Transport and economic development

Whilst development of transport has historically been seen as a response to demand, it is also clear today that the relationship is a two way one. Where accessibility to an area containing resources is improved, development will be further stimulated. There are many instances of this happening. One of the most notable is the part played by the development of the transcontinental railway network in the commercial exploitation of the prairies in North America allowing beef, wheat and other agricultural produce to be shipped to eastern markets and the ports. Also the development of the motorway network in the United Kingdom has prompted further growth of economic activity in the vicinity of motorway junctions.

But embarking on a programme of transport development does not automatically lead to further growth. The current demand and a realistic level of future demand must be assessed. Over-investment in transport can lead to insufficient finance being left over for developing the actual resources and economic activities for which the transport network is intended. Brazil, for example, has been criticised for over heavy investment in grandiose highway schemes such as the Trans-Amazonian highway and neglecting the needs of the thousands of settlers encouraged to take up plots of land in the vicinity of the highway.

The building of a route for a particular object such as developing a mineral resource or as a link to an export point, can only have a limited effect on development. It may stimulate growth and settlement at either end of the route and adjacent to it, as in the case of the recently constructed Tanzam railway from Zambia north to Dar-es-Salaam, but unless it is integrated into the overall network it has little effect on other parts of the country and on the lives of the mass of lower income households most in need.

In the past transport networks have developed in a piecemeal fashion since there was no overall planning oversight. Each development was usually a response to some sporadic event or some specific economic social or political force. The opening up of a mining area or the clearance of land for commercial agriculture was accompanied by the building of a transport route, as for example in the case of rail lines developed in West Malaysia to link tin mines and rubber plantations to ports.

But over time if economic growth and spread of settlement occurs some integration of one mode of transport with another will occur, such as feeder roads built to the main rail lines which in turn link to a port outlet. But deficiencies will be present. The network will be a response to market demand forces and a variable population distribution with most demand being in the densely settled areas whilst others will be inadequately served.

A model for transport development

Even allowing for deficiencies in networks, there have been a number of attempts by geographers to idealise the way in which a transport network may develop over time in relation to the economic development of a country. One of the most well-known is that by Taaffe, Morrill and Gould for the

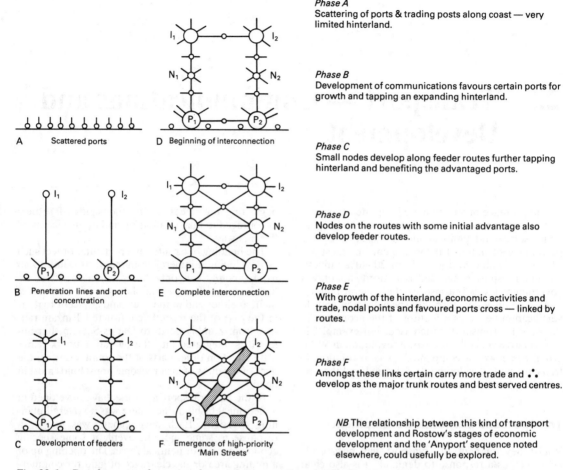

Phase A
Scattering of ports & trading posts along coast — very limited hinterland.

Phase B
Development of communications favours certain ports for growth and tapping an expanding hinterland.

Phase C
Small nodes develop along feeder routes further tapping hinterland and benefiting the advantaged ports.

Phase D
Nodes on the routes with some initial advantage also develop feeder routes.

Phase E
With growth of the hinterland, economic activities and trade, nodal points and favoured ports cross — linked by routes.

Phase F
Amongst these links certain carry more trade and ∴ develop as the major trunk routes and best served centres.

NB The relationship between this kind of transport development and Rostow's stages of economic development and the 'Anyport' sequence noted elsewhere, could usefully be explored.

Fig. 22.1 Development of a national transport network — the Taaffe, Morrill and Gould model

economic growth of an underdeveloped country in which they saw the improvement of internal accessibility through the expansion of a transportation network as a critical factor.

For many developing countries colonialism and the exploiting of primary products for export were seen as the major forces leading to the initial development of a transport network. Thus the sequence of development is seen as starting with routes leading inland from the ports and ultimately on to the development of an integrated network including major nodal points inland as well as at the ports (Fig. 22.1). In the network the most important primary routes could be identified as those linking the major population and economic centres, with secondary and minor routes linking much of the remaining areas of the country to them. Thus the network could be regarded as a system along which the flows of materials, goods and people reflected the interdependence of different areas within the country and its external links through trade and travel. The development of such a system is illustrated in the following Case Study on East Africa.

Exercise

Comment on the usefulness of the Taaffe, Morrill and Gould model in trying to understand the way in which one developing country's network has been established. What factors might in reality interrupt such an idealised development sequence?

Factors affecting the development of a transport network

Human factors

The model essentially sees the development of the transport network as a response to the way economic growth occurs. This does make it useful as a

22:1 EAST AFRICA

Transport and network development based on the Taaffe, Morrill, Gould model

OUTLINE OF EACH STAGE

Stage (a) Scatter of small isolated ports linked to Indian Ocean trade mainly by Arab merchants.

Stage (b) Zenith of Arab trade based on Zanzibar with trade routes radiating into the continent and well beyond East Africa e.g. Tabora slave route. Inland mainly human porterage along trackways.

Stage (c) Colonial powers establish two rail routes — Dar es Salaam to Kigoma, Mombasa to Kisuma (plus less successful Tanga to Moshi line).

Largely motivated by political needs but influenced where economic development occurred — cash cropping and minerals.

Stage (d) Branch and feeder lines to Arusha, Mwanza and Kampala to cope with increasing crop production and the spread of settlement.

Stage (e) Extension to West and North of Uganda to tap cotton and copper producing areas. One South from groundnuts area to Port Mtwara — shortlived as groundnuts went by road route North to Lindi.

Stage (f) Intensification of road and rail network especially along main Mombasa Nairobi axis, and the Tanzania to Zambia extension — most recently Tanzam rail, road and oil pipeline added.

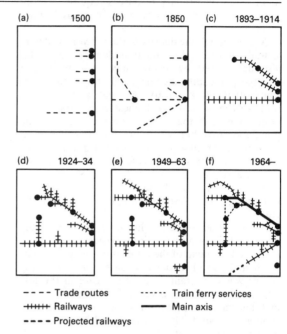

Hoyle's application of the model to East Africa

- - - - Trade routes   ------ Train ferry services
+++++ Railways   —— Main axis
- - - Projected railways

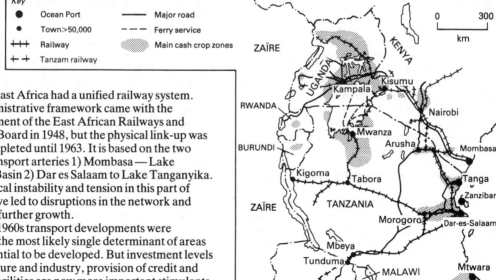

Note

By 1965 East Africa had a unified railway system. The administrative framework came with the establishment of the East African Railways and Harbour Board in 1948, but the physical link-up was not commpleted until 1963. It is based on the two major transport arteries 1) Mombasa — Lake Victoria Basin 2) Dar es Salaam to Lake Tanganyika. But political instability and tension in this part of Africa have led to disruptions in the network and hindered further growth.

To the 1960s transport developments were probably the most likely single determinant of areas with potential to be developed. But investment levels in agriculture and industry, provision of credit and training facilities are now more important stimulants. However transport network improvements and extension must follow to permit a higher level of economic development.

The Network by 1965

context for analysis of the way transport networks develop, but the relationship is not a simple one. Apart from the influence of other types of factors certain kinds of economic activity require a different level and pattern of transport from others. Development based on primary resources requires a more basic network than one where the economy is more diversified.

Again, though the density of the network will vary spatially according to population density, demand is also determined by income levels — the higher average per capita income level, the greater the transport network density. Alluvial lands in Monsoon Asia may have the highest concentrations of population, but the poverty of the mass of the population together with a greater dependence on subsistence farming, limits transport development. Network densities are greatest in the populated industrial regions of developed countries — in areas such as the north east United States and the industrial triangle of Western Europe centred on the Ruhr.

At the other extreme, however, even sparsely populated areas may require a basic network, and measured per head of the population, may be greater than the level of demand based on purchasing power would warrant — as is the case in the less populated areas of Australia. This emphasises the fact that transport provision is not solely decided on economic grounds. It is also guided by social and political requirements.

Physical factors

Besides human factors, the other most influential set of forces determining the nature of the transport network is that of the physical environment.

The natural resource of an area exerts an influence, since the level and character of economic activity as well as population numbers are to some extent determined by the resources in an area. A more direct relationship is evident where the discovery of minerals in an otherwise harsh and difficult physical environment will lead to the building of a transport artery, as in the case of iron-ore development in the desert area of Mauritania (North Africa).

Some positive aspects of the environment may, however, have a negative effect. This is increasingly so where areas are designated as areas of natural beauty and safeguarded by conservation measures. There have been a number of cases where this has so far either delayed motorway construction or caused deviation from a planned route. In the UK the parallel route to the M62 is scheduled to run through the Derbyshire Peak District but its construction has so far been prevented by the action of conservationist groups. The extension of the M40 to link with the Birmingham ring road system was the subject of controversy because it was projected through Bernwood Forest west of Oxford, one of the best known butterfly habitats in Europe. However, on economic and social grounds including the alleviation of noise and traffic hazards in country towns and villages from heavy traffic along the present routes between Southampton and the Midlands, the M40 extension could be described as essential.

Difficult physical conditions do generally deter the development of an integrated transport network. The sheer size and shape of a country are obvious but important influences. The vast distances in Australia for example make transport costs high whilst the heavily indented coast of Japan directly affects the cost and shape of the network.

Broad rivers may provide waterways as in the case of the Rhine and the Amazon, but they increase the cost of transport routes needing to cross them to link one part of a network with another. Moreover river crossings funnel part of the network creating nodal points at bridging points or river tunnels. This is well illustrated from the transport network either side of the lower Thames.

The most widespread effects are exercised by difficult terrain, whether it be marshland and ice regions as in North Siberia or the mountainous uplands as in Central Europe and down the west coast of the Americas. Such regions exercise a twofold influence. They deter settlement anyway and reduce the demand for transport, but also they make the building of the network extremely costly. Also mountainous areas have adverse weather conditions making the maintenance of routes also costly. However, if the demand is there, adverse physical conditions will be overcome. One of the clearest illustrations of this is the comprehensive network which exists in Switzerland despite its mountainous nature. Important populated regions either side, including the Ruhr to the north and the North Italian plain to the south, have needed increasingly efficient transport links. In addition Switzerland itself has a high level of economic activity particularly in the northern plateau region. This has led to a dense network of transport routes in this area.

In areas of more favourable terrain, networks are generally more efficient, directly linking areas of greatest population and economic activity as seen in the north west European lowlands and in the pampas region of Argentina and Paraguay.

Transport planning

In the modern world the organisation of the economic, social and political life of a country is very complex and governments have increasingly found it necessary to exercise some control over development. Since transport is so important a factor in this development, it is not surprising that it is subject to close planning legislation and direct government investment.

Achieving a balanced and optimum network suited to the needs of a country is fraught with problems. Investment needs in this sector must be balanced against investment needs in other sectors such as agriculture, industry and welfare. In the past over-investment in transport has occurred in some newly independent countries, with too little investment in stimulating economic activities which could make use of the new routes.

One of the most major criticisms of newly independent countries is that larger transport schemes do little for the mass of the people engaged in the rural sector where subsistence farming is combined with some cash cropping. These people cannot afford motorised transport and their essential needs are to do with carrying materials and produce on the farm, from the farm to the roadside and then from the roadside to a local market or co-operative centre.

In Kenya surveys have shown that the greatest need is for improved ways of carrying small loads of 10 to 140 kg in weight over short distances of between 1 and 25 km. The vast bulk of this kind of carrying is still by human porterage, bicycle and animal cart over rough tracks unsuitable for the usual motorised vehicles. International agencies are therefore increasingly trying to direct aid, loans and

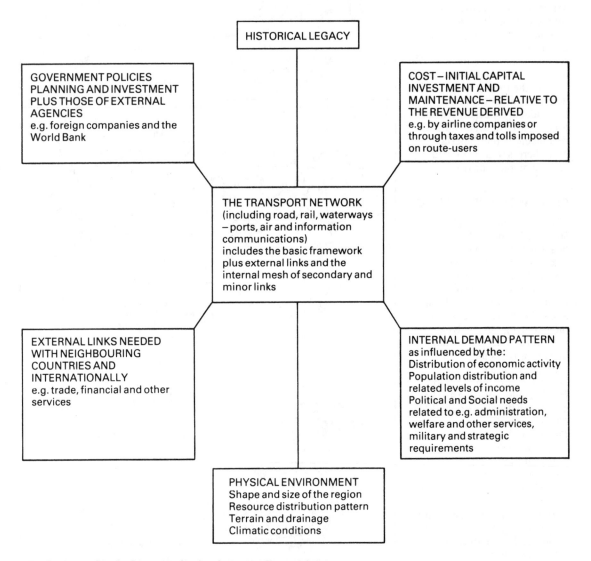

Fig. 22.2   Factors influencing the development of a transport system

22:2 THE SOVIET UNION

Transport network

NATURE OF THE NETWORK

The railway network remains the dominant form.

A fully augmented network is found at present only in European Russia and this is focussed on the capital — Moscow. In Asiatic Russia the network is skeletal with feeder routes leading off to link specific locations of economic activity whether primary producing centres e.g. minerals, or manufacturing.

Since the 1960s a well developed air network has been added, especially crucial for linking remote and difficult regions e.g. Arctic Siberia. Now there is well developed telecommunications too.

CHARACTER OF TRAFFIC

The rail network in 1980 carried 56% of all freight. Most is of heavy bulk materials e.g. coal, coke, ores, metals, building materials, timber and grain. Especially developed in Central Siberia between Urals and Lake Baykal to serve industrial regions e.g. Kuzbass — Karagand. Baykal-Amur line recently opened to tap Siberian minerals.

Waterways are important for freight hauls averaging 460 km. The Volga system carries 50-60% of the traffic. The Dnieper waterway is also significant. Siberian rivers are only useful in summer.

Road system — mainly useful within urban regions — largely unsurfaced elsewhere.

Airways — carry passenger and valuable freight, especially for mining and other areas in Siberia and the remote South.

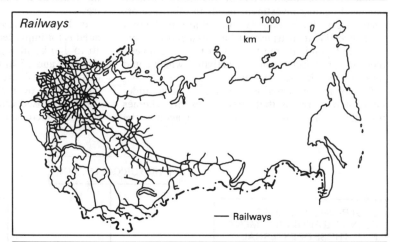

Railways

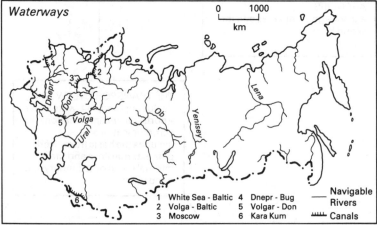

Waterways

1 White Sea - Baltic   4 Dnepr - Bug
2 Volga - Baltic   5 Volgar - Don
3 Moscow   6 Kara Kum

— Navigable Rivers
ᗤᗤᗤ Canals

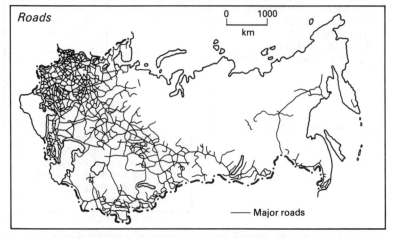

Roads

— Major roads

FACTORS INFLUENCING THE NETWORK PATTERN

Physical influences

Size — favours rail and air links.

Pattern reflects resource distribution — minerals, coal, oil, agricultural output as a reflection of soil potential variation etc.

Harsh climate — especially in Siberia and Arctic regions limits rail and road building — severe icing in winter and vast marshy tracts in spring and early summer.

Desert area to South, by its nature has a sparse population little need for an extensive transport network.

Historical and political factors

Communists in 1917 inherited a transport network established under the Czarist emperors in the 19th Century — well developed in European Russia but apart from Trans-Siberian railway little developed in Asiatic Russia.

The inherited pattern — including the Trans-Siberian railway stretching to the warm water Pacific port of Vladivostock — reflected strategic as well as economic needs.

Communist government — has had total control since. Thus under successive 5 Year National Plans the various forms have been gradually integrated to make an increasingly unified network.

It has been extended and particularly since the 1960s to open up new mineral and industrial areas in Siberia.

Double tracking and other measures on rail routes and link-ups of some water routes has improved capacity of the network.

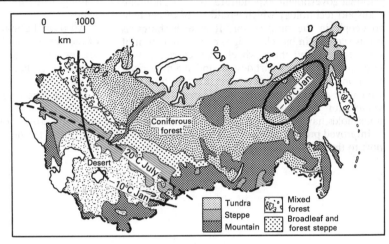

Vegetation (+ an index of climatic conditions)

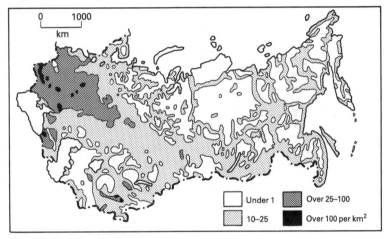

Population distribution

NETWORK REFLECTS PATTERNS OF POPULATION AND ECONOMIC ACTIVITY

Network needs are greater where most people live and the level of economic activity is the highest — hence densest in the Moscow region with extensions South to Black Sea and Eastward to and beyond Urals as new resources of coal and iron-ore tapped and industrial regions developed.

Network also reflects need to transport minerals, coal and other resources together with agricultural, goods West from Siberian to the main population and economic centres in European Russia.

Extensions — such as East into Arctic to tap new areas of development and serve some strategic outposts.

Exercise

● Comment on the main features of the Soviet Union's transport network and indicate its relationship to population distribution and the factors underlying this distribution.

national government expenditure into intermediate transport technology which would be of direct help to people in the rural sector. It is such things as improvements in bicycle design, mass production of cycle trailers and three wheel push carrier trikes, better ox and bullock cart design, and at a motorised level motor cycle carriers and tractor transport which are needed. In India the nearest thing to a vehicle for the masses is a bicycle, since 1 in 4 households have one — well over 100 million in all.

Improved public transport and other motor transport to the local market town and to reach schools, trading stores and clinics are amongst the other vital needs.

All these basic improvements on the lower order of the network and modes of transport require integrating into a larger scale network, linking larger centres together and the country to the outside world.

In conclusion we can see a range of factors affecting the way a transport system develops and these are summarised on the diagram (Fig. 22.2) and illustrated in the Case Study (22.2) of the Soviet Union.

23 The Basis and Pattern of Trade

The basis of international exchange is specialisation by countries in those economic activities for which they are best endowed by way of natural and human resources. This encourages efficient production of goods and materials i.e. theoretically maximum output at the lowest cost. Surpluses can then be traded by a country to purchase those goods and materials which are needed but not produced at all or in insufficient quantity inside its own boundaries.

In early times trade was by barter — exchange of surplus goods for wants — and to some extent still is amongst primitive societies or by special arrangement between two countries (bilateral trading). Most of today's international trade is by buying and selling — hence trade in goods and commodities is inseparably linked with international finance — world banking involving such things as foreign currency exchange, credit and debt, balance of payments. World financial exchanges are as important as trade in the modern world.

Trade itself is only partly in the form of commodities — food, raw materials and manufactures. This is *visible trade*, but increasingly trade is also in services, termed *invisible trade*. Banking has already been mentioned; others include insurance, technical advice, and tourism — here the traveller receives and pays for services in the host country.

As with household income and expenditure and in business, countries have the constant problem of 'balancing the books', i.e. selling enough by way of commodities and services to pay for the imports of the other commodities and services they need. The balance of a country's trading account at any one time is described as the *balance of payments*. Usually it will be in surplus or in deficit, since trading is unlikely at any one time to balance exactly. Clearly if a country has a balance of payments surplus it is earning more by trade than it is paying out and the reverse is the case for a deficit. Frequently the United Kingdom has a deficit on visible (commodities) trade, but a surplus on invisible (finance, insurance, services etc.) trade.

Because the price of raw materials and cash crop exports has not risen enough to keep pace with the rise in price of oil, manufactured goods and services since the 1960s, most developing countries have had serious balance of payments problems. Their main exports have been in cash crops and raw materials and thus to meet their import bills on oil, they have had to borrow from world commercial banks or institutions such as the World Bank. Consequently most developing countries are now in debt, some so seriously that a world banking crisis has occurred.

Visible trade — the pattern of world trade in commodities

Commodities entering world trade can be broadly classified as foodstuffs, raw materials, energy fuels and manufactured goods. By volume the greatest sector is that of energy fuels, chiefly petroleum. The trade in this has expanded almost spectacularly in the postwar years. The volume of manufactured goods exported has also shown a considerable increase, including now not only exports from the established industrial nations, but also a rising proportion from the newly industrialising countries of the developing world. The expansion of trade in foodstuffs and raw materials has been less substantial mainly because countries are attempting to reduce dependence on imported foods and the developing countries are processing more of their own raw materials.

Whilst the current world trading pattern is extremely complex it is possible to identify some of its basic features (Fig. 23.1).

The factors affecting the level and pattern of world trade are varied and the relationship between them complex. But an attempt has been made to indicate these in Fig. 23.2 and their effects will be explored later when some of the problems associated with international trade are considered.

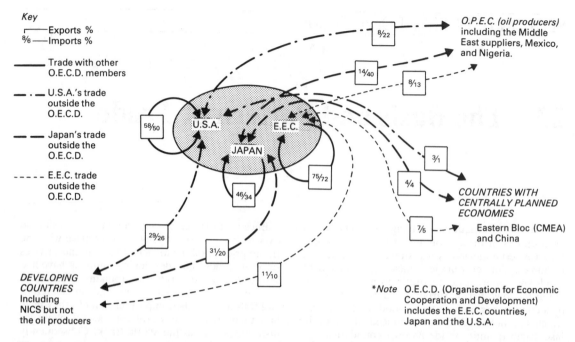

Fig. 23.1 *Patterns of international trade centred on the O.E.C.D. countries*

Domination by the O.E.C.D. countries

World trade is dominated by the developed countries of the West and Japan which together make up the O.E.C.D. (Organisation for Economic Co-operation and Development). These have high levels of national income and sophisticated economies with a high degree of specialisation. Hence they rely on international trade and have the level of income needed to finance a very large import–export trade. Indeed analysis of the expansion of world trade from the mid 1950s to the mid 1970s, which was on average 9% p.a., shows that it was largely due to trade amongst the industrial countries.

Not only do they dominate world trade, but much of the trade is between themselves. Some of this is in the form of food and raw materials, for instance the EEC members import coking coal, livestock feed grain and milling wheat from the USA. But the major part of trade within the O.E.C.D. is in manufactured goods.

It is not simply a matter of one member country importing from the others certain manufactured goods which it does not produce itself or for which home output is insufficient to meet the market demand. Much of the trade stems from competition between manufacturers of the same kind of commodity to capture a market and because buyers in advanced economies demand a choice of many types of manufactured goods. One of the best illustrations of this is the motor vehicle market. Japan has deeply

Exercises

a) Comment on the general pattern of trade between O.E.C.D. member countries and the other groups of countries.

b) Attempt to explain the differences in the pattern of trade for USA, EEC and Japan.

c) Discuss the differences in the export and import figures.

penetrated both the EEC and United States motor vehicle markets, whilst home-based producers such as Austin-Rover seek to maintain a share of the home market and themselves gain a foothold in Japan. More recently there is also fierce competition between O.E.C.D. members in the high technology market for computers and such like.

If trade is generally high between countries with advanced economies, it might be expected that the Soviet Union as a major economic power would figure prominently as a trading partner of O.E.C.D. member countries. However politics also influences trade. The Soviet Union is a planned economy controlled by the central government. As a founder and leading member of the Eastern bloc of Communist countries the C.M.E.A. (Council for Mutual Assistance) or as it is usually termed COMECON, its trade is mainly within this bloc, which functions as an economic entity.

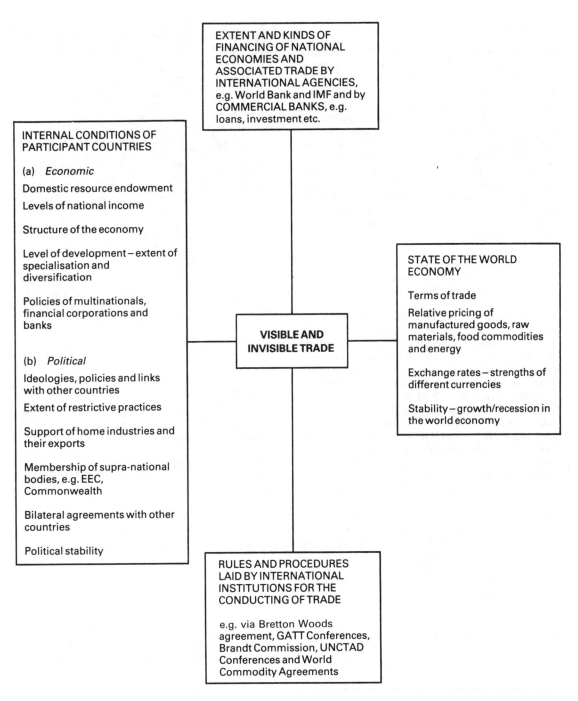

Fig. 23.2   *Factors influencing world trade*

Trade in fuel oil

Beyond the prominence of trade between developed countries, the second basic feature of the world trading pattern is the trade in fuel oil. The OPEC countries, mainly in the Middle East, are the principal exporters, whilst importers are developed countries (Fig. 23.1) (excluding the United Kingdom and Norway which now have plentiful supplies of their own from the North Sea), and countries of the developing world which have very limited energy sources of their own. These include most of the African countries and certain in Latin America such as Brazil. Since 1973 the trading pattern has changed due to the rise in world oil prices which stimulated the search for new resources of oil and alternative energy development.

Trade between developed and developing countries — the role of multinationals

The third feature of the world trading pattern is the long established exchange of manufactured goods produced in developed countries for foodstuffs and raw materials from the developing countries. Though this has relatively declined as most of the latter countries became independent of their former colonial powers and embarked on industrialisation themselves, the exchange is still prominent. It is today largely conducted by the great multinational corporations in association with overseas governments. The multinationals have invested heavily overseas in resource development ranging from oil and minerals to cash crops.

The study of transnational corporations has shown that in the flow of direct foreign investment, which is dominated by U.S.A., the share of multinational corporations rose from $83.7 million in 1970 to $814.5 million in 1981. Indeed they are held to be dominant both in world production and trade. Though a substantial amount was to develop industries, investment in raw material development also rose significantly.

Newly industrialising countries

A rather new feature in world trade has been the emergence of the newly industrialising countries like South Korea and Brazil, as exporters of manufactured goods both to other developing countries and to developed countries. Much of the latter is exports from factories established by multinational corporations with their main base in the developed countries. Lower costs, including lower wages, make it more economic to produce in the newly industrialising countries and export to the advanced economies. Many Japanese brand goods such as Panasonic tele-

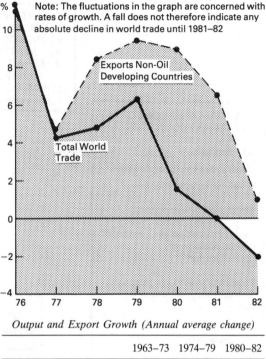

Output and Export Growth (Annual average change)

	1963–73	1974–79	1980–82
Output-Real GNP:			
World (not given)			
Industrial Countries	4.85	3.32	1.2
Non-Oil LDCs	6.00	5.1	3.45
Oil Exporting Countries	9.28	5.1	−3.6
Export Volume Growth:			
World	9.0	4.5	−0.5
Industrial Countries	10.5	5.5	1.83
Non-Oil LDCs — NICs	n.a.	8.0	6.5

Source: IMF Annual Report, GATT.

Fig. 23.3　Growth of trade volume 1976–82

Exercise

Discuss the changes in world trade indicated in the growth of trade graph and the table for output and export growth for different groups of countries in Fig. 23.3.

visions which are being sold on the United Kingdom market are in fact made in branch factories in Singapore, Hong Kong and Taiwan. Since 1976, this growth in trade between newly industrialising exporting countries and the established industrial countries has in fact been the most significant change in world trade. Even when the rate of growth in world trade declined from 1979 (Fig. 23.3) exports from the NICs continued to grow. It is estimated that they now contribute about 10% of the imported manufactured goods of the developed world.

Invisible trade with special reference to tourism

By value this now accounts for well over a quarter of world trade and is continuing to rise. As indicated earlier, invisible trade largely covers services. Those most important are a variety of financial services — insurance, banking, buying and selling of shares and trade in money currencies, loans and investments overseas. This is further increased by returns on these, including interest paid and payments from overseas governments, foreign companies and foreign personnel.

Other services include transport, carrying of goods and passengers by air and sea on behalf of overseas countries. Whilst this would include tourist travel, tourism also offers other invisible earnings because tourists pay for their accommodation in the host country and also spend a lot of currency on other services and goods during their stay (Fig. 23.4).

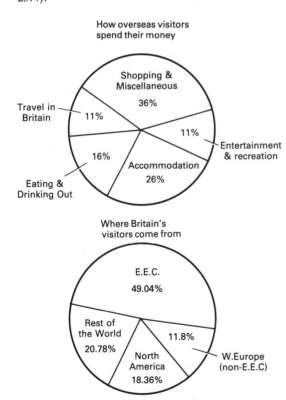

Fig. 23.4   Foreign tourists in Britain

In 1984 visitors to Britain spent £5 billion inside the country and on fares paid to British air and sea carriers. The British Tourist Authority (B.T.A.) estimates that tourism directly and indirectly provides 1.2 million people with employment.

International tourism — a foreign exchange earner

Tourism has expanded rapidly since the 1960s and the numbers visiting holiday areas overseas is rising more rapidly than internal tourism, for most West European countries. The increase can be attributed to a number of factors — increasing affluence and leisure time for populations of developed countries, cheaper and speedier travel especially by air and the entrepreneurship of tour operators, hoteliers and others engaged in the tourist industry.

Tourism measured simply in terms of numbers mainly concerns Western developed countries. They not only provide the largest number of tourists but are themselves the recipients of foreign tourists as the figures in Fig. 23.5 show. This is not surprising since accessibility is an important factor, together with the level of amenities offered by way of accommodation, infrastructure and entertainment facilities. In addition they offer coastal and other scenic attractions, as well as a rich variety of historical and cultural heritage features.

Measured in terms of its contribution towards national income and foreign exchange earnings, tourism is more vital to the less wealthy countries. It is already highly developed in Mediterranean countries such as Spain and Greece, but is also being increasingly seen as a major export earner for developing countries in Latin America, Africa and South East Asia (Fig. 23.5). Spending by foreign tourists and tour operators in the visited country, not only provides much needed foreign exchange but offers further boosts to the economy through providing employment opportunities both directly in the tourist industry and indirectly through the demand for foodstuffs, goods and further services. Because of the proximity of the Caribbean countries to the United States and their attractive climate, coasts, scenery and other tourist amenities, places such as Bermuda and Barbados have a long experience of tourism, but it is particularly since the 1960s that tourism has been a boom industry.

Taking Barbados as an example, tourism is the second largest exchange earner in the economy and contributes around 12% of the country's total income (Gross National Product). Almost 10% of the country's workforce is employed directly in tourism. Thus tourism is vital to the island's economy as well as an essential feature of its trading pattern. More recently this has also become true of other regions in the developing world, for example the Seychelles Islands in the Pacific and certain African countries such as Kenya. In 1981 tourism was Kenya's second largest exchange earner following coffee.

There are problems with tourism as a part of invisible trade. Firstly because it is a leisure industry, it is particularly susceptible to fluctuations as a result of economic recession and relative movements in currency exchange rates. Also a significant amount of income may flow back out of the country because much of the investment in tourist facilities and infrastructure, has come from foreign sources — large travel firms and also some multinationals. Tourism may also have an adverse effect both on the basic economy and the indigenous culture, by affecting the aspirations and attitudes of the local population, especially its younger elements. Contact with Western tourists has been a significant contributory factor towards the increased emigration of the younger element to the United States and other Western countries.

Thus though an important export earner, tourism needs to be part of a more diversified range of economic activities which will aid developing countries in their efforts to obtain a greater and more equitable share of world trade. As we shall see, there are severe obstacles in the way of this.

Exercise

Dealing with developed countries and developing countries as separate groups, for each table comment on both the figures for number of arrivals and receipts earned, including differences from 1977 to 1980.

Leading Developed Countries	Tourists (millions)		Receipts (£ millions)	
	1977	1980	1977	1980
France	26.2	30.1	4.3	8.2
U.S.A.	18.6	22.5	6.1	10.1
Spain	21.0	22.5	4.0	6.4
Italy	18.5	22.2	4.7	8.9
Canada	12.7	12.4	1.6	2.2
U.K.	12.3	12.3	3.4	6.9
Austria	11.7	13.8	3.7	6.4

Some Developing Countries

	1977	1980	1977	1980
Mexico	3.2	4.1	0.9	1.7
Hong Kong	1.7	2.3	0.7	1.3
Singapore	1.6	2.5	0.4	0.8
Morocco	1.4	1.4	0.4	0.4
Egypt	1.0	1.3	0.7	0.6
Republic of Korea	0.9	1.0	0.4	0.4
Philippines	0.7	1.0	0.1	0.3
Colombia	0.7	1.2	0.2	0.4
Bermuda	0.4	0.5	0.2	0.3
Barbados	0.3	0.4	0.1	0.3
Kenya	0.3			

Source: 1981 Statistical Yearbook

Fig. 23.5   Foreign tourist arrivals and income

24 Trade, Aid and Indebtedness

PROBLEMS

The actions of the industrialised countries

The actions of the industrialised countries of the Western world have had the greatest effect on the volume and character of world trade since these countries account for three quarters of it. The Soviet Union, one of the world's most powerful countries, and Eastern bloc countries have largely opted out of any major role in world trade and this in itself has meant a reduced volume of international trade.

Over the last forty years the West has pursued a blend of liberalism and interventionism towards world trade. Until 1973 the liberalist element was strongest but protectionism and other ways of intervening to control and manage international trade have since increased. This is partly a response to the world recession and partly because individual countries have tried to protect their own economies against too many foreign imports. Thus in looking at dealings connected with world trade since the war, we shall see it has never been free from restrictions and these have intensified since 1973.

Limitations of the Bretton Woods Agreement

The basis for the conditions under which world trade operated after the war was the Bretton Woods Agreement entered into by the industrialised countries of the West. Right from the start agricultural commodities were excluded from that agreement as was invisible trade. In these spheres therefore individual countries and groups of countries have been able to impose various kinds of restrictions on trade.

Thus any freer or more liberal conditions for trade largely concerned only manufactured goods. Countries therefore whose exports were mainly primary products such as foodstuffs and other agricultural raw materials, minerals, timber etc., were at a disadvantage in that they faced most restrictions on trade. These have in the main been developing countries.

But at least the Bretton Woods Agreement had the advantage of bringing in an institutionalised system of rules, conventions and procedures governing much of world trade. These were embodied in a General Agreement on Tariffs and Trade (G.A.T.T.) to which the industrialised countries of the West and later Japan were the main signatories. Periodic conferences have occurred to review and update these. Moreover the setting up of an International Monetary Fund (I.M.F.) at Bretton Woods to help provide short term financial aid in crises was also significant, especially for developing countries since these have been the main recipients of aid.

Trading blocs

In addition to the weaknesses in the Bretton Woods Agreement trading blocs have come into being within which member countries not only enjoy preferential trading terms for non-manufactured goods and services but also for manufactured goods too. Apart from the Eastern bloc (COMECON), the most powerful trading bloc is the EEC, whose members are increasingly pursuing a common policy in trade as in other economic activities. Internal tariff barriers have been lowered and internal producers have been protected from the undue competition of foreign imports. This is particularly evident in agricultural produce — quotas and tariffs on foreign imports as well as subsidies and price supports for home producers under the EEC's Common Agricultural Policy have operated against Commonwealth products such as dairy products from New Zealand and cane sugar from West Indian sources such as Jamaica.

There are also other less powerful trading blocs such as L.A.F.T.A. (Latin American Free Trade Association), and ASEAN (Indonesia, Malaysia, Thailand, the Philippines and Singapore) but their influence is not so strong.

It has been claimed that such trading blocs do bring advantages such as better bargaining for member countries, secure markets to encourage industry

271

etc. On the whole however experience has emphatically shown that these advantages do not outweigh the restrictive effects of such blocs on international or multilateral (between many countries) trade.

Interventionist measures on trade in manufactured goods

Despite the Bretton Woods Agreement expansion of trade in manufactured goods, in addition to that in other trading spheres, was being held back by a number of interventionist measures (see below). Since 1973 their effects have been intensified.

Forms of Direct Intervention

Quantitative	Quantitative restriction Voluntary Export Restraint (VER) Orderly Marketing Agreement (OMA) Tariff, Quota
Fiscal	Subsidies on exports and on export credits Discriminatory government procurement
Administrative	Import licensing

(*Note:* In addition there are a range of indirect measures such as subsidies to home industries, health and safety controls relating to goods and the technical standards which have to be met.)

The most significant intervention was through tariffs. Though most manufactured goods were affected by a tariff rate below 10% of their value, textile imports had a higher tariff imposition under international agreement for cotton textiles in the early 1960s and extended to other fibres including synthetics by the Multi Fibre Arrangement of 1974. This effectively reduced exports not only from Japan but more importantly from newly industrialising countries (NICs) such as South Korea.

Other restrictions were also imposed through the setting of import quotas particularly on goods from Japan, whose rapid rise to industrial prominence was seen as a threat to other industrial countries. In addition there have been so-called voluntary export restraint agreements (VERs) between governments or informally between industries which have affected NICs as well as Japan.

Restrictive measures taken by developing countries

Restrictions have not only been engineered by industrial countries. Indeed developing countries have built up a system of administrative controls over external trade which have been even more restrictive. The reasons for these were varied, but one motive was to protect newly emergent industries such as iron and steel in their own country against exports to them from developed countries. Restrictive measures also in part arose from the balance of trade difficulties encountered increasingly by certain developing countries — these attempted to curb foreign imports to reduce a balance of payment deficit. There was also the widely held belief that the GATT agreements and therefore the postwar general world trading conditions were advantageous to the rich and powerful industrial countries. To some extent this claim has some basis since the terms of trade in the postwar years have moved against exporters of primary materials and foodstuffs. In fact this is only one of the financial problems which together make up another and related set of constraints on the expansion and liberalisation of trade, namely a complex set of features related to financing trade and development.

World financial problems

Unfavourable terms of trade

Over the postwar years the terms of trade have generally been unfavourable to developing countries except the rich ones. This is to some extent seen as a legacy of the colonial era when colonial powers bought tropical foodstuffs and raw materials at very favourable terms to themselves from their colonial areas. During the postwar years when these areas gained independence, the rise in the price of non-manufactured commodities also failed to keep pace with that of manufactured goods. Consequently primary exporters have found themselves having to export more to import the same amount of manufactures. In addition prices have fluctuated on world commodity markets making returns on exports uncertain. This increasingly brought a number of newly independent countries into balance of payment problems (Fig. 24.1). The deficit for African countries for 1981 varied between one third and three fifths of the level of export earnings. Difficulties have been compounded by the ways in which some economies were internally managed and by external events. Internally, countries such as Brazil and Nigeria were affected by mismanagement of the financial side of the economy with rampant inflation occurring. Consequently amongst other things, rises in the cost of production made it increasingly difficult to keep exports competitively priced.

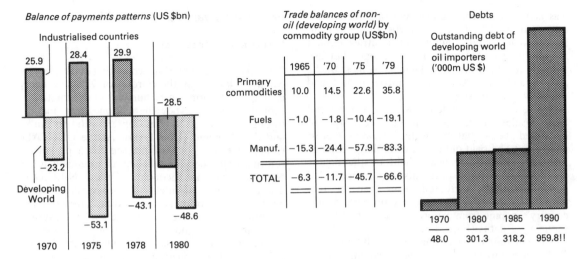

Balance of payments patterns (US $bn)

Industrialised countries

Trade balances of non-oil (developing world) by commodity group (US$bn)

	1965	'70	'75	'79
Primary commodities	10.0	14.5	22.6	35.8
Fuels	−1.0	−1.8	−10.4	−19.1
Manuf.	−15.3	−24.4	−57.9	−83.3
TOTAL	−6.3	−11.7	−45.7	−66.6

Debts

Outstanding debt of developing world oil importers ('000m US $)

1970	1980	1985	1990
48.0	301.3	318.2	959.8!!

Fig. 24.1   Debt and balance of payments problems for 'non-oil' developing countries

The oil crisis

Externally one of the most serious factors was the rise in oil prices engineered by the OPEC countries which as a group had command of the bulk of oil entering world trade and therefore could fix world oil prices. This reached crisis point in 1973 when a particularly sharp rise in price made it very difficult for importing countries to meet their energy bills. Whilst in the industrial countries inflated oil prices helped to contribute to economic crises and a drive for energy conservation, it was even more serious for those developing countries heavily dependent on oil imports. As we have seen they were already facing serious balance of payments problems and now found it impossible to meet their energy import bills. Consequently such countries borrowed even more heavily, running into heavy international debt.

Ironically by the 1980s some of the oil exporters such as Nigeria and Venezuela had also run into debt problems, having over extended imports and internal spending on the expectancy of continued high oil prices. But the world recession and cut backs on oil imports plus the North Sea oil boom has led to a world glut in oil and a fall in price.

International indebtedness

Financial support for the developing countries over the postwar years has come from a number of sources (Fig. 24.2). The World Bank and the International Monetary Fund have given loans at low rates of interest for internal projects and helped to gain better trading concessions for developing countries. Individual countries and economic blocs such as the EEC have also given aid and loans, for example the EEC funds associate developing countries (usually former colonies) through a European Development Fund (EDF) and a European Investment Bank (EIB). As developing countries further expanded, governments and private bodies also borrowed increasing sums on the world money markets from the large commercial banks. Such borrowing

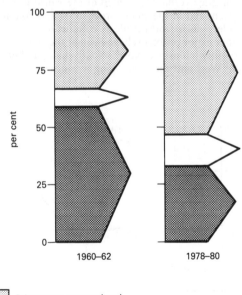

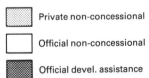

Private non-concessional

Official non-concessional

Official devel. assistance

Fig. 24.2   Net capital flows to developing countries (type and %)

273

was at the usual commercial rate of interest, frequently over 12%, during the 1970s. In the worsening economic climate a number of countries found it not only impossible to pay back these loans, but also failed to meet the interest payments — most of the African and Latin American countries have found themselves in this situation.

Before 1981 the tendency was for commercial banks to allow the debt repayments to be postponed i.e. rolled over — but this meant increased interest payments to be paid out of the dwindling exchange reserves (foreign currencies) held by the debtor countries. Interest rate payments were compounded and automatically increased faster than the real output of a country. Thus a rising proportion of a country's income from exports was absorbed by the servicing of debts (Fig. 24.3).

Not only this, it was estimated in 1980 that of the $845 billion borrowed by developing countries from the commercial banks, a staggering $837 billion was paid back in interest on loans, leaving only $8 billion to finance the further development needed to raise national income levels. Inevitably there have been serious international debt crises with a whole list of countries — Nigeria, Brazil, Argentina, Mexico, Uganda and Zambia virtually bankrupt. This state of affairs could not help but be detrimental to world trade levels and economic recovery.

Such is the seriousness of the situation today that a drastic overhaul is needed of the world monetary system and of the rules, procedures and conditions under which world trade is conducted. These and other major problems have been at the centre of the recently intensified North–South dialogue between the West and the developing world.

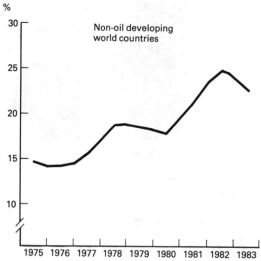

Fig. 24.3   % of export earnings needed to finance debt servicing

Progress towards a new world order

Earlier moves for reform

Since 1964 a pressure group consisting of developing countries known as the 'Group of 77' have been calling for reforms in a number of international economic areas. They have done this mainly through the United Nations Conference(s) on Trade and Development (UNCTAD). At the UNCTAD Conference in 1974 they pressed for a packet of reforms which became labelled as a demand for a New International Economic Order (N.I.E.O.). These included an integrated programme to aid world trade in primary commodities, free or preferential access to overseas markets for the exports of manufactured goods from developing countries including those from the NICs and the creation of a Third World currency and a bank to help finances.

The claims of the 'Group of 77' have been reinforced by the work of the Brandt Commission (Independent Commission on International Development) which was set up in 1977 with the approval of the Secretary General of the United Nations. It recommended a large-scale transfer of resources to developing countries (the South) from advanced countries (the North) and major reforms in the international economic system as well as a global programme for food and energy especially to help the poorest countries.

Aid programmes — their limited effect

One way of transferring resources has been through aid programmes. The aid has taken a variety of forms (Fig. 24.4), some of it done through international agencies such as the International Development Association (IDA), some of it through voluntary agencies such as Oxfam particularly for help in extreme emergencies but also over a longer term. One of the problems with such aid has been the misuse of funds when channelled through the governments of developing countries. Much of it has gone to prestige projects rather than schemes which would aid the mass of the people who are the worst off, enabling them to raise their standard of living.

Other kinds of aid have been in the form of what is known as 'tied aid' either contributed by the individual government of a developed country to one in the developing world or through private company deals, including those by multinational companies. Tied aid may be the granting of financial aid in order to buy goods from suppliers in the advanced countries. For example, in the United Kingdom the receiving developing governments channel their orders through the British Crown Agents which puts out orders for tenders among

TYPES OF AID
A guide through the maze

Official development assistance consists of grants and loans at concessional rates (low interest and long term) to promote economic development and welfare. Not included: military aid, bank loans at commercial rates and grants from non-government agencies.
Bilateral aid is provided directly by a donor to a recipient country. About 70% of all official aid.
Multilateral aid is channelled via international organisations such as the UN agencies and the World Bank. About 30% of all official aid.
Tied aid means that goods and services must be procured in the donor country; **untied** aid may be used to 'shop around' for the best deal on the open market. About half of all official aid is tied.
Project aid is for clearly defined projects, e.g. roads, water supplies and health facilities. This form of aid is attractive to donors because they can exercise greater control over its use. About 65% of all official aid.
Programme aid is non-project development assistance, usually to help countries out of balance of payments difficulties. This form of aid is most attractive to recipient countries because of its flexibility. About 35% of all official aid.
Technical assistance involves the provision of development-oriented skills by experts, the supply of relevant equipment and the training of local technical personnel. About 25% of all bilateral aid.
Food aid consists of cereals and dairy products from food-surplus countries, sent mainly to Egypt, Bangladesh, Indonesia and India. 70% is sold locally and used to support government budgets; 20% is used as project aid; 10% is used for emergency aid. Amounts to 11% of total official aid.
Emergency assistance is aid to people (e.g. refugees) in countries suffering from natural disasters, wars or other major upheavals. About 5% of official aid.

The Aid Givers

In 1981 grants and loans from 19 Western countries belonging to the O.E.C.D.* made up more than two-thirds of worldwide development assistance.
O.P.E.C. countries contributed large amounts of aid in terms of GNP per capita. Communist countries provided only slightly more aid than non-governmental agencies in the West.

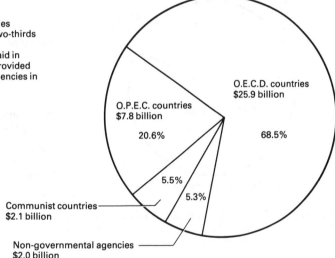

O.E.C.D. countries $25.9 billion 68.5%
O.P.E.C. countries $7.8 billion 20.6%
5.5%
5.3%
Communist countries $2.1 billion
Non-governmental agencies $2.0 billion

*Organisation for Economic Cooperation and Development

Fig. 24.4

British suppliers. In the second half of the 1970s about a third of orders were for mechanical engineering goods, including machinery and vehicles. These had to come from British suppliers who were not in some cases the cheapest suppliers of such goods.

Aid has a number of disadvantages. Though useful for specific projects the total amount of aid can be too little to have any radical effect on economic conditions. Furthermore it places the newly independent countries in a subservient position to developed countries. It does not therefore generate a positive attitude amongst the newly independent countries to promote a programme of self-help and the sustained growth needed to close the gap between the North and the South.

Exercise

Discuss reasons why the present pattern of aid giving is of only very limited value.

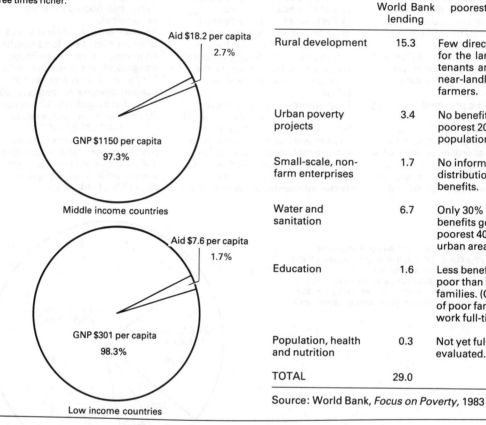

(a)

Just over 50% of all official aid from the West goes to 66 low income countries. But this amounts to only $7.6 per person compared with $18.2 per person received by people of 69 middle income countries — who are already three times richer.

Aid $18.2 per capita
2.7%

GNP $1150 per capita
97.3%

Middle income countries

Aid $7.6 per capita
1.7%

GNP $301 per capita
98.3%

Low income countries

b) World Bank lending to 'poverty-oriented' projects, mid 1970s

Sector	% of World Bank lending	Benefits for poorest groups
Rural development	15.3	Few direct benefits for the landless, for tenants and for near-landless farmers.
Urban poverty projects	3.4	No benefits for the poorest 20% of the population.
Small-scale, non-farm enterprises	1.7	No information on distribution of benefits.
Water and sanitation	6.7	Only 30% of benefits go to the poorest 40% in urban areas only.
Education	1.6	Less benefit to the poor than better-off families. (Children of poor families work full-time.)
Population, health and nutrition	0.3	Not yet fully evaluated.
TOTAL	29.0	

Source: World Bank, *Focus on Poverty*, 1983

Fig. 24.5   Aid and the poorest sectors of the developing world
(a) How much aid goes to the poorest countries?
(b) Within a country how much aid goes to the poorest?

Extent of progress

Hence the call for the New International Economic Order which will lead to a more equitable basis for world trade and a reform of the world financial order. Most immediately pressing is that of debt reorganisation and some progress has been made on this front, but as yet little has been achieved towards a more substantial long-term restructuring of the international economic order.

However all is not gloom. Some of the NICs have made substantial progress, raising their overall Gross Domestic Production and gaining a greater share of world trade. In 1981 developing countries contributed 10% of world trade in manufactures.

South East Asian countries in particular have gained a greater share of world trade. These include Singapore, the two Koreas, Hong Kong and Malaysia. There is also evidence that growth in countries such as Brazil and Mexico will also be resumed as internal inflation levels fall with stricter economic measures internally and arrangements are made to alleviate overseas indebtedness.

The situation remains most serious in Africa which contributed less than 1% of world trade in 1981. Here the rise in productivity is not keeping pace with population increase and the financial situation remains critical.

For these African and other very low income countries much more radical steps are needed, steps to which both developed and developing countries must be willing contributors, for the faults are not entirely those of the rich countries. Currently meetings are taking place to achieve progress in a number of ways. These include giving developing countries a greater say in the international agencies which help to regulate trade, in particular in the actions of G.A.T.T. There are also moves to reduce the number and level of interventionist measures against manufactured goods from the newly industrialising countries (as well as Japan). Most importantly for the developing countries as a whole, strenuous efforts are being made to liberalise trade in non-manufactured commodities and raw materials.

But improvements in world trade and more equality of opportunity for poorer nations depend also on other important world issues as well as progress within individual countries. Recently there are encouraging signs towards a transfer of resources from developed countries to help long-term development amongst developing countries, especially those in Africa. There is also some likelihood of a slowing down in the arms race between East and West, thus possibly releasing more finance for economic and social development. Further the rapid progress made by the newly industrialising countries and recently by India and China, including a slowing down of population growth, gives some grounds for believing other developing countries can also make further steps towards sustained growth and a more equitable distribution of income across society.

Further Reading

General

Leong G.C. and Morgan G.C. *Human and Economic Geography* (O.U.P.) 1982

Haggett H.P. *Geography: A Modern Synthesis* (Harper and Row) 1983

Lloyd P.E. and Dicken P. *Location in Space* (Harper and Row) 1977

Dicken P. and Lloyd P.E. *Modern Western Society* (Harper and Row) 1981

Dickenson J.P. (et al) *A Geography of the Third World* (Methuen) 1983

Mabogunge A.L. *The Development Process — A Spatial Perspective* (H.U.L.) 1980

Walmisley D.J. and Lewis G.J. *Human Geography — Behavioural Approaches* (Longman) 1984

Slater, F. (Ed) *People and Environments* (Collins) 1986

Theoretical and statistical basis

Bradford M.G. and Kent W.A. *Human Geography — Theories and Their Applications* (O.U.P.) 1977

Chorley R.J. and Haggett P. (Ed) *Socio-Economic Models in Geography* (Methuen) 1967

Gold J.R. *An Introduction to Behavioural Geography* (O.U.P.) 1980

Tidswell V. *Pattern & Process in Human Geography* (U.T.P.) 1979

Mowforth M. *Statistics for Geographers* (Harrap) 1979

Ebdon *Statistics in Geography* 2nd Ed (Basil Blackwell) 1985

Regional Africa

Udo R.K. *The Human Geography of Tropical Africa* (Heinemann) 1982

Asia

Aiken S.R. (et al) *The Development and Environment of Peninsular Malaysia* (McGraw Hill) 1982

Fryer D.W. *Emerging South East Asia* (Philip) 1979

Johnson B.L.C. *Bangladesh* (Heinemann) 1975

Johnson B.L.C. *India* (Heinemann) 1979

Johnson B.L.C. *Sri Lanka* (Heinemann) 1981

Latin America

Bromley R.D. and Bromley F. *South American Development — A Geographical Introduction* (C.U.P.) 1982

Cole J.P. *Latin America — Economic and Social Geography* (Butterworth) 1975

Williams V. *Brazil — A Concise Thematic Geography* (U.T.P.) 1981

North America

Patterson J.H. *A Geography of Canada and the United States* (O.U.P.) 1985

Watson J.W. *The United States* (Longman) 1982

Watson J.W. *A Social Geography of the United States* (Longman) 1979

Western Europe

Iberry B.W. *Western Europe — A Systematic Human Geography* (O.U.P.) 1981

Minishull G.N. *Western Europe* (Hodder and Stoughton) 1984

Johnston R.J. and Doornkamp J.C. (Ed) *A Changing Geography of the United Kingdom* (Methuen) 1982

Statistical and information sources

World Development Report — World Bank O.U.P.
  (Annual)
The Geographical Digest — Philip (Annual)
Statistical Yearbook — United Nations (Annual)
The Statesman's Yearbook — Macmillan (Annual)

Journals

Monthly: *New Internationalist*
          The Geographical Magazine
Quarterly: *Geography* (Geographical Assoc.–
          Sheffield)
          Geofile (Mary Glasgow Publications —
          London)

Daily Newspapers (including special supplements)

The Times
The Guardian
The Financial Times

Section 1

General

Gibson C. *Population* (Basil Blackwell) 1983
Hornby W.F. and Jones M. *An Introduction to
  Population Geography* (C.U.P.) 1980
Jones H.R. *A Population Geography* (Harper and
  Row) 1981
Ogden P. *Migration and Geographical Change*
  (C.U.P.) 1984

Thematic

Dwyer D.J. *People and Housing in Third World
  Cities* (Longman) 1979
O'Connor A. *The African City* (Hutchinson Uni-
  versity Library) 1983
Mabogunje A.L. *The Development Process* — Part
  3 (Hutchinson University Library) 1980
Simmons I.G. *Ecology of Natural Resources* — Part
  3 (Edward Arnold) 1974
Tarrant J.R. *Food Policies* — Chaps. 6 and 8 (John
  Wiley) 1980
World Bank *World Development Report* (O.U.P.)
  1984
The New Internationalist — (monthly) 1984
World Health — *The Water Decade* Aug and Sept
  1980 (bimonthly)

Section 2

General

Everson J.A. and FitzGerald B.P. *Settlement Patterns* (Longmans) 1969
Meyer I.R. and Huggett R.J. *Settlements* (Harper
  and Row) 1979

Rural

Phillips D. and Williams A. *Rural Britain — A
  Social Geography* (Blackwell) 1984
Pacione M. *Rural Geography* (Harper and Row)
  1984

Urban

Burtenshaw D., Bateman M. and Ashworth G.S.
  The City in West Europe (J. Wiley and Sons) 1981
Carter H. *The Study of Urban Geography* 2nd Edi-
  tion (Edward Arnold)
Clark D. *Urban Geography* (Croom Helm) 1982
Dwyer D.J. *People and Housing in Third World
  Cities* (Longmans) 1979
Hartschorn T.A. *Interpreting the City* (J. Wiley and
  Sons) 1980
Harvey D. *Social Justice in the City* (Edward
  Arnold) 1973
Jones E. *Readings in Social Geography* (O.U.P.)
  1976
King L.T. *Central Place Theory* (Sage Publications)
  1984
Knox P. *Urban Social Geography* (Longmans) 1982
Lloyd P. *Slums of Hope* (Manchester University
  Press) 1979
Short J.R. *An Introduction to Urban Geography*
  (Routledge, Kegan Paul) 1984
White P. *The West European City — A Social
  Geography* (Longman) 1984

Section 3

General

Bale J. *The Location of Manufacturing Industry*
  (Oliver and Boyd) 1981
Dickenson J.P. and others *A Geography of the
  Third World* Ch. 6 'Mining, Energy and Manufac-
  turing' (Methuen) 1983
Estall R.C. and Buchanan R.O. *Industrial Activity
  and Economic Geography* (4th Edition, Hutch-
  inson) 1980 including Case Studies of Iron and
  Steel Ch. 10 and Motor Vehicles Ch. 11

Hoare T. *The Location of Industry in Britain* (C.U.P.) 1983

Hodder B.W. *Economic Development in the Tropics* Chap. 10 Industrialisation (Methuen) 1980

Horsfall D. *Manufacturing Industry* (Basil Blackwell) 1982

Huggett R. and Meyer I. *Industry* (Harper and Row) 1981

Specialist

Hamilton F.E. and Linge F.J.R. *Spatial Analysis, Industry and the Industrial Environment* especially Ch. 4 — 'A Critical Evaluation of Industrial Location Theory' by D. Massey (John Wiley) 1979

House J.W. *The U.K. Space — Environment and the Future* Ch. 1 'U.K. at the Cross-Roads.' Ch. 4. 2 'Manufacturing Industry' (Weidenfeld & Nicolson) 1982

Section 4

General

Association of Agriculture *Sample Farm Studies from the U.K. and Commonwealth*

Bayliss Smith T.P. *The Ecology of Agricultural Systems* (C.U.P.) 1982

Chisholm M. *Rural Settlement and Land Use* (Hutchinson) 1978

Duckham A.N. *Farming Systems of the World* (Chatto and Windus) 1971

Farmer B.H. (Ed) *The Green Revolution* (Macmillan) 1977

Grigg D. *An Introduction to Agricultural Geography* (Hutchinson's University Library) 1984

Haines M. *An Introduction to Farming Systems* (Longman) 1982

Hall P. (Ed) *Von Thunen's Isolated State* (Pergamon) 1966

Hawkes J.G. (Ed) *Conservation and Agriculture* (Duckworth) 1979

Manshard W. *Tropical Agriculture* (Longman) 1974

Morgan W.B. *Agriculture in the Third World — A Spatial Analysis* (Bell and Hyman) 1980

Newbury P.A.R. *A Geography of Agriculture* (MacDonald & Evans) 1980

Scott P. *Australian Agriculture* (Akademai — Budapest) 1981

Symons L. *Russian Agriculture — A Geographic Survey* (Bell and Hyman) 1978

Section 5

General

Powell J.M. *Approaches to Resource Management* (Longmans) 1984

Mercer D. *In Pursuit of Leisure* (Longmans) 1984

Minerals

Spooner D. *Mining and Regional Development* (O.U.P.) 1981

Warren K. *Mineral Resources* (Pelican) 1973

Energy

Hardy D.A. *Energy and the Future* (World's Work Ltd) 1979

McMullan J.T., Morgan R., Murray R.B. *Energy Resources* (Edward Arnold) 1977

Odum H.T., Odum C. *Energy Basis of Man and Nature* (McGraw Hill) 1976

Fishing

Levihan J. and Fletcher W. *The Marine Environment* Ch. 1 *Marine Production* (Blackie) 1977

Hjul P. *Focus on Fish* — Geog. Magazine Oct 1977

Forestry

Leong G.C. and Morgan G.C. *Human and Economic Geography* — section on Forestry and Forestry Industries (O.U.P.) 1982

White P. *Dwindling Rain Forests* — National Geographic 1983

Hiraoka M. *The Development of Amazonia* — Geog. Review Jan 1982

Water

Jones P. *Hydrology* (Blackwell) 1983

Water — Special Topic — *Geog. Magazine* May 1977

Section 6

Hoyle B.S. (Ed) *Transport Development* (Macmillan) 1973

Hurst M.E. (Ed) *Transportation Geography — Comments and Readings* (McGraw Hill) 1974

Robinson H. and Bamford C.G. *Geography of Transport* (MacDonald and Evans) 1978

Robinson R. *Ways to Move* (C.U.P.) 1977

White H.P. and Senior M.L. *Transport Geography* (Longman) 1983

Section 7

Geofile No. 8 *Brandt, Cancun and After* Jan 1983

Geofile No. 26 *Tourism in the Third World* Jan 1984

Henderson P. *Trade Policies: Trends, Issues and Influences* Midland Bank Review — Winter 1983

New Internationalist *Rules for Real Aid* Aug 1983

The South — *'Unctad Rocks the Boat'* Special Report Oct 1981

Index

289